Oracle Press™

Oracle JDeveloper 3 Handbook

About the Authors

Dr. Paul Dorsey is the founder and president of Dulcian, Inc., an Oracle consulting firm. Paul is coauthor with Peter Koletzke of *Oracle Developer Advanced Forms & Reports* (2000) and *The Oracle Designer Handbook* (now in its second edition, 1999), and with Joseph R. Hudicka of *Oracle8 Design Using UML Object Modeling* (1999)—all from Oracle Press. Paul is executive editor of *SELECT* Magazine and president of the New York Oracle Users Group. A frequent speaker at various Oracle users group conferences, Paul has won awards such as Pinnacle Publishing's Technical Achievement, IOUW's best speaker award, and ECO's best speaker award. He spends most of his time working on Dulcian's business rules repository product suite. You can email Paul at paul_dorsey@dulcian.com.

Dulcian, Inc., specializes in Oracle client/server and web custom application development using object-oriented thinking implemented in a traditional relational database. The company provides a wide variety of consulting services, customized training, and products for the Oracle development environment. Dulcian builds extremely flexible and generic systems that adapt easily to changing business rules using an object-relational approach to database design and a business rules repository product suite. The company website can be found at www.dulcian.com.

Peter Koletzke is a technical director and principal instructor for the Enterprise e.Commerce practice at Quovera, in San Jose, California. Peter is executive vice president and web initiatives director for the International Oracle Users Group – Americas and columnist for the *ODTUG Technical Journal*. A frequent speaker at various Oracle users group conferences, Peter has won awards such as Pinnacle Publishing's Technical Achievement, ODTUG Editor's Choice, and the ECO/SEOUC Oracle Designer Award. You may find his website at ourworld.compuserve.com/homepages/Peter_Koletzke.

Quovera provides strategy, systems integration, and outsourced application management to Fortune 500, high-growth middle market and emerging market companies. The firm specializes in delivering intelligent solutions for complex enterprises, which improve productivity within the customer's business and optimize the customer's value chain, through integration of its customers and suppliers. The company also outsources the management of "best of breed" business applications on a recurring revenue basis. Quovera refers to its business model as "Intelligent Application Integration and Management." The company website can be found at www.quovera.com.

Oracle JDeveloper 3 Handbook

Dr. Paul Dorsey
Peter Koletzke

Osborne/**McGraw-Hill**

New York   Chicago   San Francisco
Lisbon   London   Madrid   Mexico City
Milan   New Delhi   San Juan
Seoul   Singapore   Sydney   Toronto

Osborne/**McGraw-Hill**
2600 Tenth Street
Berkeley, California 94710
U.S.A.

To arrange bulk purchase discounts for sales promotions, premiums, or fund-raisers, please contact Osborne/**McGraw-Hill** at the above address. For information on translations or book distributors outside the U.S.A., please see the International Contact Information page immediately following the index of this book.

Oracle JDeveloper 3 Handbook

1234567890 CUS CUS 01987654321

ISBN 0-07-212716-3

Publisher
Brandon A. Nordin

Vice President & Associate Publisher
Scott Rogers

Acquisitions Editor
Lisa McClain

Project Editor
Madhu Prasher

Acquisitions Coordinator
Ross Doll

Researcher
Roger Dorsey

Technical Editors
Derek Ashmore
Srinivasan Arun
Brian Fry
John Jannatpour
Blaise Ribet
Chris Schalk
Laura Sherman

Roel Stalman

Technical Contributor
Gnana Supramaniam

Technical Reviewer
Mari Cobb

Copy Editor
Judith Brown

Proofreaders
Pat Mannion and Paul Tyler

Indexer
Caryl Lee Fisher

Computer Designers
Elizabeth Jang
Roberta Steele

Illustrators
Lyssa Sieben-Wald
Beth E. Young

Series Design
Jani Beckwith

This book was composed with Corel VENTURA ™ Publisher.

Dedicated to the memory of Leonard G. Rubin

Contents at a Glance

vii

PART III

Implementation Techniques

Contents

PART I
Overview

PART II
JDeveloper and the Java Environment

PART III

Implementation Techniques

Foreword

There is something very powerful here which I think many of us are missing completely...
—kkirk, JDeveloper Forum, posted February 09, 2001 11:58 a.m.

t was the fall of 1999 at the Oracle Open World conference and I was lurking in the back of the room of a packed technical session. The speaker was one of the most prominent and experienced users in the Oracle Tools community: Paul Dorsey. Never known for mincing words, Paul was summing up the last three releases of my product: "JDeveloper 1.0—useless. JDeveloper 2.0—useless. JDeveloper 3.0—now that's interesting!" Ouch. I wasn't sure whether to slink out of the room over the first two pronouncements or to hold my head up high because of the third.

From the perspective of somebody accustomed to the maturity and productivity of traditional client-server database tools like Oracle Forms, PowerBuilder, and VisualBasic, I knew that Paul was absolutely right about the first two releases of the product. Prior to 3.0, JDeveloper was easily dismissed as yet another Java IDE (Integrated Development Environment). Despite its numerous powerful and innovative capabilities for Java programmers (such as the fastest debugger on the market and the unique CodeCoach feature that catches and corrects suboptimal Java coding practices), the early versions of JDeveloper did very little to simplify the critical task of building a scalable multi-tier database application. This fact certainly was not going to escape someone like Paul.

Fortunately, the fact that JDeveloper 3.0 was fundamentally different from its predecessors had not escaped Paul either. The inclusion of Business Components for Java—our new component-based application framework—plugged the hole that Paul had identified and spurred the quantum leap from "useless" to "interesting." Now we were finally able to demonstrate our vision of providing *both* a powerful programming environment *and* a productive application framework. This was something that Paul, an experienced database application developer applying his skills in the new Internet era, could appreciate.

In the year following the debut of JDeveloper 3.0 in late 1999, we have further refined both the framework and the development environment through two successive point releases. I think you will find that the product has progressed well beyond "interesting." Those that take the time to learn JDeveloper by reading books like this one and experimenting with the product will discover that we have produced something very powerful.

Before you delve in for yourself, allow me to highlight just a few of the key ingredients that make JDeveloper and Business Components for Java particularly compelling:

- **Standard platform**   The framework is built from the ground up on Internet standard protocols, languages, and APIs. Java itself is an immensely popular and powerful modern object-oriented programming language that is uniquely tailored for the Internet. Having a standard platform means that educational resources for the underlying technologies are readily available, the skills you will develop while using JDeveloper are broadly applicable, and the applications you deploy will be highly interoperable.

- **"White box" framework**   Unlike the traditional black box 4GL engines of the client-server era that are largely opaque to the developer, component frameworks implemented in a standard object-oriented language like Java provide a "white box" environment in which the inner workings can be examined, debugged, and even specialized or overridden when necessary. This approach yields the ultimate balance between the flexibility of a 3GL programming environment and the productivity of a 4GL Rapid Application Development tool.

- **Multi-tier component-based architecture**   The framework is designed to encourage a clean logical separation between the client, application, and database tiers. This is particularly crucial in the Internet environment where massive throughput requirements typically demand independent scaling of the application tier. The clean separation also enables the reuse of complex, expensive-to-develop business components across the ever-expanding array of Internet clients—from desktop to browser to handheld.

■ **Flexible deployment**   Determining the optimal deployment configuration for a multi-tier Internet application can be immensely complex. Do I really need a separate distributed object server? If so, should it be EJB or CORBA? Or should I just deploy my application logic locally within the same Java Virtual Machine as my servlet engine or Java UI? The framework eases these tough decisions by separating deployment considerations from application logic design. The same business components can be deployed in a variety of configurations. This allows you to start with the simplest or cheapest configuration first and evolve it later without recoding.

In this book, Paul and Peter delve into these key elements of JDeveloper and much, much more. The book provides an excellent cross-section of the knowledge you will need to be successful with JDeveloper. It covers the underlying Internet technologies, the application framework, and the IDE that houses them all. Most importantly, it is written from the perspective of two client-server database application development experts who have made their own journey to the brave new multi-tier, component-based world of the Internet.

As the quote at the opening of this foreword indicates, there is indeed "something very powerful here." Don't miss it. Read this book and let Paul and Peter help you discover how to harness the power of JDeveloper and Business Components for Java. Then please come share and expand your newfound wisdom with the rest of the JDeveloper community on http://otn.oracle.com.

Bill Dwight
Vice President, Java Tools
Oracle Corporation

Acknowledgments

hen I am writing a book, there are a number of things I get out of the experience. The biggest value is a deeper understanding of the subject. Heaven knows it's not the relatively insignificant royalty checks that result from these efforts! Unlike the past Designer and Developer books, this book was a foray into a brand-new product for me in a new area, namely, Java and all of its associated cousins (HTML, XML, etc.). It took me much longer to get a handle on this topic, whereas with Designer and Developer, my years of experience using these tools made the writing easier. This time, we were far along into the project before I felt that I had a good understanding of the JDeveloper product.

At the end of my first book with Peter, I looked forward eagerly to our next project. However, after each successive book, I am more impressed with the amount of work and frustration that these efforts require. I fully recognize that these projects would not happen without the support of a small army of people who are not adequately recognized. Perhaps listing only two names as authors on this book is unfair. Peter and I owe a serious debt of gratitude to a number of people who made crucial contributions to this project. Writing, assembling, and editing a manuscript to create a published book requires contributions from many people. It is important that these contributions do not go unrecognized.

First and foremost, I would like to thank my assistant Caryl Lee Fisher. In all fairness she should be listed as a coauthor on this book. Her tireless (literally) dedication to this project made it happen. She acted as one of the project managers for the book and helped keep me on schedule. She helped write much of the text that I was responsible for and did one of the appendixes more or less on her own. She handled all of my interactions with the publisher (a role that the publisher should be gratefully acknowledging rather than I). Thanks for another great job. Thanks also to Charlie Fisher for waiting patiently to play games with your mom while she was working on this book. I promise that we won't start another book for at least two weeks.

I would like to thank Roger Dorsey for his invaluable assistance with this project. He spent countless hours with the JDeveloper product, going back to its early versions, learning all of the ins and outs of the tool and creating many of the useful tutorials in this book. Without his technical knowledge and expertise, this project would never have come to fruition.

I initially started this project as a solo effort, but then thought better of it. With a little arm-twisting, I coerced my favorite coauthor to sign on to this endeavor. (To be honest, Caryl Lee figured that I needed the help and did the coercing on my behalf.) Many times when the project was in danger of veering off course or needed a boost, Peter provided his usual expert navigation and got the project back on course. As always, his efforts have helped to make this book a much more thorough and valuable addition to any Oracle developer's bookshelf.

Because the JDeveloper product is so new, we needed a lot of technical advice and support. Our technical editor, Derek Ashmore, of Delta Vortex Technologies, provided valuable feedback and advice throughout the process. We also greatly appreciate the unprecedented cooperation we received from many people at Oracle, namely, Srinivasan Arun, Sandeepan Bannerjee, Bill Dwight, Brian Fry, John Jannatpour, Vishu Krishnamurthy, Geoff Lee, Steve Muench, Blaise Ribet, Chris Schalk, Laura Sherman, and Roel Stalman.

Thanks to the OMH team, Jeremy Judson, Lisa McClain, Ross Doll, Madhu Prasher, and Judith Brown, for doing their usual professional jobs to create a quality product.

As always, finally, I need to thank my dog Popper. Since my last book, like me, Popper is a little older, a little grayer, and, although he moves more slowly now, is still usually willing to lumber to the door to greet me from his favorite napping spot on the couch whenever I come home.

Dr. Paul Dorsey
Colonia, NJ
February 2001

Travel Log   We're driving down a gravel highway in southeastern India. Two-cylinder Ambassador, top speed, 50 kph. Occasionally, a herd of goats or cattle crosses the road and the car stops as the shepherds clear the way. Meanwhile, we sit and enjoy the beauty of the scenery and the moment. Up ahead is an overturned truck with its contents strewn across the highway, so we stop again. Magically, a team of village residents appears, sets the vehicle upright, and clears the road enough that a car can pass. Eventually, we reach our destination intact and greatly enriched by the experience.

Writing this book was much like that travel experience. Our ride was longer than expected and understandably bumpy, but as we sit at our final destination and reflect, we feel greatly enriched due to the efforts of many people. Great thanks are due to them, as we would not be intact or even at our destination at all if it had not been for their interest in and dedication to this project.

My deepest gratitude goes to Caryl Lee Fisher, Paul's administrative assistant, who kept the momentum of Paul's chapters going during the days that Paul was attending to the necessary duties of running his consulting firm. Phone calls at least once a day to Caryl Lee were necessary to keep the book on track. Caryl Lee, I trust that our phone bills will return to the low three digits now that we are finished. Thanks, too, to Paul, for hiring Caryl Lee and for the superhuman endurance to stay on the long and arduous course that this book laid out.

The ride was made all the more enjoyable and successful due to the efforts of all our technical collaborators who steered, corrected, and instructed us. Roger Dorsey was our key research person and successfully guided both of us into the area of Java development—a topic fairly new to both Paul and me. His selfless dedication, sage advice, humor, and drive were much appreciated and were *instrumental* to the successful completion of the book.

Our gratitude goes to the technical editor, Derek Ashmore, who provided direction and kept us aware of how an expert Java programmer would view the tasks and strategies we describe.

We were blessed in this book with a dedication from Oracle Corporation that exceeded the excellent help we have received in our other books. We really appreciate the time and effort that Bill Dwight, vice president of Java Tools, Oracle Corporation, allowed his team (mentioned in Paul's acknowledgments before) to devote to this project. Bill's team spent time with us in conference calls to help clear the road when we were stuck. The team also participated in technical reviews (many times using their weekend or evening hours), and we must thank them greatly for their sometimes challenging and always grounding comments and corrections. This was greatly appreciated, as is the excellent foreword that Bill wrote for this book.

Many thanks to friends from the Columbia University Computer Technology and Applications program, Gnana Supramaniam and Alice Rischert, who arranged for a class of eager students to test-drive the book material as part of their JDeveloper training. Gnana was also a key editor and technical writer for the debugging chapter and devoted long hours to testing the technical content throughout the book. Dr. Thomas Smith also provided some starting material for the debugging chapter.

The Osborne/McGraw-Hill folks that Paul listed deserve extra mention. Lisa McClain, acquisitions editor, and her excellent assistant, Ross Doll, calmly adjusted our deliverables when life crises threatened to overturn the book project. Madhu Prasher, project editor, was very patient with our schedules as well, when we closed in on the end of the writing and editing. Judith Brown expertly copyedited our text to help keep continuity and consistency in the text through the long writing process.

Our gratitude also goes to many others who participated in some aspect of the book process. My Quovera boss, Guy Wilnai, gave me the freedom to supplement the personal and vacation hours spent on writing the book with many hours of otherwise billable "company time." Our technical reviewer, Mari Cobb of Ms Mari Consulting, took on a Herculean task and worked through the entire book to help us check the technical continuity. Her comments and frustrations gave us a needed reality check and helped improve the quality of the material. Nancy Taslitz, formerly of Oracle Corporation, directed us to the proper Oracle resources in the critical startup phases of the project. Rob Weaver and Will Andrews, colleagues from Quovera, assisted with details on the Java language. Jeff Jacobs, formerly of Quovera, also helped open some doors at Oracle. Thanks, too, to Joe Greenwald, President of ODK Incorporated, for the excellent Java course that gave me a solid foundation for working in JDeveloper.

My parents, Jan and Max, and brother, Mark, helped the book by sympathizing with me on the challenging deliverables and phases of the project. Finally, many thanks to my wife, Anne, who contributed to the book by being patient and understanding about the weekends and evenings that I could not spend with her and by shoving food under the office door when book deadlines made non-working meal times a luxury.

Peter Koletzke
San Carlos, CA
February 2001

Introduction

Better to do without books
than to believe everything they say.

—Chinese proverb

his is not the only book you will need to read to learn about Java-based web applications. After reading this book, you will not be able to build complex, sophisticated Java applications. We thought that you should know that up front.

As the cover indicates, this book will help you get started creating Java-based web applications. This introduction will give you a good picture of the contents of the book and whether this is the right book for you. When we started writing the book, we were relatively new to the Java world. Our background was in "traditional" application development in the terminal server minicomputer and client/server environments. We wanted to know how to apply that knowledge to this new environment. We also wanted to share our perspective with those who were in the same category—developers who know how to create applications in "other" languages but who are relatively new to the web development environment.

This book is a reflection of our transition to this environment. In a way, it documents our learning experience in the hope that this will assist others in making a similar journey. We realize that there is more to learn, and the next edition of the book will see a maturing of the environment as well as our experience in it. We have written this book to help traditional relational database developers who are accustomed to the client/server environment make the transition to a Java environment.

This is not to say that you need to be proficient with a traditional Oracle development product such as Forms to receive value from this book. However, it is important that you understand why the material that you see in this book has been included.

What You Will Find in This Book

We believe that the best way to learn a new tool is with a combination of overview information and hands-on practices. We have included both types of sections in almost every chapter. The overview material orients you to the tasks and the way that they are performed in JDeveloper. The hands-on practices help you to understand the JDeveloper environment and the basics of building applications. Although you will not be able to reach the goal of creating entire production systems upon completing this book, the book will take you some distance down that road.

If you just buy JDeveloper, load it, and begin working, you may end up like many users, playing with the product for weeks, if not months, trying to make it do something useful. This environment is complex, and you will need some help getting started. This book will hold your hand and help you take the first few steps in learning about Java and using JDeveloper. It will provide a foundation for becoming skilled in this new environment. We encourage you to go through the chapters sequentially to help build the skills necessary to begin creating systems. We also strongly encourage you to complete the hands-on practices. You would even be well served to go through each one several times. The only way to learn a new product is to use it.

What Is JDeveloper?

Before explaining details of the book's contents, we need to explain a bit about the tool. JDeveloper is a development environment designed to help you write Java code of different types and build an object layer that accesses the database. The tool does these two things very well. Although products such as Visual Café or Borland's JBuilder are also good products, what makes JDeveloper stand head and shoulders above other web development tools such as these is the database

Note for Oracle Developer Users
Since one objective of this book is to orient developers who may know how to create systems with Oracle Developer, some chapters contain special boxes like this one that explain how the JDeveloper concepts discussed relate to work in Oracle Developer.

objects layer—called Oracle Business Components for Java (BC4J). The wizards in JDeveloper allow you to quickly and easily build Java applications that will easily connect to a relational database. Prior to BC4J, building Java applications for a relational database was a challenging experience.

In addition to BC4J, JDeveloper offers a feature called *Data-Aware Controls* (DAC) that allows you to connect a GUI object to a database (BC4J) object with a single property setting. This feature is found only in JDeveloper and is extremely useful and highly productive. The DAC controls have a counterpart in *web beans* that provide the same easy-to-use connection for HTML-based applications.

JDeveloper is essentially an Integrated Development Environment (IDE) that allows developers to build, debug, and deploy various types of Java code. Its development interface looks a bit like other Oracle development tools such as Forms and Reports. However, JDeveloper generates portable 3GL code, whereas Forms and Reports generate code in a proprietary 4GL format. One of the strengths of JDeveloper is that it generates and manages Java code that is totally nonproprietary and portable. The 4GL work areas of JDeveloper that make it look like Forms and Reports exist to generate this code. This means that you are working in a 3GL environment, and 3GL environments require a different level of skill and a different method of development. This is a difficult but quite important concept to grasp. If you keep in mind that JDeveloper manages 3GL code, you will be less frustrated when it does not always work like 4GL tools with which you may already be familiar. The advantage of working with a 3GL environment is that you have ultimate control over the behavior of your applications because you have access to all of the code. However, with this freedom come new challenges of more low-level code to write and manage.

The Contents of This Book

As mentioned, the chapters in the book build on one another and are intended to be read in order. In Part I, we introduce the JDeveloper tool and the environment with overviews of the project and the IDE. A typical approach for a Java development

Note for Oracle Developer Users

Just as trying to make Forms do something it was never designed to do caused many forms to consume hundreds of additional development hours, you will be more productive in JDeveloper if you restrict your development standards to standard Java components that are easily generated and supported by the product.

book is to introduce how to create code without the complication of connecting to a database and accessing the data layer. However, in the Chapter 1 and Chapter 2 hands-on practices, you will work with database objects right away because, as a developer of Oracle web applications, you need to access data. Since your work in JDeveloper will create numerous objects, one of your first tasks should be to develop naming conventions. Chapter 3 provides some samples and a suggested approach to this task. Chapters 3 through 5 have no hands-on practices because they discuss orientation material that you will use throughout your JDeveloper work. Chapters 4 and 5 discuss the Java language and JDeveloper from the standpoint of territory that is probably familiar to you—PL/SQL and Oracle Developer.

Part II consists of two chapters that orient you to the way that JDeveloper relates to the Java environment. Chapter 6 explains the BC4J framework that is the basis for many applications demonstrated in the book. There are many options when deploying Java code, and Chapter 7 explores the major options that are available and how JDeveloper implements them.

The chapters in Part III provide selected implementation techniques. This section is where the book could be extended to fill many volumes. We had to make difficult choices about which techniques would be most useful to developers of Oracle web applications. There are subjects that we intentionally omitted (as mentioned in the later section "What You Will Not Find in This Book"). Chapter 8 explains how you create JavaServer Pages (JSPs)—dynamic HTML pages that connect to the database.

Chapters 9 through 11 discuss components that you can use in JDeveloper to create more traditional Java applications and applets. The available component toolset is explained in Chapter 9. Chapter 10 discusses how you can create pulldown and popup menus and button toolbars to make your applications more user friendly. Chapter 11 explores the JDeveloper layout managers that take care of automatic sizing and placement of components. This is a powerful Java feature that will be of great interest to developers of Oracle applications. Because the Web is a more accessible environment, you need to consider and design extra security features into your application.

Chapter 12 explains the requirements, strategies, and techniques that apply to this subject. It will help you to create the desired level of security for your applications. This topic is more advanced than some of the others in this book, but it is crucial to web applications. Chapter 13 discusses how to use JDeveloper's debugger to help you fix problems in your code.

The appendixes contain supplemental material that you may require. JDeveloper is filled with wizards that help you create code. Appendix A contains a concise list of the main wizards and how to find them. Appendix B explains the types of customizations and extensions that you can make to the JDeveloper IDE to allow you to work with maximum efficiency. Appendix C provides a brief explanation of how Java security works in the Oracle8i database.

Do I Have to Know Java?

Since JDeveloper generates 3GL Java code, it is important that you have a basic understanding of the Java language before beginning serious development work. The introduction to Java in Chapter 4 can assist in explaining some of the concepts and elements of the language, but you will want to obtain some training or study a book such as *Thinking in Java, Second Edition*, by Bruce Eckel (Prentice Hall, ISBN 0-13-027363-5), which is also available as a free download from many web sites.

The JDeveloper wizards create a lot of code for you. This code is completely functional and well formatted. You can learn a lot by examining and analyzing the code that the wizards create. Chapter 4 contains a section, "Skeleton of a JDeveloper Class File," showing the structure of a class file that the wizards create. Examining a file with this description in hand will help you understand the code and one method for constructing Java files. We learned much about Forms code from examining the code that the Designer Forms Generator created in its early days. You can use the JDeveloper-generated code for the same type of instruction.

What You Will Not Find in This Book

As mentioned, this book is not the source for all information that you will need to create an enterprise-class web application. Because of limitations on length and time constraints, we could not explain every task that you can complete in JDeveloper. Many of the tasks that are not in the book fall into four categories:

- **Advanced material**   The book is intended to get you started working with JDeveloper, and some material (such as the details about creating your own wizards) is only understandable after you have mastered the basics.

- **Complex deployment options**   Other than a brief discussion in Chapter 7 of the different tiers on which you can deploy code, the book does not explain all possible strategies for locating the code you create in JDeveloper. For example, there is no discussion about how you would develop Enterprise JavaBeans (EJBs) or database-deployed beans. It also does not describe methods for deployment into a Common Object Request Broker Architecture (CORBA) environment.

- **Server-side application code**   There is no discussion about writing Java code for deployment in the database, even though JDeveloper is capable of writing and debugging such code. In addition, the support for writing and checking XML files within JDeveloper is omitted. The emphasis in the book is on front-end user interface development.

■ **JDBC database connections** The authors believe that BC4J offers the easiest solution to the problem of connecting Java to an Oracle database. Therefore, the book only presents BC4J as the connection method. There are development shops that have used Java Database Connectivity (JDBC) as their standard, and this work is fully supported in JDeveloper. The later section "Other Resources" lists a book to assist in this pursuit.

NOTE
The 3.2 release of JDeveloper interacts with the Oracle Repository (the same database structures that Oracle Designer uses to store its metadata). The help system topic "Using JDeveloper Source Control" explains the repository support.

Oracle Database Objects and JDeveloper

Java is an object-oriented development language. Oracle8*i* has many great extensions to the database. The object-relational paradigm is one of the most exciting trends in database design and development to come along in a long time. The object extensions that were included with the Oracle8 8.0 release have matured into viable and useful extensions to the database that are likely to be universally adopted in the next few years. These will be even more robust in the Oracle9*i* database. JDeveloper support for the existing object features is quite good. It supports building BC4J objects that access the database using most of the Oracle database object types.

However, in this book, we do not discuss how to use JDeveloper with the Oracle8*i* object extensions. The reason is that the object support is not a complete solution; there are no data-aware GUI widgets (JavaBeans or web beans) to display the data from these components. At this time, building JDeveloper front-end applications to access Oracle objects would require a great deal of front-end coding.

The Oracle user community is very unforgiving when presented with an incomplete solution. It took years to overcome our experiences with Forms 4.0 and Reports 2.0, even though the Forms 4.5 and Reports 2.5 releases became competitive and Developer is arguably the best product on the market for development. The situation is similar in JDeveloper with the support for objects. If you are interested in working with the JDeveloper object extensions, run the Business Components Project Wizard against Oracle8*i* objects. You will find that the generated code is exactly what you would expect. By the time the next edition of this book is written, there is likely to be a strong focus on these objects and more emphasis in the next edition on this topic. Currently, support for object extensions in JDeveloper is a work in progress.

How Hot Is Your Cup of Java?

It is no surprise that Java is a hot topic in the Information Technology (IT) community. It is the first new, popular, mainstream development language to emerge since C++. There is probably as much hype about Java as any of the previous, overly famous buzzwords like relational database, object-oriented programming, natural language queries, CASE, artificial intelligence, and decision support systems. Some of these buzzwords lived up to their hype and more, whereas others failed to meet the expectations of the IT community.

To be honest, the jury is still out on Java. Is it the next wave in the development environment, or five years from now, will it merely be an interesting footnote in IT history? We don't think there is an answer to this question right now. Unfortunately, the answer will be driven more by market forces than by the quality of the technology. Clearly, Java is a viable contender. We think that it is one of the best programming languages ever developed. The strength of the object-oriented approach is undisputedly solid and deserves to take over the market.

What many of us want is to move away from client/server to more Internet-based applications where Java, because of its portability, promises to be a solid part of the solution. Also, the IT world is moving in a more object-oriented direction. The slow evolution toward object-oriented development, which is now overtaking the application development community, seems to be finding its way into the database community. There is a great deal of talk about object-relational databases and business rule systems, which have their conceptual foundations in object-oriented thinking. All of this strengthens the case for moving to a more object-oriented environment.

The Java environment is still in its infancy relative to other languages. Java is starting to show some maturity, but interacting with a database is still uncharted territory for most Java beginners. The whole Internet development environment has more components and is much more complex than older environments. Internet applications are not only built in Java; it appears that in order to build e-commerce front-end applications, you not only need to know Java but you also need significant experience with HTML and JavaScript. In comparison to more traditional application development environments that often require only one proprietary language, e-commerce applications require at least three languages—Java, HTML, and JavaScript. In addition, some knowledge of XML may be necessary, and this makes development a daunting task for "legacy" client/server developers. In addition, system architects need knowledge of Secure Sockets Layers and firewalls to build Internet-safe systems. We are moving to a world that is much more complex, less mature, and, as of this writing, potentially less efficient.

You can still build an internal payroll system for an organization faster by using Oracle Forms (and PL/SQL code) than by using any other tool suite because this is a mature 4GL environment that is built for rapid application development.

The dominance of Developer in this arena is not assured. The new Java-based environment shows great promise. In Java, we can build very complex objects that can be nicely encapsulated and connected to build applications faster than ever before. However, before this brave new world exists, these objects and wizards must all be created. At this point, such an environment is a technologically achievable dream. But there is a great deal of work still to be done.

Note that we haven't even mentioned JDeveloper in the context of Java yet. The focus of this discussion is centered on the industry and technology rather than a particular tool. However, once you decide that Java is the environment you want to use, JDeveloper is the best tool to use for creating web applications that require access to an Oracle database. (It can also connect to other databases through JDBC.)

About the Hands-on Practices

At first glance, the hands-on practices in this book may look similar to tutorials that you have seen elsewhere. The practices use the same Employee and Department (EMP and DEPT) tables as many Oracle examples (although JDeveloper contains sample applications that contain a more challenging data model). The reason these tables are used in this book is that they are familiar to most Oracle developers and are simple enough that no time will be spent pondering the data model. The difference between the practices in this book and other tutorials is that the practices are annotated. That is, they contain extensive explanations to help you understand the purpose of the steps you are taking. Each major section or phase contains a summary so that you can relate the instructions to the task at hand. By the time you complete the practice, with a little review, you should be able to accomplish the same task in a real work situation. (Refer to the sidebar "The Demo Tables" for information about installing the EMP and DEPT tables.)

Do I Need to Install JDeveloper?

The practices are intended to be hands-on, so it does not make much sense to read through the practices without trying out the steps. If you do not read the hands-on practices, you will be missing some key information because some topics are discussed only in the context of particular hands-on steps. Since experience is the best teacher, you should follow all of the practices to receive the full benefit from this book.

The book was written using JDeveloper 3.2. Although most practices will work with release 3.1, you will want to load JDeveloper 3.2 to take advantage of more features and so that your experience in the tool will correspond most closely with the text in the book. If you do not have JDeveloper installed, you may order a trial

The Demo Tables

The hands-on practices assume that you have access to the Scott schema that is installed using DEMOBLD.SQL (in the ORACLE_HOME\sqlplus\demo directory on the machine containing the Oracle database). Typically, you create a user called "Scott" who owns the demonstration tables. After running this SQL script in the Scott schema, you need to create primary and foreign key constraints. The following statements will create the constraints required for this book:

```
-- Primary key constraints
ALTER TABLE emp
    ADD CONSTRAINT emp_pk
    PRIMARY KEY (empno);
--
ALTER TABLE dept
    ADD CONSTRAINT dept_pk
    PRIMARY KEY (deptno);
--
-- Foreign key constraints
--     EMP to DEPT
ALTER TABLE emp
    ADD CONSTRAINT emp_dept_fk
    FOREIGN KEY (deptno)
    REFERENCES dept (deptno);
--
--     EMP to EMP
ALTER TABLE emp
    ADD CONSTRAINT emp_emp_fk
    FOREIGN KEY (mgr)
    REFERENCES emp (empno);
```

version (for evaluation only) for a minimal cost by ordering the CD pack for IDS from store.oracle.com. You may also download the JDeveloper install file (over 200MB) from the Oracle Technology Network (OTN) web site (otn.oracle.com). After downloading the file, you unzip it into a new directory and run the setup program that is unzipped into that directory.

Installing JDeveloper is relatively easy. Be sure to read the install.html file in the root installation directory for details before starting the installation. The following are a few notes to supplement the material in that file:

■ Oracle recommends that you install JDeveloper into a top-level directory (such as C:\JDev) whose name contains no spaces. The authors have successfully used JDeveloper in the default directory suggested in the installation program, but you might want to consider this advice from Oracle.

■ When you install JDeveloper, you will have the option of installing HTML Help or Web Help. If you have the space (requirements are listed in install.html), install HTML Help because it contains more features. Be sure that Internet Explorer is installed before installing HTML Help. Chapter 2 contains more information about the help system.

■ If you are installing onto a machine that has no Oracle products and you use Designer and Developer, be sure to install Designer and Developer before installing Oracle8*i*. Then install JDeveloper.

TIP
In addition to using as fast an Internet connection as possible, when you download large files such as JDeveloper, it is worthwhile to use a download manager program that allows you to restart an aborted session. Your browser may support download restarts, but programs such as Go!Zilla (www.gozilla.com) or GetRight (www.getright.com) will also accomplish the same goal.

Other Software Requirements
The best release of the database to use with JDeveloper is 8.1.7 or later. If that release is not available on your platform, you may use release 8.1.6, although some features such as EJB and CORBA deployment (as listed in the Release Notes) may not work.

What Happens if the Practices Do Not Work?
Although it is not expected that you will have problems, there is always a risk in basing book material heavily on hands-on practices. With the variable conditions that are possible in system configurations, you may experience a problem (or even a bug in the practice description) at some point. While the authors or publisher cannot provide support for your work in the practices, here are some ideas for resolving any problems that you experience in the practices:

■ **Slow down.** Read the instructions carefully to determine the exact operation that you need to perform. As is true with most programming languages, Java is not forgiving if you skip a step or miss a setting. If you slow down and assimilate the meaning of the step, you are more likely to experience success.

■ **Start over** with a new workspace. Sometimes a wrong step early in the practice can cascade into a larger problem later. You may even want to restart your system before doing this in case you have a memory area that has not been cleared correctly.

■ **Use the quick troubleshooting tips** described at the end of Chapter 2 to determine where the failure is occurring.

■ **Step back and look at the process** to see if it makes sense from what you know. If there is a wrong step in the practice, try to skip or work around it.

■ **Download the sample solution** from the authors' web sites (listed in the author biographies at the beginning of the book). Compare your code with the solution (using a file comparison utility such as Microsoft Word's file comparison tool) and determine where the differences occur.

■ **Consult the list of other resources** (in the next section) for more help. Particularly helpful will be discussion forums where you can compare notes with other users.

■ **Use the JDeveloper debugger** (described in Chapter 13) to determine the problem area, and exercise your troubleshooting skills to work on a solution.

Starting Over

At this point, you will probably not have worked through any practices. However, when you do follow the practices and experience difficulties, there are two possible ways to start over.

Delete the Old Files and Directories   If you have stored the workspace file and all project files inside one directory, you can just delete the directory to delete the workspace and its related files. Before deleting the directory, check to see if projects in any other directory references that directory using the following steps in Windows NT 4.0 or Windows 95. (Windows 98 and 2000 have similar fields in the main search pane.)

I. Navigate to the JDEV_HOME\myprojects directory in Windows Explorer.

2. Click F3 to display the file search utility and enter "*.jpr" in the Name & Location tab's *Named* field.

3. Enter the name of the directory in the Advanced tab's *Containing text* field. Click Find Now. This will find all project files that contain the text string of the directory name. You can open the project .jpr file in Notepad if you want to confirm the name of the file that is inside the project.

4. If you find any references to the directory, you need to decide whether the projects that reference that directory are important enough that you need to keep the directory. If the references to the directory are not important or if you found no references, you may delete the directory.

> ### What Is JDEV_HOME?
> When you install JDeveloper, you get a chance to name the directory in which the files are placed. By default, this directory is C:\Program Files\Oracle\JDeveloper 3.2. Since this directory is installation specific, this book refers to the directory in which JDeveloper is installed as *JDEV_HOME*. For example, the "myprojects" directory under this directory is referenced in this book as JDEV_HOME\myprojects, but the actual file system path may be C:\Program Files\Oracle\JDeveloper 3.2\myprojects.

NOTE
The Package Browser is displayed when you click the Browse button on the default package field in the Project Wizard. The list of directories that appears in that dialog is a combination of the directories in the myclasses and myprojects directories in JDEV_HOME. If you delete a directory in myprojects, you need to delete any corresponding directory in myclasses if you do not want to see it in the Package Browser list. If there is no directory in myprojects, you need to delete the directory in myclasses to remove it from the list.

Rename the New Files and Directories   If you want to keep the old files and directories but still want to start over with a practice, you can leave the original files and follow the practice steps as written. When you reach a step where you need to name a file or directory, add a number to the name (for example, empapp2). The main part of the name will be recognizable, but you will be able to start fresh in a particular practice. While this is not a recommended production practice, it will suffice for the purposes of learning JDeveloper.

CAUTION
Be aware that JDeveloper automatically writes the names of files and directories into the project and workspace files (described in Chapter 1). Therefore, if you rename a file or directory outside of JDeveloper, a reference in a JDeveloper file may no longer be valid. Therefore, use JDeveloper to rename files whenever possible.

Other Resources

By spending the time to search out what has already been written, you will probably find that others have spent many hours doing just what you want to do. With the extensibility of Java classes, you can use, modify, and extend the existing code with a fraction of the effort that would be required to develop it from scratch.

Scattered throughout the book are references to online web sites, both Oracle and others, that you can visit, and books that you can refer to for more information about the material introduced in the text. There are several other resources that are generic to the topics of Java and JDeveloper, and these are worth special mention here.

The JDeveloper Help System

The JDeveloper help system (introduced in Chapter 2) contains a wealth of information. You will need to go beyond the help system for many subjects if you want to fully explore the topics. There are low-level details such as Javadoc references on the Java language and Oracle-created classes used in various objects. There are also descriptions of the steps used to create specific components or full applications. The help system is a good companion to this book because, although there is some overlap, each contains different tutorial and descriptive material. You will be exposed to many of the tasks that you need to perform by using both resources.

NOTE
Throughout the book are references to help system topics. The references include the location or name of the help topic, but this is subject to change as JDeveloper is upgraded. The best strategy is to use the Search or Index tab in the help system if you cannot find a help topic in the referenced location.

JDeveloper Tutorials and Samples

The help system contains some key tutorials and sample applications under the Contents node "Tutorials and Sample Applications." The best way to learn a technique is to examine a sample application to determine how its creator solved a specific problem. There are several examples of specific techniques in this area. The sample files are loaded into the JDEV_HOME\samples directory.

JDeveloper Release Notes

The Release Notes are installed with the product and are available in the same Windows Start menu group as JDeveloper. You can also access the Release Notes from the JDeveloper Help menu. The Release Notes contain useful information that is not included in other sources, and you should become familiar with them. Some of the notes refer to limitations or workarounds that you would not know about if you tried and failed with the expected or documented method. For example, one of the notes, "Updating Business Components for Java Libraries on Oracle9*i* Application Server (*i*AS)," discusses how to set up the Oracle9*i* Application Server so that it can find the proper libraries to support BC4J objects. If you do not make these modifications, your remotely deployed BC4J application may not work.

Other Books

As mentioned in the beginning of this introduction, this is not the only book you will need to read to create Java-based applications using JDeveloper. A Java programmer's bookshelf should contain at least six other reference books in addition to the texts that are available on the Web. The actual books required will depend upon your knowledge base. The following list contains several books that the authors found useful in understanding various concepts. Other chapters contain different references and also mention some of these books in specific contexts.

- *Java How to Program*, Harvey M. Deitel and Paul J. Deitel, Prentice Hall, ISBN 0-13-899394-7

- *Java Black Book*, Steve Holzner, The Coriolis Group, ISBN 1-57-610531-8

- *JDBC API Tutorial and Reference, Second Edition*, Seth White, Maydene Fisher, Rick Cattell, Graham Hamilton, and Mark Hapner, Addison-Wesley, ISBN 0-201-43328-1

- *Refactoring: Improving the Design of Existing Code*, Martin Fowler, Kent Beck, John Brant, William Opdyke, and Don Roberts, Addison-Wesley, ISBN 0-201-48567-2

- *Java 2: The Complete Reference, 4th Edition*, Herbert Schildt, Osborne McGraw-Hill, ISBN 0-07-213084-9

TIP
Another resource is an online magazine called "Java Developer's Journal." It features detailed technical articles on the language and is available at www.javadevelopersjournal.com.

Oracle User Groups

One resource of which you must avail yourself is other users of Java and JDeveloper. The process of learning and using these tools is a challenging one, and it is likely that another user somewhere has already solved a problem you may be having. There are many online forums where the experts congregate, particularly, the International Oracle Users Group – Americas (IOUG-A) discussion forums (www.ioug.org), where users discuss Oracle web development topics. In addition, the Oracle Development Tools User Group (ODTUG) hosts list serves for a wide range of Oracle development topics, including Web and Java (www.odtug.com). You will also want to hook up with your local Oracle users group (the IOUG-A office can help you locate the nearest group) and discuss issues face-to-face with Oracle users in your area. OTN also has an active JDeveloper forum (otn.oracle.com) that is monitored by and contributed to by the JDeveloper product team.

What's Coming Up?

JDeveloper is part of a product package, currently called Internet Developer Suite (IDS). The suite contains other Oracle web development tools such as Oracle Forms Developer, Oracle Reports Developer, Oracle Portal (formerly WebDB), Designer, and Discoverer.

The 3.2 release of JDeveloper that is the topic of this book is a mature product containing many productivity enhancers. We can also look forward to other features that are in the pipeline for future releases. The only word that we can offer for the time frame for some of these features is "soon," and for others, it is "later." Here are several enhancements that will be included in upcoming releases:

- **UML modeling**   JDeveloper will contain a diagrammatic modeling feature with which you can create Unified Modeling Language (UML) representations of your data structures. JDeveloper will generate code based on these diagrams in the same way that Oracle Designer generates front-end code with its generators.

- **A 100% Java IDE**   An upcoming release of JDeveloper is being rewritten totally in Java. This means that you can develop Java applications on any system that has an updated JVM. Development work using JDeveloper will be supported on Solaris, Linux, and Windows NT. Of course, now you can develop Java applications for any Java platform using JDeveloper on the Windows platforms (NT, 9x, and 2000).

- **GUI object support**   At some point in the release cycle, we can look to JDeveloper for generation of front-end code that will access Oracle8*i* (or Oracle9*i*) objects.

- **Enhanced Database Browser features**   The Database Browser that exists in JDeveloper now will be enhanced with an editing environment for PL/SQL code as well as a SQL Viewer for executing SQL statements and generating Explain Plan results for performance tuning.

- **Extended Data-Aware Controls (DAC)**   A new release will add the ability to store session, row set, and attribute information in an independent XML file that can serve many panel and frame classes. In the current release, this information is not shared between frame classes. In addition, you will be able to base a panel on a row set and have the layout of the panel dynamically generated at runtime instead of having to define individual elements within the panel.

PART

I

Overview

CHAPTER
1

Working with
JDeveloper—Logical
Concepts

*"Contrariwise," continued Tweedledee,
"if it was so, it might be; and if it were so,
it would be; but as it isn't, it ain't.
That's logic."*

—Lewis Carroll (1832–1898), *Through the Looking Glass*

he Java environment is much richer and more complex than the traditional development environment. With terms like web-based deployment, Java Foundation Classes, Java Server Pages, encapsulation, Java Virtual Machine, Abstract Windowing Toolkit, inheritance, Common Object Request Broker Architecture, HTML, polymorphism, XML, application servers, Java Database Connectivity, JARs, Swing, SQLJ, applets, servlets, JavaBeans, multi-tier, and enterprise, all of the possibilities can be a bit daunting. However, the Oracle JDeveloper product can assist you in creating, debugging, and deploying Java business components and database applications for the Internet.

This chapter provides an overview of the logical concepts you need to keep in mind when creating an application using JDeveloper. To enforce these concepts, the chapter ends with a hands-on practice to demonstrate how to create a simple, working Java application that interacts with the database.

Overview

As mentioned in the Introduction, this book does not discuss everything that you can do with JDeveloper. The primary focus is to help client/server developers who use products such as Oracle Forms, Visual Basic, or PowerBuilder make the transition into Java using JDeveloper. What will you need to learn? Is building systems in JDeveloper significantly different from using other tools? After wading through all of the confusion, there are not as many differences as you might think. For example, in designing and building a payroll system in a more traditional environment such as Oracle Forms Developer, there is no notion of an "application system." You create some number (perhaps hundreds) of smaller applications that coordinate and call each other. Together, these form the application system. Similarly, in the JDeveloper environment, there is no such thing as an "application system." You will still be creating a number of smaller applications that fit together.

The first major difference between the traditional environments and the JDeveloper environment is that in some development environments, the user interface and its interaction with the database are inseparable. For example, in Forms, blocks hook directly to database objects. In the JDeveloper environment, the user interface (UI) and the database interaction are separated. In JDeveloper, you create files in logical containers called *projects*. Each program will usually consist of two types of JDeveloper projects:

- **User interface components and logic** built and written mainly using Java and Java components

- **Business Components for Java (BC4J)** built and written using Java and XML to provide the database interaction components

Using this architecture, for most of the UI project, you do not actually communicate with the database. Instead, the UI communication with the database is done in the middle-tier, BC4J objects. This is not to say that the UI project cannot contain Java Database Connectivity (JDBC) code that communicates directly with the database, but the primary GUI objects (such as multi-record screen objects) will usually communicate with the database using BC4J objects.

Using JDeveloper

JDeveloper is an application development tool that can support your first steps in the Java world. It can act as a blank sheet of paper for the sophisticated do-it-yourselfer, or as a code generator for those who prefer developing applications by using 4GL techniques such as drag and drop. JDeveloper can also automatically generate basic database interface code, allowing you to customize the results to your heart's content.

Coming to an understanding of JDeveloper and Java is like trying to learn English and a computer word processing program at the same time. You should have some experience with other computer languages and application conventions before you leap into this type of effort. It is a good idea to actually build the items and structures in the hands-on practices presented in this book as you read the chapters. In this way, you can quickly get a feel for the development environment by trying out real code. Depending upon how successful you are, you will also get a chance to do some real-time debugging and troubleshooting.

If you are building Internet applications, you will probably not be using only Java, but HTML code that is possibly enhanced with JavaScript. A complete discussion of these languages is beyond the scope of this book but Chapter 8 provides an introduction.

The Multi-tier Approach to Application Development

JDeveloper is optimized to assist you in producing a multi-tier architecture for your database applications. The unique power behind JDeveloper to produce a multi-tier application is centered on BC4J. A multi-tier architecture encourages the logical separation of the following elements:

■ **Client tier**   The client tier supports the data access requirements of the end user. Complex GUIs can be supported using application code over the Internet, browser-scripting capabilities, and/or by installing application code on the client's desktop and running it outside of the browser.

■ **Application tier**   The application tier is where the business logic is generally enforced and data access is coordinated. Application servers contain business logic that can be reused across a wide variety of clients and applications, thus making it possible to share physical and logical resources across multi-tier architectures. The application tier can also contain specialized reporting and analysis tools to handle complex business intelligence requirements.

■ **Database tier**   The database tier is where the data is stored and queried. This layer may also contain links to other external data sources and applications, which may be members of the overall architecture.

Hands-on Practice: Create a Java Application Using the Wizards

Now that you have an idea about the approach to working in JDeveloper, it is time to try it out. The following practice shows how JDeveloper can be used as a code generator. In later chapters, more details will be presented about how to use JDeveloper as a code editor. When you complete this practice session, you should have a good idea of how JDeveloper's user interface works. The JDeveloper user interface (the Integrated Development Environment or IDE) is discussed in more detail in Chapter 2.

NOTE
*After you open JDeveloper for the first time, look at the Welcome page. (Select **Help | Welcome Workspace (Sample)** if you need to reload it.) This page provides numerous links to helpful documents and online resources to help you get started. As mentioned in the Introduction, users groups, newsgroups, and company web pages are good resources to guide you down the Java path.*

In this first practice, you will create a Java application using the wizards in JDeveloper. This Java application will display employee information by department, in a simple master-detail relationship. The data for this application is from the Scott schema (part of the starter database), which comes with all Oracle databases. If you do not have access to these tables, please contact your database administrator, or you can install them from the starter database that comes on the Oracle distribution CD as mentioned in the Introduction.

This practice session consists of the following phases:

    I. **Set up the workspace**

   II. **Create a business components project**

       ■ **Create a project file**

       ■ **Create a connection**

       ■ **Complete the Business Components Project Wizard**

  III. **Create a user interface project**

  IV. **Define a master-detail data form**

       ■ **Launch the Business Components Data Form Wizard**

       ■ **Select attributes**

       ■ **Add an application wrapper**

       ■ **Compile and run the application**

When you run the Java application, it will look similar to Figure 1-1.

I. Set up the Workspace

To get started with your own code development, you will need to close any open workspaces and create a new one.

Working within JDeveloper, everything happens within the confines of a workspace. A *workspace* is a logical construct that houses all of the elements of an application. A workspace can conceivably hold any number of projects; however, experience dictates that you should have a separate workspace for each significant

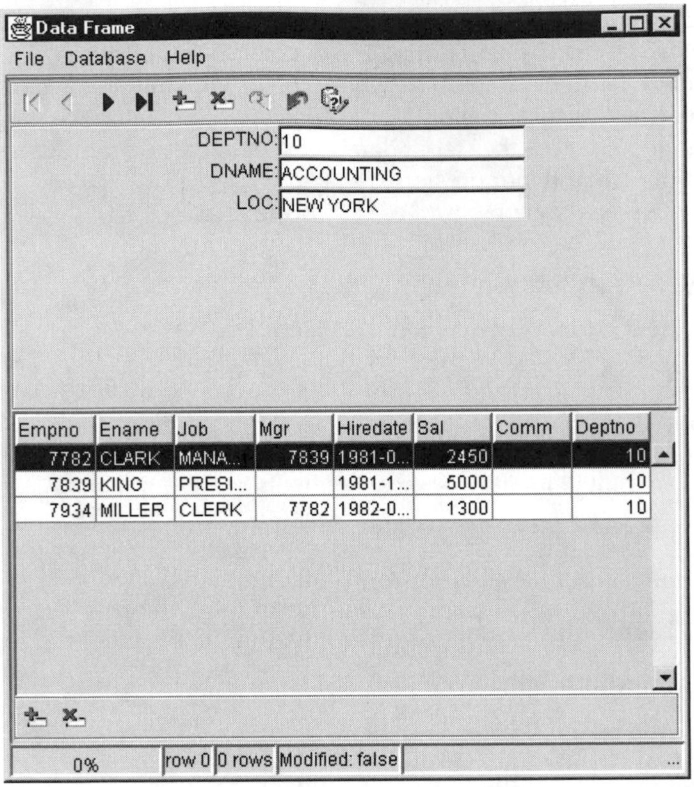

![Data Frame application window]

Data Frame

File   Database   Help

DEPTNO: 10
DNAME: ACCOUNTING
LOC: NEW YORK

Empno	Ename	Job	Mgr	Hiredate	Sal	Comm	Deptno
7782	CLARK	MANA...	7839	1981-0...	2450		10
7839	KING	PRESI...		1981-1...	5000		10
7934	MILLER	CLERK	7782	1982-0...	1300		10

0%   row 0 | 0 rows | Modified: false

FIGURE 1-1.   *The completed Java application*

screen application (corresponding to one form in Oracle Developer or a single Visual Basic project).

NOTE
You can only have one workspace open at a time in JDeveloper. This is a limitation of the product that will hopefully be changed in future releases.

Physically, a *workspace* is a text file (with a .jws extension) that contains information about the projects and applications you are building. In this practice session, you will create a workspace named EmployeeWS to track the files and settings you use while developing your first Java application. The workspace file will be stored with your other project-related files in one or more folders (operating system directory). During your development effort, the physical subdirectory/folder (path) where groups of related files are stored is referred to as a *package*. The term package also refers to a duplicate structure that exists in a class library file (.jar or .zip) that represents the storage paths within the library. The *JAR* (Java archive) is basically a compressed file containing the compiled code that you wish to deploy or share and an extra file that describes the contents of the JAR. Your workspace file can maintain information about files stored in many different packages. Whenever you save the workspace, all current open files and windows are updated and saved for you.

1. If you have an existing workspace open, select **File | Close Workspace**. The Navigation pane will display a new default workspace named "Untitled1.jws."

2. Select **File | Save Workspace**.

3. To create a new folder for your application, click the Create New Folder icon in the file dialog and name the New Folder "myempapp."

4. Double click myempapp to navigate to it.

5. To name the workspace file, click in the *File* name field, rename Untitled1 to "EmployeeWS" to see something similar to Figure 1-2. Then click Save.

6. Select **File | Save All**.

What Just Happened?   You created a workspace and a folder/package to hold the workspace file and all of the associated files that you will need for your project.

The next step in building your application is to capture the metadata for the tables you wish to access in what Oracle calls the BC4J layer. JDeveloper has provided a Business Components Project Wizard to help you with this task. Customizing the BC4J layer will be discussed in detail in Chapter 6, but for now you can view this code simply as a framework to develop, deploy, and customize your multi-tier business applications. For this practice, the Wizard will build predefined views of the business data for the Employee and Department tables. The BC4J layer will maintain the parent-child association rules for the tables and be responsible for updating the database when you insert, delete, or change rows.

The source code for the Java code (classes) must be stored in files with the extension .java. Each source file is given the same name as the class that it is defining, and a project file is used to reference each of the source files. When you compile your code, JDeveloper will save the resulting *bytecode* (code ready to be run in the Java Virtual Machine or JVM) in a file having the same name as the source, but using the extension .class. When you compile a Java program, it does not generate a .exe file and is not directly callable. Instead, to execute your Java program, you run the JVM and pass the name of the class file as a parameter. This is

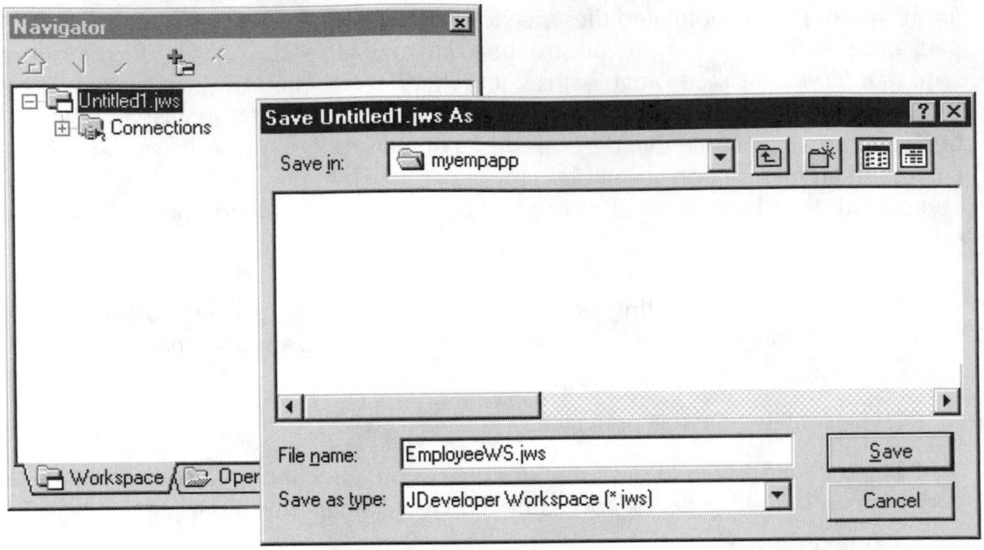

FIGURE 1-2. *Creating a workspace*

not an insurmountable requirement since all modern operating systems come equipped with their own JVM.

II. Create a Business Components Project

Within the workspace, files are logically divided into *projects*. A project has little significance from a code perspective but merely functions as a logical grouping container for files.

Physically, a project is a file with the extension .jpr, or extensions .jpr and .jpx for BC4J projects. In this phase of the practice, you will create the BC4J project that contains a list of source files (with a .java extension) and metadata files (with a .xml extension) for the business components layer. This separation of the two projects helps to create a clean and well-structured application by encapsulating most of the database access in one place.

You will always need to set up a workspace and project file before you do any work in JDeveloper. These files provide a logical way to organize your code during its development and act as tables of contents for your work.

You can create any number of projects that point to the same class files. Also, you may store your project files in any location, independent of the class files to which they point. However, you should carefully consider the scalability of how

Note for Oracle Developer Users

The BC4J handling of database access is analogous to how blocks in Oracle Forms access the database. The event code in the primary application is analogous to the handwritten triggers and program units that access the database in Forms.

you plan to store your Java workspace, project, and class files. If you put all of these files into one location (such as JDEV_HOME\myprojects), you will soon find yourself overwhelmed by the number of files in your root directory. It is a good idea to organize your files in a directory hierarchy that puts the workspace and project files in the same folder as their associated source code.

Create a Project File

When you create a project file, you will have the opportunity to run additional wizards, such as the Business Components Project Wizard, to generate other application files that will be referenced in your project.

   1. Select **File | New Project** to display the Welcome Page of the Project Wizard. Click Next to display the Project Type page.

NOTE

JDeveloper wizards that contain more than one page start with a Welcome Page that provides a brief introduction to the purpose of the wizard and the types of details that you will need to specify. You can uncheck the "Display this page next time" checkbox if you do not need this information later. Clicking Back the next time you start the wizard will display the Welcome Page if you have unchecked this checkbox. The practices in this book assume that this checkbox is checked in all wizards. Similarly, the Finish page in each JDeveloper wizard provides a summary of the settings that you specified in the wizard and indicate what you will create when you click the Finish button. In most wizards, the Finish button is enabled on the next to last page and you can skip the Finish page by clicking this button (if you know which page is next to last).

2. Click Browse to display the Select Project dialog. Doubleclick myempapp to navigate to the folder/package to store your project files.

3. To name your project, rename MyProject1 to "MyDeptEmpBusCompPRJ," and click Open. JDeveloper will apply the extension .jpr to the project file name and return you to the Project Type page. (Chapter 3 contains a discussion on naming conventions for files that you create in JDeveloper.)

4. On the Project Type page, under *What type of project would you like to create?* select "A Project Containing Business Components," and click Next.

5. On the Project Options page, click Browse, next to *What is the name of the project's default package,* to start the Package Browser. Select "myempapp" as the default folder/package for your project, and click OK. Leave the project's source and output directories/paths at their default values.

6. Click Next to complete the Project Options page.

7. On the Project Information page, you may enter information to describe your project. Leave the *Generate project HTML file* checkbox unchecked. When you have finished, click Next to continue.

8. You will now see a summary of the options you have selected. Briefly examine the contents of this page to confirm your selections.

9. Click Finish to create the project and invoke the Business Components Project Wizard. Click Next if the Welcome page appears.

Create a Connection

When you are asked to create an application, you generally have access to a limited number of database instances. Connecting to these databases is a repetitive task that you will perform over and over again. To facilitate this task, JDeveloper has implemented a definition called a *connection* that is shared across all development sessions. This definition is used to store the user names, passwords, URLs, and related parameters for your database connections. You can expand the Connections node (in the Navigator Pane), to view the connections you have already implemented. By doubleclicking a connection, you can obtain immediate access to the Database Browser that allows you to view database objects.

1. In the Connection page, click New to open the Connection dialog. This is where you can define the database connection that you want to use.

NOTE
Verify the information for the Connection dialog box from your database administrator.

2. Fill in the fields as follows. This assumes that the database is on your PC:

Connection Name as "ScottConnectionAuto"

User as "SCOTT"

Password as "tiger"

Connection Type as "JDBC"

Include password in deployment archive (check this checkbox)

JDBC Driver as "Oracle JDBC Thin"

Connection method as "Named Host"

Host ID as "localhost"

SID as "ORCL"

Port as "1521"

Row Prefetch as "10"

Batch Value as "1"

Report TABLE_REMARKS (leave this unchecked)

3. Click Test Connection. If you entered the appropriate information, you will see the message "Success!" returned to the right of the Test Connection button.

Click OK to complete the Connection dialog. You will see the settings appear in the Connection page as follows. Click Next.

If the connection tests successfully, the Package Name page opens. If the connection fails, JDeveloper displays an exception message and remains on the Connection page. In the case of an exception, confirm and update the connection information, and click Test Connection to make sure that the connection is working. Your connection must test successfully before the wizard will proceed.

Complete the Business Components Project Wizard

The previous section created a connection. This is normally a one-time operation.
If you need this connection in subsequent projects, you can just select it from the
pulldown list in the Connection page. The next steps finish the business components
definition and generate the code.

1. On the Package Name page, accept the default package name myempapp.
   Click Next.

2. On the Business Components page, the schema field should show "SCOTT"
   and the Tables checkbox should be checked. Select DEPT and EMP (using
   CTRL-click) from the *Available* field and move them to the *Selected* field by
   using the > button.

3. Check the *View Objects and View Links* and *Application Module*
   checkboxes. Click Next.

4. Click Finish to create the business components and add them to your project.

5. To save your work, select **File | Save All**.

What Just Happened?   You used the wizard to create a BC4J project that
connects to a database schema and defines metadata for the EMP and DEPT tables.
This will supply the data elements that you need to create the user interface project
in the next phase.

> **NOTE**
> *Take a look at the code that JDeveloper has generated
> so far. You now have over 1000 lines of code that can
> be modified and extended to obtain the results that
> precisely meet your needs. Browse the Navigation
> Pane and double click on file names to open them
> in the Source Editor. Be sure to look at the XML files,
> which hold the definitions for the BC4J objects. You
> will undoubtedly see many terms, tags, specifiers,
> classes, and language constructs that are new to you.*

III. Create a User Interface Project

The next project that you will add to the workspace will be used to store the GUI
code to display the data from DEPT and EMP. This project will logically isolate the

GUI code from the business components code since each of the projects represents a different functional area and may be deployed separately. Projects can have one or more deployment profiles that designate how to deploy the project. Chapter 8 discusses deployment alternatives and profiles in more detail.

Even though you are creating a second project to track the files for this application, you will note that all source files for this practice session are being stored in the same physical location. Since this practice session is using a single package (subdirectory) to store its source files, you must create unique file names for each new piece of code that you intend to add to this subdirectory.

1. Select **File | New Project** to display the Project Wizard. Click Next to dismiss the Welcome page.

2. On the Project Type page, click Browse to display the Select Project dialog. Double-click "myempapp" to navigate to the project's folder.

3. Name your project "EmpAppPRJ," and click Open.

4. On the Project Type page, under *What type of project would you like to create?* select the *An empty project* field and click Next.

NOTE
At this point, if you were to select "A project containing a new" and specify "Application," the Business Components Data Form Wizard that is run in the next phase would start. While this bypasses a number of steps (and is the way that the tutorials in the JDeveloper help system are written), that path does not show as clearly the different objects that you are creating.

5. On the Project Options page, click Browse, next to *What is the name of the project's default package,* to start the Package Browser. Select "myempapp" and click OK.

6. Leave the project's source and output directories/paths at their default values. Click Next to complete the Project Options page.

7. On the Project Information page, you may enter information to describe your project. Leave the *Generate project HTML file* box unchecked. Click Next to continue.

8. You will now see a summary of the options you have selected. Click Finish to create the project. If all went well, you should see a project file (EmpAppPRJ.jpr) shown here with Connections in the Navigation pane.

```
□ 📁 EmployeeWS.jws
  ⊞ 📁 Connections
    └ 📁 EmpAppPRJ.jpr
  □ 📁 MyDeptEmpBusCompPRJ.jpr
```

9. Select **File | Save All**.

What Just Happened?   You created another project to contain the GUI code and files for the application that you are building.

NOTE
For simplicity, this practice places the BC4J project in the same folder as the application. However, a better production practice is to place the BC4J project in a separate folder. This makes reusing the BC4J project for other applications a bit cleaner. Other practices in this book follow the path of creating a separate folder for the BC4J project.

IV. Define a Master-Detail Data Form

The Business Components Data Form Wizard will now walk you through the steps to create the basic user interface. This UI will be based on information from the DEPT and EMP tables that are joined in a master-detail relationship, and it will use the database interface that was developed in your Business Component project to access this data. After you finish responding to the choices provided, the Wizard will generate the Java source code required to implement the UI in a Java frame. Later you will create an application class that calls this frame to display the Business Form.

Launch the Business Components Data Form Wizard

The following steps start the wizard that creates a frame class file in the UI project.

1. Select EmpAppPRJ.jpr in the Navigation pane. Select **File | New** to display the Object Gallery.

2. Select the Business Components Data Form icon. Click OK. The Welcome page of the Business Components Data Form Wizard is displayed.

3. Click Next to display the Data Form page to define a form.

4. Select "Master-Detail" to specify the type of form you want to create.

5. Select "Frame" for your implementation preference. Click Next to display the Frame page.

6. Name the frame as "MyEmpFrame," and accept the defaults for the *Package* and *Title* fields. Click Next to display the Form Layout page.

The Business Components Data Form Wizard allows you to choose the default look and feel of the layout for your form based on UI templates. In this practice, you will display the Department columns using single fields at the top of the form. The Employee columns will be displayed in a multi-record grid control at the bottom of the form. The "Frame with Navigation Bar" template provided by JDeveloper will manage the form's default look and feel.

7. For the Master table, select "Vertical" for the *Layout*. Select "Left" for *Label Position* for each field.

8. For the Detail table, select "Grid" for the *Layout* field. Check that the *Label Position* field is set to "Above." The page should look as follows:

9. Click Next to display the Template page.

10. Select "Frame with Navigation Bar" as the template and click Next to display the Business Components page shown here:

11. Accept the default application module and click Next to show the Database Objects page.

    You will now establish a master-detail relationship between the DeptView and the EmpView objects that were generated in the Business Components project. These view objects provide access to the underlying data from the Scott schema.

12. Click DeptView(ViewObject) to select the master object.

13. Click EmpView(ViewObject) to select the detail object. The page should look as follows:

14. Click Next to display the Join Condition page. The default join condition will serve to synchronize the employee records as the user browses through the department records.

15. Be sure that both views are highlighted and click Next to accept the association.

Select Attributes

The wizard lists all of the attributes belonging to the master and detail view objects. These attributes represent the database columns in DEPT and EMP. The information after the attribute name indicates the datatype and size of that column in the table. The following steps are used to select columns for the form.

1. On the Master Attributes page, click the >> button to move all available attributes to the *Selected* list as shown here:

The following is a screen capture of the Business Components Data Form Wizard, Step 8 of 10: Master Attributes dialog, showing "Which master attributes do you want to include in your form?" for DeptView, with an empty Available list and a Selected list containing DEPTNO: NUMBER(2, 0), DNAME: VARCHAR2(14), and LOC: VARCHAR2(13).

2. Click Next to display the Detail Attributes page.

3. Click the >> button to move all attributes from the *Available* list to the *Selected* list.

4. Click Next to display the Deployment Connection page. The connection that you created earlier (ScottConnectionAuto) should be selected.

5. Click Next to go to the Finish page. You will see a summary of the definitions that you have entered in the Wizard.

6. Click Finish to generate the frame and UI code for your Business form.

7. After designing the user interface, save all of your work by selecting **File | Save All**.

Add an Application Wrapper

The final piece of code that needs to be generated for your UI project is a class called an *application* that is the executable code responsible for displaying your frame. You can use the Application Wizard to generate a class that checks your screen size and then uses an appropriately sized window to display your frame.

1. Click EmpAppPRJ.jpr in the Navigation Pane.

2. Select **File | New** to display the Object Gallery.

3. Select the Application icon under the Objects tab. Click OK. The Application Wizard is displayed as follows:

4. Change *Class* to "MyEmpApp," and accept the default for the *Package* field (myempapp).

5. Under *Add a default frame,* click "An existing frame," and click the Browse button to the right of the empty field to open the Class Browser.

6. In the Class Browser, click the + icon to the left of myempapp to expand the node, and then click MyEmpFrame to select the frame you previously created for your UI components.

7. Click OK to dismiss the Class Browser and return to the Application Wizard. Leave the *Center frame on screen* checkbox checked and click OK to complete the Wizard and generate the code.

8. Save all of your work by choosing **File | Save All**.

Compile and Run the Application

You will now compile each of the projects that you have created in preparation for running your Java application. When you compile the projects, JDeveloper will generate a duplicate project folder structure under your output directory (JDEV_HOME\myclasses) and fill it with the compiled bytecode files with a .class extension for your application.

Use the following steps to compile and run the projects that make up your Java application:

1. In the Navigation pane, click MyDeptEmpBusCompPRJ.jpr, and then select **Project | Rebuild Project "MyDeptEmpBusCompPRJ.jpr"**.

2. Click EmpAppPRJ.jpr, and then select **Project | Rebuild Project "EmpAppPRJ.jpr"**.

3. Save all of your work by selecting **File | Save All**.

4. Click the MyEmpApp.java file under EmpAppPRJ.jpr in the Navigator pane.

5. Select **Run | Run "MyEmpApp"**. Accept the Java copyright notice if displayed.

6. Click OK on the login dialog. (Enter a password if necessary.)

   JDeveloper will compile your source code and, if no errors are generated, run the application. Take some time to investigate the operational characteristics of your Java application. You will find that you can rearrange the column order of the detail area by dragging and dropping; sort rows by clicking the headings of various columns; hide and display columns by selecting the column name from the right-click popup menu; and resize the window.

What Just Happened?   You have just completed your first Java application using JDeveloper, generating nearly 40 pages of code. This is no small feat, but there is still a great deal of work to do if you wish to build even the simplest real-world business application. You will quickly find that the wizards cannot generate everything you might want. However, this is not a significant problem because, in this flexible environment, you can literally edit every line of generated code. The only limit placed on your final product is simply your skill in writing Java code and your ability to implement what you envision.

CHAPTER
2

The Integrated Development Environment

Beware the ides of March.

—William Shakespeare (1564–1616), *Julius Caesar* (I, ii, 18)

ll serious development languages feature an integrated development environment (IDE). It is a selling point for the language because it allows developers to quickly produce massive amounts of code that are debugged and optimized. The generated code is available to be modified or used as is. In general parlance, an *integrated development environment (IDE)* is a cohesive set of programs that automates and centralizes the lifecycle of program code creation and deployment. As with all third generation languages, you can create Java programs using a text editor, and there is no inherent requirement for using an IDE for Java development. The choice of which tool and development method to use is one that you have to make at the start of any project. It helps to have an understanding of what IDEs offer.

What's the Big IDEa?

When examining what benefits IDEs offer, it is useful to explore the alternatives. The standard Java development process without using an IDE consists of the following steps:

1. Write the source code (.java file) in a text editor such as Notepad.

2. Compile the source code at the command line using the javac program.

3. Run the compiled .class file using the java runtime program.

4. Make note of the errors and use the debugger, jdb, to determine the causes.

5. Repeat steps 1 through 4 until the code works satisfactorily.

This is the traditional method that many developers start with because it is a no-cost path. The Java Development Kit (JDK) that is available as a free download includes a command-line compiler, runtime program, and debugger as well as standard class library files. Therefore, however ponderous the steps are, there is no cost for the required tools. Countless Java programmers today still use this "traditional" method with variations, such as the use of a more fully featured text editor.

The development path is different with a Java IDE. It consists of the same steps (create the source code, compile, test, and debug), but all steps are accomplished using an easy-to-use windowed environment. Java development using an IDE is different from the traditional path for the following reasons:

■ **You do not need to be an expert in the language to create basic applications.** Proponents of IDEs argue that this allows more novice developers to be effective in creating code for a particular purpose. Critics of IDEs argue that it is a dangerous situation because, if the programmer is not fully aware of all of the detailed ramifications of the generated code, the programmer will not be able to make decisions on how to modify it or enhance it.

■ **You can do everything within the tool.** The major steps of compile, run, and debug are available with a click of a button. There is no need to type commands on the command line.

■ **You can work on different levels.** In addition to being able to write the code within the tool's code editor, you can use the declarative style of development, in which you define an object by name and assign values to properties. These definitions will create source code. The code and declarative areas will stay in sync so that when you change one, the other changes.

■ **You can easily visualize the code structure.** Many IDEs include navigator interfaces that allow you to see the many files that are required to implement a full Java application. This task is a significant one without an IDE.

IDEs may not be right for all developers. A true expert in the language has probably developed techniques that help in quickly creating efficient and complete code. The code that the expert creates has few bugs because it is written with care and an awareness of the libraries and other files that are required to place the code in production. This type of user may not require an IDE to assist in the familiar tasks of creating and compiling code. However, this type of expert is rare in the industry, although many may claim to have that status. In addition, many expert developers rely on enhanced tools; for example, instead of using Notepad to write code, the developer will use a more fully featured text editor that can automate some of the tasks. The more automated the text editor becomes, the closer it gets to a full IDE such as JDeveloper.

A traditional measurement for the output of a developer in "heads-down" development mode (when the developer is just coding based on a set of requirements) is the number of lines of code produced. In the past, the rule of thumb is that the developer is sufficiently productive if she or he creates 100 lines of debugged code in a day. Creating code in an IDE has a much greater output because much of the manual effort that coding requires is automated. As a comparison, the hands-on practice at the end of this chapter takes an hour or two to create more than 1500 lines of working code—the equivalent of 15 days of effort by the old rule of thumb. While the traditional measurement of a developer's output is a bit dated and rarely followed today, the point of the potential productivity increase is not.

If the developer's skills are anything less than expert, an IDE will assist greatly. An IDE can even make an expert more efficient by off-loading some of the tedious manual tasks such as tracking the source code required for a project and building command-line scripts to facilitate the compile process. In addition, the code that an IDE generates can assist this type of expert user because it is completely debugged and integrated with the other components that the application requires. The IDE will create a complete set of files that are required for deployment and track them effectively. Those tasks are difficult and tedious in a manual situation.

The JDeveloper Environment

The key to working with the JDeveloper IDE is in knowing how it is organized and what facilities it offers. If you understand the setup of the major areas of the tool, you will be able to work more efficiently when creating the code. The major areas that you will be working with are the following:

- Menus and toolbars
- IDE work areas
- Wizards
- The help system

The following discussion will focus on each of these. This section will not focus on how to use a toolbar and menu because it is likely that you are already well versed in those skills. One of the benefits you will receive from this section is a basic understanding of the range of features and functions that are available in the tool. This understanding will serve you well in future JDeveloper work. This section will not cover the exact actions you need to perform in each area since that subject is well handled in the help system. It will introduce the major areas and explain some details about the contents of each. At the end of this chapter is a hands-on practice that you can use to try out most of these main areas.

Menus and Toolbars

The JDeveloper IDE has a standard windowing interface and makes use of toolbars and menus for commands. (The help system calls these two facilities the *command area*.) The following shows a standard arrangement of the main menu and toolbars at the top of the main window:

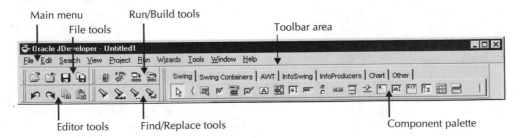

Menu Operations

The menu is arranged in logical pulldowns. Although you can access a description of each menu item by selecting it (without releasing the mouse button) and pressing F1, it is worth the time to examine some of the items.

File This contains the main operations for different files that you use in the tool (for example, workspaces and projects). It contains a Reopen item that lists the latest files that you worked on. This is handy for reloading a recently accessed project or file.

The File menu contains a selection for Remove File that disassociates the file from the higher-level file such as a workspace or project. This function is also available in the Navigation Pane of the Navigator.

CAUTION
Removing a file means that the file will no longer open when you open the workspace or project. However, the file will not be deleted from the file system. If you want to delete the file, you need to use Windows Explorer to navigate to the directory where the file is located and delete the file. For .java files, the default directory node is myprojects. You also need to delete the compiled .class files located by default in the myclasses directory node. If the wizard generated an HTML file, it will be located in the myhtml directory node.

TIP
*You can delete a file without leaving JDeveloper by selecting **File | Open**, right-clicking the file, and selecting **Delete** from the popup menu. This saves having to open Windows Explorer to delete the file.*

You can add a file to the opened (working) set using the Open item in this menu. For example, you can add a project to a workspace by selecting the workspace, selecting **File | Open**, and finding the file in the dialog. In this dialog is a checkbox for *Add to Project* (or *Add to Workspace*) that you can check to open the file under the selected object. If you uncheck this checkbox, the file will open into the Opened tab. The Rename item will change the name in the file system and in the workspace or project definition.

CAUTION
If you change the name of a file that is used by another higher-level file or project, that file will not update automatically. Although the old file name will show in the Navigation Pane, there will be no file in the file system to support it. Therefore, when you open that workspace or project, you have to remove the old file and open the new file so that the file is properly updated.

When you need to create a new file under an existing file, you select that file (such as a project file) in the Navigation Pane, select **File | New**, and the Object Gallery will appear, as in Figure 2-1. The Object Gallery is a repository of types of objects that you can create in JDeveloper. There are tabs for Objects, Business Components, Web Objects, Beans, and Snippets. These are detailed in the help system. (You can add your own snippets—pieces of code—by selecting Add Snippet from the right-click menu in the Object Gallery.)

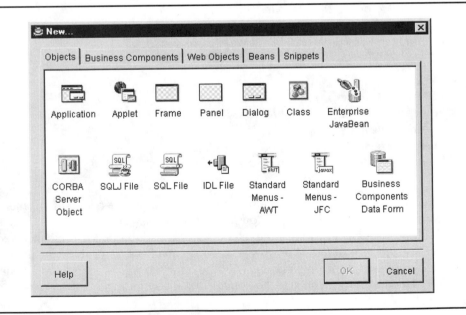

FIGURE 2-1. *The Object Gallery (New) dialog*

After selecting an object and clicking OK, the file node will be created in the Navigation Pane under the file that you selected.Depending on the object, the appropriate wizard may appear and prompt you for properties.

The New Project item in the File menu starts the Project Wizard, which prompts you through the process of creating a project. The project will be created under the workspace node regardless of what you selected before starting the process.

Save Modified Files

When you exit JDeveloper or open another workspace, the tool will save the state of the workspace even if you do not save the files explicitly. Therefore, if you add a project to a workspace and navigate to a new workspace, that project will open when you reload the original workspace. However, the contents of the files will not be saved unless you answer the Save Modified Files dialog that pops up when you navigate out of the workspace, as shown here:

```
┌─ Save Modified Files ──────────────────────────────────── [X] ─┐
│ ┌──────────────────────────────────────────────────────────┐ │
│ │ ☑ d:\program files\oracle\jdeveloper 3.1.1.2\myprojects\deptempbuscomp\Deptempl │ │
│ │ ☑ D:\Program Files\Oracle\JDeveloper 3.1.1.2\myprojects\deptideapp\Frame1.java │ │
│ │                                                          │ │
│ │                                                          │ │
│ │                                                          │ │
│ │                                                          │ │
│ │                                                          │ │
│ │                                                          │ │
│ │                                                          │ │
│ │                                                          │ │
│ │                                                          │ │
│ │                                                          │ │
│ └──────────────────────────────────────────────────────────┘ │
│  [ Select All ]  [ Select None ]    [   OK   ]   [ Cancel ]   │
└────────────────────────────────────────────────────────────────┘
```

You can select to save the changes to all or only some files using this dialog.

When you save a file that has been changed, the name of the file in the Navigator Pane changes from italics to non-italics as below:

Before saving   After saving

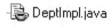

Edit   The Edit menu provides the standard window edit features. All items here have keypress shortcuts (such as CTRL-Z for Undo) that are faster to use than the menu selections.

Search   This menu contains standard search facilities. Most items have shortcut keys (such as CTRL-F for Find). Incremental Search (CTRL-E) is extremely handy for finding text in a large body of code. After pressing CTRL-E, you can start typing, and the tool will find the first occurrence of whatever you type. Pressing F3 will repeat the find.

Another extended search item is Search Source Path, which allows you to find an occurrence in any file in a particular directory. The Browse symbol button loads the package or class that matches the names of matching class, package, or interface code into the Opened tab of the Navigator. The search only works on code that is referenced in the import section.

View   The View menu allows you to display or hide the main windows and toolbars in the tool. The Open Viewer As submenu will display the Viewer window navigated to a specific page that you select (such as Source Editor, Visual Designer, Class Editor, JavaDoc Viewer). The Customize window will display a window containing a special property wizard or viewer if you have defined them for a specific component.

The View menu also contains selections for the debugger. The Tracing Disabled Classes item displays a dialog that specifies which classes will not be traced in the debugger. There are also selections for navigating to the next and previous error message in the Message View. The Breakpoints item will display the Breakpoints window that shows where the code will stop for examination during debugging. The Debugger Context Browser shows a window containing details of the code that is running when you are in debugging mode.

Project   This menu contains a selection (**Project | Deploy | New Deployment Profile**) for setting up a *deployment profile*—a definition of the .jar, .zip, or other file that will contain the .class and other runtime files. There are also items for Make and Rebuild that act on the currently selected file or the entire project. Both are available on the toolbar, and you can also execute Make by pressing CTRL-F9. Make will compile all .java files under the selected node with .class (compiled) files that are out of date or that do not exist. Rebuild compiles all .java files under the selected node regardless of the .class files. In both operations, any files referred to in the import section of the code will be compiled unless they are system packages (such as java.awt). Check the JDeveloper status bar at the bottom of the window for verification that the compilation succeeded.

TIP

*Although Make is faster than Rebuild, Rebuild is
always safer. If you have a problem with a file on
which you used the Make operation, try using
Rebuild as the first troubleshooting technique.*

The Project menu also allows you to display the Project Properties dialog, as
shown in Figure 2-2. This dialog allows you to change settings for the project file
with which you are working. The settings you use here will be used for all files in
the project even if they are used by another project. Therefore, you have to be a
bit careful with files that are shared between projects that have different project
properties. The properties you set here are stored in the project .jpr file.

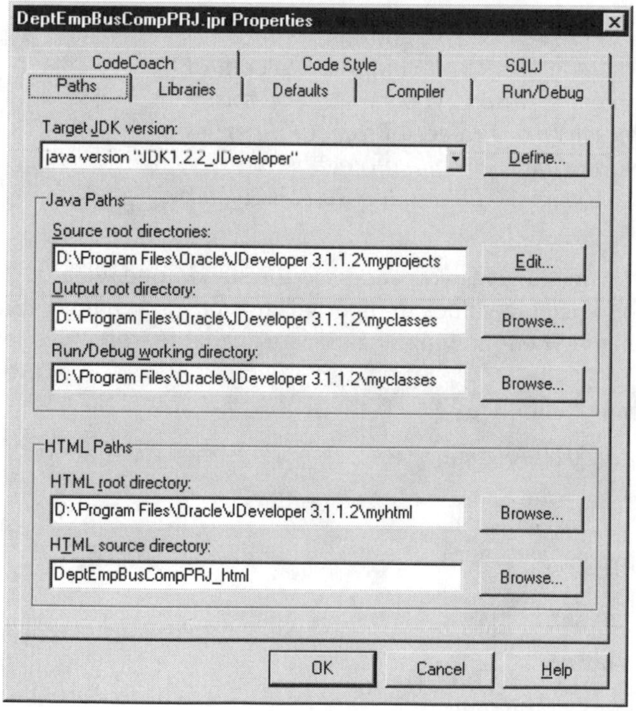

FIGURE 2-2. *Project Properties dialog*

CAUTION
When you make changes to the properties of an existing object, be sure to compile that project so that the changes will take effect.

Run   The Run menu contains items for running and debugging the project files. When you select Debug to run the file, the debugger will open, and many of the items in this menu will become enabled. Clicking the Debug toolbar icon or pressing F9 will also run the file in debug mode. Chapter 13 describes the debugger in detail. If you select Run in this menu, the file will execute without the debugger. You can also run a file by clicking the toolbar icon or by pressing SHIFT-F9. The Terminate item will stop a file that you are running, debugging, or CodeCoaching. (Chapter 13 contains a description of CodeCoach.)

NOTE
*When you run a file, the entire project will be recompiled automatically. If you prefer to control compilation more closely, you can turn off this behavior by selecting **Project | Project Properties** and unchecking the "Compile project before running or debugging" field in the Run/Debug tab.*

Wizards   This menu gives you access to the standalone wizards. Some wizards are executed by selecting values in other wizards or by creating a new object using the Object Gallery. The following wizards are available from this menu:

- Implement Interface
- Override Methods
- Resource
- BeanInsight
- Generate Javadoc
- IDL to Java
- Business Components
- Business Components Properties
- Web Object Manager
- JSP Element

As mentioned, other wizards start up from settings within these wizards or from the Object Gallery. For example, the Application Wizard is not available in this menu. You can access this wizard by selecting an application from the Object Gallery or specifying that you want to create a new application in the Project Wizard (that you call by selecting **File | New Project**). Appendix A lists the wizards and how to access them.

The functionality of the wizards available in this menu is well documented, and this book will touch on specific wizards in later chapters.

Tools   The Tools menu contains the following items:

- **IDE Options**   Defines how the IDE is displayed. Figure 2-3 shows the Editor tab of this dialog. This allows you to customize the editors (Editors and Fonts tab), the Navigator window (Navigator tab), and how the Code Insight feature works (Code Insight tab). This feature automatically pops up lists that help you enter code in the Source tab of the Viewer window. The Tools menu also contains an Environment tab for general IDE interface settings, such as which windows appear on top in a modal display.

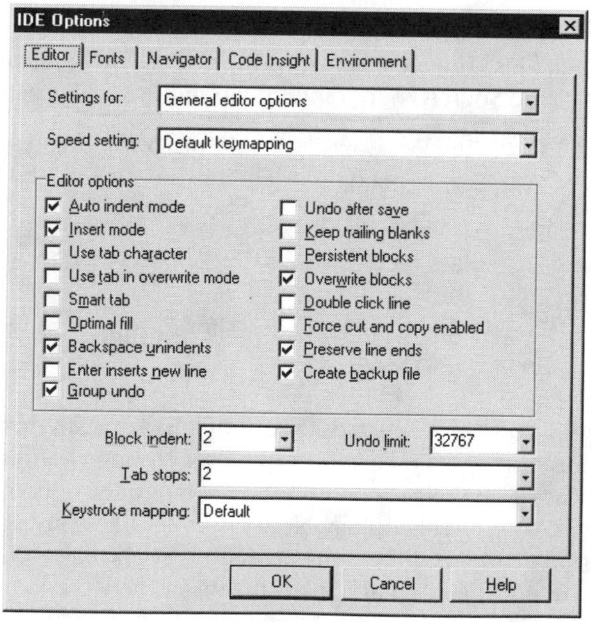

FIGURE 2-3.   *IDE Options dialog*

■ **Default Project Properties**   Allows you to set default values, such as the paths, libraries, compiler, project information, code style, and SQLJ style, that will be used for new project files. The Project Wizard uses these defaults when creating a project.

■ **Connections**   Displays the Connection Manager dialog, where you can add and modify connections. You can also display this dialog by doubleclicking the Connections node in the Navigation Pane or selecting Properties from the right-click menu on a particular connection. You can use the Export and Import buttons in this dialog to save and reload connections from other JDeveloper configurations (for example, from another machine).

■ **Invoke SQL*Plus**   Shows a dialog where you define the connection that you want to use and the location of the SQL*Plus executable. When you click Connect, SQL*Plus will run and log in as the user associated with the selected connection.

■ **Configure Palette**   Displays the same Palette Properties dialog that you see when you select Properties from the component palette popup menu. This allows you to add and modify the contents of the component palette toolbar.

■ **Treat as Text**   Allows you to add file extensions to the list that JDeveloper sees as text files. The file extensions in this list will be displayed and editable in the Source Editor (Source tab of the Viewer window).

■ **Notepad**   Loads the Windows Notepad program. If you selected a file in the Navigation Pane, when you select this menu item, the file will load into Notepad.

■ **Calculator**   Displays the Windows Calculator program.

Window   The Window menu contains items for closing, arranging, and switching focus to open windows.

Help   This menu contains expected items for Help Topics, which displays the opening page, and About, which displays version and trademark information. It also contains access to the release notes and Java language documentation stored locally. Two items, Oracle Technology Network and Oracle Java Education, will link to the appropriate Internet sites. The Welcome Workspace (Sample) menu item closes the workspace that is open and loads the welcome workspace. This workspace includes HTML files that provide an overview of JDeveloper features. You can navigate among the topics using the links in the text.

TIP
When you want to return to the workspace you were using after selecting **Help** | **Welcome Workspace (Sample)**, *select* **File** | **Reopen** *and find the workspace you were using. It will probably be the first item in that list.*

Toolbar Operations

As you would expect, all toolbar icons have tooltips that appear when you hold the mouse cursor over the icon. The toolbars contain icons for the most common commands as follows:

- **File tool**   Contains File Open, Close, Save, and Save All.

- **Editor tool**   Contains Copy, Paste, Undo, and Redo.

- **Run/Build tool**   Contains Run, Debug, Make, and Rebuild (compile for the entire project).

- **Find/Replace tool**   Contains Find, Replace, Search Again, and Browse symbol. The first three of these will work only if the Viewer window is open. Browse symbol works in any window as described in the Search menu section later.

- **Component palette**   Contains controls you use in the UI Designer. These controls are arranged into tabs based on the control's source. For example, there is a Swing tab that contains controls from the swing libraries. You can add to and modify the contents of these tabs as described in Chapter 9. The tooltips for these icons contain the library information for the class name (such as javax.swing). Right-clicking any non-icon area inside the component palette will show a popup menu (also called a *context menu*), where you can display the Palette Properties dialog. This dialog allows you to modify the contents of the palette.

Rearranging the Toolbars

There is a toolbar area that houses the tools. You can resize this area by dragging any toolbar drag handle (vertical lines on the left side of the toolbar) down. You can also detach any toolbar from the toolbar area by grabbing its drag handle and moving it outside the toolbar area border. Moving the detached toolbar window inside the toolbar area border will reattach it.

You can turn the display of any toolbar on and off choosing **View** | **Toolbar**. This menu command is also available by right-clicking any toolbar drag handle. If you uncheck the name of any toolbar in the menu, it will be hidden. You can also hide the entire toolbar area using this menu.

IDE Work Areas

When you open JDeveloper from the Windows Start menu, you will be presented with an outer window containing a number of IDE work areas. (The help system calls these the *development area*.) This section explains the purpose and functionality of the major areas shown in Figure 2-4.

Each work area represents a window or a *pane* (section of a window). The windows are called by various names in the documentation, but the names in this diagram are the most common.

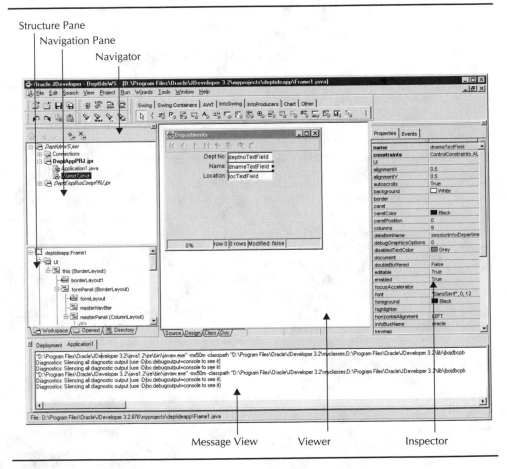

FIGURE 2-4. *Standard JDeveloper window arrangement*

Monitor Size and Resolution

There are many work area windows in JDeveloper, and you will probably want to have most of them open at the same time. Running a high resolution such as 1280x1024 (or 1600x1200) gives you more screen real estate in which you can place windows. Figure 2-5 shows JDeveloper running in this resolution. Compare that with Figure 2-4, where the screen is running a 1024x768 resolution.

As in most modern GUI development tools, a large monitor and high resolution are best. Although most of the screen shots in this book use a 1024x768 resolution for clarity, you will be more productive with a 1280x1024 resolution because you will be able to open more windows and leave them arranged in a certain way. With lower resolutions, you will spend time moving windows around on the screen so they are visible or sized correctly. This is time that you could spend on other tasks. As a rule of thumb, a 19-inch monitor is a minimum size for 1280x1024 resolution. 1600x1200 works on a good 21-inch monitor but may not be comfortable for some people.

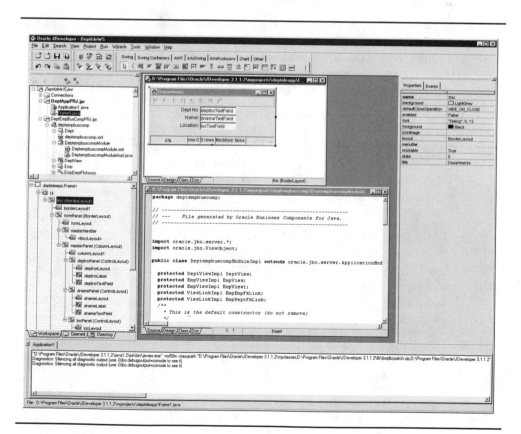

FIGURE 2-5. *JDeveloper running in a 1280x1024 resolution*

NOTE
Some of the wizards in JDeveloper do not display optimally when your screen colors are set to 256 or less. If possible, set the number of colors option (on the Windows Control Panel's Display application Settings tab) greater than 256 to avoid color problems. If you have problems with the display, switch to small fonts on this same tab.

Navigator

The Navigator window contains a number of tabs that offer different functions as follows:

- **Workspace**   This tab shows hierarchical tree views of the open files in two panes—the Navigation Pane and the Structure Pane. These panes are described in more detail later.

- **Opened**   This area shows files that you need quick access to. They do not have to be part of the currently open workspace. You can drag files on top of the Opened tab while working in the Directory tab or Workspace tab. For example, if you find a text file in the Directory tab, you can drag it on top of the Opened tab and it will be added to the Opened list.

  You can also add files by selecting **File | Open** when this tab is active or by using the Open into Opened List button. Files will be placed here if you select an inappropriate file type for a particular context. For example, if you select the workspace node in the Navigation Pane and open a .gif file, that file will be placed in the Opened tab because it must be housed within a project, not a workspace. You can remove files from the opened list using the Remove from Opened List button in the Navigator.

- **Directory**   This tab is a file browser that you can use to navigate through the file system. When you find a file, you can drag and drop it into the Opened or Workspace tab. If you drop the file on the Workspace tab, it will be added to the currently selected project. Alternatively, you can use Windows Explorer to find a file and drag and drop it into a project in the Workspace tab.

- **Hierarchy**   If you select Class Hierarchy from the right-click menu of a .java file, the Hierarchy tab will display the parent (and all ancestor) classes that the file inherits from.

- **Search**   The **Search | Search Source Path** item that finds files in a set of subdirectories will display that file list in this tab.

- **Debug**   When you are running in debug mode, this tab displays the main debugging session.

- **Watch**   When you are running in debug mode, this tab displays the list of variables that you are examining.

TIP
Doubleclicking a file in any of these tabs opens it in a Viewer. If the file is a graphics file (such as a GIF or JPG), the Viewer will display the graphic in read-only mode.

You can display the Directory, Hierarchy, and Search tabs by selecting the View item from the right-click menu that appears in the tab area. You can remove any of these tabs using the Drop item from the same right-click menu.

In all tabs, the Navigation Pane and Structure Pane display information about the file or hierarchy. The following sections describe how these panes work for the Workspace tab. The panes work similarly in the other tabs.

TIP
If you need to search for a specific item in the Navigator, click somewhere in the Navigation Pane and start typing the name of the item. The cursor will jump to the first occurrence of that name. Press the DOWN ARROW *key to find the next occurrence of the name.*

Navigation Pane   The Navigation Pane appears at the top of the Navigator window. It shows a hierarchical view of the selected object. For example, the following shows a portion of the hierarchy that appears when you expand a business component package. The top nodes are the workspace, DepIdeWS.jws, and projects such as DeptEmpBusCompPRJ.jpr. The bottom levels are the .xml and .java files for an entity, Dept, under a package, deptempbuscomp.

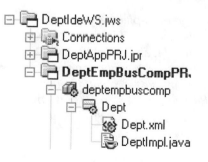

Each listed item type has an icon associated with it (listed in the help topic called "The Workspace Tab"). You can also hold the mouse cursor over the icon, and a tooltip will pop up indicating the object type. When appropriate, the organizational levels are displayed in the Navigation Pane so you can see the files that are in a parent-child relationship.

Structure Pane   The Structure Pane contains a view of the items within the file that is selected in the Navigation Pane. The form that this view takes depends on the selected file type and the tab that is active in the Viewer. For example, if you selected an .xml file for an entity in the Navigation Pane, the Structure Pane would display a list of the attributes and keys for that entity as this shows:

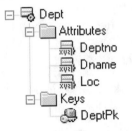

If the selected file were a Java class file, the Structure Pane would display the details of the class, such as the imports, methods, superclass, and properties. When you are designing visual classes such as a Java application and select the Design tab of the Viewer window, the Structure Pane will contain a hierarchy of the UI objects. You can drop components from the palette into the Structure Pane, and they will be added to the code and the UI. The practice at the end of this chapter provides an example.

When you click a Structure Pane object, the corresponding object will be selected in the Viewer (if the UI Designer or Menu Designer is visible). If the Source tab is displayed in the Viewer, the code line that defines the selected object's method will be selected.

TIP
You can take advantage of in-place editing in this window when you display the UI Designer (Design tab of the Viewer). Clicking an item once and clicking it again (or pressing F2*) will open the name-editing box and allow you to edit the name property directly. Pressing* ENTER *stops the editing.*

Navigator Operations   The purpose of the Navigator is to allow you to browse the workspace files. Doubleclicking a code file such as a Java or XML file will open the source code in the Viewer. Clicking a Navigation Pane node will load the Structure Pane with information about that node.

Doubleclicking a code item (such as a method name) in the Structure Pane will move the cursor and highlight the applicable line of code in the Viewer. If the source code Viewer is not open, it will be opened as a result of this action.

NOTE
You can think of the two panes in this way: the Navigation Pane shows a file and directory view of the open files. The Structure Pane shows the major code items and the organization for a selected file.

When you select a file in the Navigation Pane, the name and path of the file are displayed in the status bar at the bottom of the main window.

The Database Browser   You can view objects in the database using an action in the Navigation Pane. Expand the Connections node and doubleclick a Connection, such as ScottConnection. The Database Browser will open, as shown in Figure 2-6. This window allows you to view database objects in a navigation pane on the left and in an information pane on the right. For example, if you select a table from the hierarchy, the table structure will display in the information area. If you select a package, the code will appear in the information pane. You cannot add or modify definitions here, but you can refresh the view if the structures have changed.

Inspector

The Inspector window (also referred to as the Property Inspector in the documentation) is active when you have displayed the Design tab of the Viewer window. The Inspector automatically appears when you select this tab. You can also display it by selecting **View | Property Inspector**. This window contains two tabs—Properties and Events.

The Properties tab shows a list of properties for the class that is selected in the Structure Pane. When you modify the property value of a component, the code will be changed to reflect the new value. There are various ways to change a value based on the property. Some properties allow you to type in a value; other properties supply a fixed list of values from which to select; still others present a "..." ellipses button in the property value area. Clicking this button loads another dialog where you set the required values.

```
ScottConnection                                                    _ □ ✕

□ ⚏ Database Schemas            ▲   ▥ EMP
  ⊞ ♣ CTA                            PK    Name     Type     Size   Scale  Allow Nulls
  ⊞ ♣ DBSNMP                         ✓    EMPNO    NUMBER   4      0      ✕
  ⊞ ♣ DEMO                           ✕    ENAME    VARCHAR2 10            ✓
  ⊞ ♣ OUTLN                          ✕    JOB      VARCHAR2 9             ✓
  ⊞ ♣ REPOS                          ✕    MGR      NUMBER   4      0      ✓
  ⊟ ♣ SCOTT                          ✕    HIREDATE DATE     7             ✓
    ⊟ ▦ Tables                       ✕    SAL      NUMBER   7      2      ✓
       ▦ BONUS                       ✕    COMM     NUMBER   7      2      ✓
       ▦ DEPT                        ✕    DEPTNO   NUMBER   2      0      ✓
       ▦ DUMMY
       ▦ EMP
       ▦ SALGRADE
    ⊞ ▦ Views
    ⊞ ▦ Synonyms
    ⊞ ▦ PL/SQL Packages
    ⊞ ▦ PL/SQL Package Bodies
    ⊞ ▦ PL/SQL Functions
    ⊞ ▦ PL/SQL Procedures
    ⊞ ▦ Triggers
    ⊞ ▦ Sequences
    ⊞ ▦ Object Types
    ⊞ ▦ Deployed Java Classes   ▼

Browser
```

FIGURE 2-6.   *The Database Browser*

TIP
You can create customizers that handle a number of properties in a single interface. You can define a customizer that works like a wizard or like a dialog with a set of properties. You can also define your own property editors for editing individual properties. Appendix B provides some details on customizers and property editors.

The second tab, Events, displays a list of events for the component that is selected in the Structure Pane. You can add code to handle any event in this tab by typing an event name as the value for an event in the list and pressing the ENTER key. The Source tab will open and navigate to the code stub that was added, so you can type in an event handler.

The properties and events in these tabs appear in alphabetical order. To set a property value, first click the property name; then type in a value, select from the pulldown, or click the ellipsis button as appropriate to the property. To finalize the property value, press ENTER or click another property. The code will be changed to reflect the new value.

NOTE
There are preferences in the Environment tab of the **Tools | IDE Options** *dialog that specify which windows appear on top of other windows.*

Viewer

The Viewer is another multi-tab window. You interact with the first two of these tabs, Source and Design, more frequently than the last two tabs, Classes and Doc. Not all tabs are applicable to all types of files. For most file types, doubleclicking the file name in the Navigation Pane will open the Viewer and load the file's source code into the Source tab. The window name contains the path and file name. As mentioned, the initial viewer type depends on the file type. For example, if the file is a graphics file, the Viewer will open with a graphical display of that file. If the file is a Java file, the Viewer will open with the source code loaded. If the file is an HTML file, there will be the usual Source tab and a Viewer tab that shows the HTML as it would appear in a browser. Descriptions of the most common tabs follow.

NOTE
Remember that JDeveloper keeps the contents of the work areas in sync. Therefore, updating a property in the Inspector will update the code in the Source tab as well as the display in the Design tab. When you make a change in the Design tab, the code in the Source tab will change.

Source Tab   This tab contains the code editor (called the *Source Editor*) for the Java files represented in the Navigator. XML files created by the wizard may be viewed but not edited in the Source tab. Each file you open for editing opens another Viewer window. You can highly customize this editor by selecting **Tools | IDE Options**.

Normal editing keys, such as CTRL-X for Copy and CTRL-V for Paste, work as expected in the editor. You can change the indent level of a particular block of code using the following steps:

1. Press ALT and select the text. Start at the widest line, if possible, so that you can grab the entire block.

2. Cut the text, move the cursor to the desired indent level, and paste it. Be sure there are enough empty lines below where you paste to handle the number of pasted lines.

   Remember that CTRL-Z (Undo) will reverse the last editing change.

TIP
If you want to record and play back keystrokes for more complex editing sequences that you need to repeat, you can press a key combination to start recording, enter the keystrokes, and press the same key combination to stop recording. Another key combination will play back the recorded keystrokes. The keys you use to activate this feature vary depending upon the editor style you set in IDE Options. The following lists the keys and the editors:

Function	Default or IDE Classic	Brief
Record and stop recording	CTRL-SHIFT-R	F7
Play back	CTRL-SHIFT-P	F8

JDeveloper offers a feature called Code Insight to help you write code for Java source files. This feature pops up context-sensitive lists of methods, constants, imports, and method parameters as you type. The contents of the lists provided by Code Insight are based on the libraries in your project's *classpath* (a list of code directories defined in Project Properties) that have Javadoc available to them. You can manually pop up the lists using CTRL-ALT-SPACE for the Class Browser and CTRL-SPACE for a methods list, as shown here:

```
frameSize = frame.get
```

Method	**getAlignmentX** : float
Method	**getAlignmentY** : float
Method	**getBackground** : Color
Method	**getBounds** : Rectangle
Method	**getClass** : Class
Method	**getColorModel** : ColorModel
Method	**getComponent** : Component
Method	**getComponentAt** : Component
Method	**getComponentCount** : int
Method	**getComponentOrientation** : ComponentOrie
Method	**getComponents** : Component[]
Method	**getCursor** : Cursor
Method	**getCursorType** : int

JDeveloper caches a large number of edits so you may undo changes as far back as the last time you saved the file. You can reduce the number of undo levels to save memory by selecting **Tools | IDE Options** and modifying the *Undo limit* field. The default is the maximum of 32,767, and normally there should be no need for reducing this number. When you save a file, by default, the undo cache is cleared, although if you check the *Undo after save* checkbox in the IDE Options dialog, a save operation will not clear this cache. In any case, compiling the file will clear the undo cache.

NOTE
Look in the help system Index tab for the words "source code editing." This topic provides details about all aspects of the code editor.

Design Tab   This tab is also called the *UI Designer* or the Visual Designer. It shows a graphical view of the UI layout if there is one, for the selected class. For example, if you doubleclicked an application Java file in the Navigation Pane, the Viewer would open up on the Source tab. Clicking the Design tab will display the UI Designer with a graphical representation of the frame or other object.

When you add objects to the layout, you can drop them into the Structure Pane (at the correct node) or onto the UI Designer. When you make a change to the layout in this tab, the code will be updated.

If you need to refresh the display of the UI, minimize the Viewer window and restore it. There is no Redraw function.

NOTE
*You can view the UI Designer using a particular appearance ("look and feel"). You may be coding your applications to use the CDE Motif, Metal, or Windows look and feel and want to view the UI Designer in that same look and feel. Select the **Look and Feel** submenu from the right-click menu in the UI Designer and select one of the possibilities. This will not alter the way the application runs. To specify a look and feel at runtime, you need to write some code. (Chapter 9 provides examples of this code.)*

Class Tab   The Class tab opens an area called the *Class Designer* or *Class Editor*. This is somewhat like a wizard for manually created class files. It will prompt you through some common tasks such as creating and viewing methods and fields, creating BeanInfo for JavaBeans, and creating events. Figure 2-7 shows the Class tab opened to the methods editing area.

Doc Tab   This tab displays the Javadoc that you generated for the displayed source code. Figure 2-8 shows an example of generated Javadoc.

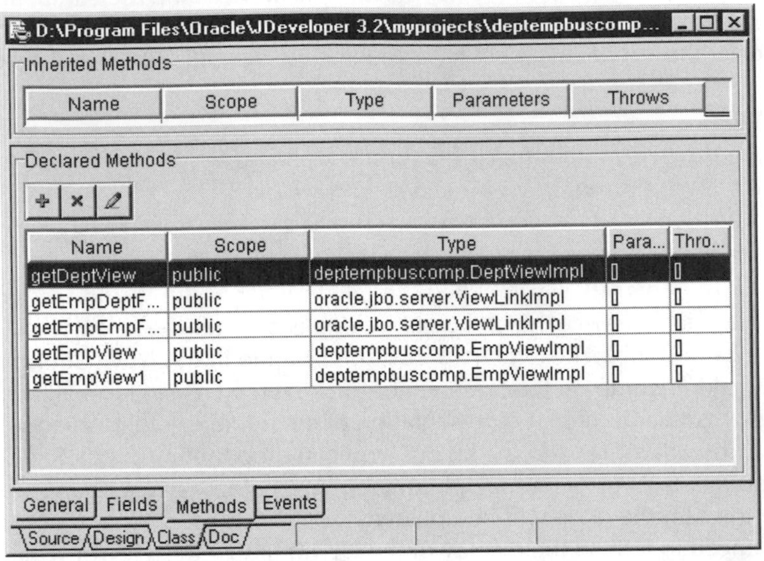

FIGURE 2-7. *Class tab, Methods area*

Generating Javadoc

Javadoc is a generated help file created from special comments in your code. The Doc tab displays previously generated Javadoc for the class. Generating the Javadoc is a manual process that starts in the Navigation Pane using the following steps:

1. Include documentation comments using the /**marker to start the comment and */ to end the comment. You can include any HTML tags, including those for embedded graphics, in these comments.

2. In the Navigation Pane, select a .java file that represents the class you want to document.

3. Select **Wizards | Generate Javadoc** from the menu. The wizard will appear.

4. Leave the defaults and click OK. A command window will open up to generate the doc and then close on its own.

If you want to see the Javadoc, doubleclick the .java file in the Navigation Pane. The Viewer window will open up. You can then click the Doc tab to view the documentation.

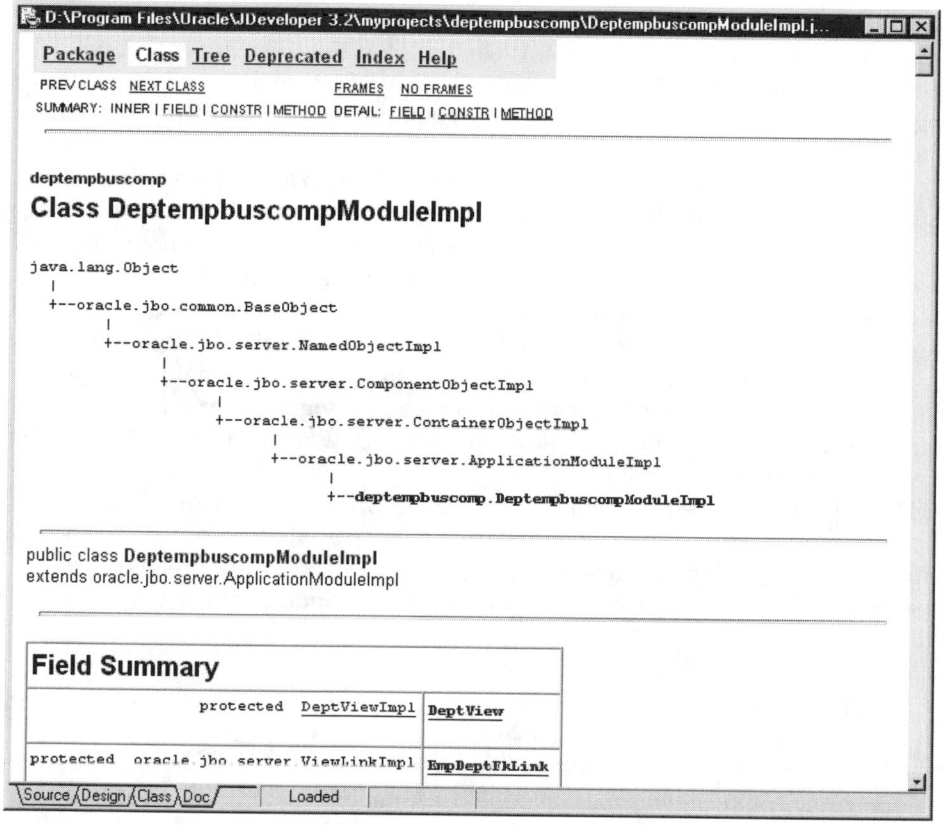

FIGURE 2-8.   *Generated Javadoc in the Doc tab*

Message View

This window shows messages that occur when you run, debug, or compile your code. If the message is an error, you can doubleclick on the error text in this window and the problem code will be highlighted in the Source tab. This gives you a quick way to navigate to the problem area.

Arranging the JDeveloper Windows

When you work with the JDeveloper IDE, you have to handle many work area windows. You will waste time arranging windows if you do not have a scheme for how windows should be placed in the tool. Here is one suggestion for that kind of scheme. You can adjust it as required. An example of how the windows appear is shown back in Figure 2-4.

The main arrangement is to anchor the Navigator to the left side of the main window and the Inspector to the right side of the main window. The area in between is reserved for the Viewers. When the Message View appears, it will automatically pop up at the bottom of the window. Be sure that the Navigator and Inspector windows are set to stay on top (as defined in the **Tools | IDE Options** dialog's Environment tab).

The easiest way to accomplish this arrangement is to anchor the two windows, then resize them so each has enough viewing space but there is room between them for the Viewer. Select **View | Property Inspector** if the Inspector is not displayed. Follow the instructions in the sidebar for *Anchoring a Floating Window* if you need help with that. When you open more than one Viewer window, you will find it useful to maximize the Viewer using the window maximize button in the upper-right corner of the window. This will give you the maximum amount of space between the Navigator and the Inspector. You can navigate between open Viewer windows using the list of open windows in the Window menu or by double-clicking the file name in the Navigator.

When you have the arrangement set, save the workspace you are working on. Opening a previously created workspace will revert the windows to the arrangement saved with that workspace, so you may need to repeat this procedure. If you start a new workspace from one that has properly arranged windows, the new workspace will inherit the arrangement.

NOTE
When you exit JDeveloper or close a workspace, JDeveloper will save the window sizes and cursor location. The next time you open the workspace, the windows will rearrange based upon this saved information.

Anchoring a Floating Window

Anchoring a floating Navigator or Inspector window requires a special technique. If the Navigator is floating (not docked), it will have a title bar. Grab the title bar and move the window to the left until the mouse cursor reaches the left border of the outer window. You will see the window outline click into place on the left side of the outer window. Release the mouse button and the window will stick. Use a similar technique to anchor the Inspector window to the right side of the outer window.

> **Note for Oracle Developer Users**
> You will notice obvious parallels between the JDeveloper IDE work areas and
> the Form Builder and Report Builder tools. The JDeveloper Inspector corresponds
> to the Property Palette in Forms and Reports. The Navigator is a more fully featured
> version of Developer's Object Navigator. The UI Designer corresponds to the
> Layout Editor, and the Menu Designer parallels the Developer Menu Editor. The
> Message View corresponds to the compiler error window in Developer. The
> Source tab in the Viewer is like the PL/SQL Editor in Forms and Reports. The
> JDeveloper wizards are similar in effect to the Developer wizards, although they
> manipulate very different objects. Chapter 5 contains more discussion on
> comparisons of thse tools.
>   A big difference between development in Developer Forms and Reports
> and JDeveloper is that JDeveloper creates one file for each class that is required.
> Therefore, there are many files for each application, whereas in Developer, one
> file is considered an application unit. Another big difference is that, in JDeveloper,
> you can see the source code for each property and layout change that you make.

Wizards

A *wizard* in JDeveloper is a dialog that steps you through the complexity of creating
an object. Typically, a wizard presents the required properties in an easy-to-understand
way, supplies default values where appropriate, and ensures that the values you enter
are appropriate and complete. The wizard dialog usually presents a series of pages
that step you through the process of creating an object. Next and Back buttons allow
you to navigate between pages. A Finish button closes the dialog and accepts all
values. There is usually a Help button that presents specific instructions on the step
you are performing. You can see these features in Figure 2-9, which is a page of the
Project Wizard.

Wizards Are for Real Programmers

Many programmers think that wizards are useful only for inexperienced or novice
users. That may be your perception, too, but JDeveloper wizards have so many
benefits that it is well worth changing your perception. The main benefit is that
wizards allow you to define an object completely and quickly. For example,
without a wizard, completely defining a multi-table Business Components for Java

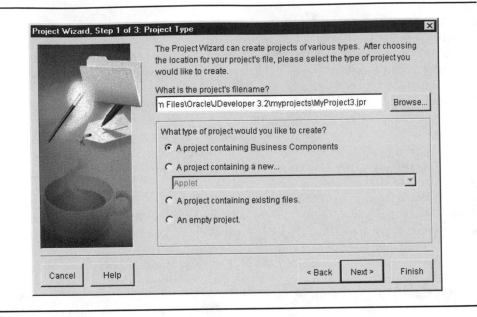

FIGURE 2-9. *Project Wizard's Project Type page*

(BC4J) project has many steps and some intricate relationships. It could take you hours to set up this kind of project manually. If you use the Business Components Project Wizard, you will have working code in a matter of minutes. The wizard approach also ensures that your definitions are complete and working. A manual approach requires debugging and a detailed awareness of all the related objects that need to be created.

CAUTION
Wizards hide the complexity of the code they are creating. While this is the main purpose of the wizard interface, it is important that you have an understanding of what you are creating and how it fits into the general context of the application.

Modifying What the Wizard Created
Different wizards create different types of objects. The details that you enter in a wizard are translated to code or project properties. Although some wizards are not *reentrant*—that is, you cannot open them to modify a created object—you can

always change properties after an object has been created. In most cases, the way you change properties is to doubleclick the object node in the Navigation Pane to show the properties dialog.

For example, the Business Components Project Wizard creates a large number of code files to access the database. Although you cannot modify the business components project in the same way after the wizard is finished, using the Navigation Pane, you can doubleclick any object that it creates and adjust the properties. Figure 2-10 shows a dialog that appears when you doubleclick the application module node in the business components project. You can also load this dialog by selecting Edit from the popup menu on the object. Other types of objects have similar menus, although the actual dialog will look different. This example is taken from the practice application at the end of this chapter.

This property dialog has a wizard-like interface that includes the same buttons. It does have tabs so that you can navigate freely between pages of the dialog. The wizard that originally produced the module, the Business Components Project Wizard, had a different interface for filling in the properties.

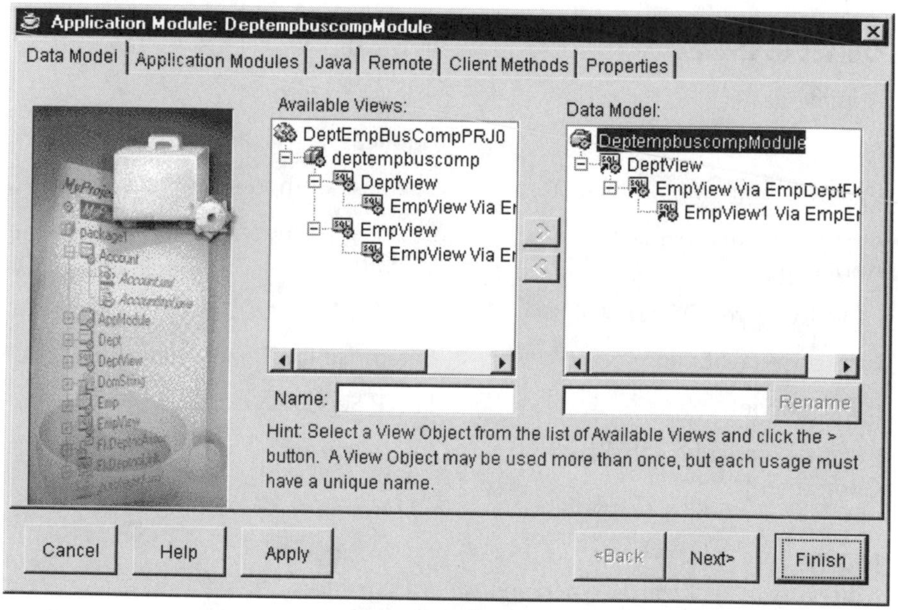

FIGURE 2-10. *The Application Module dialog*

NOTE
*You can define the formatting of the code that the wizards create to some degree. Selecting **Project | Project Properties** and navigating to the Code Style tab will allow you to specify some details for the code formatting. These properties can be changed for all new projects using the dialog in **Tools | Default Project Properties**.*

What Can Wizards Accomplish?

A list of JDeveloper wizards appears in Appendix A. Other chapters in this book give examples and hands-on practice for some of these wizards. However, it is useful at this point to get a feel for the different types of wizards that are available. The Project Wizard (shown in Figure 2-9) allows you to specify the contents of the project by selecting from the pulldown list. Depending on your selection, the Project Wizard will automatically run one of the following wizards when it has finished creating the project. This gives you a seamless transition into creating a particular object.

Object to Create	**Wizard**
Applet	Applet Wizard
Application	Application Wizard
Business Components Data Form	Business Components Data Form Wizard
Business Components JSP Application	Business Components JSP Application Wizard
CORBA Server Object	CORBA Server Object Wizard
Enterprise JavaBean	Enterprise JavaBean Wizard
HTTP Servlet	HTTP Servlet Wizard
Oracle Forms Pluggable Java Component	PJC Wizard

NOTE
You can create wizards to accomplish tasks that the native wizards cannot accomplish. Check the help system index for "Addins - about" for details.

The Help System

The JDeveloper help system can greatly facilitate your work in learning the tool and in accessing reference information.

Installing the Help System

When given a choice as you are installing JDeveloper, specify "HTML Help" as the style of help. (You can specify this if you select the type of install to be "Custom.") HTML Help is available if your system has MS Internet Explorer (4.0 or later) installed. If you do not have Internet Explorer installed, it is advisable to load it before installing JDeveloper because you will then be able to install HTML Help. If you select the "Typical" type of installation, the installer will automatically load WebHelp if Internet Explorer is not on your system.

If you do not have or do not wish to install Internet Explorer, you can specify that the installer load WebHelp, but you will be more limited in search capabilities. HTML Help allows you to perform full text searches. It also takes less hard disk space than WebHelp because it uses compressed .chm files to supply the text.

Help System Viewer

JDeveloper HTML Help contains a tab search area on the left and a text area on the right, as shown in Figure 2-11. The tab area contains the methods for navigating to a particular topic as follows:

- **Contents**   Use this tab to drill down through various levels of books that contain other books or pages. This is the same mechanism used for the MS help systems used by other Windows programs. When you find a topic, click it once to display the text in the text area.

- **Index**   You type in a keyword or phrase for the topic in this tab. As you type, the list under the search field reduces to match the words. The words in this index are preloaded by the help system's author. When you find a match In this tab, doubleclick it to display the text. Alternatively, you can select the matching topic and click the Display button.

- **Search**   This tab allows you to perform searches of any text in the help system. After typing the words, you click the List Topics button, and all matching topics are displayed in the list. Doubleclicking or selecting and clicking Display will show the topic in the text area.

- **Favorites**   When you find a topic that you would like to bookmark, navigate to this tab and click the Add button. This acts as a personalized list of topics that you can display at any point without drilling down or entering search words.

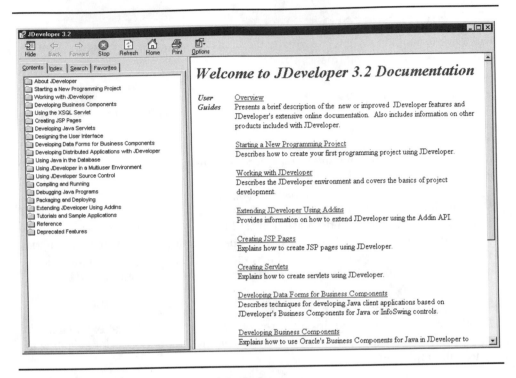

FIGURE 2-11. *Opening page of the help system*

The help viewer contains standard browser buttons that allow you to navigate through the pages that you have viewed. There is also a button, Hide, that removes the tab area in case you want to expand the text area. You redisplay the tab area by selecting the Show button. There is also a button, Print, that allows you to print the topic that is displayed in the text area.

TIP

If you need to print a portion of a help topic, select it and press CTRL-C *to copy the text to the clipboard. You can then paste the text into a text editor or word processor. If you paste into MS Word, the formatting will be preserved as it is in the help system. If you want to print a graphic in the help system, select Copy from the right-click menu and paste it into a graphics-aware editor such as MS Word.*

When you navigate to a topic that you found using the Search tab, the word or phrase that you entered as search criteria will be highlighted. If you want to turn this highlighting feature off, click the Options button and select **Search Highlight Off** from the pulldown menu.

TIP
Click an object in the UI Designer and press CTRL-SHIFT-F1 *to load the class information about the component into a help window.*

How to Display the Help System

You can display the HTML Help viewer using a number of methods:

- Selecting **Help | Help Topics** will display the opening page of the help system.

- Pressing F1 at any time in the tool will show a help topic that is as closely related as possible to what you are doing. Since many different topics may fit the current task, you may not see the topic that helps you at first. If you do not see the correct topic, use the search facilities to find what you are looking for once the help system has opened.

- Clicking the Help button in a dialog will show context-sensitive help.

- Navigating to a menu item, holding down the mouse button, and pressing F1 will display a help topic on the menu item.

TIP
Leave the help system window open once you have accessed it. The next time you need it, you will not have to wait for the window to load again.

Help System Contents

The help system Contents tab contains the following major topic categories:

- **Introductory topics**   There are headings for "About JDeveloper," "Starting a New Programming Project," and "Working with JDeveloper" that will get you started working with JDeveloper.

- **Specific techniques**   There are a large number of headings such as "Developing Business Components" and "Creating JSP Pages" that contain overview information and steps you may follow to create specific types of code for your application.

- **Tutorials and Sample Applications**   A single heading that contains step-by-step instructions for creating complete applications. The tutorials give practice with a particular style, such as a Java applet, and the sample applications demonstrate a particular technique, such as creating your own wizard.

- **Reference**   This is a heading that contains Oracle, Sun, and Other nodes for basic documentation on the libraries that each vendor supplies. For example, the Sun reference area contains a section on the Swing classes that Sun supplies. The format is the same as a standard reference guide, with API information about arguments, dependencies, interfaces, classes, and exceptions. There are no step-by-step guides here.

- **Deprecated Features**   A heading that refers to features in the product that were once part of the product, but are now obsolete. The features are supported with the current version, but you should avoid using them in new development work because they may be unsupported in a future release.

TIP
When learning the tool, it is a good use of time to spend 20 minutes exploring the help system to understand how it is organized. This time will pay back manyfold when you have to find a particular subject while working with the tools. In that 20 minutes, you will also pick up some useful information about JDeveloper.

About the Hands-on Practice

Now that you have toured the main areas of the tool, it is time to put the IDE to use. The hands-on practice that follows steps you through the process of creating a Java application. It is unlike many normal tutorials because it spends time explaining the objective of what you are accomplishing and provides a review to describe the objects that you are creating. Therefore, it may take you some time to complete the practice.

Steps for Creating a User Interface

When you set up objects for a user interface, you follow these steps for each object in the application:

1. **Create a container**, such as a frame or panel. You also set up its layout characteristics.

2. **Place the component into the container**, by dropping it from the component palette onto a node in the Structure Pane. The component will appear as a child object of the object that it was dropped on. Alternatively, you can drop the component on the UI Designer, and the component will be added under the object you dropped it on. The final variation is to select the node in the Structure Pane that will become the parent to the new object and drop the object into a blank area in the Structure Pane. The effect is the same regardless of the technique.

3. **Set the properties** of the new object to customize it for your requirements. You also set the component's constraints, which determine where the component will display.

4. **Attach event handlers**, if the object requires. In addition, you may need to write some code to modify or set properties outside of the Inspector.

The hands-on practice provides examples of this set of steps for many objects.

Projects and Workspaces

You will be creating a workspace and two projects. As a review from Chapter 1, a *workspace* is a collection of projects and other files that have a name. The workspace represents a file that you create in the file system. JDeveloper stores the names and details of all files in the collection in the workspace file.

A project is a collection of files that can contain Java, XML, HTML, text, and *graphics* (.gif, .jpg, .bmp, .au, and .wav) files from different locations in the file system. The project file stores the names of all files you create or open in the project. You can edit this project information using the navigators. The file JDEV_HOME\lib\jdeveloper.properties also stores information about projects. You can change this file, but it is best to make a backup before you do so.

What the Practice Creates

You will create *Java classes*—collections of methods and attributes or properties—contained in a package. The package name is stated at the top of the source code for the class.

When you run the application that you will create, the runtime calls the `main()` method, which creates the application object (via the constructor method). This constructor calls the frame class to create the frame and display the window.

Figure 2-12 shows the basic parts required for the application as they will appear in the Navigator. The application code is generated for you when you define the project and the frame. Each part represented has either Java, XML, or both types of code to implement it. In addition, the workspace and projects are represented by files (.jws and .jpr, respectively) that contain the definitions of the parts within them. The Connection box in this diagram represents the Connections node in the Navigator that you use to test the application code by connecting it to the database. When the code is deployed, you have many options for how the connection is made. Chapter 6 discusses business components concepts further.

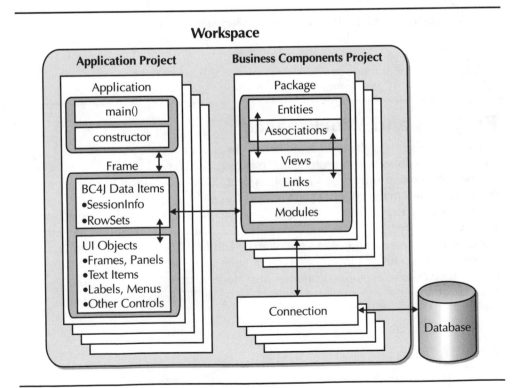

FIGURE 2-12. *Hands-on practice components*

It is useful to remember that the package represented by the diagram is a directory. JDeveloper uses this directory to store other files such as the .jpr file that defines the project. However, when the code is deployed, the package will contain the Java class files that implement the package but will not include the JDeveloper-specific definition files such as the .jpr.

TIP

If you want to clean out old practice sessions, you can delete the appropriate files and subdirectories from the myprojects directory. To completely remove the practice sessions, you also have to delete the corresponding directories and compiled files from the myclasses directory. If you created HTML files, you need to remove them from the myhtml directory. If you want to delete a connection, doubleclick the Connections node in the Navigation Pane, select the connection, and click the Delete button. Connections are stored in the connections.properties file in JDEV_HOME\myclasses directory.

Hands-on Practice: Creating a Java Application Using the IDE Tools

In this practice, you will use the IDE tools to build a Java application based on the DEPT table. Since the steps to create a workspace and projects are very similar to those in the Chapter 1 practice, the instructions are somewhat abbreviated here. There is a similar tutorial in the JDeveloper help system if you need more practice.

The drag-and-drop approach to development using the IDE tools gives you much more flexibility than the pure wizard approach. By nature, this flexibility requires more steps to reach the final goal. Regardless of whether you use the wizard approach or the IDE tools approach, you always have the option of editing the generated code. In this practice, you will complete the following phases:

I. Create a workspace

II. Create the business components project

■ **Create a project**

■ **Create a connection**

■ **Define the business components code**

   III. **Create the user interface project**

- **Create another project**
- **Add an application and frame**

   IV. **Add the data-layer controls**

   V. **Add the user interface controls**

- **Check the window called "this"**
- **Add a status bar to the panel**
- **Add panels to control the layout**
- **Add a navigation bar**
- **Add additional panels**
- **Add labels and fields**
- **Add a login dialog**

   VI. **Compile and run the Java application**

The completed application will look something like the one shown in Figure 2-13. If you need to stop in the middle of this practice or any other practice, click Save All in the toolbar before you exit. When you return to JDeveloper, the tool will open the same workspace that was open when you exited. If you need to reload the workspace for this practice, select **File** | **Close Workspace** and **File** | **Open**. Navigate to the deptideapp folder and open the DeptIdeWS.jws workspace file.

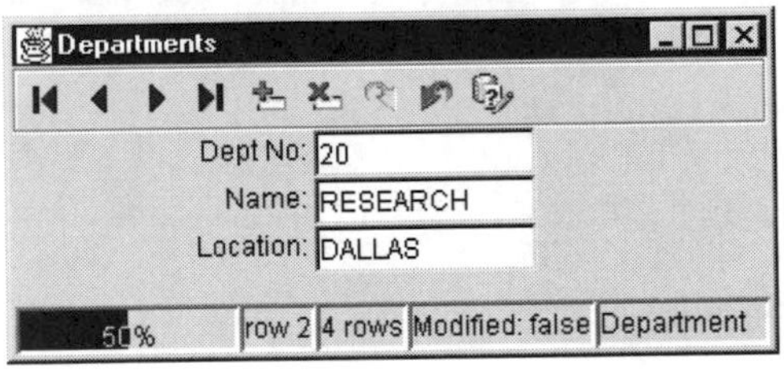

FIGURE 2-13. *The completed application*

CAUTION
Before starting, be sure that your sample database contains foreign key constraints for the DEPT and EMP tables because the wizard in this practice will use them. There should be a foreign key constraint defined on EMP.DEPTNO referencing the DEPT.DEPTNO column. In addition, there should be a foreign key constraint on EMP.MGR that references EMP.EMPNO. A script to create those constraints may be found on the web sites mentioned in the author biographies.

I. Create a Workspace

This step creates a workspace named "DeptIdeWS" to store the files and settings you use while developing the sample application. The workspace file will be stored with other files for this application in a folder named "deptideapp" that stores the application code. You will also create another folder, "deptempbuscomp," which stores the business component code. These folders correspond to the Java packages that are created to contain the code.

1. If you have an existing workspace open, select **File | Close Workspace**. If you have files that are not saved, you need to respond to the Save Modified Files dialog. The Navigation Pane will display a new default workspace named "Untitled1.jws."

2. Choose **File | Save Workspace**.

TIP
*Instead of step 1, you can select **File | New Workspace** from the menu.*

3. Click the Create New Folder icon in the Save As dialog and name the folder "deptideapp." This folder will be a subdirectory of myprojects.

4. Doubleclick "deptideapp" to make it the current directory.

5. To name the workspace file, click the *File name* field, and change the default to "DeptIdeWS."

6. Click Save to dismiss the file dialog. The Navigation Pane will now look like this:

What Just Happened? You created a workspace that will contain the JDeveloper projects used for the application. The workspace file (with the .jws extension) stores a list of files that make up the workspace. This file and other code files that you will create are stored in a subdirectory that you created to represent the Java package (deptideapp).

II. Create the Business Components Project

You will now create a project file to store the business components. You will also create the business components that represent the DEPT and EMP tables. The business components will be virtually the same as in Chapter 1, but in this practice, the code will be assigned to a separate folder so that it may be easily reused in other applications. The Project Wizard will start the Business Components Project Wizard that will create the code files for the BC4J layer.

This practice will not display the EMP table in the user interface, but the business component that you create in this step will contain both tables and will be used for applications in other practices.

CAUTION
Be sure to arrange your windows as suggested in the earlier section "Arranging the JDeveloper Windows." Otherwise, you may see dialog windows that pop up underneath the Navigator window or Inspector.

Create a Project
Now you need to create a project for the business components.

1. Choose **File | New Project**. The Project Wizard will start. If the Welcome page is displayed, click Next.

TIP

Uncheck the checkbox on the Welcome page if you
want to bypass this page in the future.

2. In the Project Type page, click Browse to display the Select Project dialog. Create a new folder called "deptempbuscomp" under myprojects and navigate to the new folder. Your business component code files will be stored in this folder and become part of the package.

3. In the *File name* field, replace the default value with **DeptEmpBusCompPRJ**, and click Open. JDeveloper will apply the extension (.jpr) to the project file name and fill in the appropriate project name field in the wizard, as shown here:

Project Wizard, Step 1 of 3: Project Type	☒

The Project Wizard can create projects of various types. After choosing the location for your project's file, please select the type of project you would like to create.

What is the project's filename?

`'projects\deptempbuscomp\DeptEmpBusCompPRJ.jpr`   Browse...

What type of project would you like to create?

- ⊙ A project containing Business Components
- ○ A project containing a new...
  - [Applet ▾]
- ○ A project containing existing files
- ○ An empty project

Cancel	Help		« Back	Next »	Finish

4. Leave the default selection for *A project containing Business Components* so the Business Components Wizard will display at the appropriate moment. Click Next. This will display the Project Options page.

5. Click Browse next to the field called *What is the name of the project's default package* to display the Package Browser. Select "deptempbuscomp" as the package for this project, and click OK.

6. Leave the defaults for source path and output directory. Click Next to move to the Project Information page.

7. Enter information to describe your project (*Title, Author, Copyright, Company,* and *Description*). Leave the *Generate project HTML file* box unchecked.

NOTE
*You can change the default values that appear in this page using the Defaults page on the **Tools** | **Default Project Properties** dialog.*

8. Click Next to continue. You will now see a summary of the options you have selected as follows:

```
Project Wizard: Finish                                      [X]

            You have completed the Project Wizard.
            You have selected the following options for your Project:

            Project File
               D:\Program Files\Oracle\JDeveloper 3.2\myprojects\deptempbusc
            Project Type
               Business Component
            Project Options
            ⊟ Default Package
                  deptempbuscomp4
            ⊟ Source Path
                  D:\Program Files\Oracle\JDeveloper 3.2\myprojects
            ⊟ Output Directory
                  D:\Program Files\Oracle\JDeveloper 3.2\myclasses
            Project Info
            ⊟ Project HTML file

            Click Finish to create your new Project.

  Cancel      Help                    < Back    Next >    Finish
```

9. Click Finish to create the project and invoke the Business Components Project Wizard.

Create a Connection

You need to create a definition that links the BC4J project to a database schema. The following steps accomplish this task.

1. Click Next if the Welcome page appears. This will display the Connection page.

2. The next steps will create a connection like the one you created in Chapter 1 but with a different name.

3. Click New to open the Connection dialog and set up the database connection. Fill in the following properties:

- *Connection Name* as "ScottConnection"

- *Username* as "SCOTT"

- *Password* as "TIGER"

- *Include password in deployment archive* Leave this unchecked. If this were checked, the database login would occur automatically and you would not need to create a login box for the application.

- *Select a JDBC Driver* Leave the default of "Oracle JDBC Thin."

- *Select a connection method* Select "Named Host" (the preferred value) and fill in the Host ID, SID, and Port fields. If you have set up Net8 or SQL*Net on your machine, you can use "Existing TNS Names," and the Host ID, SID, and Port details will be filled in based on your selection. If you need further help with the values, ask your DBA for details. Leave the other defaults as they appear.

4. Click Test Connection. If you entered the appropriate values, you will see a success message to the right of the Test Connection button.

NOTE
Remember that if your connection fails, you will not be able to continue with the wizard.

5. Click OK to dismiss the Connection dialog. Click Next to continue with the Business Components Project Wizard.

Define the Business Components Code

The following steps complete the business components project by defining the data elements that it will access.

1. If a login dialog appears, click OK.

2. In the Package Name page, accept the default package name, "deptempbuscomp," and click Next.

3. In the Business Components page, the top pulldown list should indicate that the database schema is SCOTT. If your tables are owned by another user, select that user from the pulldown list.

4. Be sure that the *Tables* checkbox is checked. If you had other object types (such as views or synonyms to another schema's tables) that you wanted to include in this component, you would select them here.

5. Select "DEPT" and "EMP" (using CTRL-click) in the *Available* field's list, and use the " >" button to move them to the *Selected* field, as shown here:

6. In the *Create default Business Components* area, be sure that the *View Objects and View Links* and *Application Module* checkboxes are checked. The former will create the .xml and .java code needed to access the tables (entities). This application will not work without the View Object for the DEPT table. The *View Links* are used to implement the entities' *associations—* objects that represent the foreign keys on the tables. Checking the *Application Module* checkbox causes the .xml and .java code to be created for the *application module—*an overall container that holds the view objects and view links.

NOTE
A view object represents a query consisting of one or more entities. The entity represents a database object (table or view). A view link represents an entity association, which could represent a foreign key constraint. The application module holds the view and view link objects as well as the database session information. (Refer to Chapter 6 for details on these BC4J concepts.)

7. Click Next to display the Finish page. Click Finish to create the business components and add them to your project.

TIP

Remember that you can click Finish on most pages in the wizards, and the other pages will fill in with default values.

8. To save your work, select **File | Save All**, or click the Save All icon in the toolbar.

What Just Happened?   You created a project inside the workspace using the Project Wizard. This project was earmarked for Business Components for Java, which started the Business Components Project Wizard. The wizard created business component .java and .xml files that represent the database objects to be used in the application. You will see the files that were created if you browse the nodes in the Navigation Pane, as shown in Figure 2-14.

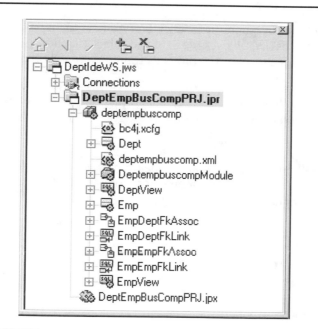

FIGURE 2-14.   *The Business Components project*

III. Create the User Interface Project

This stage uses the Project Wizard to create a project for the user-interface code. You then create an application class using the Application Wizard. The *application* is an executable program that runs within a Java Virtual Machine (JVM). The Application Wizard then calls the Frame Wizard to create a frame class that is attached to the application class. The *frame* is a window that acts as a container for the user interface objects.

Create Another Project

Now you need to create another project for the application.

1. Choose **File** | **New Project** to display the Project Wizard. Click Next if the Welcome page appears.

2. In the Project Type page, click Browse and navigate to the folder called "deptideapp."

3. Replace the default *File name* value with "DeptAppPRJ," and click Open.

4. In the *What type of project would you like to create?* area, select "An empty project." Click Next.

5. In the Project Options page, click Browse next to the *What is the name of the project's default package* field and select "deptideapp." Click OK in the Package Browser. The project's source path and output directory will remain at their default values.

6. Click Next to move to the Project Information page. On this page, enter information to describe your project.

7. Click Next to continue.

8. You will now see a summary of the options you have selected. Click Finish to create the project. You should see a project file (DeptAppPRJ.jpr) listed below Connections in the Navigation Pane.

9. Click Save All.

Add an Application and Frame

The following steps create the application and frame using wizards for each object.

1. Select the new project file.

2. Select **File** | **New** to display the Object Gallery shown here:

3. Select the Application icon. Click OK. The Application Wizard will open as shown here:

4. Leave the default names for the package (where the code will be stored) as deptideapp and the class (the name used in the code) as Application1. If there were more than one application, it would be important to use a descriptive name.

5. Leave the *Add a default frame* field selected, but select "A new empty frame." This will cause the Frame Wizard to appear after the next step.

6. Be sure that the *Center frame on screen* checkbox is checked, and click OK to create the Application1.java file. The Frame Wizard will now display as shown next.

7. Accept the default values for *Class* as "Frame1," *Package* as "deptideapp," and *Extends* as "javax.swing.JFrame." If you were creating more than one frame in the application, it would be important to name each frame descriptively. The class and package names have the same purpose as in the application. The *Extends* field indicates which existing class will serve as the superclass (master) for the user interface frame.

8. Fill in the *Title* field with "Departments." This will become the window title.

9. Leave all other *Optional attributes* fields blank. In the future, if you want the wizard to create default code for a menu bar, toolbar, status bar, or About dialog, you would check the appropriate checkboxes.

10. Click OK to generate the Frame1.java file. The Navigation Pane should look like this:

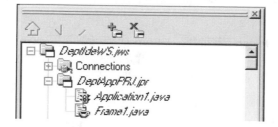

11. Select the project node and click the Make icon in the toolbar to compile the project.

12. Save your work by clicking the Save All icon in the toolbar.

TIP
It is a good habit to compile projects as you create them. This not only helps check the syntax of the code but also allows the project's objects to become available in selection lists for other objects.

What Just Happened?   You created another project that contains the code files for classes representing the application and the frame. These will hold the user-interface classes that are created in the next step.

IV. Add the Data-Layer Controls

This step adds two controls that the form will use to access the database. Both are data-layer controls that are built on the InfoBus standard, which defines how data is passed to Java controls. The two controls that you will use follow:

A **SessionInfo** component establishes a connection path to exchange data with the BC4J application module. It can contain one or more RowSetInfo components.

The **RowSetInfo** control works with the SessionInfo object to supply and cache the data for the user interface objects. Each business component view object (a representation of the table) is represented by a RowSetInfo component.

The following steps will create the code to implement these controls.

1. Double-click "Frame1.java" in the Navigation Pane. The Viewer window will open.

2. Click the Design tab at the bottom of the frame's Viewer window to display the UI Designer. JDeveloper will parse your source code and display the frame graphically. The Inspector window should pop up at this time.

NOTE
If the Inspector is not displayed, you can select **View | Property Inspector** *from the menu. Once again, be sure that you have set up your windows as described in the earlier section "Arranging the JDeveloper Windows."*

3. Click the SessionInfo icon in the InfoProducers tab of the palette. Click anywhere in the Structure Pane. This will add a data item called sessionInfo1 to the frame, as shown here:

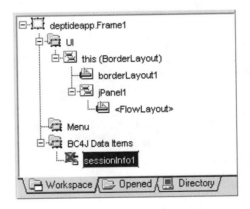

NOTE
The "x" on the SessionInfo data item indicates that the session has not been associated with a database connection.

4. In the Inspector, change the *name* property of the SessionInfo object to "sessionInfo." Change the *bindName* property to "sessionInfo."

5. Click the *appModuleInfo* property in the Inspector window. Click the "…" button to open the appModuleInfo dialog.

6. Accept the default module name by clicking OK.

7. Click the *connectionInfo* property and click the "…" button to open the connectionInfo dialog. In the *Deployment Type* field, be sure that "Local" is selected. This means that the application logic will reside on your machine. The *Deployment Mode* field will remain empty.

8. In the *JDBC connection* pulldown list, verify the selection of the connection you defined in the Business Components Project Wizard, "ScottConnection." Click OK. The icon for the SessionInfo item will no longer have a red "x," as shown here:

9. From the InfoProducer tab, click the RowSetInfo icon.

10. Click anywhere in the Structure Pane to add the RowSetInfo control to the application.

11. Be sure the new item is selected and change the following properties:

- *name* to "deptRowSet"
- *bindName* to "department"
- *session* to "sessionInfo"

12. Click the "…" button on the *queryInfo* property to open the queryInfo dialog, as shown in Figure 2-15.

13. On the Definition tab, be sure that "Single Table (Master only)" is selected.

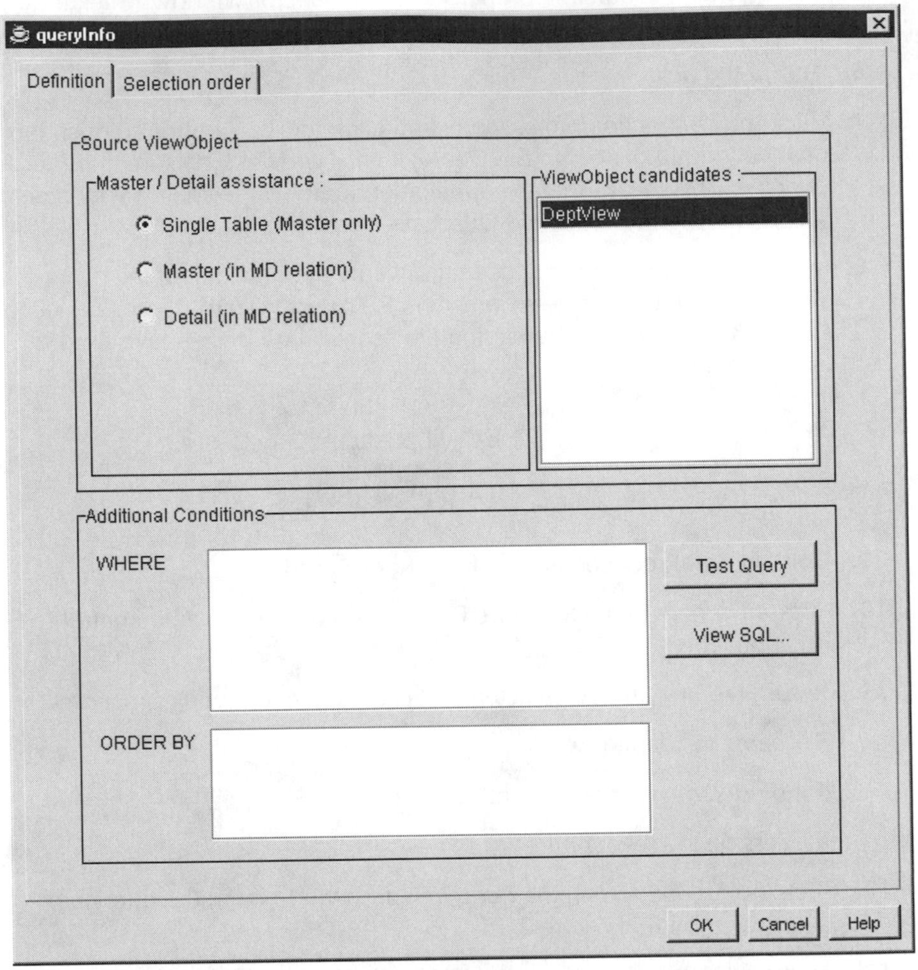

FIGURE 2-15. queryInfo *dialog,* Definition *tab*

14. In the *ViewObject candidates* list, select "DeptView" and click the Selection order tab.

15. Move all columns (Deptno, Dname, and Loc) to the *Selected Columns* list using the ">>" button.

16. Click the Definition tab, and click Test Query to test the query. Click OK to confirm success.

NOTE
Additional clauses of the query can be entered in the WHERE and ORDER BY fields. This RowSetInfo component provides the final filter for the rows that are to be returned to the client application from the Business Components layer.

17. Click OK to exit the queryInfo dialog.

NOTE
Clicking OK will test the query again. If you had entered a WHERE or ORDER BY clause that was syntactically incorrect, you would receive an error message when clicking OK. If you receive an error message that there are no columns selected, revisit the Selection order tab and reselect the columns before clicking OK. Columns must be selected before proceeding.

18. Click Save All. The Structure Pane should now look like this:

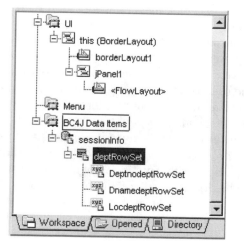

What Just Happened?   You just created the data-layer controls that are responsible for connecting the application's interface controls to the business components and, therefore, to the database objects. The next step will create the interface controls and hook the data controls to them.

V. Add the User Interface Controls

The frame to which you will be adding objects appears in the Viewer window's Design tab. Now you will use the following controls to define the look and feel of the Java application:

 StatusBarControl to display a progress meter and other information such as the current record number and total number of records

NavigationBar control to allow scrolling between records, adding, editing, deleting, and locating records

JPanel controls to contain the objects and provide automatic layout

 TextFieldControl controls to display data

JLabel controls to identify the fields

LoginDlg to prompt the user for input on the database connection

All of these controls except JPanel and JLabel must be bound to the data-layer controls you added in the previous step. This data awareness is indicated by the control's icon. All controls in the InfoSwing tab (see examples in the preceding table) contain a database "drum" symbol indicating a *data-aware control* (DAC).

The default behavior of this form is to automatically execute a query upon startup and allow the user to scroll through the records. Data returns to the BC4J layer that links to the user interface controls through the data-layer controls.

Java uses *layouts* (or *layout managers*) to control how the objects within the user interface arrange themselves. Each layout has a particular appearance and behavior. For example, setting the *layout* property of an object to "ColumnLayout" will automatically stack all objects that are inside of it. If you want to keep the objects inside fixed to a specific location, you set the outer object to have an XYLayout. A BorderLayout layout manager will expand objects inside it to fill the entire outer object. (Chapter 11 discusses layout managers in more detail.)

For this practice, you will designate one of several layouts for each panel that you add. The panels act as containers for the interface objects and provide this automatic layout functionality. Figure 2-16 shows how the main panels and some other controls will be nested using the steps in this section.

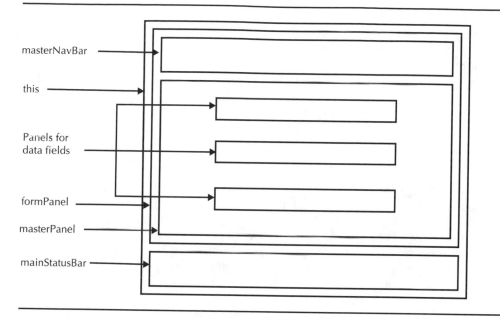

FIGURE 2-16. *User interface layout components*

Check the Window Called "this"

Now you have to verify that the default layout property is set for the main window.

1. In the Structure Pane under the UI node, select "this."

2. In the Inspector, be sure that the *layout* property is set to "BorderLayout."

Add a Status Bar to the Panel

The next steps add the control that shows the status of various objects at runtime.

1. Click StatusBarControl in the InfoSwing tab and click "this" in the Structure Pane.

2. Select the status bar and change the following properties for the status bar:

   ■ *name* to "mainStatusBar"

   ■ *constraints* to "South" to anchor the status bar to the bottom of the panel

TIP
If a property value is contained in a pulldown list, you can press the key of the first letter of the value after clicking the property name. If there is more than one match, you can press the same key again. For example, to set the constraints properties to "South," you can click the property, and press the "s" key. You can also doubleclick the property value to cycle through the list.

Add Panels to Control the Layout

The best way to control the layout is to place objects into containers that have automatic layout capabilities. The following steps create panel containers for this purpose.

As mentioned earlier and shown in Figure 2-16, there are a number of nested panels in this example. The first panel to add will fill the entire portion of the form above the status bar.

1. Click Jpanel1 in the Structure Pane and change the following properties:

   ■ *name* as "formPanel"

   ■ *layout* as "Border Layout"

   ■ *constraints* Be sure that this is set to the default of "Center."

2. Use in-place editing to change the name of formPanel's layout object to "formLayout." (Hint: In the Structure Pane, click the layout object name under formPanel. Then click the name again to open an edit box.)

Add a Navigation Bar

The navigation bar provides a set of buttons for manipulating the records displayed.

1. Click the NavigationBar icon in the InfoSwing tab, and drop it on the formPanel in the Structure Pane. This will add the bar to the frame.

2. Select the navigation bar and change the following properties:

   ■ *name* as "masterNavBar"

   ■ *dataItemName* as "deptRowSet" (selected using the dialog accessed with the "..." button on that property)

   ■ *constraints* as the default "North"

Add Additional Panels

To control the display further, you need to create additional panels that have automatic layout capabilities.

1. From the Swing Containers tab, click JPanel and click formPanel in the Structure Pane. Change the following properties of the new panel:

- *name* field to "masterPanel"

- *constraints* to "Center"

- *layout* to "ColumnLayout"

JPanel is not a data-aware control, so you do not need to bind it to data.

2. Name the new layout object "masterLayout."

3. In the Structure Pane, select masterNavBar and ensure that its *constraints* property is set to "North." This may have changed after you dropped in the navigation bar.

4. From the Swing Containers tab, click JPanel, and then click masterPanel in the Structure Pane to add a panel.

5. Select the new panel and change the following properties:

- *name* to "deptnoPanel"

- *layout* to "ControlLayout"

NOTE
The JDeveloper wizards use a slightly different naming convention. For example, the wizards call this panel "panelDEPTNO." The naming conventions used in this practice follow the guideline of a type or class suffix that is presented in Chapter 3.

6. Change the name of the new layout object to "deptnoLayout."

7. Repeat steps 4–6 for the DNAME and LOC fields. Use panel names that correspond to these fields (for example, dnamePanel and locPanel). Change the layouts and rename them appropriately (for example, dnameLayout and locLayout).

CAUTION
*Be sure that the object is selected in the Structure
Pane before changing its properties.*

Add Labels and Fields

The following steps add the data fields and their prompts (labels).

1. In the Swing tab, click JLabel, and then click deptnoPanel in the Structure
   Pane to add the label. Change the following properties of the
   new label object:

   - *name* to "deptnoLabel"

   - *constraints* to "ControlConstraints.ALIGN_RIGHT, 0, 0, -1, -1"

   - *text* to "Dept No: " (there is a space after the ":")

2. From the InfoSwing tab, click TextFieldControl, and then click deptnoPanel
   in the Structure Pane to add the field. Change the following properties of
   the new field:

   - *name* as "deptnoTextField"

   - *dataItemName* as "deptnodeptRowSet" (set using the dialog accessed
     with the "..." button in that dialog) in the dataItemName dialog.

3. Click OK.

4. Repeat steps 1-3 for DNAME and LOC using appropriate field names (such
   as dnameTextField and locTextField), label names (such as dnameLabel and
   locLabel), label text (such as "Name:" and "Location:"), and data bindings.

5. Click "this" in the Structure Pane and resize the "this" window in the
   Design tab so it looks like the following:

Departments	_ □ ×
I⟨ ⟨ ▷ ▷I ⟰ ✕ ⟲ ⟳	
Dept No:	deptnoTextField
Name:	dnameTextField
Location:	locTextField
0%	row 0	0 rows	Modified: false	...

6. Click Save All.

TIP

To make the window automatically resize based on its contents, add pack () *in the frame's constructor method. For example:*

```
try {
      jbInit();
      pack();
}
```

Add a Login Dialog

The last step is to add the login dialog object that will make the connection to the database.

1. Click the LoginDlg control in the InfoSwing toolbar and click on the frame object in the Design tab. This will add a LoginDlg under the Other node in the Structure Pane.

2. Change the *dataItemName* property of the new object to "sessionInfo." This represents the session, which this login dialog will connect to and verify.

3. Switch to the Source tab in the Viewer window and add the following code to the imports list at the top of the file:

   ```
   import oracle.dacf.control.LoginFailureException;
   ```

   This will ensure that the code can find the code that manages this control.

   Find the line that calls `loginDlg1.setDataItemName()` in the `jbInit` function. Add the following after that line:

   ```
   if (loginDlg1.showDialog() == JOptionPane.CANCEL_OPTION) {
       throw new LoginFailureException();
   }
   ```

   This line displays the login dialog and defines what will happen when the login fails or is canceled.

4. Click Save All.

What Just Happened?   You just added panels, labels, and fields to represent the data. You also added a status bar and navigation bar to assist the user, and a login box with some code so the user can specify a database connection. The Structure Pane nodes are shown in Figure 2-17.

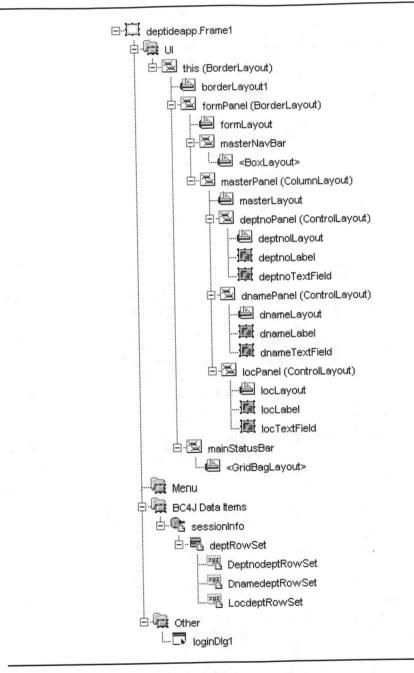

FIGURE 2-17. *Frame objects in the Structure Pane*

VI. Compile and Run the Java Application

In JDeveloper, you need to compile each project separately. Running the application is a simple button click once you have compiled it.

1. Select DeptAppPRJ.jpr in the Navigation Pane and select **Project | Rebuild Project "DeptAppPRJ.jpr"** from the menu. Alternatively, you can click the Rebuild toolbar icon or right-click and select Rebuild from the popup menu.

2. Select DeptEmpBusCompPRJ.jpr in the Navigation Pane and select **Project | Rebuild Project "DeptEmpBusCompPRJ.jpr"** or use the Rebuild toolbar icon. This is a redundant step if you compiled the project as instructed in the preceding steps and did not change the project after compiling. It is essential to have the business components project compiled before running the application, so when in doubt, rebuild.

CAUTION
Be aware of where the cursor is when you compile. If you click on the frame and compile, the application will not be compiled. The best method is always to select the project node in the Navigation Pane before compiling.

3. Click the Save All icon.

4. In the Navigation Pane, select Application1.java and select **Run | Run "Application1"** or click the Run icon.

5. When the login dialog appears, log into the database with the proper ID and password.

What Just Happened?   You just compiled and ran the code that was generated in the preceding steps. You can now experiment with the Java application. For example, you can navigate through the department records using the navigation bar, and you can test the other icons on the navigation bar. If there are errors, you need some simple techniques to debug the application. Exit the application when you are finished by closing its window.

Troubleshooting the Java Application

When you test code such as the code in this practice, you are testing the user interface, its binding to the data control layer, the data controls, and the business components. JDeveloper presents error messages for all problems in a separate window as you compile and run.

Although the process and concepts of this practice are more important than correct results, you will probably want to see a working application. Chapter 13 explains the JDeveloper debugger, but you can use the techniques here to identify common problem areas.

NOTE
When all else fails, it is possible that your JDeveloper installation is suspect. If you cannot successfully create an application using the wizard as described in Chapter 1, the easiest solution is probably to uninstall and reinstall JDeveloper. This is actually easier than it sounds.

General Debugging Tips

The following are some standard techniques you can use to troubleshoot the application.

■ A Message View window will pop up if there are compile errors. The message text should indicate the line in which the error occurred. Doubleclick the error message to navigate to the problem code. This should help you identify and fix code syntax problems.

■ The first thing to do is to ensure that all projects have a current build. Click on each project node one at a time and click the Rebuild icon.

■ You can also doublecheck that all properties and objects have been correctly defined by comparing the instructions with the properties and objects.

■ Check that you have properly defined the frame. Check the hierarchy of objects in the Structure Pane, as shown in Figure 2-17. Check your structure against this one. If something is out of place, you can right-click it and select Cut from the popup menu. Select the node that the object should appear under. Right-click and select Paste so that it will appear under that node.

Testing and Editing the Connection

There are some tests that become part of the normal development process. For example, when you define a connection, you can test it to ensure that it accesses the database. If you need to test it after the initial definition, use the following steps:

1. Right-click the Connections node in the Navigation Pane and select Connections from the menu. Alternatively, you can select **Tools | Connections** from the menu.

2. Click a connection and click the Edit button.

3. Click the Test Connection button in the Connection dialog. You can modify and save the definition here as well.

Testing and Editing the Row Set

When you define a row set, you click the Test Query button to check that the SELECT statement is properly written. After the RowSet is defined, you can double-check this by returning to the queryInfo property dialog as follows:

1. Doubleclick the Frame object in the Navigation Pane and click the Design tab of the Viewer window. The frame's interface objects will be displayed in the Structure Pane.

2. Select the RowSet node in the Structure Pane and open the queryInfo property's dialog from the Inspector. Check that you have the proper column list defined and that the Test Query routine indicates a successful query.

Testing with the Oracle Business Components Browser

After defining a business components project, you can test its code using the Oracle Business Components Browser. Use the following steps:

1. Open the business component's project node in the Navigation Pane and find the node that represents the application module. You will be able to identify this because it is named the same as the name you gave the subdirectory but with a suffix of "Module," for example, "DeptempbuscompappModule."

2. Right-click the application module node and select Test from the menu. The Connect dialog will open. Verify the settings and click Connect. If another login dialog appears, enter the password and click OK.

3. The Oracle Business Components Browser window will appear, as in Figure 2-18. This window contains an Object Navigator and a Viewer pane. For testing purposes at this point, you just need to doubleclick a node for one of the View Object Members or select Show from the right-click menu.

The view area should be filled with an application that you can use to test the data view as Figure 2-19 shows. The application contains a navigation bar that you can use to test the data browsing features. If this application works, you can be certain that your business components are working. There are other features of this application that you can learn by reading the help topic that appears when you select **Help | Contents**.

```
┌─────────────────────────────────────────────────────────────────┐
│ [■] Oracle Business Component Browser (Local)        [_][□][X]    │
├─────────────────────────────────────────────────────────────────┤
│  File   View   Create   Help                                      │
├─────────────────────────────────────────────────────────────────┤
│  [◄]  [▶]                                                          │
├─────────────────────────────────────────────────────────────────┤
│  [■] DeptempbuscompModule                                         │
│  ├─[■] View Object Members                                        │
│  │    ├─[■] DeptView                                              │
│  │    ├─[■] EmpView                                               │
│  │    └─[■] EmpView1                                              │
│  ├─[■] View Link Members                                          │
│  │    ├─[■] EmpEmpFkLink                                          │
│  │    └─[■] EmpDeptFkLink                                         │
│  └─[■] Application Module Members                                 │
│                                                                   │
├─────────────────────────────────────────────────────────────────┤
│  Name: DeptempbuscompModule  Definition: deptempbuscomp.Deptempbuscomp
└─────────────────────────────────────────────────────────────────┘
```

FIGURE 2-18.   *Oracle Business Components Browser*

TIP
*Using this browser tool, show the EmpEmpFKLink
member that represents the foreign key link between
manager and employee. The tool will create a
master-detail application with a navigator for
browsing the employee hierarchy. You get all
of this without writing any code!*

NOTE
*You can extend and customize the JDeveloper IDE
to match your preferences. Appendix B provides
information on the extension and customization
features.*

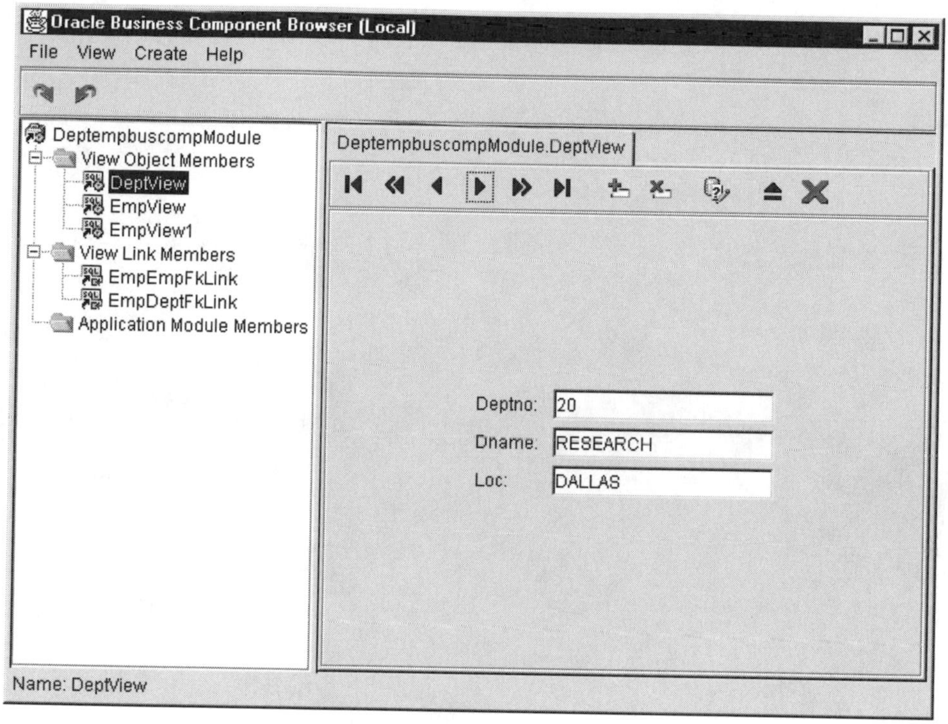

FIGURE 2-19. *Application for a View*

CHAPTER
3

Naming Conventions

Java, Java bo bava
Banana Fanna fo fava
Fee Fi Mo mava
Java.

—Apologies to Shirley Ellis, *The Name Game*, 1965

onsistently applied naming and coding conventions are critical for the success of any system. Given the enormous number of elements available in Java and the JDeveloper environment, it is even more important to have a clearly defined set of conventions to follow. Unlike many earlier development environments that included a relatively limited set of components to name, the Java environment includes an almost limitless range of objects. Although the sheer number of objects is advantageous for development, it poses special challenges for creating consistent naming standards. Using previously developed Java elements from different sources will yield a hodgepodge of naming standards because the standards of those sources may be quite diverse. In addition, even elements from the same manufacturer may not be named consistently. This chapter provides some insights into what standards have been used by others as well as some recommendations for structuring your own naming and coding conventions.

The Importance of Using Naming Conventions

Creating naming conventions for your Java applications has several benefits. First, when you review your code, you will be able to quickly grasp the meaning of a particular element simply by seeing its name. Also, by knowing how elements are named, you will be able to locate specific elements more efficiently, making your applications easier to maintain. Another benefit of using a naming convention is that it frees you from having to re-create ways to name elements. By having a naming framework, you will not have to stop and think about how to name each new element.

Ultimately, consistent naming conventions in a Java environment are even more important than they are in traditional development environments such as Oracle Developer. Not only is there a wider variety of elements from which to choose, but behind the scenes is a straight 3GL environment. This means that, at some point, you will be opening up large blocks of code to edit. All of your program elements will not be neatly organized into an object navigator. You want to be able to scan through the code and quickly identify the type of element you are looking at. By using distinctive naming conventions with consistent prefixes or suffixes for the elements, you can quickly and easily search all of the elements of a particular type using an automated search routine.

If you don't use very precise naming conventions, you may end up spending time unnecessarily searching for a particular element. Consistently named elements applied throughout an organization also make it easier for developers to work on each other's code.

Even though elements imported from other sources may not adhere to these conventions, enforcing a naming standard makes it easier to identify those elements that are imported from outside sources as well as better organizing those created internally.

The goals you strive for should follow the four Cs adapted from *Oracle Developer Advanced Forms & Reports* (Koletzke and Dorsey, Oracle Press, 2000) as follows:

- ■ **Consistent**   The way that you name elements should remain the same within an application and throughout all of your applications. You should create complete naming standards for everything at the same time. You cannot create database-naming standards and then later create development standards since these two standards categories interact. The standards must be set for the entire development environment and lifecycle.

- ■ **Concise**   The names that you give elements should be short, but not so short that their meaning is not quickly understood. Short names make repeated typing easier and less prone to errors. Also, short names ease the burden on others who may need to read your code. If you use concise and consistent names, you will be able to scan through your code quickly, find the necessary elements, and determine their basic functions.

  JDeveloper allows you to select classes, methods, and parameters from lists that pop up automatically or by using a keypress such as ALT-CTRL-SPACEBAR to display a package and class browser. You can save the typing necessary for long names using these features. However, it is usually faster to type a shorter name than to browse or select from a list. If you use shorter names, you can still use the automatic completion features.

- ■ **Complete**   If you use naming conventions at all, you should use them for everything. This means that you need to adopt or develop a naming standard before any coding begins. If you leave out a particular element from your standard, when it comes to your attention you should develop a standard for that element before including it in your development effort.

- ■ **Clear**   Select meaningful names for your variables to aid in the "self-documentation" of your programs. For example, when naming Boolean methods, use a name beginning with "is," such as "isOpen."

Naming conventions are part of your overall standards effort and, as such, will be included in your standards strategy. As with other components of your standards strategy, you have to consider how you will document your naming conventions, train developers how and why to use them, and use code reviews to enforce the naming conventions that you develop.

This chapter discusses how to create naming standards for the elements you will use when developing applications with Oracle JDeveloper. This chapter suggests

Note for Oracle Developer Users

Although the elements that you are naming in Java are very different from the elements you name in Forms and Reports, the main goals are the same. In Forms and Reports, some objects exist outside of PL/SQL and SQL code that you create. In JDeveloper, all elements are represented by lines of Java code. Therefore, even though you may think of your naming conventions as handling visual objects in the UI Designers, everything you define works into the actual code that JDeveloper generates. You are therefore defining naming standards for code.

the types of names you need to consider and provides examples to help in developing your own standards.

Naming Convention Considerations

When you are making decisions about what standards to create for naming JDeveloper elements, you will need to consider the capabilities of the language. For example, Java identifiers are limited to strings that include characters, numbers, underscores (_), and dollar signs ($). These identifiers cannot begin with a number, nor can they contain any white spaces and usually do not contain underscores. Java is also case sensitive, which may be a source of some initial confusion for those who are not accustomed to worrying about upper- and lowercase letters in their code. However, case-sensitive names actually help the readability and comprehension of your code. For example, if you use a lowercase letter as the first character of each class instance and an uppercase letter at the start of each class, it is easy to distinguish between objects and classes.

Even though Java is case sensitive, keep in mind that Oracle products are not. EMP, Emp, and emp are the same in Oracle but different in Java. When dealing with objects that will be mapped into PL/SQL elements or database tables or columns, remember that PL/SQL is case insensitive. However, Oracle string comparisons are case sensitive. If you query any system views in Oracle, the names of the Oracle elements are usually returned in uppercase. For those developers experienced in the Oracle environment, this will be routine. Java developers should take special care with any elements that will be translated into Oracle elements.

NOTE
JDeveloper uses the prefix "my" for many of its examples as does this book. This is not a useful practice for production code. When you are thinking of a naming convention, you might want to use an application prefix for classes that will only be used for a specific application. Choose the prefix carefully because an application-specific class today may prove useful for another application in the future and, for this reason, may require a more generic prefix.

The Consistency Issue

As you develop Java applications, you will use elements from libraries that someone else created. You will also use the JDeveloper code generators to write code. Both of these sources use some type of naming convention. For consistency, it would make sense, when you are writing your own code, to use naming conventions that are similar to those employed by these sources. The good news is that there is some consistency regarding the general structure of a name. For example, a fully qualified name such as `java.lang.String.trim` is consistent among all Java vendors. (This structure is discussed further in the following section.)

While most vendors try to be concise and clear when naming code elements of the fully qualified name, there is inconsistency among them as to how to name those elements. You will find naming inconsistencies in how code is generated, even within JDeveloper. In addition, there is inconsistency regarding how concise the names will be. For example, you will find the use of acronyms, full names, and abbreviations mixed together but not consistently applied. Some names are only marginally understandable.

Generally you can identify the library author by looking at the way its components are named. The following are some examples of how various companies name their code groupings:

- **Sun Microsystems**   `java.io`
  `java.lang`
  `java.math`
  `java.net`

- **Oracle**   `oracle.jbo`
  `oracle.dacf`
  `oracle.jdeveloper`

■ **Borland** `borland.jbcl`
`borland.sql`
`borland.javaport`

■ **Objectspace** `com.objectspace.jgl`

■ **Three D Graphics** `tdg, tdg.event`

Just by looking at the way the groups are named, you will notice that each company uses slightly different standards. These variations occur at almost every level of Java; so where significant variations exist, you will need to come up with a viable standard. In the case of naming functional groups in Java libraries, most companies will use their company name or abbreviation, which adds a little advertising to their code. Sun Microsystems owns the core Java classes, and they simply use the names java or javax to identify their code.

When you are creating your own naming conventions, you need to examine the names that are used for existing code and apply general rules that you create to come up with a fully defined naming convention. It is useful to base your naming conventions on ones that are generally recognized by Java programmers. This should be familiar territory if you have studied the Java language.

Recognized Naming Conventions

Most Java professionals follow the established conventions for naming basic Java elements. By following similar patterns in your own code, you will be able to produce a final product that is not only functional but also integrates well with established conventions.

The following sections examine basic Java code elements and the generally recognized naming conventions. General naming conventions usually define case usage (uppercase or lowercase). There are a number of categories of elements, each of which has a recognized naming convention.

Keywords

Keywords are named with all lowercase letters; for example, `abstract`, `boolean`, `if`, `import`, `int`, `public`, `switch`, and `try`. Since the names are part of the language, you have no options for spelling or case usage.

Constants

Constants are identified by all uppercase letters. When the name of the constant contains more than one word, the words are separated using the underscore character (_); for example, `MAX_LOAD` and `MIN_SIZE`. It is important to follow this standard when you define your own constants.

Classes

Classes use an initial capital letter for each word in the class name; for example, `JavaFirstClass`, `EmployeeHistory`, and `CustomerOrder`. Note that there are no spaces or underscores between the words making up the class names.

Class Instances, Exceptions, Methods, and Variables

These elements all use mixed case and always start with the first letter in lowercase and the remaining words using an initial capital letter. There are no spaces or underscores between words; for example, `javaFirstObject`, `printHistory`, and `customerName`.

A common practice among Java programmers is to use short, meaningless variable names such as "x" or "y." This is not useful and violates the goal of clarity in naming elements. Meaningful names such as "price" or "totalPrice" can make the usage clearer. An exception to this rule might be loop counter variables. A common practice in most languages is to use "i" as the name of an integer counter in a loop (for example, `for (int i=0; i < 10; i++)`). If there is a nested loop, you would use "j" as the counter for the inner loop. Although these variable names are not clear, they are generally recognized in the programming community, and your standard could document and accept them.

There are methods that are named to comply with standards in the language. For example, if you had a class called Address that contained methods for assigning a city name and retrieving a city name from an object instantiation, you would name the methods `setCity()` and `getCity()`, respectively. These implement a standard feature of the language—getters and setters that the language knows how to handle. The names of these methods use the "get" and "set" verbs combined with the property name (city).

Constructors

Constructors have exactly the same name as their class. For example, if your class is named `ClassName`, its constructor must also be named `ClassName`. You may not use any variation in either case or spelling.

Packages

Generally, packages are named using all lowercase letters, but you will find many exceptions to this convention because the package standards have continued to change as the popularity of Java has grown. Follow the all lowercase standard when you create code. There is also a recognized standard of how a fully qualified name is constructed. A *fully qualified name* contains the names of all elements that specifically locate it. For example, `java.lang.String.trim` points to the method `trim` that is part of the class `String`. The class is contained in a package `java.lang`. Because of the word "java" the name also indicates that the vendor for this library is Sun Microsystems. This type of fully qualified name is logical and universally recognized.

Since the standards mentioned here are well established, the main topic of discussion when it comes to naming standards for Java is in how to name the components that make up the qualified name (for example, the actual class or method).

A sensible strategy is to start with some general guidelines and add specific rules for each type of element that needs to be named.

General Guidelines

The task of defining and implementing a standard of your own can be formidable. It is easy to espouse the principle of using a naming standard, but attempting to encompass all of the possibilities can be very difficult if you try to create a list of naming methods for each element used in your development effort. Many developers attempting their first Java project have expressed their frustration when trying to apply standards they have used in the past to the Java environment. Numerous projects have fallen behind schedule and exceeded their budgets with little to show in terms of completed work. In the Java environment, it is clear that you must be ready to change the way you think and work, or you may find yourself buried in so many details that you literally cease to make any headway with your overall project.

It is a good idea to learn and use the recognized conventions for the major items as just discussed. To complete your naming convention, you need to add some general guidelines and specific rules to the generally recognized conventions for naming all elements.

It is best to use a pre-defined, structured approach for your standard. By defining a simple naming structure that fits most situations, you will be free to add new components to your design without having to stop and think about how to name them.

Use Meaningful Names for Clarity

The name must be absolutely understandable to anyone who knows the language or the application. Avoid ambiguous names such as "x" or "abc" that do not suggest a meaning. For example, if you need to represent the DEPTNO column, use the word "deptno." Case usage and placement in the name depend on the actual element, as described later.

Use Acronyms and Abbreviations for Conciseness

The name should be long enough to represent meaning, but as short as possible to fulfill the goal of conciseness. For example, to represent a table called APP_EMPLOYEE_SALARY_HISTORY, you can use the word "EmpSalHistory." If you need to designate a name to represent the table called ACCOUNTS_PAYABLE, you can use "AP" since this is a generally recognized acronym. As with table and column aliases and abbreviations, you should create a list of words and valid abbreviations for use in all of your enterprise and application names.

Use Suffixes to Imply Type

Some elements are more clearly named if they contain the class or type to which they belong. For example, a panel that you create in the JDeveloper design area to hold information about the master table of a master-detail form would be called "masterPanel." The suffix indicates the type. This makes the code easier to read because you can distinguish the category that the component fits into by looking at the suffix. Without the type, you might have both a master panel and a master navigation bar that use the word "master," but do not include the element type. A reader might be confused if the name has no suffix.

Using a suffix instead of a prefix is an arbitrary decision, but it follows the naming convention that JDeveloper most commonly uses when its wizards generate code. If you are using a combination of wizard code and self-named code, there may be a disparity of suffixes and prefixes in your application. However, the reader will be able to rely on the fact that your code always uses suffixes.

NOTE

Naming elements with a suffix that denotes the component type, such as deptnoTextfield, has a potential danger. If you decided to change the item type after you have written code based on the component name, you will either need to rename the item and update all of its references, or leave the item with a wrong and potentially confusing name. Fortunately, JDeveloper can make the code changes automatically, if you change the name in the UI Designer. This effect is not severe enough to change the suffix standard.

It is useful to list the main categories of names and apply these general guidelines to describe how you might assign specific naming conventions to these categories.

Specific Rules

There are different types of elements that you use in Java. The following sections describe each of these and suggest standards that you can use to extend the general guidelines discussed so far.

Libraries and Packages

If you work in an area with wide Internet visibility, you should adhere to the practice used by vendors of naming the libraries so that readers can tell the exact source of the code. To avoid conflicts with packages created by other developers, the current convention is to use your reversed Internet domain name as the package root in your library. For example, if you wanted to store the doJob() method, from class MyBusTask, in the mybusinessutil package, use the following naming structure in your library: com.company.mybusinessutil.MyBusTask.doJob(), where "com.company" is a reversed domain name—for example, "com.mcgraw-hill."

If your code has more limited visibility, as in an intranet system, you should keep the names as short as possible to make the typing easier and faster. By convention, library and package names use all lowercase.

Files

JDeveloper uses a multiple directory structure on your hard drive to store Java-related code. Separate structures exist for source code, compiled code, documentation, and HTML files. In order to keep all of these files in sync, JDeveloper creates several overhead files as well. Although many of these files are automatically named for you, it is necessary to understand their naming conventions so that you can quickly locate, view, and/or edit them as necessary. As you become more proficient in using JDeveloper, you will be creating and naming many of these files on your own. A quick review of the structure is useful at this point.

JDeveloper stores your source files under a source code root directory that has the default path (JDEV_HOME\myprojects). This is the default anchor point for all of your source packages. In practice, you will probably set up different project directories for each application. Each subdirectory created under myprojects represents a new Java package where you can store related application files. After you compile your code, you will find that JDeveloper has created a duplicate structure under (JDEV_HOME\myclasses) where it has stored the compiled version of your code in files using the extension ".class." Where appropriate, there is a similar structure in the "myhtml" directory.

The source and overhead files use different file extensions to distinguish them, as shown in Table 3-1.

File Type	Extension
Business components	.xml and .java
Class source	.java
Connections and other properties	.properties
HTML and XML files	.html and .xml, respectively
Java Server Pages (JSPs)	.jsp
Libraries	.jar or .zip
Packages	(no extension)
Project	.jpr
Workspace	.jws

TABLE 3-1.   *JDeveloper File Extensions*

JDeveloper will present a default name (such as Untitled.jws) when you first save a file. Be sure to change this to a descriptive name in the Save dialog. JDeveloper will fill in the file extension automatically in most cases if you save without a particular extension. This feature saves you from having to type the name in and worry about the exact extension. Using the default extensions allows you to use the file filters in the save and open dialogs to help locate a file. The descriptions and suggested standards for each file type follow.

Workspaces

Name these files using a descriptive base name and an uppercase WS suffix; for example, EmpDeptWS. The suffix is helpful when looking at a long list of files in the Navigator and makes a particular file easier to find when you select **File | Open**. Workspace files may be stored anywhere but should ideally be stored in the same directory as your source code when you start using JDeveloper. The workspace should be named the same as the directory with a .jws suffix.

Projects

Use the suffix PRJ to name the project file, and, as always, name it descriptively: for example, EmpAppPRJ. An additional file, using an extension .jpx (an XML file), is automatically created with BC4J projects.

Class Source

JDeveloper's IDE creates class files for you based on the name that you use in the wizard. If you need to create your own class file, the file name must have the same name and case assignment as the class name; for example, EmployeeHistory.java. The Java language imposes this rule.

Libraries and Packages

Libraries are zipped (compressed) collections of packages that are stored in files with the extension .jar or .zip. Libraries do not have any consistent naming conventions; thus you will find a wide variety of naming styles from different vendors. In JDeveloper, you can give each library a file name and an alias that is more readable. Since the library file names must follow the naming conventions of your operating system, you will find that the alias provides a user-friendly way to identify your library. The alias may also refer to a group of library files, allowing you to store a single logical library in multiple physical files. For example, the Java Business Object runtime library for JDeveloper has the alias JBO Runtime. It is stored in the following physical files: jbomt.zip, jboorasql.zip, jboremote.zip, jndi.jar, and xmlparserv2.jar. Name library files with lowercase names, using an acronym or abbreviation with the same pattern. The abbreviation or acronym must be documented if it is specific to your application or enterprise. Library file names need no suffix because they are distinguished in the context of their usage.

Packages correspond to directories (or folders) in the operating system file structure and usually have no suffix. If you are creating a business component package, it is useful to denote the package type with a suffix; for example, "empdeptbuscomp." Otherwise, package names follow the same convention as libraries and use documented abbreviations and acronyms.

HTML

JDeveloper creates a few types of HTML files as described next.

HTML to Call Java Applets   These files run an applet in your web browser. When you use the Applet Wizard in JDeveloper, the generated HTML files are automatically named using a pattern based on a concatenation of the following: Project Name + " _ " + Applet Class Name; for example, BusPRJ_BusApplet.html. These files are stored under the HTML root directory, which has a structure that is very different from the other root directories in JDeveloper. Instead of being based on packages, the HTML root directory is organized around project names.

So the preceding example would automatically be stored in the directory JDEV_HOME\myhtml\BusPRJ_html.

Javadoc   JDeveloper gives the Javadoc HTML files the same base names as their parent classes with an .html extension. These files are stored in a structure similar to the source root directory, but are under the doc generated root directory; for example, JDEV_HOME\doc\Generated\myempapp\DeptImpl.html.

Project Notes   JDeveloper gives project notes the same base name as the project and an .html extension; for example, EmpAppPRJ.html. It stores them in the same directory as the associated project file.

Connections and Other Properties

JDeveloper stores connections information in a file called "connections.properties" in the JDEV_HOME\myclasses directory. This is an editable text file as are other .properties files that JDeveloper creates (such as jdeveloper.properties). Properties files are stored in various directories under JDEV_HOME, such as the lib directory.

Business Components for Java

JDeveloper uses the following naming conventions to create elements in the BC4J layer. This information will be helpful if you need to find a specific element and its associated files or if you wish to add your own custom BC4J component.

You can distinguish the basic elements from their associated files because the basic elements have no file extension. For example, the Dept entity is a basic Java business object, and Dept.xml is its associated XML file. Also, you will notice that the elements are displayed in the Navigator one level higher than their associated files. Some BC4J elements use a suffix and some do not. You can identify those without suffixes by the context within the code. All BC4J objects use a mixed-case naming convention with initial uppercase letters. The following are specific standards that the tool uses to name the BC4J elements:

■ **Entities**   Entities are generally named after the database table that they represent; for example, "Dept" represents the DEPT table. BC4J entities are defined in an XML file (for example, Dept.xml), which holds the metadata from the database. Entities are also used by one or more .java files that implement the object-specific code (for example, Dept.java). If you create one on your own, be sure to use an initial uppercase letter for each word in the name, no underscores, and a name that reflects the source of the associated data. As with other names, documented abbreviations and acronyms are allowed. For example, the EMPLOYEE_SALARY_HISTORY table would be represented by an entity called EmpSalHistory.

■ **Attributes** Entity attributes are named after the database column that they represent or a user-defined function or value that has been specified. The naming convention is the same as for the entity; for example, Deptno.

■ **Associations** The generated name for an association is a concatenation of Foreign Key Constraint Name + "Assoc." The "Foreign Key Constraint Name" is the database name of the foreign key constraint in mixed case with underscores stripped out. There is an associated XML file that uses the same name and a .xml extension. For example, if the foreign key constraint for the DEPTNO column in the EMP table were EMP_DEPT_FK, the association element would be named EmpDeptFkAssoc, and its XML file would be named EmpDeptFkAssoc.xml.

■ **Domains** Domains are user-defined. When you create a domain, replace the default name "Domain" to reflect its intended usage. Use initial uppercase and a suffix of Domain; for example, MaxSalaryDomain. The Domain will have two files associated with it—an .xml file for data definition and a .java file for the object-specific behavior. These associated files are named automatically with the name of the domain; for example, MaxSalaryDomain.xml and MaxSalary.java.

■ **Application modules** The generated name for an application module is a concatenation of the package name and the word "Module" in mixed case; for example, myempappletModule. As with other BC4J objects, there is a .xml and a .java file that have the same base name with appropriate file extensions.

■ **Views** The JDeveloper wizard automatically names views using a concatenation of the entity name and the word "View"; for example, DeptView. The .xml and .java files use the same base name and appropriate file extensions.

■ **View links** The generated name for a view link follows the same naming convention as the association, but uses the suffix "Link" instead of "Assoc"; for example, EmpDeptFkLink.

Lookup Values

If the column you are retrieving is not in a base table that is represented by an entity, you need to construct a name. The value could be derived from a function or subquery embedded in the SELECT list. For example, you may have a business component that includes a query such as the following:

```
SELECT  empno,
        ename,
          (SELECT  dname
           FROM    dept
           WHERE   dept.deptno = emp.deptno)
        as dept_name
FROM    emp
```

Using the default attribute name DeptName might lead the reader to think that this is a column in the EMP table. A more descriptive name would use a prefix to denote the derived source, such as DspDeptName. The "Dsp" prefix denotes that this is a display-only column value. The easiest way to do this in JDeveloper is to alias the column in the SELECT clause as DSP_DEPT_NAME.

UI Components

Java has hundreds of prebuilt classes available for your use. When the JDeveloper code generators (wizards) add UI components (controls) to your project, they will include a default name that you will override. The default name is usually a number added to the component name; for example, jPanel1. After adding several components of the same type, you will find it nearly impossible to distinguish them.

The general guidelines describe how to use a suffix to define the type or class of object. This is particularly important for UI components. For example, if in a dataform you were to add a java.awt.Button component that is intended to be an exit button, you would name it exitButton. A similar component from the Swing library javax.swing.JButton would also be named exitJButton. It is not important that you distinguish between swing and AWT components. If this distinction is important, you would name the button exitJButton.

Part of the naming convention document you create will list the suffixes used to distinguish various components. Some components will use an abbreviation of the class name. For example, a GridControl component for the EMP table would be called empGrid, not empGridControl, because the latter name is longer than is required to identify its type.

NOTE

The JDeveloper wizards create UI components using a different naming convention. For example, a text item for the DEPTNO column is called "controlDEPTNO." The naming convention suggested in this chapter and used throughout most of this book calls this control "deptnoTextItem." This maintains the standard of suffixes that represent the element type.

CHAPTER
4

Java for PL/SQL Programmers

I love coffee, I love tea
I love the java jive and it loves me.

—The Ink Spots (1940), *The Java Jive*

oth Java and PL/SQL are ALGOL-based languages with the standard structures of many programming languages, including code blocks, control structures, and so on. However, there are some significant differences between Java and most third generation languages (3GLs). Java is very much a modern programming language for several reasons:

■ It fully supports object orientation.

■ It explicitly supports multi-tasking.

■ It is platform independent (the code is portable).

■ It has enhanced memory management and garbage collection.

There is a serious temptation to treat Java as just another programming language. From this viewpoint, you would think that you simply need to learn a new syntax and notation differences such as using curly brackets { } instead of BEGIN and END statements. Thinking only along these lines would not be productive. Approaching Java with the same frame of mind that you use with non-object-oriented languages will result in the creation of much more code than would be necessary with a true object-oriented approach. Object orientation isn't necessarily more efficient from a performance point of view. In fact, it is common to make object-oriented design concessions in the name of performance.

Remember learning to code? In writing early programs, you probably copied and pasted a lot of code in various places until you learned how to use local functions and procedures, explicit exception handling, and anonymous blocks of code. In comparing a novice programmer with someone having five years of experience, the quality of the algorithms will vary greatly. This is true even if the novice programmer is skilled in another programming language.

Although this chapter was written with a PL/SQL programmer in mind, you do not have to be a PL/SQL programmer to understand it. PL/SQL has traditionally been Oracle's primary programming language. All writing must make assumptions about its audience. However, the points discussed will be equally applicable to users of any standard third generation language.

For each language, there is an optimal style of learning. This chapter does not substitute for learning Java thoroughly. Rather, it will teach you a few basic things that are different about Java and point out some places where you will want to pay careful attention as you study Java. This chapter should provide enough basic information about Java to enable you to understand how it is used in the rest of this book. After reading this chapter, you should feel comfortable picking up a Java book and reading it through.

NOTE
Throughout this chapter, the names of some objects include the prefix "my" to indicate that they have been created by the programmer. As mentioned in Chapter 3, this practice is not recommended for production systems but was used for the purposes of clarity in the examples shown to distinguish between language elements and user-defined elements.

Programming with Objects

The fundamental building block of an object-oriented language like Java is a user-defined datatype called *Class*. This construct, in its simplest form, acts similarly to the datatypes used in most other procedural languages. Java has both *primitive datatypes* (sometimes called either *simple* or *built-in*) and user-defined datatypes. The primitive datatypes were implemented for performance reasons and each has a sister class available when a fully functional class is required (for example, Integer is a class, whereas int is a primitive datatype). The word *instance* is used to denote a specific instance of an object in a class. The instantiation of a Java primitive datatype is called a *variable*. The following are characteristics of primitive datatypes:

- The Java primitive types are byte, short, int, long, char, float, double, and boolean. An example of declaration and initialization of the integer variable age follows:

  ```
  int age = 38 ;
  ```

- Primitive types in Java can hold only a single value, and they cannot be passed by reference or by using explicit pointers as in C or C++.

The architecture of procedural languages such as C and PL/SQL diverges from Java at this point. Procedural languages rely on functions and procedures as their basic programming units, whereas Java and other object-oriented languages build upon user-defined datatypes (classes) as their basic programming structures. Java shifts the programmer's attention from function-like behavior to object behavior by basing its code on classes.

The following are object concepts used in Java:

- An instance of a user-defined datatype is called an *object*.

- An object is passed by reference and may be as complex as desired.

■ To use a class, you must declare an instance of it like any other datatype; for example,

```
Integer age = 38;
```

where Integer is the class, and age is the object.

■ Each public class definition is stored in its own source file (ASCII text), which has exactly the same name as the class with .java as the file extension. The compiled version of this is called a *class file* and uses a .class file extension.

■ Related class files are stored in libraries of packages. These libraries are stored in zipped files with the extension .jar.

Although the terminology may differ in places, the underlying concepts of Java programming reflect those in other languages. For example, procedural language functions and procedures are called *methods* in Java. Methods are defined within classes and work the same way as functions and procedures within a package in PL/SQL. Just as you can define variables within a procedural language package, you can also define them in a Java class.

The Basic Parts of Java

Java, like most programming languages, is composed of comments, executable program blocks, variable and object declarations, control statements, and exception handling.

Comments

Commenting code is an important practice. You need to set standards for both inline and block comments just as you do for other aspects of system development. As in other programming languages, the syntax for inline and block comments is slightly different as shown here:

```
/* This is a long comment or
     multi-line comment in Java. */
// This is a single line or short comment.
-- THIS IS NOT A LEGAL COMMENT IN JAVA, double dashes won't work.

/** There is a special type of comment used in JDeveloper to automatically generate
documentation. This special syntax is a Javadoc comment.
**/
```

This special comment called *Javadoc* uses a slash and a double asterisk and each additional line begins with a single asterisk. A Javadoc is a reference document for a class that you can generate dynamically in JDeveloper. The Javadoc Wizard parses the packages and/or source files that you designate, to automatically produce HTML pages describing the basic elements in the source code for your classes. To create or update a Javadoc for a class, select **Wizards | Generate Javadoc** after you have created and commented your source code.

NOTE
Access to Java objects is controlled through the use of the keywords public, private, *and* protected, *and a default value when no specifier is given. The levels of encapsulation around which access control is built are method, class, and package.*

The Basic Executable Program Block

The basic executable program block is a collection of declarations, specifiers, and methods. *Specifiers* are added to the *class* declaration (the first line of code), to modify the class's visibility and functionality. Consider the following code:

```
public class MyFirstExample {
  public static void main ( String args[] ) {
    System.out.println("Hello World");
  }
}
```

The first line of code, public class MyFirstExample, represents the declaration of a new class given the name MyFirstExample. The access specifier *public* indicates that this code can be used anywhere within a program that calls it. The specifier public provides the widest access. Public allows a class member to be accessed from anywhere in your program.

The other two choices for access specifiers are *private* and *protected,* which limit external access to the object. The most limiting access occurs when the keyword private is used. In this case, access for a class member is limited to other members of the same class. The specifier protected is slightly less open than public. When the keyword protected is used, you can access a class member anywhere except from a non-subclass or class that is in a different package.

The final possibility is to use the default access, which is granted when no specifier is used. If you do not specify an access modifier, you will only have access to objects in the same package. The sets of curly brackets represent the start and end of each code block. The code within each block has its own scope. As you can see in the example, code blocks can be nested within each other.

Now look at the second line, `public static void main (String args [] )`. This line declares a method called `main()`. The `main` method will handle the code we want to be executed when our class `MyFirstExample` is executed. The Java Virtual Machine (JVM) specifically looks for a method called `main()` when any application starts. To meet the basic requirements for the JVM to call the `main()` method from outside of the class `MyFirstExample`, `main()` must have an access specifier of `public`. Also, `main()` must be declared static, which means that the method can be run without instantiating the class defining it. The `static` declaration is necessary because the Java interpreter calls the `main()` method before any objects are created. The third term, `void`, is a declaration of the return type since `main()` does not return any values. A void return value acts like a procedure in PL/SQL. As you build methods that return values, you can use any valid datatype or class as a return type.

The remainder of the line is used to pass parameters to the `main()` method. The set of parentheses `()` that follow the method's name is used to hold these parameters. As you view the parameter declaration for `main()`, you will see that only one parameter is used. Its datatype is String, and its name is "arg." The square brackets [ ] after arg indicate that arg is being declared as a String array. (*Arrays* are collections of similar objects.) The String array arg is used to pass any command-line arguments that exist when the class is executed.

The third line, `System.out.println("Hello World") ;`, is a call to a library that is distributed by default with all JVMs. The method `println()` will generate the line "Hello World" with a carriage return and send it to the console. A similar method `print()` would produce the same text but without the carriage return.

Support for Inheritance and Polymorphism

The object-oriented concept of *inheritance* means that properties and behaviors are derived from the parent object. *Polymorphism* refers to the ability to send a message to an object without being concerned with the details of the object, such as a datatype.

Additional keywords that can be added to class definitions give them specific capabilities in an object-oriented structure. When you use the keyword `extends` in the declaration of a class, it allows you to inherit methods and variables from a parent class. This gives you the opportunity to reuse, extend, or modify the existing code without the need of rewriting it. The parent class is referred to as a *superclass*, and the child is known as a *subclass*. A superclass can have any number of subclasses, but a subclass may only extend a single superclass. There is no multiple inheritance. If you reuse the same name for a variable in both the parent and child classes, the child definition will override the parent definition. When you use the same name for multiple methods, with different kinds or numbers of datatypes, you effectively overload the functionality of a given name. Overriding and overloading are known as forms of polymorphism. The following examples illustrate the concepts of inheritance and polymorphism:

```
// A parent class for a 2-Dimensional object
public class Box {
  int width  = 2;
  int length = 3;
}


// A child class for a 3-Dimensional object, which inherits a parent class
public class Cube extends Box {
  int height = 4;
  int width  = 1; //polymorphism - this variable is set to 1.
  int volume = super.width * length * height;
  public Cube() {
    System.out.println("The volume of the cube is: " + volume);
  }

  public static void main(String[] args) {
    new Cube();
  }
}
```

This cube will have a volume of 24, because super.width references the width defined in the superclass Box. If you change 'super.width' to just 'width' in the volume calculation for the cube, you will have a new volume of 12.

Variable and Object Declarations

The creation of an object or variable in Java is an inherently dynamic process and can take place anywhere in your program whereas in some programming languages, there is a formal declaration section with a separate section where you manipulate these variables. In most programming languages, this is considered good coding style since this makes the code easy to read and maintain.

This presents an interesting challenge in setting coding standards. There is a temptation to be lax about declaring objects. Experience has shown that declaring objects and variables in the same way as in a traditional programming language provides an appropriate natural structuring for your Java code. This is not to say that you will not also create objects elsewhere in the program.

If you embrace the philosophy of creating objects in a pseudo-declaration section as in the past, the code will be more consistent. Using this approach will also support situations where objects are created on the fly. Embedded in program logic, this code will stand out and make programs easier to maintain.

CAUTION
When identifying objects in Java, you may use a combination of uppercase and lowercase letters, numbers, the underscore, and the dollar sign. However, you may not begin names with a number.

Variable Types

Java is a semi-strongly typed language—every variable has a type and every type is strictly defined. All parameters passed to classes are checked for type consistency. There is no automatic modification of one variable type to another. However, in practice, Java is not as restrictive as you might think since most built-in methods are heavily overloaded. For example, you can combine strings, numbers, and dates together using a concatenation operator (+) without formal variable type conversion. This is similar in philosophy to the way that PL/SQL works but is much more restrictive than languages like C or C++.

In PL/SQL, you are limited to a few datatypes for variables. Java has a much richer and more varied set available to developers. More details about these datatypes will be discussed later in the chapter. A number of datatypes exist in Java. Each will be discussed separately.

Boolean   There are two logical values for boolean operators in Java: true and false. The boolean values do not have any numerical counterparts (such as 0 or 1), as do other programming languages. The following are examples of some boolean operators in Java and PL/SQL:

```
class MyBooleanOperators {
    public static void main (String args[]) {
        boolean myTestCondition = true;
        if (myTestCondition)  System.out.println("My condition was TRUE");
        myTestCondition = false;   //Now reset test condition to FALSE
        if (myTestCondition)  System.out.println("This line Never prints");
    }
}
-- PL/SQL Example: BOOLEAN operators may be TRUE, FALSE or NULL.
v_test_condition BOOLEAN := TRUE;
```

Character   The Java datatype char consists of a single byte (a 16-bit number with a value between 0 and 65,000), representing the Unicode international character set. Char variables can be treated transparently as numeric or character datatypes. A char datatype in Java is very different from a CHAR datatype in PL/SQL. A CHAR datatype in PL/SQL is closer to a Java String than a Java char, as shown in the following examples:

```
/* Java Example: The char datatype can only represent a single character or
symbol, and may be initialized as follows: */

char myFirstChar = 97 ;        // decimal equivalent of letter 'a'
char mySecondChar = 'a' ;      // using a character
char myThirdChar = '\141' ;    // octal equivalent of letter 'a'
char myFourthChar = '\u0061' ; // Unicode (Hex) value for letter 'a'

--PL/SQL Example:  In PL/SQL the CHAR datatype is a fixed length string.
v_string_char CHAR(48):= 'Datatype CHAR is a fixed length string in PL/SQL';
```

NOTE
*You can find more information about the Unicode
character sets at www.unicode.org.*

Strings   The *String* type in Java defines an object. In its simplest form, the
String type can be used to declare string variables, which can be assigned a
quoted string constant. In this respect, the String type can handle string literals
in the same way that a VARCHAR2 datatype does in PL/SQL as shown here.

```
//The Java String type:
String myString = "This is a Java test string";
System.out.println(myString);

--A PL/SQL VARCHAR2 example:
v_string VARCHAR2(200) := 'This is a PL/SQL test string';
dbms_output.put_line(v_string);
```

Java implements a string as an object instead of just a character array. The String
class includes a full complement of features to support string construction and
manipulation. These features include methods to create strings from literals, chars,
char arrays, and other string reference objects. The following Java Strings all store
the value "Java" using a character array.

```
char myChars[] = {'J', 'a', 'v', 'a'};
String myString = new String(myChars);

// using a string literal
String myString = "Java";

// using decimal values for the ASCII characters
byte myASCII [] = {74,97,118,97};
String myString = new String(myASCII);
```

```
// using the concatenation operator (+)
String myLetter = "v";
String myString = new String("Ja" + myLetter + "a");

// using method concat()
String myLetters = "Ja";
String myString = myLetters.concat("va");
```

You can compare, concatenate, change the case of, find the length of, extract characters from, search, and modify strings. Although strings cannot be changed in Java, this does not present a real problem. Whenever you alter a string through a string operation, you simply get a new string that contains the modifications. The language was constructed this way to increase its overall efficiency. When you need a string to be implemented as a modifiable object with its associated overhead, you can use a sister class for strings called StringBuffer. Actual performance differences between these classes will depend upon the implementation and tasks that are being performed. Some examples follow:

```
//Java performs automatic datatype conversions in String methods.
String myAge = ("Myage is " + 2 + 35);   //This produces "My age is 235"
//If you wish to add 2+35 to indicate an age of 37, then use:
String myAge = "My age is " + (2 + 35);   //This produces "My age is 37"

//In Java:
String myString = "This is a Java xxx string.";
myString = myString.substring(0,15) + myString.substring(19, 26);
System.out.println(myString); //This will print "This is a Java string"

-- In PL/SQL
v_string VARCHAR2(50) := 'This is a PL/SQL xxx string.';
...
v_string := SUBSTR(v_string, 1, 17)||SUBSTR(v_string, 22, 7);
dbms_output.put_line(v_string); //Print "This is a PL/SQL string"
```

NOTE
In Java, the method substring(int startIndex, int endIndex) *returns a portion of a string from the startIndex to the (endIndex –1). In PL/SQL, the SUBSTR function returns characters from a start position for a given length.*

CAUTION
Java strings and arrays have indexes that start with zero (0), just as in C and C++. This is different from PL/SQL where they start with one (1).

The String class uses two overloaded methods for locating characters and substrings within a string. The first method, indexOf(), will search for the first occurrence of a character or substring, by searching from a given index and working toward the string's end. The second method, lastIndexOf(), performs a similar search in the reverse direction, beginning at an index and searching backwards until it reaches the beginning of the string. Both methods will return the index where a given character or substring was found, or –1 if no match is located.

Java and PL/SQL search methods for strings are shown in the following examples:

```
class MyStringSearch {
  public static void main (String args[ ]) {
    String sourceString = "This a Java string to be searched";
    System.out.println( sourceString.indexOf("Java", 0) +
          " is the starting position for the word (Java)" );
  }  // This search reports that Java starts at position 7
}
```

```
--In PL/SQL a string search can be performed with the INSTR function.
--This PL/SQL code fragment shows a starting position of character 8.
v_index INTEGER;
v_source_string VARCHAR2(200) := 'This a PL/SQL string to be searched';
...
v_index := INSTR( v_source_string, 'PL/SQL' );
```

StringBuffer   StringBuffer is a sister class to String and represents character sequences that can change size and/or be modified. What this means to the developer is that methods such as append() and insert() are available to modify a StringBuffer, whereas in String you are limited to the concatenation operator (+). Thus, the StringBuffer class may be used when the character sequences being stored need to have substrings inserted or appended.

```
//The Java StringBuffer append()

class MyAppend {
  public static void main (String args[ ]) {
    String myString = "This is my string";
    StringBuffer buff = new StringBuffer(50);
    myString = buff.append(myString).append(", my append.").toString();
    System.out.println(myString);
  }  //This produces "This is my string, my append."
}
```

The Java `String` concatenation operator (+) can also be used to append as follows:

```
class MyAppend {
   public static void main (String args[ ]) {
     String myString = "This is my string";
     myString = myString + ", my append.";
     System.out.println(myString);
   }  //This also produces "This is my string, my append."
}
```

In PL/SQL, an append is performed using the concatenation operator (||) as follows:

```
v_string VARCHAR2(50) := 'This is my PL/SQL string';
...
v_string := v_string || ', and append.';
--This will produce "This is my PL/SQL string, and append."
```

Numeric   There are several subtypes of numeric datatypes. For whole numbers, these include

- long ($\pm \sim 9 * 10^{18}$)

- int ($\pm \sim 2{,}000{,}000{,}000$)

- short ($\pm \sim 32{,}000$)

- byte (-128 to 127)

For numbers with fractional precision, the datatypes include the following:

- float ($\pm \sim 3.4 * 10^{38}$)

- double ($\pm \sim 1.7 * 10^{308}$)

Floating-point literals (such as 34.5) default to datatype *double*. If they are of datatype `float`, you must add an "f" suffix (for example, 34.5f), or you may *cast* (convert) them to the datatype `float` explicitly: for example, (float) 34.5. Some examples follow:

```
//Java Example: longs end with 'L' and floats end with 'f'

long population = 1234567890123456789L ;
int age = 38 ;
float price = 460.95f ; //or float price = (float) 460.95
...
double area, length = 3.15, width = 4.2 ;
area = length * width ;

--A PL/SQL Example:

v_population DOUBLE PRECISION := 1234567890123456789 ;
v_age INTEGER := 38 ;
v_price NUMBER := 460.95 ;
```

CAUTION
*Java is case-sensitive, so, unlike PL/SQL, you must
be extremely careful about the use of capitalization
in the naming of objects as well as keywords. See
Chapter 3 for suggestions about naming
conventions.*

As mentioned earlier, although Java is strongly typed, you do not need to
perform your datatype conversion manually in all cases. Frequently, you can be a
bit "sloppy." With numeric variables, you can always assign a narrower variable
type (such as byte) to an int variable or anything to a `double` datatype. The
opposite situation does not work. You cannot assign a broader, less restrictive
variable type to a narrower, more restrictive one. The reason that this works in Java
is that Java automatically promotes datatypes based upon the operation being
performed. This can often lead to very confusing behavior, as shown in the
following code:

```
byte b = 10;
byte c = 2 * b;
```

This code will fail because 2 * b is automatically assigned to an internal int
variable. In this example, you would have to explicitly cast the resulting expression
back into a variable of type "byte," as shown next:

```
byte b = 10;
byte c = (byte) (2 * b);
```

NOTE
Java has a number of wrapper classes, such as
Boolean, Byte, Character, Double, Float, Integer,
Long, and Number, that provide full object-oriented
support for simple types like byte, char, *and* int.
These classes provide the ability for the simple types
to be passed as objects.

Arrays

Arrays in Java are similar to arrays in other languages. They are collections of objects of similar type and may have one or more dimensions. Elements within an array are accessed by indexes, which always start at zero [0]. To create an array, you must declare a variable, allocate memory, and initialize the elements. These operations can all be performed in two basic steps. First you must create an array variable, by adding a pair of square brackets to the end of a type declaration. For example, the following line declares a string array named myAnimals:

```
String myAnimals[];
```

The second step is to set the size of the array, which allocates memory and initializes the elements. To create a string array with enough room to store ten names in myAnimals, we use the following:

```
myAnimals = new String[10];

// Or we could declare and allocate in one line
 String myAnimals[] = new String[10];
```

In the string array myAnimals[ ], we can now access ten elements, which are numbered 0 to 9. To store the name of an animal in a given element, just include the index number within the square brackets. For example, here's how to store "Cat" in element 3:

```
myAnimals[3] = "Cat";
```

In Java, you can create arrays of arrays…of arrays, more commonly known as *multidimensional arrays*. Since each array can be independently created, you can even create irregular combinations where array sizes vary within a given dimension. However, keep in mind that most small arrays are coded as rectangular objects for ease of implementation. Thus, extra care must be taken with irregular arrays to prevent problems with out-of-range index values. In practice, you may not wish to implement this type of structure as part of your regular coding style.

In addition, you can create multidimensional arrays. These are similar to PL/SQL tables of records. Here is an example of a two-dimensional irregular array. The first dimension will store four pet owner names and the second will store the type of pet that they own.

```
// A Java 2-dimensional irregular array.

class MyTwoDimensionArray {
  public static main (String args[]) {
    String myPetFriends[ ][ ] ={  //This declares, allocates and initializes
      {"Arlette", "Cat", "Alligator" },
      {"Paul",    "Dog"},
      {"Eddie",   "Goldfish"},
      {"Yalim",   "Camel", "Dolphin", "Parrot"}  };
  }
}
```

In addition to arrays are other groups of objects, such as collections. Java provides a framework to handle these groups of objects. The powerful classes in this framework provide functionality for grouped objects such as dynamic arrays, vectors, linked lists, trees, and hash tables. In addition, Java2 has implemented *maps* that associate key/value pairs. The enhanced interface provided by these tools brings a rich assortment of methods for handling object groups in Java. A full discussion of these complex objects is beyond the scope of this book.

Global Variables

Because Java is an object-oriented language, you usually instantiate a class before it, or anything it contains, can be used. But in the case of global variables, you may want to have some methods or variables that are independent of the instantiations of the class. This is accomplished by the use of the keyword static. When static is used with a class member, the member is instantiated when the class is referenced for the first time. Since these members are already in existence when you create new instantiations of the class, they remain intact and are in essence global variables that can be accessed by all instances of the class. Static is also used with the main() method in the case of an application class. This is necessary because the main() method must be instantiated when the class is loaded so that the class can be executed at run-time.

The following is a demonstration of a global variable using get() and set() methods:

```
//The setx() and getx() methods are public globals
public class MyGlobals  {
  private static int x = 3;
    public static void setx (int y){
```

```
    x = y;
  }
  public static int getx (){
    return x;
  }
}
```

Constants

At times, it is desirable to have constants within your program. The concept of having something that cannot change is meaningful at the variable, method, and class levels. In the case of variables, using the keyword `final` is similar to using the keyword `constant` in PL/SQL. Variables declared with `final` must be initialized in the same statement. It is a common coding practice in Java to use all uppercase when naming a constant—for example INCHES_PER_FOOT as explained in Chapter 3.

When a method has the specifier `final` in its declaration, it means that you cannot override the method in a subclass. Thus, if class A has a `final` method B(), and if class C extends A, then C cannot override the inherited method named B().

When a class has the specifier `final` in its declaration, it cannot be inherited. Since inheritance is used to extend or modify an object, it makes sense that you would be blocked in this way. In addition, all of the class's methods are implicitly `final` as well. This example illustrates different uses of the specifier `final`:

```
//Using final in the declaration of constants
class MyConstants(){
  final int FEET_IN_MILE = 5280;
  final int FEET_IN_YARD = 3;

  final void printMe() {
    System.out.println("You CANNOT override this method");
  }
}
```

CAUTION
When considering inheritance, the keyword `final`
applies only to method and class declarations. If you
declare a variable as `final`, *you can override it in a*
subclass. This is contrary to what you might assume
from the way inheritance is otherwise implemented
in Java. When methods and classes are declared as
final, they cannot be extended in subclasses.

Control Statements

Java uses traditional `if-else`, `switch`, `loop`, and three jump statements: `break`, `continue`, and `return` to control program flow during run time.

The following is an example of a Java program control using `if-else`.

```java
class WhichTaxQuarter {
   public static main (String args[]) {
     int taxMonth = 10;   //October or 4th Quarter
     String taxQuarter;
     if (taxMonth == 1 || taxMonth == 2 || taxMonth == 3)
       taxQuarter = "1st Quarter";
     else if (taxMonth == 4 || taxMonth == 5 || taxMonth == 6)
       taxQuarter = "2nd Quarter";
     else if (taxMonth == 7 || taxMonth == 8 || taxMonth == 9)
       taxQuarter = "3rd  Quarter";
     else if (taxMonth == 10 || taxMonth == 11 || taxMonth == 12)
       taxQuarter = "4th  Quarter";
     else
       taxQuarter = "Not Valid";
     System.out.println("Your current Tax Quarter is: " + taxQuarter );
   }
}
```

The same business logic can be programmed using a `switch` statement as shown here:

```java
class WhichTaxQuarter {
   public static main (String args[]) {
     int taxMonth = 10;   //October or 4th Quarter
     String taxQuarter;
     switch (taxMonth) {
       case 1:    case 2:    case 3:
         taxQuarter = "1st Quarter";
         break;
       case 4:    case 5:    case 6:
         taxQuarter = "2nd Quarter";
         break;
       case 7:    case 8:    case 9:
         taxQuarter = "3rd  Quarter";
         break;
       case 10:   case 11:   case 12:
         taxQuarter = "4th  Quarter";
         break;
       default:
         taxQuarter = "Not Valid";
     }
```

```
      System.out.print("Your current Tax Quarter is: ");
      System.out.println(taxQuarter);
  }
}
```

Loop Controls

As in other languages, the iterative control structures for Java are known as *loops*. They provide control for repeated execution of specific code segments. The extensive set of loop controls is very effective for implementing almost any type of loop structure. The basic loop statements include `for`, `while`, and `do-while`. Their functionality can be extended using Java's three jump statements: `break`, `continue`, and `return`. In addition, you can modify the various portions of the loop to handle almost any valid Java expression to meet your programming needs.

The following is an example of a basic Java `for` loop:

```
class MyLittleCounter {
   public static main (String args[]) {
      int i;
      for ( i=1; i<=10; i++ )
         System.out.println("My count is: " + i);
   }
}
```

The following is an example of the corresponding PL/SQL FOR loop:

```
PROCEDURE little_counter
IS
BEGIN
  FOR i IN 1..10
  LOOP
     dbms_output.put_line('My count is: '|| TO_CHAR(i));
  END LOOP;
END;
```

The following is an example of a variation of the Java `for` loop. Most programmers would use a `while` loop in this situation but this example was used to show this type of variation on a Java `for` loop.

```
class MySimpleLoop {
   public static main (String args[]) {
      int i = 1;
      boolean isCounting = true;
      for ( ; isCounting ; ) {    //Only the Boolean condition test is used
         System.out.println("My count is: " + i);
         if( i == 10 ) isCounting = false;
```

```
      i++;  //This increments the variable used for counting.
    }
  }
}
```

The following example is a variation of the PL/SQL loop:

```
PROCEDURE simple_loop
IS
  i INTEGER := 1;
BEGIN
  LOOP
    dbms_output.put_line('My count is: '|| TO_CHAR(i));
    EXIT WHEN i = 10;
    i := i + 1;
  END LOOP;
END;
```

Exception Handling

Exceptions can occur in the Java environment when undefined conditions are encountered. You may also generate an exception by using the keyword `throw` anywhere in your code. The five statements associated with Java exception handling are `try`, `catch`, `throw`, `throws`, and `finally`. The first two statements, `try` and `catch`, define the block of code that is in focus and the block of code to execute when a given exception occurs. The statement `finally` is used to identify an additional block of code to execute after the try/catch blocks, whether or not an error occurs. This is useful to close file handles in the event of an error.

When defining a method, you must use the statement `throws` to identify the exceptions that cannot be handled by the standard libraries. Exception types for `RuntimeException`, `Error`, and their subclasses are included in the libraries and do not need to be identified. If you attempt to compile a method in which you have not listed all the exceptions that need to be handled, you will receive a compile-time error.

The following example demonstrates try and catch exception handling.

```
public class MyRatio extends Object {
   public MyRatio() {          //this is the start of the class constructor
     int numerator = 5;
     int denominator = 0;
     int ratio;
     try {                     //This is the beginning of a try block
       ratio = numerator / denominator ;
     }
     catch (Exception e)  {        //This is the start of the catch block
```

```
        e.printStackTrace();              //This sends the error msg to the screen
    }
    System.out.println("This prints because the error is handled correctly");
    }    // end MyRatio() method
  public static void main(String[] args) {      //This is the main method
    new MyRatio();                              //This calls the constructor
    }      // end main()
}        // end MyRatio class
```

The following is an example of a PL/SQL exception handler for a divide-by-zero error.

```
DECLARE
  v_numerator    INTEGER = 5;
  v_denominator  INTEGER = 0;
  v_ratio        INTEGER;
BEGIN
  BEGIN                                    //This is the start of the (try) block
    v_ratio := v_numerator / v_denominator ;
  EXCEPTION                                //This is like the catch block
    WHEN OTHERS
    THEN
dbms_output.put_line('Exception: ' || SQLCODE ||', '|| SQLTERM);
END;
  dbms_output.put_line('This is printed because the error is handled correctly');
END;
```

Skeleton of a JDeveloper Class File

JDeveloper has adopted a common style and skeleton for generating code. You will find that the classes generated by the wizards all have the same look and feel. Understanding this implied coding standard is very helpful if you wish to find a particular piece of code. You have a great deal of latitude when using the code editors, but if you can adopt a similar coding style to the one that the wizard uses, you will find your code easier to extend, edit, and maintain. The generated code follows the following skeleton:

- **package xxxx**   First line of the file (giving the storage location of the class file)

- **import yyyy**   Several import statements (adding stored classes in libraries)

- **class zzzz**   Assigns class name, interfaces, and inheritance

- **Variable and Object instances**   Declare instances of other classes and variables

- **Constructor** Executes automatically each time an instance of the class is declared
  - Provides automatic initialization of selected class variables
  - May be overloaded
  - Is named the same as the class
- **Methods** Generated by JDeveloper and written by the user
  - `main()` and `init()` (only needed for executable classes for Java application or applet)
  - Java applications start execution with the `main()` method.

    Applications run on a client machine, under the operating system of that machine.
  - Java applets start execution using the `init()` method.

    Applets that run stand-alone will begin by using `main()` to call `init()`.

    Applets run under a browser via the Internet/intranet.
  - Add other user-defined methods as necessary.

Interfaces

An interface is like a skeleton for a class, somewhat like a PL/SQL package specification. You can use an interface to specify what a class will do, without defining how it will accomplish it. The interface must include a declaration statement for each of the class methods you wish to implement, but the method bodies and instance variables for the class are not included. Thus each of the methods defined in an interface are abstract by definition, meaning that the developer must provide a definition for the method when the subclass references an abstract object. Creating an interface allows you to compile code that depends on a class while deferring the writing of the method bodies until you implement the interface. Having abstract methods defined in an interface instead of a class gives you the freedom to combine as many interfaces as necessary when defining a new class; whereas you are limited to a single class when you use direct inheritance. Interfaces provide a workaround for Java's lack of support for multiple inheritance (many parents for one child).

If you include variable declarations in an interface, they are final and static by definition. Variables defined in an interface act as constants that can be shared by all classes implementing the interface.

An example of an interface follows:

```
Interface MyArea {
    int length = 3;
    int width  = 2;
    double area();
}

class MyBox implements MyArea{
    public MyBox() { }
    double area(){ return (length * width); }
}

class MyTest {
    public static void main (String args[]) {
        MyArea boxArea = new MyBox();
        System.out.println("Test box area is: " + boxArea.area() );
    }
}
```

Garbage Collection

Java automatically handles the deallocation of memory for objects that are no longer referenced by a variable. This is performed by what is called the *garbage collector*. In some instances you may wish to perform some explicit activities, such as releasing a file handle as part of the garbage collection for a given object. This can be handled through the `finalize` method. You should remember that the `finalize` method is called just before the garbage collector destroys an object. Since you have no control over the garbage collector, you have no guarantee as to when your `finalize` method may be executed. If you need to have an action performed at a precise point in your program, you should not rely on `finalize` to execute it.

CHAPTER
5

JDeveloper for Oracle
Developer Programmers

Real programmers can write assembly code in any language.
—Larry Wall, author of the Perl language

f you have been working in the traditional Oracle Developer world, you are accustomed to creating systems in certain ways. Learning another way takes a bit of thought and training. The easiest way to make a transition such as this is to relate the new concepts to something familiar. Now that you have had introductions to JDeveloper and the Java language, it is useful to examine how development activities in this tool relate to the activities that Oracle Developer programmers are familiar with. This should make the transition to JDeveloper easier and faster.

Specific hints about how the concepts being discussed relate to a specific concept in Oracle Developer are scattered throughout this book. This chapter discusses the overall differences and similarities of creating a system using JDeveloper and Oracle Developer. The term, Oracle Developer, used in this chapter is a combination of the products known (at this writing) as Oracle Forms Developer and Oracle Reports Developer. Oracle Developer has evolved from development tools that Oracle has offered for many years under names such as IAD, SQL*Forms, Cooperative Development Environment (CDE) Forms, Oracle Forms, Oracle Developer Forms, Developer/2000 Forms, and Form Builder (and variations on all of those names for the report development tool). This chapter also discusses how to decide which language and which programming environment to apply to a particular system in case you are the one whose task it is to make (or influence) that decision.

If you have used client/server development tools other than Oracle Developer, the following discussion will still be of some use because the tasks and considerations for work are similar regardless of the development product.

Which Development Tool to Use?

The answer to the question of which is better for you, Developer or JDeveloper, will always be "It depends." The products are intended for different uses. However, if you are currently working in an Oracle Developer environment, you might wonder which tool to use for a specific application. If you decide that Java is the direction to follow, JDeveloper is the best choice. If you have access to Oracle Developer talent and only need to deploy your system internally, your decision is similarly easy.

The authors have used and promoted Oracle Developer for many years (and have even written an Oracle Press book on the subject). They feel that the product has many compelling strengths and is the tool of choice in many situations. They also feel that JDeveloper has many compelling strengths and is the tool of choice in many other situations. The two products are not in direct competition—they are complementary parts of a suite of development products that is marketed and sold (at this writing) as Internet Development Suite (IDS). There is no purchasing decision to be made; when you purchase IDS, you have all of these tools at your disposal.

The first thing you do when creating a system is to examine the business requirements and issues. Then, you must select a particular technology (for example, Java or more traditional client/server) that will best satisfy these requirements. You then choose a tool that fits that technology and your environment. Java is now a technology to consider. Therefore, one of the first steps after determining the requirements of the business is to decide whether to launch into the Java environment.

Why Use Java?

Java is an emerging language that provides many advantages over other programming languages. Java offers a modern, fully object-oriented environment for development and web deployment. The object orientation provides you with benefits in analysis and design because you can more easily match business concepts with objects than with standard relational structures.

The biggest drawback of Java is its newness. There is less technical expertise available, and the environment is nowhere near as mature as the traditional client products that access a relational database. It is the authors' opinion that there are relatively few Java-based production systems built to run against an Oracle database.

Working in a Java environment is very different from working with Oracle Developer, PowerBuilder, or Visual Basic (VB). It will take time to learn the nuances of this environment. If you are committed to creating an organization-wide Java environment, building a traditional client/server application still makes sense under certain circumstances. If your development team has skills in another language, Java will require some retraining and ramp-up time. However, building applications directly in Java provides improved flexibility and the ability to build sophisticated applications. It also makes the transition of your business to the Web easier because Java is a primary language of the Web.

Deciding to Move to a Java-Based Development Environment

Most developers have experience building systems. Many shops, whether they are using Oracle Forms Developer, C++, VB, or PowerBuilder, are building client/server applications successfully and efficiently. This book discusses the JDeveloper environment, which can be used in place of all of the previous development efforts. Does this mean that you should abandon your old development environment?

Probably not. It is possible to set up a largely Java-based development environment (JDeveloper coupled with HTML, JavaScript, and XML) that can be used to support an entire organization's development needs. However, no organizations that the authors are aware of have fully made this transition. This is still very much bleeding-edge technology. However, very soon, it is likely that the development community will shift in the direction of Java-based tools and applications. In the long term, many organizations will move into an entirely Java-centric development environment.

Keeping it Simple

It is very difficult to maintain and support disparate development environments, even for large organizations. Organizations with applications built using whatever was the fashionable tool of the moment usually ended up with systems in chaos. It is preferable to work in a development environment that allows you to minimize the number of different tools and languages required to build a system.

One reason that the Oracle Developer environment has such an advantage over VB and PowerBuilder is that you can use PL/SQL for both front- and back-end development. However, there is a huge startup cost to becoming efficient in any programming environment. Requiring developers to work in two programming languages is not advantageous. This is why the Oracle Forms Developer environment is so compelling—it uses only one language.

In the Java environment, knowledge of Java is not sufficient. Coding complex applications for e-commerce still requires knowledge of HTML (and JavaScript) as well as one of the associated editors such as Macromedia Dreamweaver or Microsoft FrontPage. Ultimately, it will be possible to leave the existing tools behind and move to a strictly Java-based environment. However, rushing too quickly toward such a decision is not advisable.

Which Is Best?

With all of the current development tools trying to improve their web-enabled capabilities, it becomes increasingly difficult to make a compelling argument to abandon these technologies. For example, following a long and difficult transition, Oracle Developer running over the Web is now a stable and viable environment. Oracle has not stopped there. A new project currently called "Cherokee" promises to provide yet another alternative for deploying Forms applications over the Internet.

The ability to cleanly and seamlessly deploy reasonably sophisticated applications using Developer talent is already available. The best bet at this point is to leave the core application development in whatever legacy environment you are comfortable with and build a few limited-scope systems in the Java/JDeveloper environment. Once you have some experience in building and deploying production applications, you can make an informed decision about whether your organization is ready to make the transition to an entirely Java-based environment. There may still be good reasons to stick with your legacy environment for core applications and only use a Java-based environment for e-commerce and other web-based applications.

Decision Points

The tool that you select for a particular application is a decision that requires careful deliberation because the tool, or at least the language or environment, that you select will become integral to the system. If you make a mistake, or change your mind after development is complete, a major effort and cost will be required to modify the language or environment. You need to consider many aspects of your situation, such as the intended audience (for example, web or client/server) and the talent available for development, deployment, and maintenance. Other factors that can influence your decision are the stability of the company behind the tool (to help you predict whether support, bug fixes, and enhancements will be available in the future); market direction (to lead to an assurance that there will be development talent available); and the stability of the code (so that you are comfortable that the development tool will not require you to spend time finding and reporting bugs in the tool). An additional factor to consider in this decision is the hardware and software environment that your target audience uses.

User Environment Considerations

Your application must support the equipment available to your target audience. For example, if you are deploying an Oracle Developer application to a client/server environment, you need to ensure that the users' PCs have enough memory and disk space for the runtime executable.

You also need to be certain that the screen resolution for which you develop the application is supported. For example, you might develop an Oracle Developer application for a screen resolution of 1024x768 and develop the window and canvas sizes accordingly. If users are not able to set that resolution because of hardware limitations, they will need to use the window scrollbars in all screens in your application. This is not a desired effect and will frustrate users quickly. A fix for this condition would require significant effort.

This consideration is not as important for HTML-based code such as JSP applications because the browser size can determine how the elements are laid out inside of it. Java client/server-based applications can resize and reposition objects automatically if they make use of layout managers (discussed in Chapter 11). Browser support is more important than screen resolution in a Java-based application. If your users may access your system with either Internet Explorer or Netscape, you need to be sure that all of the code that you write works in both browsers.

Systems Development Methodologies

Regardless of the tool or environment, creating systems always requires good software engineering practices. Therefore, at the core, the system lifecycle phases for a project are the same whether you use JDeveloper or Oracle Developer. Based on the system requirements, you need to select a sound methodology. You may want to use a method that includes analysis, design, and development with some variation on the traditional waterfall or iterative cycle. Alternatively, you may decide to use a rapid-application development methodology. As you progress through the analysis phase, you need to decide which tool would be best for the system that you want to create. After that decision is made, you can then target the design efforts at a specific environment.

One strategy you can use to minimize your risk of wanting to change products at a later time is to build "thin" applications. You can place all major code routines in the database and base your applications on complex views (frequently using INSTEAD OF triggers). In this way, 90% or more of your program logic is not embedded in a specific product and it is relatively easy to rewrite your application if you change your deployment platform in the future. This strategy also improves the logical organization and efficiency of your applications. Code that is more closely associated with the database resides there. This strategy can be taken to its logical conclusion by placing all business rules in a repository and driving very simple applications from the repository.

In addition to the language and tool decision, in the design phase you need to decide what your intended deployment technology will be. For example, in a Java environment, you can place your application into production in one of a number of formats—Java application, applet, or JSP application. (Chapter 7 explores details on these deployment alternatives.) Oracle Developer gives you the option of deploying in client/server or on the Web using a Java applet. Your choice of a technology depends upon the same considerations of the application's audience (intranet or Internet) and the type of application (e-commerce or internal). This factor can be used to validate your tool decision or to help you make your tool decision in the first place.

The differences in system development appear for the first time, therefore, before the design phase. You identify the target audience and business requirements before proceeding. You then try to match those parameters with the tool's targeted audience and use.

Target Uses for JDeveloper

JDeveloper is intended to be the tool of choice for creating scalable, web-based systems with a wide range of audiences—intranet (and extranet) and Internet—and with any business purpose, including departmental applications, internal corporate applications, and e-commerce.

JDeveloper is primarily a Java-based development tool. Java applications naturally support all types of media files that may be presented on the Web. They can be relatively undemanding of the client machine. For example, if you deploy a JSP application, the only requirement on the client side is an HTML-aware browser.

JDeveloper is primarily a 3GL code-generation tool that requires some coding by hand but offers many wizards that assist greatly with this task. It requires a different kind of development skill (low-level Java programmer), and this requirement must be a key factor in deciding whether to use Java technology, in general, and JDeveloper, as a development tool.

JDeveloper can also be used to create client/server applications using Java. This is particularly important for shops that have programmers who are skilled in Java development and need a client/server–style application.

Another strength of the tool is its ability to easily create BC4J code that you can use to separate data access and business logic from the user interface. BC4J provides a common layer that different kinds of applications with different target users can access.

Target Uses for Oracle Developer

Oracle Developer is intended to be the tool of choice for creating scalable, web-based and client/server systems with an intranet audience and with specific business purposes: departmental applications and internal corporate applications. The primary example of the use of Oracle Developer is its largest user—Oracle ERP (prepackaged applications such as Financials and Manufacturing), although future releases could use JDeveloper.

Oracle Developer has evolved from a long line of development products that have transitioned from mainframe to client/server to web architectures. The modern release of Oracle Developer runs on the Web in a Java applet that closely emulates standard client/server applications. Therefore, developers who are accustomed to creating client/server applications will find that there is virtually no learning curve to deploy those applications on the Web. Users who are accustomed to client/server applications will have less of a learning curve with an Oracle Developer application than with a JDeveloper JSP application (although JDeveloper can also create Java applications and applets that emulate client/server).

True to its heritage, Oracle Developer is also extremely strong in implementing client/server applications. The primary scripting language is PL/SQL, but much of the programming work is declarative in nature. Instead of writing lines of code, you work in a 4GL programming environment that uses definitions and declarations of objects. Oracle Developer also supports multimedia files, such as those found in all web applications, through extensions to the tool. Oracle Forms Developer applications running on the Web can even incorporate JavaBeans created in JDeveloper.

Other Comparisons

To help you in the decision of which tool to select, you need information about the similarities and differences between the tools. This type of information will also be helpful if you have a background in Oracle Developer and need to supplement your development skills with knowledge of JDeveloper. There are two categories of comparisons that will help you better understand JDeveloper and the differences between it and Oracle Developer.

- Programming environment
- Work in the tool

Comparing Programming Environments

JDeveloper creates applications within a Java environment. This environment is different from the "traditional" Oracle Developer environment because of the way that projects employ files, the languages, and the kind of code that the tools create.

Projects and Files

JDeveloper creates a number of different types of files for a specific application. Each Java class file that you create can contain a number of methods and other objects. In Oracle Developer, the application is contained in a single file (for example, a Forms .fmb file). A single Java class has a specific purpose that is usually more granular than a single Oracle Developer file. Therefore, there are inherently more files in a Java project than in an Oracle Developer project. You can combine these files into a single unit—the package—that is deployed, but the package is made up of a number of distinct files.

The Languages

Java is an object-oriented language. Oracle Developer provides some object-oriented concepts such as subclassing, but is more accurately termed an "object-based" or "object-friendly" tool. Object orientation requires a different way of thinking. Thinking in Java means that you need to think about objects. An object in Java is an instantiation of a class. (An *instantiation* is a programmatic declaration that creates something new. A *class* is a user-defined data structure that has attributes and methods and acts as a pattern from which the object is built.) Objects are created using programmatic declarations. In PL/SQL a user-defined datatype is implemented as a class in Java. PL/SQL variables are implemented as objects in Java. For example, the following code creates a text field object called "empnoTextField" from a class called JTextField.

```
JTextField empnoTextField = new JTextField();
```

Once the object is created in this way, you can assign values to its attributes (properties) using set() methods and call its other methods programmatically. If you want to see the object on the screen, you call an add() method on the container that will visually contain the object. The code to create and manipulate objects is always exposed. This gives you the ultimate in flexibility because you can code almost anything you want. However, as with any other tool, this flexibility comes with the price of responsibility. You are responsible for more of the low-level details in Java because they are available to you. JDeveloper eases this responsibility by supplying wizards that generate much of the basic code for you.

NOTE
Chapter 4 contains details about the Java language.

Oracle Developer and the PL/SQL language do not use this concept of wizards as heavily. You do not create most objects programmatically; instead, you create them in the Object Navigator or Layout Editor. Some objects such as timers, parameter lists, and record groups can be created, maintained, and destroyed programmatically without being represented in the Object Navigator. The nonprogrammatic objects are visible in the Object Navigator, and you can assign property values to them at design time. You can also call built-in procedures to modify their property values programmatically, but you cannot create or destroy nonprogrammatic objects at runtime. The built-in procedures that modify property values are like the set() methods for Java classes. Since you cannot break into the code that creates objects (it is there in the runtime file but hidden from the designer), you do not have the responsibility for ensuring that all requirements of the object are met. That responsibility is handled under the covers by the tool.

JDeveloper generates the "add" and "set" code for you when you interact with its UI Designer. The code is available for you to modify and supplement. In fact, although JDeveloper generates completely working applications, it is likely that you will have to modify almost every file it creates to fit your application's requirements. Oracle Developer does not provide access to the code to create each object in the designer interface. When you create an object, there is nothing to modify other than its properties.

Both Oracle Developer and Java contain rich event models. When the user acts upon the screen objects, an event (called a *trigger* in Oracle Developer) occurs that can be handled by code that you write.

NOTE
Another effect that you will experience when starting to work in a Java environment is the shock of new terminology. There are lots of new terms, many of which are from the world of object orientation. To assist in your learning process, do not be afraid to ask questions when a new term is used.

The Code

JDeveloper creates Java-based code. The source code (.java) files are normal Java files that you can open and modify in any text editor. JDeveloper also creates files in a number of other languages such as XML, JSP, and HTML. All files are plain text files. Oracle Developer creates source code files (.fmb for Forms and .rdf for Reports) in tokenized binary formats that are proprietary to the tool. In both tools, you compile the files into runtime files that you use for deploying the application. In Oracle Developer, the runtime file (.fmx for Forms and .rep for Reports) is run by the proprietary Developer runtime engine. In Java, the runtime bytecode is a .class file that runs in a standard (nonproprietary) JVM or other engine. XML, JSP, and HTML files are all run from their source code files since they are purely interpreted tag language files.

There are no standalone executables created by either tool. Both tools use some kind of runtime program to interpret the compiled runtime files. Oracle Developer uses a runtime program that corresponds to the JVM (or server-side JSP container) in Java.

Comparing Work in the Tools

One way to understand the differences and similarities between JDeveloper and Oracle Developer is to take a quick tour through their development work areas and describe how the development process is different in each. Both are full-featured IDEs, as described for JDeveloper in Chapter 2, and, therefore, support the basic operations of code development, compiling, debugging, and packaging. So that the following discussion can be reasonably brief—it will focus on the development of a Java application in JDeveloper and a form in the Oracle Forms Developer. Developing reports in Oracle Developer is a bit different, but the Oracle Reports Developer IDE also has many similarities to the Forms IDE.

The first comparison to discuss is the IDE window. In JDeveloper, you can anchor windows to the outer frame so that they do not float within the frame. Oracle Developer presents all internal windows as separate windows without the ability to anchor the window to a particular side of the outer frame although you can maximize the window to fill the outer frame. There are additional comparisons possible in different areas inside the IDE window.

NOTE
Another difference between JDeveloper and Oracle Developer is their help systems. Since you have to work with lower-level code in JDeveloper, you need to know how to use the Javadoc documentation for class libraries that you are using in JDeveloper (such as Swing and AWT components). There is also a wealth of information about these non-Oracle class libraries on many Java developer web sites. As a Java programmer, you need to have this information at your fingertips. In Oracle Developer, the help system is relatively complete. All reference material for the built-in procedures is available directly in the Oracle Developer help system.

The Navigators

The JDeveloper and Oracle Developer navigators are similar in appearance, as Figure 5-1 shows. The objects displayed in each are arranged in a hierarchy. Oracle Developer organizes the objects so that the file type is the top-level node and the file is the next node. Objects can have child objects represented under them. JDeveloper uses the workspace as the top-level node. This workspace corresponds in Oracle Developer to a set of open files. It allows you easy access to a number of files by opening one file. There is no parallel to the single-file workspace concept in Developer. The Navigation Pane (top part of the window) shows project files and their child files. The workspace is also stored in a file, which means that the main objects represented in the Navigation Pane are files.

The bottom part of the window, the Structure Pane, displays the objects inside each file. In summary, both navigators show files and objects in the files using a hierarchical tree structure. You can add objects to the application by dropping them into the Structure Pane. Both Oracle Developer and JDeveloper allow you to cut and paste objects in the navigators. JDeveloper does not allow the same drag-and-drop reordering of objects that Oracle Forms Developer allows, but you can use Cut and Paste to accomplish the same task in JDeveloper.

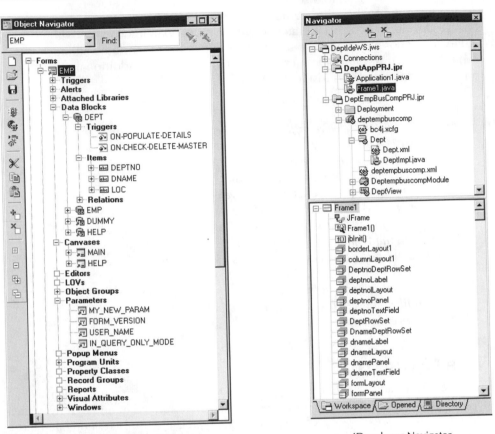

Oracle Forms Developer Object Navigator   JDeveloper Navigator

FIGURE 5-1. *The navigators*

The Structure Pane changes to something like the following display when the Design tab of the Viewer window is active. This view represents the objects in a hierarchical structure so that you can see the relationship between objects.

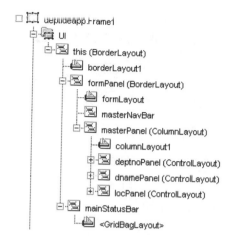

In both tools, selecting an object in the navigator will select the object in the UI Designer and load the property inspector with the object's properties.

The JDeveloper Navigator also contains Opened and Directory tabs (described in Chapter 2) that have no equivalent in Oracle Developer. Both tools offer toolbar buttons within the navigator window to act upon objects in the window. The menu in both tools contains the same actions as the toolbar buttons. In addition, both tools offer toolbars under the menu bar for common main menu selections.

UI Designers

When you create a Java application or applet in JDeveloper, you can view the frame as it will be displayed at runtime using the UI Designer. You can also use this tool to add or modify objects on the frame. The changes that you make to the objects in this window will be represented by code in the Source Editor. The UI Designer is very similar to the Oracle Forms Developer Layout Editor. These tools are shown in Figures 5-2 and 5-3. There is also a Menu Designer that corresponds to the Oracle Forms Developer Menu Editor.

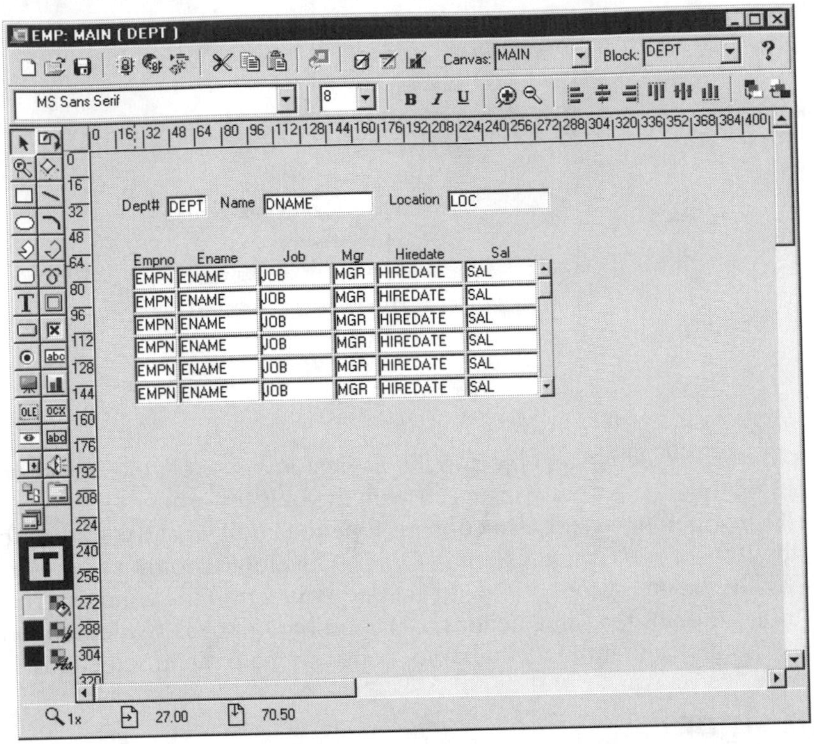

FIGURE 5-2. *Oracle Forms Developer Layout Editor*

One difference between the tools is in the dependency between the source code and layout editors. JDeveloper will only display either the UI Designer or the source code editor for a particular file. Oracle Developer can display both PL/SQL Editor and Layout Editor at the same time. Since changing an object in the JDeveloper UI Designer will change the code, you are essentially rewriting and editing the source code when you make a change to the layout. Similarly, when you make a change to the code, the UI Designer will reflect that change if it affects a visual object.

NOTE
JSP code does not use the UI Designer for emulating the runtime display. Therefore, most of your JDeveloper work on JSP applications is done using the Source Editor.

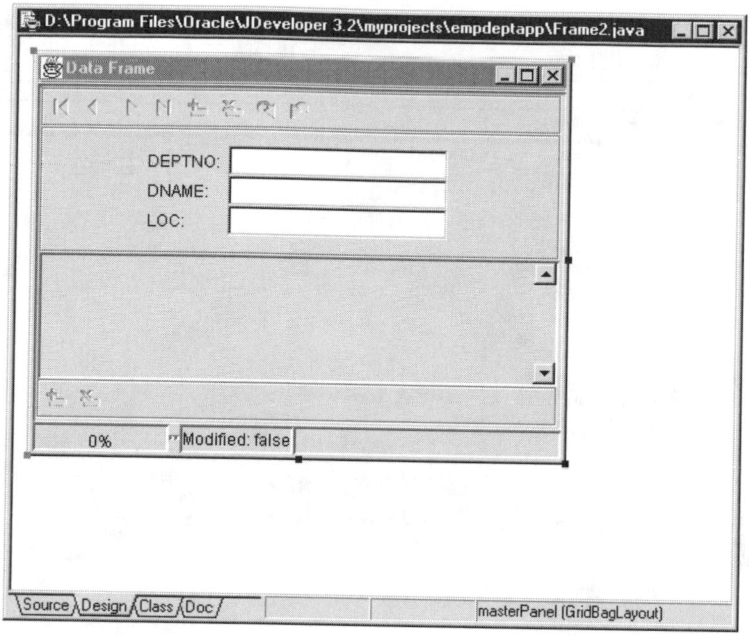

FIGURE 5-3. *JDeveloper UI Designer*

Source Code Editors

Both tools contain source code editors that represent keywords and comments in different colors. Figures 5-4 and 5-5 show the source code editors in both tools. Both tools provide assistance in filling in syntax (the Syntax Palette in Oracle Developer and Code Insight in JDeveloper). Both tools also allow you to open more than one source code window at the same time.

Property Inspectors

JDeveloper provides an Inspector window that allows you to set property values easily. The property values consist of characters that you type in, selections from a pulldown list, or additional dialogs that help you fill in the proper values. This is similar to the Property Palette in Oracle Developer. Figure 5-6 shows the property windows from both tools.

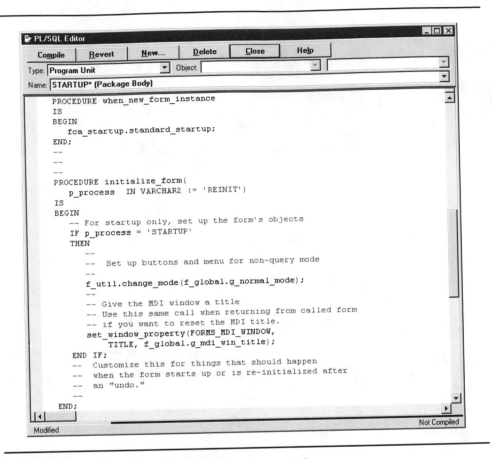

FIGURE 5-4. *Oracle Forms Developer PL/SQL Editor*

The JDeveloper Inspector provides an Events tab for adding code for specific events. This facility adds listener code and a code stub for the event that you click in

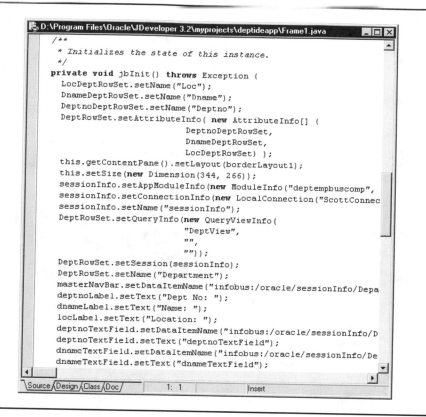

```
D:\Program Files\Oracle\JDeveloper 3.2\myprojects\deptideapp\Frame1.java
/**
 * Initializes the state of this instance.
 */
private void jbInit() throws Exception {
  LocDeptRowSet.setName("Loc");
  DnameDeptRowSet.setName("Dname");
  DeptnoDeptRowSet.setName("Deptno");
  DeptRowSet.setAttributeInfo( new AttributeInfo[] {
                              DeptnoDeptRowSet,
                              DnameDeptRowSet,
                              LocDeptRowSet) };
  this.getContentPane().setLayout(borderLayout1);
  this.setSize(new Dimension(344, 266));
  sessionInfo.setAppModuleInfo(new ModuleInfo("deptempbuscomp",
  sessionInfo.setConnectionInfo(new LocalConnection("ScottConnec
  sessionInfo.setName("sessionInfo");
  DeptRowSet.setQueryInfo(new QueryViewInfo(
                          "DeptView",
                          "",
                          ""));
  DeptRowSet.setSession(sessionInfo);
  DeptRowSet.setName("Department");
  masterNavBar.setDataItemName("infobus:/oracle/sessionInfo/Depa
  deptnoLabel.setText("Dept No: ");
  dnameLabel.setText("Name: ");
  locLabel.setText("Location: ");
  deptnoTextField.setDataItemName("infobus:/oracle/sessionInfo/D
  deptnoTextField.setText("deptnoTextField");
  dnameTextField.setDataItemName("infobus:/oracle/sessionInfo/De
  dnameTextField.setText("dnameTextField");
```
Source / Design / Class / Doc /   1: 1   Insert

FIGURE 5-5.   *JDeveloper Source Editor*

the Inspector window. It also switches cursor focus to the code stub so that you can easily find it and fill in the required functionality.

There are some cosmetic differences in the windows of both tools. For example, the JDeveloper palette lists properties in alphabetical order, whereas Oracle Developer organizes the properties into groups with headings.

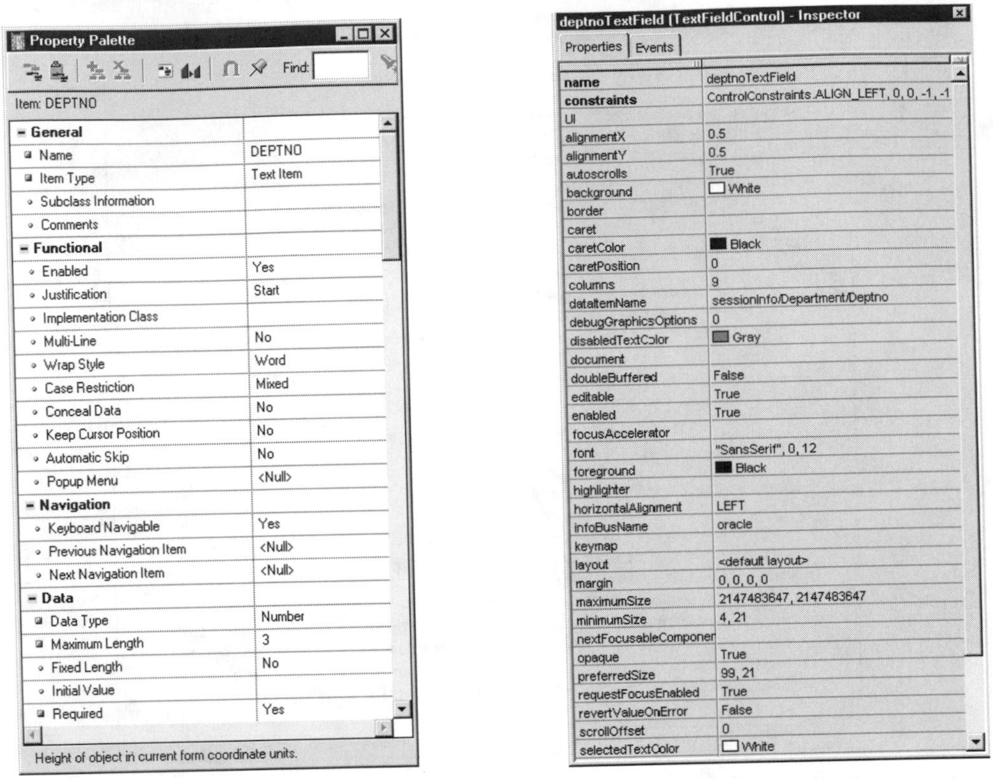

Oracle Forms Developer Property Palette

JDeveloper Inspector

FIGURE 5-6. *Property windows*

Message Windows

Both tools offer message windows that display compilation and runtime status messages. Oracle Developer uses two areas—the bottom part of the PL/SQL Editor window that displays the results of a compilation problem in the program unit and a Compile window that shows the results of compiling all code in the form. These windows are shown in Figure 5-7.

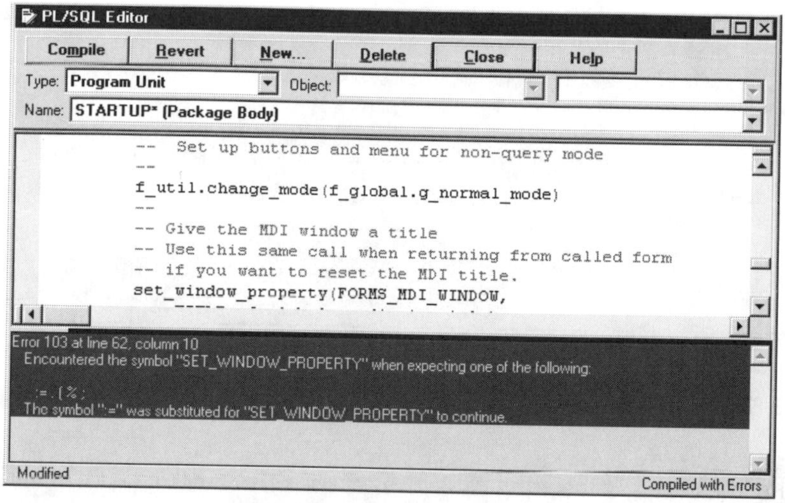

PL/SQL Editor message pane

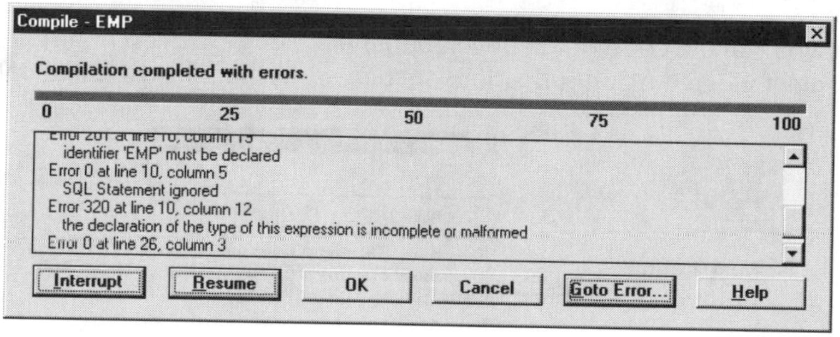

Compile window

FIGURE 5-7. *Oracle Developer message areas*

JDeveloper contains a similar message window that allows you to view compilation errors, as shown in Figure 5-0. This window also allows you to display messages from the code on a separate tab page. You can use this feature for simple

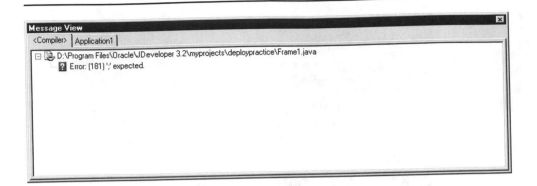

FIGURE 5-8. *JDeveloper Message View*

debugging messages by inserting calls to `System.out.println()` at various points in the code, for example:

```
System.out.println("*** After pack.");
```

When you run the code from JDeveloper, the Message View will display the print statement when it reaches that line of code, as in the following illustration:

Message from
println() ⟶

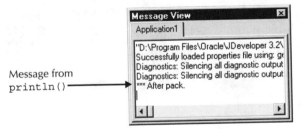

In addition to these message areas, both tools provide a status bar at the bottom of the main window that displays the file name or status of a compilation or save operation.

NOTE
Chapter 13 contains a description of the primary debugging features supplied by JDeveloper. In general, the debugger in JDeveloper can accomplish the same tasks as the debugger in Oracle Developer but contains features that are closer to other 3GL environment debuggers. A more detailed comparison of the two debuggers would not be useful because the development environments (3GL for JDeveloper and 4GL for Oracle Developer) are so different.

Wizards

JDeveloper contains a large number of wizards (most of which are listed in Appendix A). There are wizards for creating a default BC4J project, a Java application, an applet, and a JSP file, as well as for lower-level objects such as frames, applications, web beans, and so on. The wizards are key to starting a particular task and are a true benefit of using JDeveloper because they create bug-free code that is as complete as possible. You will need to add application-specific logic and objects that cannot be handled by defaults. However, the wizards create a lot of code for you and allow you to concentrate on customizing the application for the business needs.

Since Oracle Developer is a higher-level development environment, it does not supply as many wizards. There is no need for a separate database access layer, so there is nothing like the Business Components Project Wizard. There are wizards in Oracle Developer for defining a data block and its source database objects (table, view, procedure, REF CURSOR, or SELECT statement). There are also wizards for block layout, LOV definition, reports, and charts. There are no wizards for lower-level objects because the work that you are doing is declarative in nature; it does not create lines of code for everything that is required in the application.

Figure 5-9 shows a corresponding wizard page for defining the data source of a single-table application in Oracle Developer and in JDeveloper.

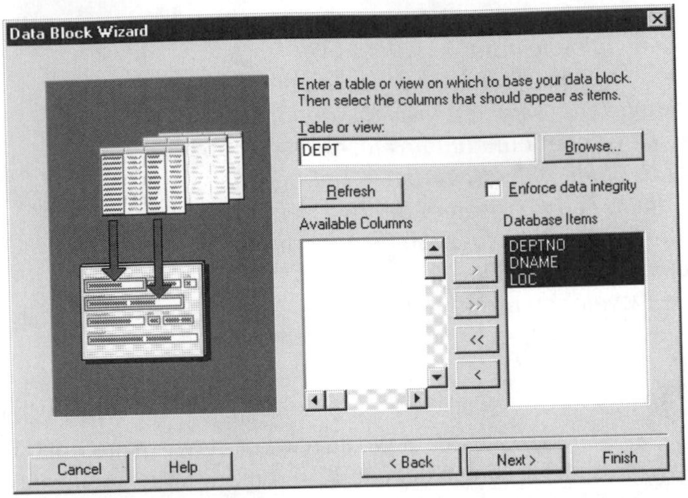

Oracle Forms Developer Data Block Wizard

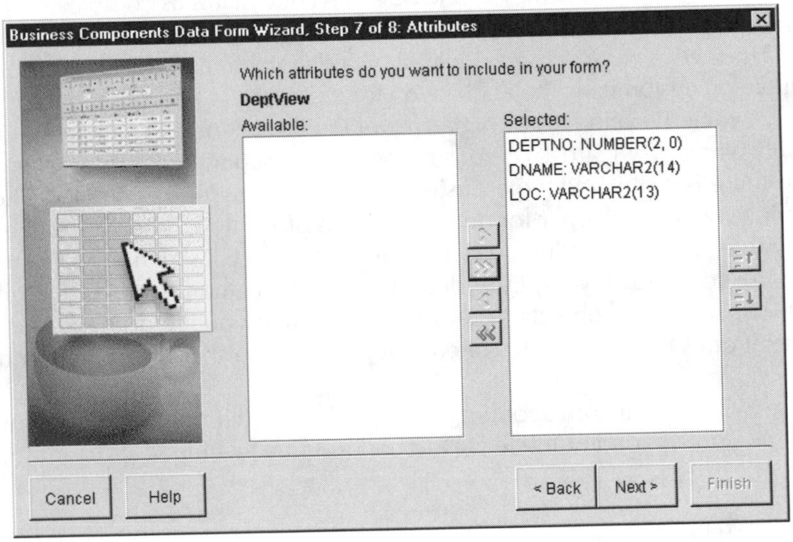

JDeveloper Business Components Data Form Wizard

FIGURE 5-9. *Defining a data source using a wizard*

NOTE

As you work with JDeveloper, you will find differences in the behavior of some controls. For example, when you create a multi-record block in Oracle Developer, you can modify any item type. You can change a text item to a poplist or checkbox control with one property setting. In JDeveloper, the grid control that emulates the multi-record block in Oracle Developer requires some nondefault code to modify the item types. (There is an example of this on the authors' web sites.) However, the grid control allows users to resize, hide, and display items at runtime—a feature that would require a significant amount of code in Oracle Developer.

Development Method

As you would expect, the steps you need to follow in creating an application are different for each tool. The method you use in JDeveloper requires a specific order, as with any tool. Table 5-1 shows the major steps you would follow to create a Java application in JDeveloper. Java applications contain many of the same elements as applications that you create in Oracle Developer, and the table lists the corresponding steps that you would take in Oracle Developer. Other variations on Java code (such as applets or JSPs) would use some different steps.

Note for Oracle Developer Users

You have many choices for the style of application you are creating in JDeveloper (for example, Java application, applet, or JSP). When learning JDeveloper, it is best to stick with the basics and create a sample Java application first. The Java application has many similarities with the applications that you create in Oracle Developer, so you will not have to make the transition step of learning a new architecture for deployment. After you feel comfortable with this style of application and with the way that JDeveloper works, you can branch out and explore the other styles.

JDeveloper Steps	Corresponding Step in Oracle Developer
1. Define a connection object to access the database schema through JDBC.	Normal database grants and a Net8 connection.
2. Create a workspace to contain project files.	Create a file system directory to organize the source code files.
3. Create a data access project (BC4J) using the Business Components Project Wizard to set up the data layer.	(none)
4. Create a Java application using the Project Wizard and Business Components Data Form Wizard (or just the Application Wizard and Frame Wizard).	Create a form using a template and use the Data Block Wizard and Layout Wizard to define and lay out a block that connects to a database table or other data source.
5. Add and modify objects in the UI Designer and Menu Designer.	Add and modify objects in the Layout Editor and Menu Editor.
6. Modify object properties using the Inspector.	Modify object properties using the Property Palette.
7. Set other properties using code in the Source Editor.	(none)
8. Add event-handling code using the Source Editor.	Add trigger code using the PL/SQL Editor.
9. Add code using the Source Editor to enforce business rules and set object properties at runtime.	Add code using the PL/SQL Editor to enforce business rules and set object properties at runtime.
10. Compile, test, and debug the code using the IDE tools.	Compile, test, and debug the code using the IDE tools.
11. Create a deployment set with files to be copied to a production location.	Create a deployment set with files to be copied to a production location.

TABLE 5-1. *Steps for Creating a JDeveloper Application Compared to Steps in Oracle Developer*

PART
II

JDeveloper and the Java Environment

CHAPTER

6

Business Components
for Java

Talk of nothing but business and dispatch that business quickly.
— Aldus Manutius (1450–1515), placard on the door of the Aldine Press

Developer's main advantage over other Java development tools is its Business Components for Java (BC4J) framework and associated code generators. BC4J is the heart of the JDeveloper product that sets it apart as the tool of choice for Oracle developers building Java or web-based applications. At its roots, BC4J is supported by a programming protocol or standard that describes how to build classes that will interact with a relational database.

JDeveloper uses BC4J as the primary way of handling database DML operations (queries, inserts, updates, and deletes). Prior to the existence of BC4J and similar products, connecting a Java-based application to the database was an extraordinarily difficult task. You needed to write complex JDBC and SQLJ code in order to coordinate your Java front-end with the database. In addition, you had to maintain your own data caching, batch your own updates, and keep track of table locks and commits. This complex interface with the database has proven to be one of the biggest hurdles to building web-based applications. Organizations that attempted applications projects without a product such as JDeveloper were frequently over budget and found their applications difficult to maintain. The BC4J components in JDeveloper provide a functional interface to the database and can be constructed using the built-in code generators or wizards.

This chapter presents only an overview of the BC4J components. In Chapter 7, you will find a discussion of deployment options for these components. The hands-on practices in this chapter show how to build and modify BC4J components. Hands-on practices in other chapters will demonstrate how these components can be used in conjunction with data-aware components, Java Server Pages (JSPs), and other JDeveloper-generated code.

Overview

When you use BC4J, you are building a set of Java classes that wrap the DML commands and reference an XML document that stores the data structure. These Java classes make the JDBC calls to the database that take over all of the insert, update, delete, and lock functions required to make the applications run. This enables you to completely encapsulate the logic associated with database access and provides developers a similar ease of application development to that of basing blocks on tables in Oracle Forms Developer.

However, BC4J does more than this. Frequently, complex validation is placed in database locations such as triggers on tables, or views with INSTEAD OF triggers. Complex data validation can also be implemented within BC4J classes. Despite this additional option, it is still difficult to set guidelines for what circumstances lead you to place data validation logic in the database as opposed to placing it in the BC4J components. In an environment that is not 100 percent Java, placing validation in BC4J components may be dangerous. Some applications will access the validation through BC4J, whereas other applications written in different products may not even have the ability to access the validation logic through BC4J. If you are working in a completely Java-based environment, JDeveloper makes the creation and manipulation of BC4J components easy enough that you may choose to use BC4J over server-side validation due to the cost savings realized through reduced development time. However, this is only appropriate if you can guarantee that all data-modifying DML operations will use the BC4J components.

BC4J classes can also cache data to be shared among multiple users, allowing for many tuning capabilities since no access to the database is required.

While using BC4J, developers create or utilize three types of files:

- An XML document that redundantly stores the data structure of the relational database

- Java classes themselves containing complex logic along with the application calls used by other parts of the application

- A sophisticated Java library provided by Oracle that handles the JDBC generation

BC4J Structure

BC4J is a well-constructed and carefully thought out component of JDeveloper. Only the sophisticated JDeveloper user will be aware of any of the underlying structure since the BC4J wizards provide a simple mechanism for modifying the underlying Java classes and XML documents.

From the developer's perspective, you will only need to think in terms of logical BC4J objects. You manipulate the Java classes only where complex validation or coding capability beyond what the wizards can handle is required.

The BC4J components allow you to conceptually divide your application into two major parts, as shown in the following illustration:

- User interface and client logic

- Database interface and business logic

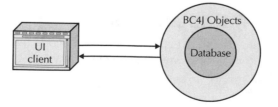

Using this object-oriented framework will help you create reusable business components that can effectively communicate between the database and your user interface (UI). The BC4J wizards read the Oracle system views to obtain metadata representing the database structure. Using this metadata, the wizards generate XML and Java code that provides a customizable framework to which you can add data validation or other business logic.

The BC4J components provide a number of benefits. First, simplicity and organization are easier to achieve using these components. The inclusion of a BC4J project in an application means you can optimize overall performance and reusability of code depending upon where you choose to deploy your BC4J components. Second, you can improve code maintainability by moving shared code such as data validation into the BC4J layer. Third, BC4J classes can be deployed on the database server, application server, or locally on the client. This portability can have a significant performance benefit for applications that are validation intensive.

How BC4J Works

Behind the scenes, BC4J uses a series of wizards to generate both XML files that define the structure of the data and also Java classes to control what is done with the data. This provides a portable interface to the database and a sophisticated structure to which you can add your validation and business rules.

Your initial creation of the BC4J layer is accomplished using the wizards. You can modify the generated code by re-entering the wizards and modifying your selections. If you open any of the generated XML files directly in JDeveloper editor panes, you will find that you can only view the source code files. The only way to change these files is to use the Business Component wizards.

CAUTION
In the case of the XML definition files, all manipulation should be handled through the wizards.

The structure in BC4J enables you to add complex validation in the application layer. This allows developers to write applications where complex data validation is handled without database access. This validation may be quite sophisticated. In addition to declarative validation using XML, developers may create customized programmatic validation procedures using Java.

Utilizing BC4J Capabilities

There is an extraordinary depth of capability in BC4J beyond the basic database transactions. However, it is not always entirely clear how to use this capability effectively. For instance, moving complex validation out of the database and into an application layer has both pros and cons to consider. Over the last few years, Oracle Forms Developer has evolved into an environment where more and more logic and validation can be moved into the database, frequently employing updateable views and INSTEAD OF triggers in order to consolidate the validation in one place. There is a conceptual purity in this approach that also carries over to JDeveloper. However, in JDeveloper, there are several additional options for placement of complex validation. The one you choose is dependent upon several factors:

- Hardware configuration
- Deployment strategy
- Number of and types of clients
- Ease of debugging and maintenance

In general, placing validation closer to the client will allow you to display and handle errors immediately, whereas placing the validation code closer to the database provides for more reusability.

The BC4J code itself can be placed in one of three basic places:

- Database tier
- Middle tier (application or web server)
- Locally in the client

The distinction between the various locations for validation deployment is not as clear-cut as it might first appear. For example, performing complex validation in the database may impact performance due to network limitations. More code in the client means faster performance and easier debugging and maintenance if the code is not duplicated in multiple locations. However, if you are using multiple clients that are pulling data from different kinds of Java applications, having the validation code in a common BC4J layer would provide better code reuse. You may want to use multiple application modules to implement the business logic for a particular application screen or task in its own module. Typically an application module would contain three to four view objects, although it might contain many more. A large application could have 20 or more application modules, each containing the appropriate views for a given task.

A sample data model is shown in Figure 6-1 in both ERD and UML formats.

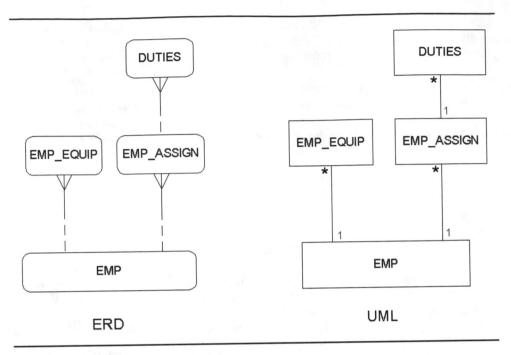

FIGURE 6-1. *Sample data model*

Specific Application Example

Using the model shown in Figure 6-1, BC4J would require four entities corresponding to the four tables, and three associations corresponding to the three foreign key relationships. In order to determine what BC4J views and links are required, you must assume a specific application. In this case, a four-tab application for employees and the equipment and assignments associated with them would include the following:

- **Tab 1**   A locator set up to search for and display a specific list of employees.

- **Tab 2**   After an employee is selected in Tab 1, Tab 2 is used to edit the existing employee or to create a new one. If you doubleclick an employee name in Tab 1, Tab 2 will automatically return the detailed information for the selected employee.

- **Tab 3**   Shows the associated equipment attached to the employee record.

- **Tab 4**   Shows both the employee assignments for selected employee on Tab 2 and the duties associated with each assignment in a master-detail relationship.

Even though there are five groups of data, you will only need four BC4J views.

Building Applications Using BC4J

You can quickly build an entire application by connecting your user interface to BC4J objects. In the past, the client and database were required to communicate many times to complete even the simplest transaction. However, with today's web and wide area networks, this style of high-volume system traffic is not practical. The BC4J components solve this problem by providing alternative locations for the traditional client/server logic, resulting in shorter data paths to your business rules and data validation code. Using a BC4J layer is like having a virtual database (tables - columns - synonyms - metadata) adjacent to the client application. You can think of BC4J as simply a black box database. It can interact with one or more clients to synchronize data, manage the cache, and implement the basic functionality of your data model, as shown in Figure 6-2.

Once you investigate the extensibility of the BC4J components, you will realize that they can provide more functionality than just acting as a virtual repository. BC4J provides an extensible framework that can take you far beyond the traditional relational database constructs by including elements such as complex business rules. For example, you can implement logical "OR" ref-constraints without the need for BEFORE INSERT triggers. By including a bit of extra code and leveraging the deployment options, you can optimize the overall performance of a system.

Virtually every application will need some modification to the basic BC4J components. Thus, it is very important to understand how the BC4J components are designed and interfaced.

Java and XML

BC4J components are built using a combination of Java and XML. Both XML and Java are open-source (nonproprietary) languages. Since both languages are operating system and platform independent, they interface well with networks and operate effectively across the Web. Each of these languages has unique strengths that complement the

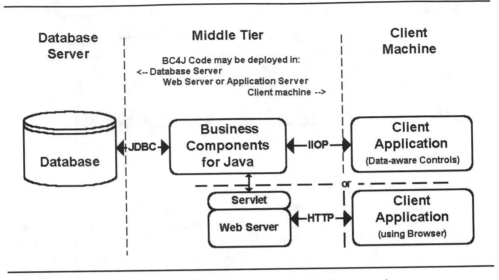

FIGURE 6-2. *Using BC4J components in a multi-tier framework*

other. Java is a modular and portable language that is ideal for communicating between business applications due to its built-in security and Internet capabilities. Yet Java lacks an effective way of exchanging data across different platforms and applications. This is where Extensible Markup Language (XML) becomes useful. *XML* is a tag or markup language that is similar to HTML; however, the XML tags are much more powerful because the basic tags can be extended to meet your evolving needs. In HTML, you use tags to describe how you want things displayed, whereas in XML you create tags to describe the structure and content of the text or data. It should be noted that XML is case sensitive just like Java.

XML is used to define the data, and Java is used to operate on the data. You will find that the BC4J components will have both XML and Java files associated with them. The XML file holds the metadata that defines the business component, and the Java file holds the methods that implement the business component. The .java file contains get() and set() methods, which dynamically generate insert, update, and delete statements at runtime. Also, the XML and Java files can contain more than just database table references. They may define and implement validation rules as well. Note that the terms used to describe the BC4J objects are very similar to those used in describing relational databases.

The BC4J Components

The BC4J components fit into three major groups: data definition and validation components, data manipulation and filtering components, and storage locations and containers.

For those readers familiar with data modeling, Figure 6-3 will be helpful in understanding the relationships and cardinality associated with each of the BC4J components. If you are not familiar with UML modeling, the figures can simply be viewed as block diagrams that illustrate the overall relationships in the BC4J layer. This information will help you in visualizing how these components relate to each other and how they are organized as a group.

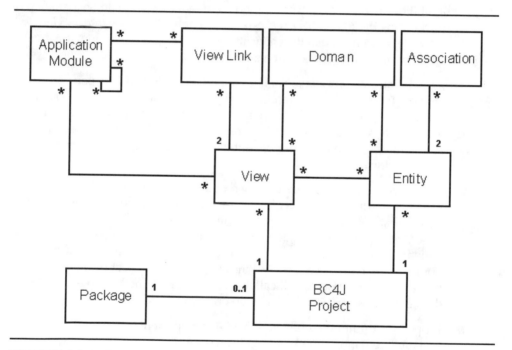

FIGURE 6-3. *BC4J components modeled in a UML diagram*

Data Definition and Validation Components

The following are descriptions of the components used in data definition and validation:

- **Entity**   *Entities* are based on database tables, views, snapshots, or synonyms and include the database storage requirements. Entities can be generated from existing database objects, or they can be manually defined and used to create new database tables. Entities contain attribute (column) definitions.

- **Attribute**   There are two types of attributes: entity attributes and view attributes. An *entity attribute* is the part of an entity that usually corresponds to a table column, and may include validation rules and business logic. Some attributes, such as BLOB types, cannot be queried and should be identified by unchecking the *Queriable* checkbox in the Entity Object Wizard. A *view attribute* is simply one of the entity attributes. You can create additional view attributes for items such as calculated columns.

- **Association**   An *association* defines the relationship between pairs of entities. Typically these represent a foreign key constraint from the database, but they may be defined for any pair of Entity Attribute components You can also specify more than one attribute on each side of the association, as long as you have the same number of attributes on each side. The association is bidirectional.

- **Domain**   A *domain* is a user-defined datatype representing the type of values an attribute can have. For example, you could create a domain to ensure that you have entered nine digits for your Social Security number. When you write the validation logic for this component, you must put it in a method named `validate()` that is called in the constructor of the domain's Java file. Each time you instantiate a new object using this domain, the constructor will call the `validate()` method to ensure that the new attribute meets your defined criteria.

- **Property**   Within the context of a BC4J component, a *property* is a name/value pair of type `String`. Properties are used to store text strings. These text strings can be used to display information at runtime, for example, to define a user's access level, to specify what type of UI control to use, and to set a domain's format mask. You can define properties for domains, entities, views, entity attributes, view object attributes, and application modules. The BC4J properties are stored in the associated component's XML file.

CAUTION
A BC4J property is not the same as a JavaBean property, even though they have the same name. Don't confuse the two.

Data Manipulation or Filtering Components
The BC4J views and links provide the appropriate data to support your UI by filtering the data returned by the Entity and Association objects.

- **View object** *View objects* use SQL queries to specify and filter data that is defined in the entity objects. Client applications can navigate, update, insert, and delete data using the view object's `get()` and `set()` methods.

- **View link** *View links* are used to express the relationships between view objects. These relationships are only implemented in one direction. Thus, in a master-detail relationship (the master being the source and the detail being the destination), only the source objects have get/set accessor methods defined. View links provide the filtered rows for the detail table, for the current row selected in the master table.

  View links link views in the same way that associations link entities. However, there is no programmatic connection between view links and associations. Associations can be used to generate view links or view links can be created independently of the associations.

Storage Locations and Containers
There are two types of locations/containers for placing elements in the BC4J layer:

- **Packages** Java classes are grouped by categories in *packages*. During development, these packages are equivalent to the subdirectories or folders on the hard disk where your source code is stored. When the code is compiled and prepared for deployment, you will find a duplicate directory structure in the output-root path JDEV_HOME\myclasses, with the compiled class files having a new extension .class.

- **Application modules** The application module instantiates the BC4J view objects and view links with which the client applications will interact. It is possible to have multiple application modules within the same BC4J layer. It is also possible to nest application modules within other application modules.

You may want to use multiple application modules to implement the business logic for a particular application screen or task, giving each logical part its own module. Typically an application module would contain three to four view objects and links, though it might contain much more. And a large application could have 20 or more application modules, each containing the appropriate views and links for a given task.

Hands-on Practice: Creating a BC4J Project

In this practice, you will walk through all of the wizards in the BC4J layer to provide insight into the circumstances under which each will be useful. Unlike most wizard-based environments, the BC4J wizards are quite robust. The number of times you will need to go beyond the capabilities of the wizards will be relatively small. However, there are still reasons why you will need to add code manually, for example, for data validation. Therefore, in order to provide examples of how to build or modify some components manually outside of the wizards, this hands-on practice includes many more steps than you would normally require when using them.

This practice session consists of the following phrases:

I. Set up the structure

- **Prepare a new work area**

- **Create a project for your business components**

- **Create or select a connection**

II. Add Components

- **Add an entity object for DEPT**

- **Add entity objects for EMP and SALGRADE**

- **Add association objects**

- **Add a view object for DEPT**

- **Add view objects for EMP and SALGRADE**

- **Add view links**

- **Create application modules**

This session was developed to give you practice with many of the BC4J wizards; some of these steps are somewhat artificial and may be unnecessary in a real project.

They do not reflect a typical BC4J development philosophy. In most cases, you would use the following overall strategy in creating a BC4J project:

■ **Generating** Use the BC4J wizards to generate the basic entities, associations, views, view links, and application modules.

■ **Testing** Use the built-in Oracle Business Component Browser to verify that you have correctly defined the appropriate views and links for your application. (See the hands-on practice later in this chapter.)

■ **Customizing components** Add calculated columns, data validation, and business logic to your entities and views. For example, to customize a view object you could perform the following activities:

1. Remove the Loc attribute from DeptView.

2. Remove the Sal and Comm attributes from EmpView, and add a calculated attribute, Earnings, whose value is Sal + Comm.

3. Remove the Mgr attribute from EmpView and replace it with an attribute that contains the manager's name. This requires adding the manager entity to EmpView's entity list.

■ **Adding objects** You may add more complex objects to your BC4J project, such as view objects, that are based on more than one entity. You can also add a WHERE or ORDER BY clause. For example, LocView may contain an employee's ID, name, job, and location; ManagerView may contain just the managers; TechStaffView may contain employees in research and operations.

■ **Testing your objects again** Before you start developing your GUI screens, retest your application modules to ensure they meet all your design criteria.

This generalized development strategy should save you considerable time in developing and debugging your BC4J projects.

I. Set Up the Structure

Before you start to build your BC4J objects, you will need to create a new work area and add the appropriate workspace and project files.

By default JDeveloper tries to place the workspace files in the default source root directory. It is usually not a good idea to put all workspace files in the same location because this strategy unnecessarily clutters the root directory, making it difficult to separate the required files.

Prepare a New Work Area

To create a new workspace file in a new folder, use the following steps:

1. If you have an existing workspace open, select **File | Close Workspace**. The Navigation Pane will display a new default workspace named "Untitled1.jws."

2. Select **File | Save Workspace**.

3. Click the Create New Folder icon in the File dialog and name the new folder "buscomppkg."

4. Doubleclick the buscomppkg folder to navigate to that folder.

5. To name the workspace file, change the *File Name* field to "BusCompWS," and click Save. JDeveloper will add the extension .jws.

Create a Project for Your Business Components

If you look at your hard drive after you create a project that contains Business Components, you will notice that the wizard has produced a slightly different set of files than it normally does. As you may recall .jpr is the extension for a project file. In the case of a Business Component Project, you will find a second project file with the extension .jpx. This extra file contains additional metadata for the BC4J projects.

CAUTION
You may find that the project file with the extension .jpx is not stored in the same location as your other project files. Do not try to move or delete it, as you may lose access to your entire project. The storage location for this file may change, depending upon which version of JDeveloper you have installed.

To create a project for your Business Components:

1. Select **File | New Project** to display the Project Wizard's Welcome page. Then click Next.

2. On the Project Type page, click Browse to display the Select Project dialog. Doubleclick buscomppkg to select the folder or package to store your project files.

3. To name your project file, rename "MyProject1" to "MyBusCompPRJ," and click Open.

4. On the Project Type page, under "What type of Project would you like to create?", select "A Project Containing Business Components" and then click Next.

5. On the Project Options page, click Browse next to "What is the name of the project's default package?" to open the Package Browser.

6. Select "buscomppkg" as the default folder or package for your project, and click OK. Leave the project's source and output directories at their default values.

7. Click Next to complete the Project Options page.

8. On the Project Information page, you may enter information to describe your project. You may generate an HTML page for your project information by selecting the checkbox *Generate project HTML file.* When you finish making changes, click Next to continue.

9. You will see a summary page showing the options you have selected. Click Finish to create the project and invoke the Business Components Project Wizard.

Create or Select a Connection
Use the following steps to create a connection for your Business Components:

1. On the Business Components Project Wizard's Welcome page, click Next to open the Connections page.

2. Select a connection you have already created for the Scott schema using the pulldown list, or click New to open the Connection dialog box and create a new database connection.

3. Click Next.

4. In the Package Name page, accept the default package name "buscomppkg." Click Next.

5. In the Business Components page, the *Database Schema* field should show "SCOTT." Do not make any selections on this page.

6. Click Next and Finish to end the Business Components Project Wizard. You will exit the wizard at this point.

7. To save your work, select **File | Save All**.

What Just Happened?   In this phase, you created the necessary workspace and project files for your BC4J objects and set up a connection to the database. The remaining portion of this practice will be used to demonstrate how to build and modify BC4J objects at the component level.

II. Add Components

The first of the BC4J objects you will add to your project is an entity object. An entity object has Attribute (column) definitions just like the database table, view, synonym, or snapshot with which it exchanges data. In addition, you can add data validation code to the entity so that remote data checking can be performed before any database transactions. By adding the data validation code to an entity, you can maintain a thin-client architecture and still reduce the required network traffic with the database. Since BC4J objects logically reside between the database tier and the client tier, they can also coordinate multiple requests for the same data by caching the results of each database transaction. Physically, the BC4J objects can reside on the client or in the database as well as in a middle tier (application server). Coordinating and synchronizing client data is achieved through the use of multiple BC4J view objects that share the same entity objects.

In each step of this process, the wizard will prompt for information. After you give your responses, the wizard will interrogate the data dictionary and build the BC4J objects for you. After the wizard completes the generation, you are free to modify the results to obtain any additional functionality that is not covered by the default capabilities of the wizard.

Add an Entity Object for DEPT

The following steps will build an entity object for the DEPT table, which was created in the Scott schema using the following DDL:

```
CREATE TABLE dept
  (
   deptno                    NUMBER(2) NOT NULL,
   dname                     VARCHAR2(14),
   loc                       VARCHAR2(13)
  )
```

1. Select **File | New.** Click the Business Components tab and select the Entity Object icon. Click OK to start the Entity Object Wizard.

2. Click Next to dismiss the Welcome page.

3. Look in the Database Objects area for the *Select object* field. Using the scrollbar, locate DEPT and select it. Leave the remaining fields with their default values.

4. Click Next to go to the Attributes page.

5. Remove the Loc attribute, by clicking Loc and then clicking Remove. This leaves only the DeptNo and DName columns for your entity object as shown in Figure 6-4.

6. Click Next and then Finish to skip the remaining screens and end the wizard.

7. To save your work, select **File | Save All**.

After you build the BC4J Entity Object for DEPT, you should see at least two new files in the Navigator Pane below the DEPT entity node:

- **Dept.xml**   This XML file contains the table metadata from the data dictionary.

- **DeptImpl.java**   A Java class, implementing object-oriented methods to process data from the DEPT table.

  Doubleclick each of these files to open it and inspect its contents.

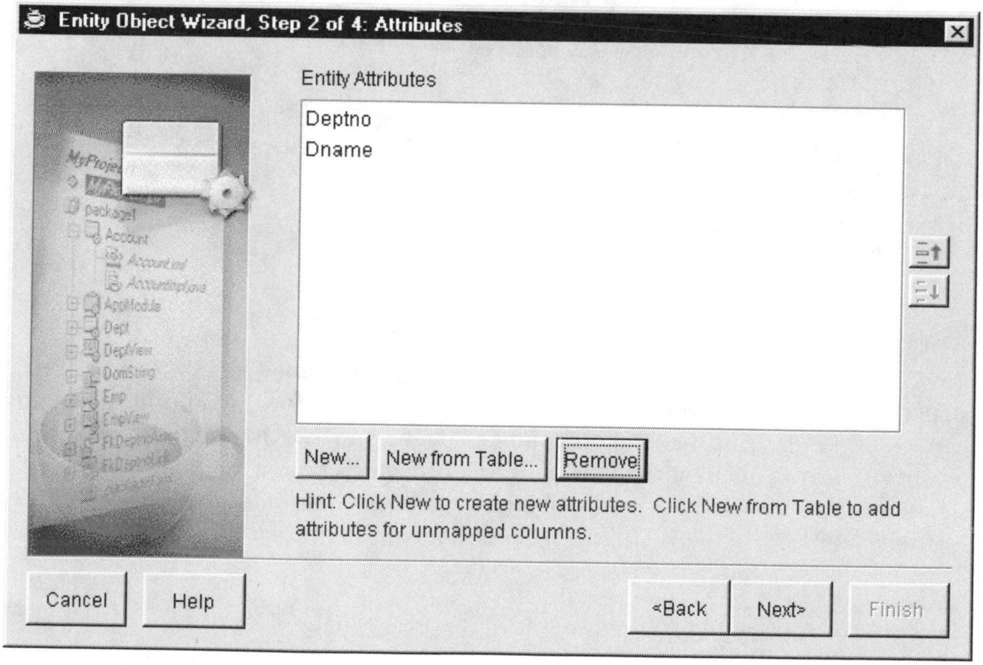

FIGURE 6-4.   *Selecting entity attributes*

XML Files   Since JDeveloper does not support direct editing of the XML code, you will find that files with the extension .xml can only be opened as read-only. When you make changes to the entity's definition, corresponding updates are automatically made in the associated XML file.

As you look at the XML code in the Dept.xml file, you will see that it looks a great deal like HTML. If you compare the DDL for the DEPT table with the XML code in the Dept.xml file, you will see how a few simple XML tags can be used to store the metadata from the data dictionary in a simple and extensible structure, as shown here in part of the Dept.xml file:

```
...
<Entity
    Name="Dept"
    DBObjectType="table"
    DBObjectName="DEPT"
    AliasName="Dept"
    BindingStyle="Oracle"
    CodeGenFlag="4"
    RowClass="MasterDetail.DeptImpl" >
 ...
    <Attribute
       Name="Deptno"
       Type="oracle.jbo.domain.Number"
       ColumnName="DEPTNO"
       ColumnType="NUMBER"
       SQLType="NUMERIC"
       IsNotNull="true"
       Precision="2"
       Scale="0"
       TableName="DEPT"
       PrimaryKey="true" >
 ...
```

Java Files   The first items you will see when you open the file are the libraries specified in the import statements at the top of the file. Below the import statements you will find the class declaration, followed by the variable and method definitions, as shown next. Notice the set () and get () methods for each column (attribute). These methods provide the read/write interface for the attributes that you selected with the Entity Wizard. The following code snippet is part of the DeptImpl.java file:

```
import oracle.jbo.server.*;
import oracle.jbo.RowIterator;
import oracle.jbo.domain.Number;
```

```
import oracle.jbo.Key;
import oracle.jbo.server.util.*;

public class DeptImpl extends oracle.jbo.server.EntityImpl {
  protected static final int DEPTNO = 0;
  protected static final int DNAME = 1;

  private static EntityDefImpl mDefinitionObject;
  /**
    * This is the default constructor (do not remove)
    */
  public DeptImpl() {
  }

  /**
    * Retrieves the definition object for this instance class.
    */
  public static synchronized EntityDefImpl getDefinitionObject() {
    if (mDefinitionObject == null) {
      mDefinitionObject =
        EntityDefImpl)EntityDefImpl.findDefObject("buscomppkg.Dept");
    }
    return mDefinitionObject;
  }

  /**
    * Gets the attribute value for Deptno, using the alias name Deptno
    */
  public Number getDeptno() {
    return (Number)getAttributeInternal(DEPTNO);
  }

  /**
    * Sets <code>value</code> as the attribute value for Deptno
    */
  public void setDeptno(Number value) {
    setAttributeInternal(DEPTNO, value);
  }
...
```

Add Entity Objects for EMP and SALGRADE

Next you will add entity objects for the EMP and SALGRADE tables. In this case,
you will tell the wizard to pass the metadata for all the columns to the BC4J layer. In
practice, however, you should consider retrieving the minimum number of columns
for any given entity. It would be inefficient to return data from all of the columns for
a given table if you didn't really need them.

To add an Entity Object for the EMP table, use the following steps:

1. Select **File | New**. Click the Business Components tab and select the Entity Object icon. Click OK to start the Entity Object Wizard.

2. Click Next.

3. Using the scrollbar in the Select Object dialog, locate EMP and click it.

4. Click Next to go to the Attributes page.

5. Click Next and then Finish to skip the remaining screens and end the wizard.

6. To save your work, choose **File | Save All**.

7. Repeat steps 1 through 6 for SALGRADE. You will need to designate GRADE as the primary key.

Add Association Objects

Relationships between entity objects, similar to the foreign keys in the database, are expressed in association objects. When an association object is identified as a "composition," it ensures that the parent-child data verification is performed in the BC4J layer, enforcing the traditional referential integrity constraint in this layer. Children or parents cannot be created, updated, or destroyed without parent-child validation.

NOTE
Some versions of JDeveloper will automatically add an association object when a foreign key exists between the tables on which your entities are based. If the `FkDeptnoAssoc` *object was automatically generated when you added the entity for Emp, you may skip to the next section or delete the* `FkDeptnoAssoc` *object and re-create it using the following steps.*

1. Select **File | New**. Click the Business Components tab and select the Association object. Click OK to start the Association Wizard.

2. Click Next.

3. Change the *Name* field to "FkDeptnoAssoc." Leave the default package as "buscomppkg" and leave the *Extends Association* field blank. Click Next to proceed to the Association Entities page.

4. In the *Select Source Entity Object* field, click Dept. Typically the source is the entity object containing the primary key.

5. In the *Select Destination Entity Object* field, click Emp as shown in Figure 6-5. Typically the destination is the entity object containing the foreign key.

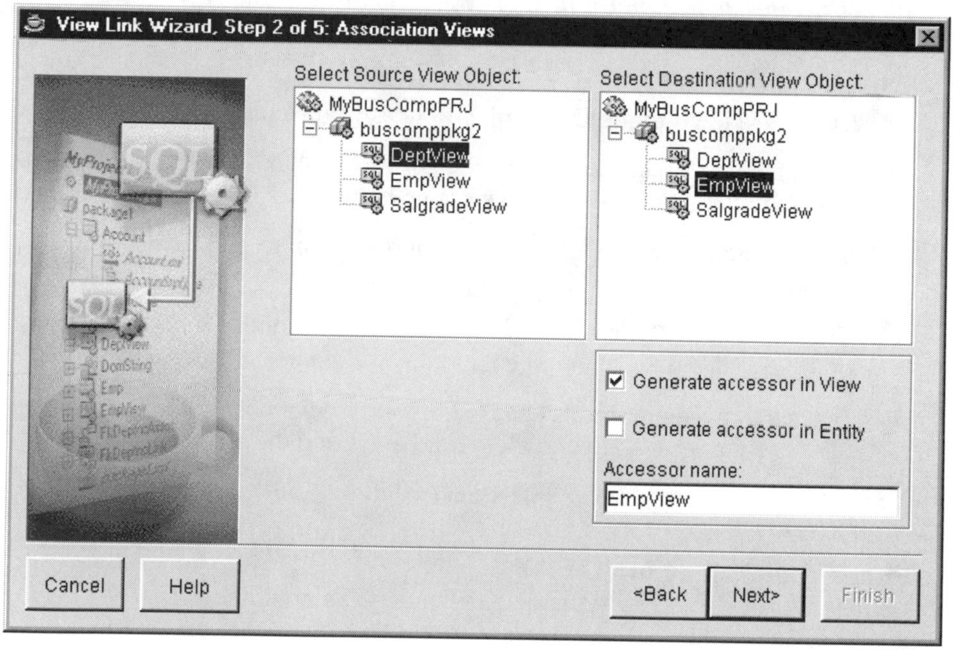

FIGURE 6-5. *Selecting entity objects*

6. Click Next to go to the Source Role Attributes page.

7. Select Deptno and click the right arrow (>) to add the attribute to the *Selected Attributes* field.

TIP

Although you can explicitly select the attributes to express a relationship, there may already be foreign keys that have appropriate attributes selected. If so, you can save time by selecting the appropriate key from this list. An advantage of using a key is that if you select a foreign key attribute on the source entity object, the matching attribute (if applicable) will be included by default on the destination object.

8. Click Next to go to the Destination Role Attributes page.

9. Select DEPTNO again, and click the right arrow (>) to add the attribute to the *Selected Attributes* field. Click Next to go to the Associations Properties page.

10. Set the cardinality for Dept to "0..1", and for Emp to "*", to match the Scott schema data model.

11. Check the *Composite Association* checkbox to enable validation checks on both Source and Destination data in the middle tier.

12. Leave the remaining boxes checked in the Associations Properties page, and click Next and Finish to end the wizard and build the associations.xml file.

13. To save your work, select **File | Save All**.

Add a View Object for DEPT

View objects provide access to the data defined by the entity objects. The client applications access the database using metadata from the entity objects and SQL queries from one or more view objects. Any number of view objects can access a single entity object, and a single view object can access any number of entity objects. This combination provides a unique opportunity to maintain a single copy of the data in the middle tier, while referencing it from several client panels. Even uncommitted data can be made visible (synchronized) across many client screens. View objects are based on SQL queries and may be as complex as necessary to return the appropriate data.

To add a view object for DEPT to your business components, the following steps are necessary:

1. Select **File** | **New**. Click the Business Components tab and select View Object. Click OK to start the View Object Wizard.

2. Click Next to dismiss the Welcome page.

3. Select View1 and change the *Name* field to "DeptView." Leave the default package as "buscomppkg" and leave the *Extends View* field blank. Click Next to proceed to the Entity Objects panel.

4. Select the Entity Object for this view by clicking Dept, and then click the right arrow (>) to add an instance of this entity to the *Selected* field as shown in Figure 6-6.

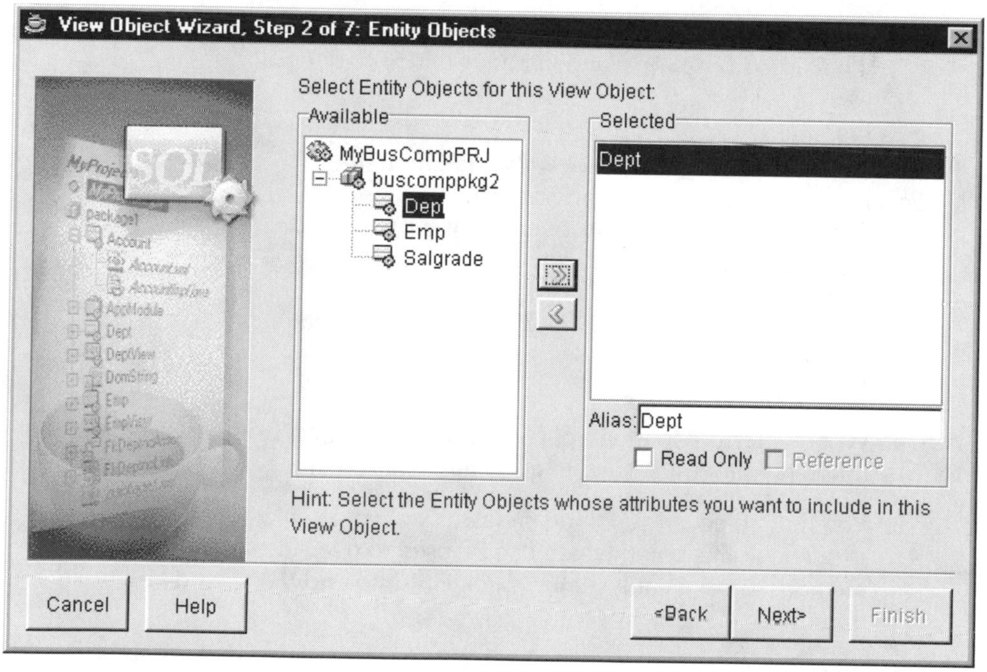

FIGURE 6-6. *Adding a view object*

5. Click Next to go to the Attributes page. This is where you select the data elements that you wish to make available in the view. If the source represented in the entity is a database table, the attributes will generally be columns for that table.

6. Click the double-right arrow (>>) to move DEPTNO and DNAME to the pane.

TIP
You may click New in the Attributes page if you wish to add a user-defined attribute to the view object.

7. Click Next to go to the Attribute Settings page. You may view or modify the attribute settings by using the pulldown list next to the *Select Attribute* field. You will generally bypass this page, and click Next to access the Query page.

8. The Query page can be used to refine the query. If you check the *expert mode* checkbox, you can enter any valid SQL query.

CAUTION
You may find it best to limit your initial queries to the default settings. Some problems may arise when using literals, functions, and complex queries. When you need to go beyond what the wizard can handle, edit the source code after the wizard has completed. Allowing the wizard to construct a basic framework can save you a significant amount of time and effort, though.

9. When you have finished refining your query, click Test to ensure that your query is valid. Click Next to go to the final screen.

10. You may select any additional classes you would like the wizard to generate at this point, which can be used to override view object methods or set default values. Click Finish to end the wizard and build the source files.

11. To save your work, select **File | Save All**.

Add View Objects for EMP and SALGRADE

To add view objects, follow these steps:

1. Select **File | New**. Click the Business Components tab and select View Object. Click OK to start the View Object Wizard.

2. Click Next.

3. Change the *Name* field to "EmpView." Leave the default package as "buscomppkg" and leave the *Extends View* field blank. Click Next to proceed to the Entity Objects page.

4. Select the entity object for this view by clicking EMP, and then click the right arrow (>) to add an instance of this entity to the *Selected* field.

5. Click Next to go to the Attributes page.

6. Click the double-right arrow (>>) to move all attributes to the *Selected* field.

7. Click Next to go to the Attribute Settings page. You will generally bypass this page. Click Next to access the Query page.

8. Click Test to ensure your query is valid. Click Next to go to the final screen.

9. Accepting the defaults, click Finish to end the wizard and build the source files.

10. To save your work, select **File | Save All**.

11. Repeat steps 1 through 10 for SALGRADE. In step 3, name the view "SalgradeView."

Add View Links

A view link defines the relationships between view objects, which delivers filtered child rows from a parent-child relationship. The supported relationships for view links include many-to-many, one-to-many, and one-to-one. View links can only be used to filter data in one direction (from source to destination), in contrast to associations for entities that are bidirectional in nature. If you need to navigate through data that is linked in two views in both directions, you must create two independent view links: one for each source-destination direction that you wish to navigate, such as from DEPT to EMP or EMP to DEPT. The following steps add a view link from DEPT to EMP.

1. Select **File** | **New**. Click the Business Components tab and select View Link. Click OK to start the View Link Wizard.

2. Click Next to dismiss the Welcome page.

3. Change the default name by changing the *Name* field to "FkDeptnoLink." Leave the default package as "buscomppkg" and leave the *Extends View Link* field blank. Click Next to proceed to the Association Views page.

4. To set the source view for the link, click DeptView in the *Select Source View Object* pane.

5. To set the destination view for the link click EmpView in the *Select Destination View Object* field. Both DeptView and EmpView should now be highlighted as shown in Figure 6-7.

6. Click Next to go to the Source Role Attribute page.

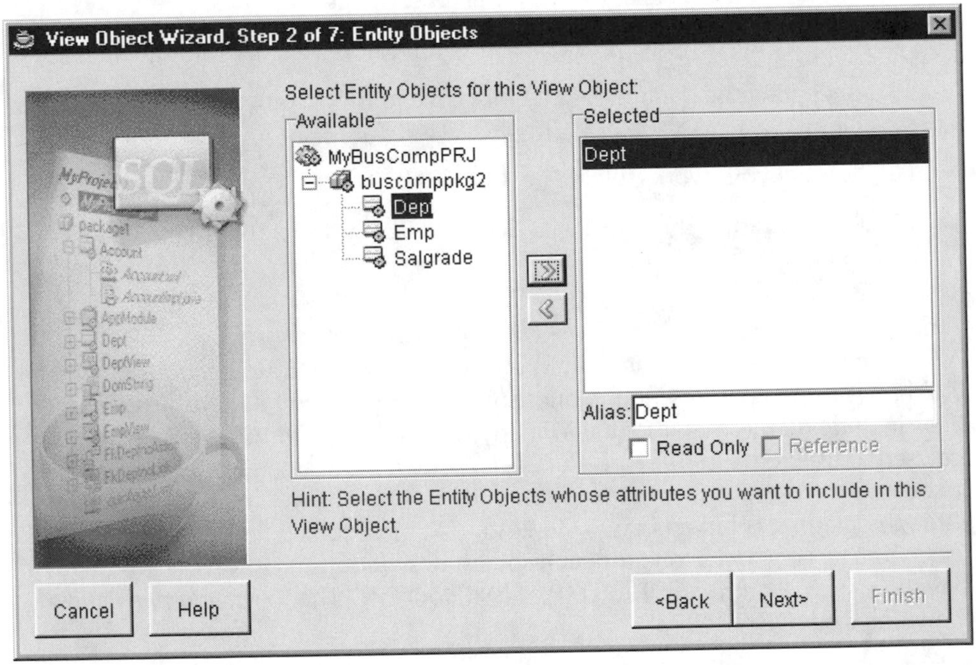

FIGURE 6-7.   *Selecting a destination view*

7. Next you will add the source attribute (column) that the view link will be based on. You can do this by selecting one of the available attributes or by pointing at a previously defined association. In this case you will use an association based on DEPTNO. Click FkDeptAssoc in the *Available Associations* dialog, and then click the right arrow (>) to add the attribute to the *Selected attributes* field. Click Next to go to the Destination Role Attribute page.

8. Now you will use the association based on DEPTNO to set the destination attribute for the view link. Click FkDeptAssoc in the *Available Association* field, and then click the right arrow (>) to add the attribute to the *Selected attributes* field.

   Click Next to go to the Association SQL page to view your results. You can test the generated query for the view link by clicking Test. If the query is properly formed, you should see a dialog with a "Valid" message. Click OK to acknowledge the message, and click Next and Finish to close the wizard and generate the source code.

9. To save your work, select **File | Save All**.

Create Application Modules

An *application module* is a logical container used to coordinate the BC4J objects that are related to a particular task. The application module includes a simple data connection and a context for defining and executing database transactions. The application module will interface with the InfoSwing classes to build the user interface. The InfoSwing components will be bound to rowsets and attribute objects to exchange data with the application module. In this example, you will be creating an application module and selecting two of the three views or view links you have constructed so far, to include in this application module. You will add DeptView to show all departments as well as the FkDeptNo view link.

1. In the Navigation Pane, right-click the buscomppkg Business Component (which is the package component shown in the BC4J project "MyBusCompPRJ"); then click Create Application Module to start the Application Module Wizard.

2. Click Next to dismiss the Welcome page.

3. Change the *Name* field to "buscomppkgModule."

4. Click Next to go to the Data Model page.

5. In the Available Views dialog, click DeptView.

   Objects placed in the data model must have unique names, which the wizard creates appropriately by incrementing a numerical suffix for duplicate objects. When you wish to name your own references, you may do so at this point. In the next step of this hands-on practice, you will rename DeptView to "MyDeptView" to demonstrate this renaming capability.

6. In the *Name* field change the name to **"MyDeptView."** Then click the right arrow (>) to move it to the *Data Model* field.

7. Next you will add the filtered EmpView Via View Link (which is in reality a view link named "FkDeptnoLink" that you just created) to the module. This view link is automatically filtered or updated to show only rows with employees assigned to the current DEPTNO that is selected in DeptView. Expand the DeptView node, then select "EmpView Via View Link" in the *Available Views* field to select the view link; then click "MyDeptView" to select the parent for the view link in the *Data Model* field. Then click the right arrow (>) to add the view link to the model as shown in Figure 6-8.

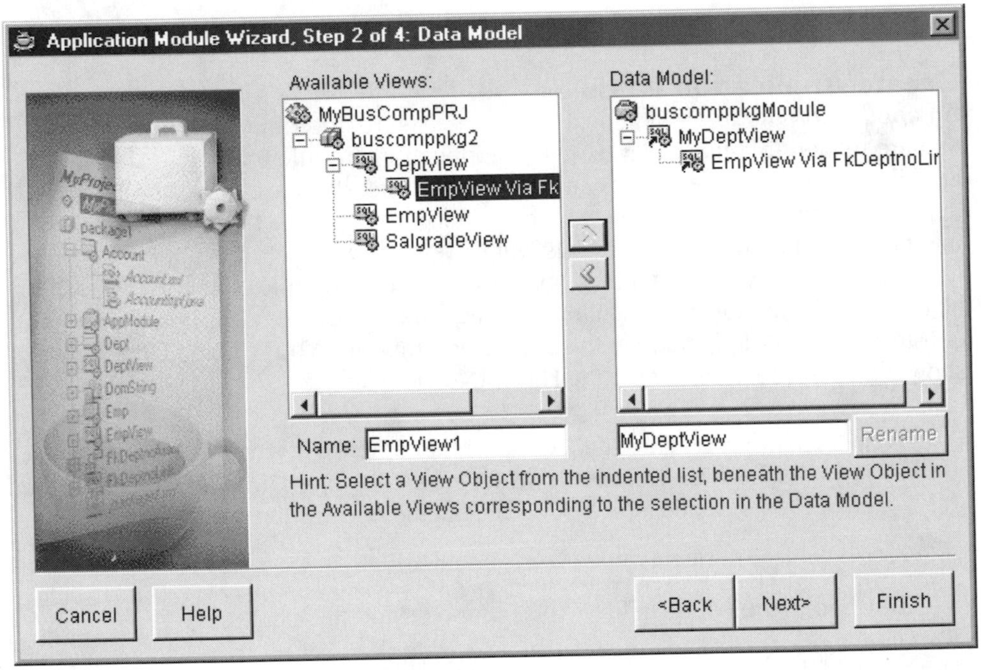

FIGURE 6-8. *Adding a view link*

8. Click Next and Finish to skip the remaining pages and create the application module.

9. To save your work, select **File | Save All**.

What Just Happened   In this hands-on practice, you added components including entity objects, association objects, view objects, and view links to your BC4J project. In addition, you created an application module to contain all of the business components and provide an interface to your UI.

Hands-on Practice: Add Data-Validation Code

The BC4J layer provides a powerful place to add validation code when the layer is deployed locally in the client or in a middle-tier application server. This works particularly well because the BC4J layer is the last common code point that the data must pass before it goes to the database. Validation code, implemented at this point, can affect all instances of a database item. This provides a useful, "write-once, use-everywhere" type of architecture. Validation code can be as complex as you need to make it, or as simple as defining a greater-than, less-than, range, or list-of-values using XML tags generated by the Validation tab in the Entity Wizard. This practice builds on the previous practice to demonstrate the following:

   I. **Create validation at the attribute level**

   - **Add a validation check using XML**

   - **Add a validation check using Java**

   II. **Create validation at the row level**

   III. **Create validation at the domain level**

I. Create Validation at the Attribute Level

The BC4J layer provides two basic processes for implementing validation checks. The first process is a wizard-driven code generator that requires little or no coding on your part. It is based on adding tags to the XML file to define basic validation rules for attributes (columns). These tags are generated when you use the wizard to specify the simple checks to see if an attribute's new value meets a simple comparison, range, list, or method test. The wizard can be displayed by right-clicking any entity object (names that have no file extension) in the Navigation Pane; then clicking Edit to invoke the Entity Object Wizard; and selecting the Validation tab. This process gives developers a quick and error-free way to implement simple validation checks.

CAUTION
Use the Query Result in the Compare With *field to obtain a single value from the first row returned from a query. This simple declarative process ignores all other rows and only uses the value from the first row for the validation check.*

One of the simplest types of data checks you can perform is validating a single row value. To demonstrate the ease with which you can accomplish this in JDeveloper, the following steps will add an upper limit for the SALARY column in the EMP table. This type of validation check works at the field level. When you navigate outside of the field, or perform a commit to the database, you trigger this validation check.

Add a Validation Check Using XML

A validation check can be performed on the SALARY column with XML using the following steps:

1. In the Navigation Pane, right click the Emp Business Component (which is the package component shown in the BC4J project "mybuscomppkg"); then click on Edit Emp to start the Entity Object Wizard.

2. Select the Validation tab to display the attributes to which you may add code.

3. Select the attribute Sal, and then click Add to go to the "Add Validation Rule for Sal" dialog.

4. Click the pull-down arrow to the right of the *Operator* field and select "LessThan."

   Leave Compare With set to *"Literal Value,"* and enter "6000" in the *Enter Literal Value* area (shown in Figure 6-9). Click OK to return to the Entity Object Wizard, and click Finish to generate the validation code.

5. To save your work select **File | Save All**.

Unfortunately, the XML code-generation approach only covers simple field-level validation checks. When you need more complex checks on a single field, you will have to revert to inserting your own Java code in the appropriate `set()` method. To show how this can be done, the following adds a validation check for minimum Salary. The attribute (column) validation code will be added to the appropriate entity implementation file. For example, the Java code for the Emp entity would be located in a file named EmpImpl.java.

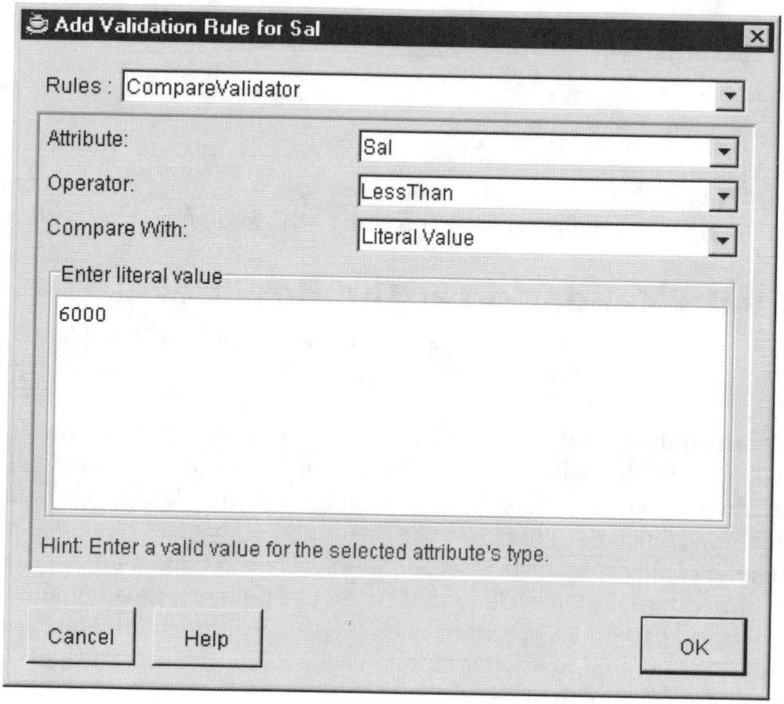

FIGURE 6-9. *Adding a validation rule for the Salary column*

Add a Validation Check Using Java

The following steps modify the Java file to add a validation check.

1. Doubleclick EmpImpl.java to open the file in the source editor.

2. To add the error handling class, locate the import statements and add the following code:

```
import oracle.jbo.JboException;
```

3. Locate setSal() method and modify it to look like the following code:

```
/**
 * Sets <code>value</code> as the attribute value for Sal
 */
public void setSal(Number value) {
  if (value.floatValue() < 500){
```

```
        throw new JboException("Salary below minimum");
   }
   setAttributeInternal(SAL, value);
}
```

4. Select **File | Save All**.

What Just Happened In this hands-on practice, you added different types of data validation at the field and row levels using XML and Java.

II. Create Validation at the Row Level

You may wish to perform row-level validation checks such as "End Date is after Start Date" or checks on SALGRADE such as "low salary is less than or equal to high salary."

To demonstrate a validation check that will be performed at the row level, this phase will add one that will check to see if LOSAL is less than or equal to HISAL. This check will be evaluated when you attempt to commit data or navigate out of the current row. Since this check is to be performed at the row level, you must add the code at the Entity level instead of at the Attribute level, as in the previous example. To add validation code for SALGRADE at the entity level, you will need to add a method named `validateEntity()` to the SalgradeImpl.java file. The body of this method will hold your custom validation code. Java Business Objects (JBO) provide special methods, such as `equals()` and `compareTo()`, for you to perform Boolean checks on the JBOs. The `equals()` method returns a boolean true or false, and the `compareTo()` method returns the following:

- ■ –1 if less than

- ■ 0 if equal to

- ■ 1 if greater than

You may also cast the JBO values back to primitive datatypes and use the traditional boolean operators.

The following steps can be used to validate the Salgrade entity:

1. Doubleclick on SalgradeImpl.java to open the file in the source editor.

2. To add an error handling class, locate the import statements and add the following code:

   ```
   import oracle.jbo.JboException;
   ```

3. Add the following code just above the `getGrade()` method.

You may implement either block of code.

```
public void validateEntity() {
   //Generated call
   super.validateEntity();

     //Custom validation is added here using special Jbo Boolean checks
     //Rule: Losal is greater than Hisal - throw exception
     if (this.getLosal().compareTo(this.getHisal()) > 0 ){
         throw  new JboException("Losal greater than Hisal.");
     }
}
```

or

```
public void validateEntity() {
   //Generated call
   super.validateEntity();

     //Custom validation is added here using type conversion
     //Rule: Losal is greater than Hisal - throw exception
if (this.getLosal().shortValue() > this.getHisal().shortValue()){
         throw  new JboException("Losal greater than Hisal.");
     }
}
```

4. When you have completed editing your source code, compile the entire BC4J project by selecting the project file in the Navigation Pane and selecting **Project | Rebuild Project "MyBusCompPRJ.jpr"**.

5. Choose **File | Save All** to save your work.

What Just Happened   In this phase of the hands-on practice, you added validation to the Salgrade entity by implementing one of two blocks of code and compiling the project.

III. Create Validation at the Domain Level

A third alternative to consider when implementing validation checks is to create a user-defined datatype called a *domain*. When you create a new domain, it can be reused to validate attribute-level data within entities, views, and even be used as a datatype on the client machine. The moment users navigate out of a field using a domain, they will receive an error message if they fail to meet the validation logic. This write-once, use-many-places type of validation is very helpful where you need to reuse the same validation logic for several attributes. To create a domain you may select **File | New**; then click the Business Components tab, and doubleclick the Domain object. Alternatively, you can right click the Business Components package in the Navigation Pane, and then select Create Domain.

After creating the domain, you may add your custom validation logic to the method named `validate()` in the .java file created for the domain.

Validation Order

When considering validation order, it is obvious that client code will come first, then the BC4J layer, and finally the database. What is less obvious is the order in which validation will occur in the BC4J components. Since you can use a number of techniques both in XML and Java to implement validation in the BC4J layer, it is necessary to understand that the order that your validation logic will trigger depends upon where you have implemented it. When you have multiple levels of validation, the validation code will trigger in the following order:

1. Domain validation methods.

2. Custom code added to the `set()` methods for the attributes in the entity implementation Java file (for example, the `setSal()` method in the EmpImpl.java file).

3. Custom code added to the entity validation method in the entity implementation Java file(for example, the `validateEntity()` method in the EmpImpl. java file).

4. Attribute validation rules in the XML file, which have been generated using the Validation tab in the Entity Wizard.

5. Associations defined as a composition to check the parent-child constraints.

Since objects can contain objects in the BC4J layer, it is important to note that the contained objects will have their validation rules triggered before the container objects have their rules triggered.

Hands-on Practice: Testing Your BC4J Components

As mentioned in Chapter 2, you can test your newly created BC4J layer without the need of a client application by using the built-in Business Component Browser (Tester). The Tester will dynamically build a default set of panels to display the data in the BC4J layer. It will generate a simple single-table UI, to test your view and entity objects, or a master-detail UI to test your view links. You can check the underlying data-validation code in your entities by entering test data in either UI. Use the following steps to run the tester on the project you created in the earlier practices.

1. In the Navigation Pane, right click the buscomppkgModule node, and then click Test.

2. On the Connection screen, accept the default connection parameters, which should still be pointing at your Scott schema connection. Click Connect and supply a password, if necessary, to start the Tester. Wait for the Tester to construct the UI.

3. Right click EmpView, and select Show to generate a test application for your BC4J components as shown in Figure 6-10.

4. You may now navigate through the Employee data and test the functionality of inserts, updates, deletes, and the validation rule you placed on Sal. Try entering an invalid salary, such as $8000, for an employee, and attempt to commit it to the database by clicking the green arrow near the upper-left corner of the Test panel. You will see an exception dialog indicating that your attempt to commit 8000 for SAL failed. As long as you enter a value less than 6000, the data is committed as expected.

Note for Oracle Developer Users

Oracle Developer contains extremely easy-to-use links to the database. All you need to do is to define the table that a block will be based on and define the items that will interact with data in the column. At runtime, the tool generates the proper SQL statement from the definitions and sends the SQL request to the database (usually through a SQL*Net or Net8 transport layer). The database sends the request back and the tool allocates the data to the proper visual controls based on the controls' properties.

An application that accesses BC4J works a bit differently. For Java applications and applets, the user interface controls are tied to InfoBus components (such as a row set) that are linked to the BC4J application module. For JSP applications, the user interface controls are tied to the Data Tag Library tags or web beans, both of which access the BC4J application module. The application module communicates via SQL with the database. Therefore, BC4J corresponds to the internal mechanism that Oracle Developer offers to connect interface objects with database objects. The difference with BC4J is that you can go behind the scenes and alter its behavior using wizards and definition screens. To alter the behavior of the data layer in Forms, you need to write triggers (such as PRE-INSERT or ON-UPDATE) that alter or replace the native mechanism.

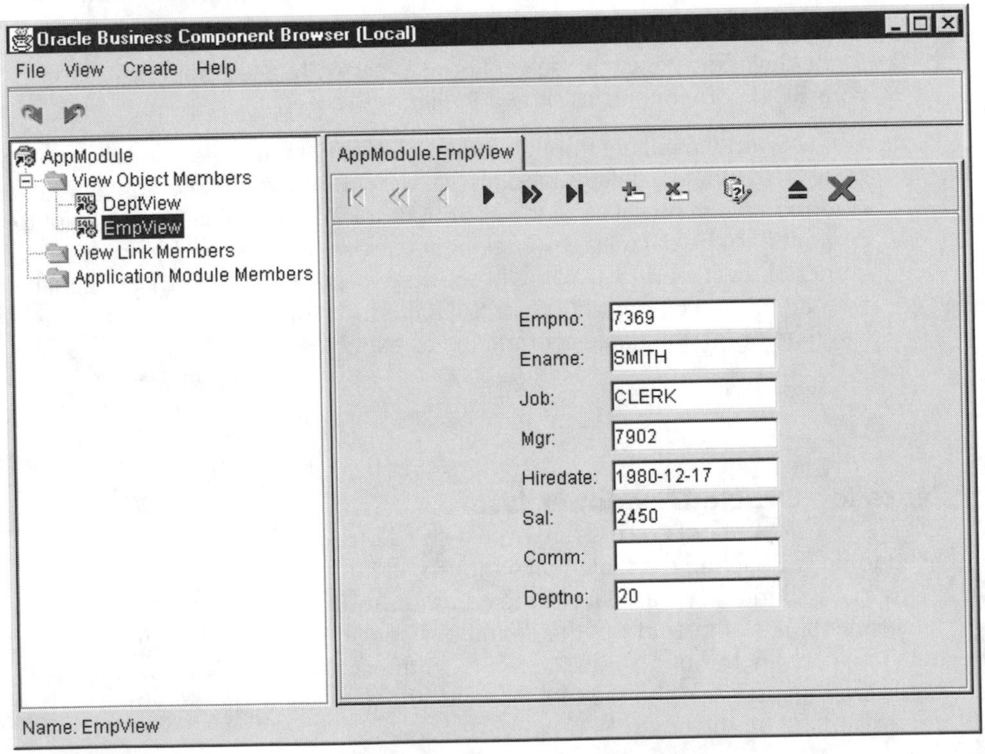

FIGURE 6-10. *Oracle Business Component Browser*

CHAPTER

7

Deployment
Alternatives

You pays your money and you takes your choice.

—Punch (1846), *X, 16*

hen you develop an application, you should choose the architecture long before you write the code. Therefore, you will know ahead of time what server will be assigned to the database, what the client platforms will consist of, what use you will make of web servers, and, in general, which system architecture the application will use. JDeveloper creates code that can be deployed on most of the modern architectures. There are several main deployment architectures and variations of each. This gives you the flexibility of selecting an architecture that best fits the requirements of your application.

You may think that JDeveloper replaces your application development environment. So the question is: can Visual Basic, Oracle Forms Developer, or PowerBuilder users throw away these tools and use JDeveloper instead until the next product comes along? Although there are only limited situations where you can use JDeveloper to completely build and deploy your web-based applications, it is still a tool that can greatly assist in this work. The reality is a bit more complex, since there are many more alternatives. An entire book could be devoted to these alternatives.

The Java environment provides a three-tier architecture in which to place code. Code may reside in the database, at the application server, or at the client. There are also a variety of products and communication protocols that enable these options. With a product such as JDeveloper, the primary goal is likely to be building e-commerce applications. Unfortunately, this is the one type of application where you must go beyond the product to support your requirements.

This chapter will discuss four alternative strategies for building applications, as follows:

- **Java application** A self-contained application that is deployed in a client/server environment

- **Applet** Java program that is located on the application server and runs using a client's web browser

- **JSP** A type of servlet that presents an HTML and JavaScript front-end

- **Terminal server** A client/server application that runs on another server but displays in a browser

Note for Oracle Developer Users

The choices you have for deployment of Oracle Developer applications are less numerous but have parallels to the choices for deployment of Java applications. The Java technologies provide the option of more granular division of the code, so there are a few more variations of the architectures that Oracle Developer supports. The Java application alternative for Java code is similar to the traditional Oracle Forms Developer client/server deployment option.

Applets correspond to Oracle Developer forms running in web-deployed mode (in fact, the Forms runtime for this mode is a Java applet). There is no current deployment of Oracle Developer that corresponds closely to the JSP solution. However, JSPs corresponds to the Oracle9*i* application server module (modplsql) that you can use to generate HTML pages from PL/SQL database procedures. A future Oracle development product, currently named "Cherokee," promises to merge JSP technology and Oracle Forms Developer design work.

This chapter also explains how the code is deployed across different tiers for each alternative. You will learn how the files you create will be deployed to the tier that you select. The hands-on practices step through how to use the Deployment Profile Wizard to create the files you need to distribute to a server. Before you make a decision about which alternative to use, be sure to read the discussion in Chapter 5 concerning which environments each tool supports. Your environment will limit and guide your choice of deployment alternatives and the tool you select.

Alternative 1: Java Application Strategy

Java is a compiled language. You can generate an application that contains information about the database connection and executes in a runtime environment, the Java Virtual Machine (JVM), against the database. This application can be deployed and maintained just like any other existing client/server application.

When you deploy a Java application as a compiled application, you do not need a browser or application server.

NOTE
The term "Java application" is used to identify the technology described in this section. In Java terms, this is really just an "application," but since that term is a common one in the IT world, it is usually qualified by the word "Java." The word "applet" is usually not qualified because it is, by definition, a Java feature and not as commonly used.

How Do Java Applications Work?

A Java application runs on the client machine in a JVM runtime environment. The compiled Java application (class) files are stored on the client, or on a local or wide area network server. There is no web server required. If the Java application uses BC4J, the BC4J layer may be located on the client side as well. As shown in Figure 7-1, the application's class files access the BC4J objects (class and XML files). The BC4J objects provide the data communication link to the database. This is called a "local" database connection because the database layer is local to the client machine.

It is also possible to locate the BC4J objects on a server that runs an application for serving code. An example would be a Common Object Request Broker Architecture (CORBA) server or an Inprise VisiBroker wrapper that connects the application to the BC4J application module located somewhere other than the client machine. This variation, depicted in Figure 7-2, allows clients to share the main connection and database layers.

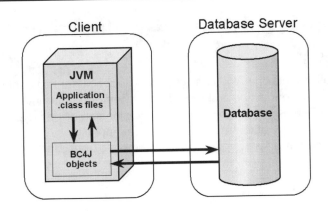

FIGURE 7-1. *Java application architecture*

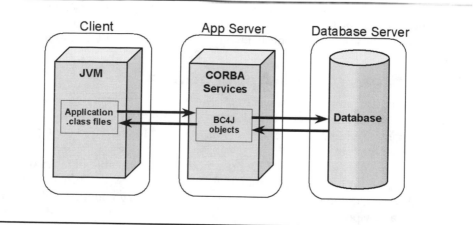

FIGURE 7-2.   *Java application with CORBA server architecture*

Java applications must have a method called `main()`. This method usually calls a constructor method (in JDeveloper this method is `jbInit()`). The constructor method creates the first object, such as a frame. All requests for data flow from the application's frame through the BC4J layer.

NOTE
For JDK 1.2 and greater, the `main()` method must be defined as `private static void`, and have an argument of `String[] args`, for example, `private static void main (String[] args)`.

To create a Java application deployment, you install java.exe (the Java runtime JVM) and supporting Java libraries on the client. You also need to install the .class files for the application and data access (BC4J) objects and set up the client's CLASSPATH so that the JVM can find the .class files. When the user needs to run the application, she or he enters the following at the command line:

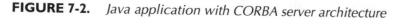
```
java MainClass
```

In this example, "MainClass" is the compiled .class file that contains the `main()` method that starts the application. The client machine would likely use a shortcut icon instead of requiring the user to type a command-line string.

Chapters 1 and 2 contain hands-on practices that focus on creating Java applications. Chapters 9, 10, and 11 provide details with hands-on practices using the Java elements and components that you can employ to build Java applications.

Advantages of Java Applications

If you are accustomed to client/server deployments, Java applications provide you with an easy architecture in which to deploy Java code. You gain all of the benefits of the Java language described earlier without the need to learn and configure the application server.

Java applications provide rich GUI possibilities. The available libraries of controls (mainly AWT—Abstract Windowing Toolkit—and Swing) provide all of the functionality of traditional windowed applications but allow you the flexibility of modifying each aspect of the control.

Disadvantages of Java Applications

Java applications also come with all of the drawbacks of client/server architecture. Larry Ellison, CEO of Oracle, stated at an Oracle OpenWorld conference recently that client/server was a mistake and for good reason. One main problem is that runtime and application code must be maintained and installed on the client. WAN servers promise to ease the burden, but the reality is that they are not responsive enough, so companies used LANs. The LAN solution for a large application is still not responsive and requires installations of the same code on more than one machine. This takes a lot of time and effort, as those who have been supporting client/server applications have experienced. In addition, the client needs a large amount of resources because the application is running in its memory and using disk space.

When the number of users grows, this architecture scales poorly. More users may require additional installations and decentralization of the runtime code. The architecture makes no use of the benefits of web server technology for centralized installation and maintenance, although the CORBA server architecture mitigates this effect somewhat.

Where Are Java Applications Useful?

Java applications are indicated for intranet or small-department solutions with a small number of clients. When the number of clients grows, you will experience all of the same problems and resource drains as in client/server applications because, for each new client, a new software installation is required.

Alternative 2: Applet Strategy

Applets are an alternative that better leverages the strengths of web technology. With a Java applet, when the application is run, the applet is copied from the application server to the client machine and run within a browser session. This gives you all of the functionality of a Java application as if you were deploying client/server but allows you to run it over the Internet. As with the first alternative, you are working entirely in a Java environment. This means that you can use JDeveloper exclusively to create complete applications that are deployed as applets.

Everything you can do in a Java application, you can deploy over the web as an applet completely transparently using JDeveloper. You will also have complete control over where the code is executed.

How Do Applets Work?

An applet offers the benefits of web technology while allowing you to use the rich user interface libraries that are offered by AWT and Swing components. The applet differs from the Java application in the location of the runtime code, which is stored on an application server. In addition, the application is started from a browser. A description of the applet startup process follows:

1. The client browser requests an HTML file from the web server through a standard URL. The HTML file may be static or dynamically generated from another application. This HTML file contains a special applet tag as shown in the following example:

```
<APPLET CODE = "empappjsp.DeptApplet"
    CODEBASE = "/applet_code/"
    WIDTH = 400
    HEIGHT = 400
    ALIGN = middle >
</APPLET>
```

2. The applet tag signals the browser to start an applet window for the JVM session and load the application's class file named by the *code attribute.* The applet tag's attribute *codebase* specifies the location of the applet's .class files relative to the physical location of the HTML file. If the HTML file is in the same directory, the codebase attribute is set to "." (the same directory).

3. The application's .class files download from the application server and are presented in the applet window. The class files may also be cached on the client machine, which means that the download may not be required in all cases.

4. Once the application has started, it runs in the JVM on the PC like a Java application. The database communication occurs between the JVM and the BC4J objects as with the Java application.

Figure 7-3 shows the communication lines for the applet architecture. As with the Java application, the BC4J files may alternatively be located on the client.

There is a hands-on practice in Chapter 12 that demonstrates how to create and run an applet. In addition, the material on UI components in Chapters 9, 10, and 11 applies equally to applets as it does to Java applications.

Advantages of Applets

A strong advantage of the Java application is its ability to use the rich user interface components that are included with the AWT and Swing libraries. This advantage is exactly the same in the applet. An applet has the additional advantage of allowing you to use the web application server to store a common set of runtime files. The client also has to have the CLASSPATH environment variable defined so that the JVM can find the required files. Although the client still needs to have the JVM runtime files installed, they are included with all popular browsers. This means that the burden of installing software on the client is greatly reduced. The main installation requirement is the client's browser, which is standard issue these days.

Disadvantages of Applets

There are several problems with the Java applet strategy. First, Java applets can be very large. The more complex the application, the larger the applet and the longer

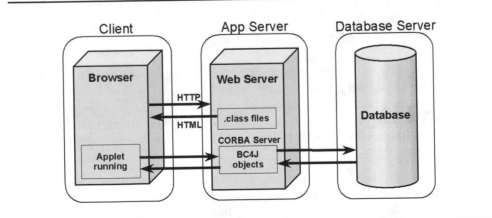

FIGURE 7-3. *Applet architecture*

the download time (although that can be mitigated if the applet is cached on the client machine). Internet users are an impatient lot. There is a trade-off in performance with this strategy. Once the application loads, unless there is a lot of required database access, the performance will be excellent. For e-commerce purposes, the load time for the applet is likely to be unreasonable.

Second, the actions that the Java applet can perform on the client are restricted by the built-in security mechanisms. If those features are circumvented, Java applets can be written to perform tasks on the client machine such as writing to the file system. In many organizations, client machines reside behind a firewall that prohibits the downloading of Java applets. Therefore, the use of Java applets is an unworkable strategy for e-commerce applications.

A restriction of the applet security mechanism is that the database and application server must be located on the same physical machine; there are workarounds for this limitation but the workarounds complicate the configuration of the server. This is a disadvantage that can be easily overcome.

Another disadvantage is that an applet uses an HTML browser to supply the JVM. Browsers do not universally support the Swing class libraries, and these are the basis for the Oracle Data Aware Controls (DAC) that have strong ties to the business components (BC4J) layer. If you do not use DAC, you are not taking advantage of one of the greatest strengths of JDeveloper and probably are writing too much code. AWT classes are fully supported but require much more coding to connect to the data layer. The impact on applet technology is that you must ensure that your users can access and install the Swing class plug-in offered by Sun. This requires a one-time step to download and install the plug-in. This is a factor to consider in your decision about deployment strategies.

Although one of the advantages of the applet architecture is its use of the web application server to store and serve the HTML file and applet class files, this is also one of its disadvantages. The application server requires additional configuration and maintenance, which, in turn, requires extra human resources and skills. While this requirement is manageable, it is one that must be taken into account.

Where Are Applets Useful?

Within an organization, using Java applets is a viable strategy. An applet gives you a client/server–style application without the overhead of maintaining a client/server environment. An intranet environment may also provide adequate bandwidth to reduce the load time for large Java applets. Even if the load time is significant, if users stay within a single application for some period of time, this may not be much of a hardship. Since an intranet system is a controlled environment, you will likely be operating behind the firewall, thus eliminating the security limitations.

Alternative 3: JavaServer Pages Strategy

The question that remains to be answered is how to safely deploy applications over the Internet so that customers can interact remotely, safely, and securely from any web browser, anywhere in the world. What is needed to implement this goal?

To build e-commerce applications you can build a BC4J project and generate JavaServer Pages (JSPs). The applications will reside on an application server such as Apache Internet Server or Oracle9i Application Server. Due to firewall issues discussed earlier, these applications cannot consist of purely Java code. They must generate JSPs, which consist of HTML code constructed dynamically by calling Java routines on the application server.

JDeveloper has limited visual editing capabilities for working with HTML pages. To build serious e-commerce or internal applications, a separate HTML product is highly recommended. The most popular alternatives are Microsoft FrontPage or MacroMedia Dreamweaver. Although you can gain some efficiency from these tools, any HTML editor will do. If you want additional client/side functionality (such as complex data validation) within your applications, you will need to extend your HTML pages using JavaScript.

How Do JSPs Work?

A JSP is an extension of servlet technology. A s*ervlet* is a program stored and run on the web application server that accepts requests from a client browser through an HTTP data stream (posted data or URL) and constructs an HTML page by querying the database and outputting the HTML tags mixed with data from the queries. The entire page is constructed dynamically by the program in a similar way to a Common Gateway Interface (CGI) program.

The advantage of servlets over CGI programs is that they only require a new thread, not an entirely new process like CGI programs. This is a significant resource savings for the application server. In addition, unlike CGI output, servlets are cached providing performance benefits such as allowing the database connections to stay open. Servlets are coded entirely in Java and are therefore portable and do not need a CGI language such as Perl.

JSPs are variations on servlet technology. They have both a dynamic and static element to them. This allows the developer to establish the parts of the application that do not change (for example, the `<HTML>` tag at the beginning and `</HTML>` tag at the end of the page). Other parts of the page that would not change would be all of the static links and boilerplate graphics and text. A servlet has to generate these each time the program is run, whereas a JSP program represents the static tag exactly as it will be output. In reality, JSPs are converted to servlets when they are run, but the cleanliness of the JSP code justifies the choice of the JSP style over the servlet style. For example, for each static tag that is built into a JSP, a `println()` statement would be required in a servlet. Here is an example of the default JSP code that JDeveloper creates when you select JSP from the Object Gallery:

```
<%@ page contentType="text/html;charset=WINDOWS-1252"%>
<HTML>
<HEAD>
<META HTTP-EQUIV="Content-Type" CONTENT="text/html; charset=WINDOWS-1252">
<META NAME="GENERATOR" CONTENT="Oracle JDeveloper">
<TITLE>
Hello World
</TITLE>
</HEAD>
<BODY>
<H2>The following output is from JSP code:</H2><P>
   <% out.println("Hello World"); %></P>
</BODY>
</HTML>
```

This sample mixes standard HTML tags ("< >") and JSP tags ("<% %>"). The file extension .jsp indicates to the web server that the page requested is a JSP file. The web server passes the interpretation of the page to a *JSP container* program that runs in a JVM on the server. The JSP container passes the HTML tags back as is and processes the JSP-specific tags, some of which may create additional HTML-formatted output. The container then sends the entire page back to the browser.

The first time a JSP page is accessed, it creates a Java file and compiles that file into a bytecode in a .class file. For subsequent accesses, the .class file is cached on the server so that this compilation is not required unless the code is changed. The JSP container runs the .class file in its JVM session. The Java and class files are generated dynamically from the JSP source code file. The BC4J layer sits on the application server and communicates with the database as in the other models. Figure 7-4 shows the main elements of the JSP runtime architecture.

Chapter 8 contains a discussion and hands-on practices that explain how to create a JSP application using JDeveloper.

Advantages of JSPs

An advantage of the JSP solution is that each page loads quickly. JSPs output standard HTML and are therefore small, compact, and universally readable in any browser. They transmit easily over the Internet. However, this ease of transfer is accompanied by limited functionality. The style of having to scroll through dozens of screens, making option selections on each one, is a familiar one for users of web applications. Simple functions such as deleting a record or changing the way information is sorted requires a reload of the page. You can increase the functionality of a JSP application

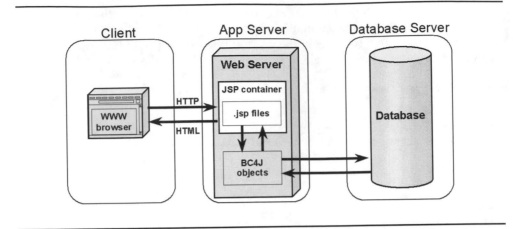

FIGURE 7-4. *JSP architecture*

dramatically by including JavaScript in the HTML page, but this solution requires that the JavaScript that you use is supported by the requirements of your users' browsers.

The client requirement is much less than with Alternatives 1 and 2 because there is no JVM running on the client. There are no application files or Java runtime files stored or run on the client, which means that the client machine has fewer resource requirements and no special application installation. This automatically makes the JSP applications you develop compatible with a larger number of users. Since the solution is more efficient on the server side, you can support a large number of users such as with an e-commerce application.

The presentation look-and-feel of a page is embedded in HTML tags and cascading style sheets. Since the HTML tags are directly embedded in the JSP source file, you can split the development work. Creating the template look-and-feel for a page may be accomplished by a web graphics designer, while the dynamic JSP-specific sections would be developed by a Java programmer. Merging the work is just a matter of embedding one in the other. JDeveloper provides the tools to create and test the JSP code. The web designer would work in another tool as mentioned before.

Disadvantages of JSPs

The main disadvantages of JSPs are in the added complexity of the JSP tags and the architecture. In addition, there is added complexity in setting up the web server to support the servlet API and the JSP container. This extra complexity is not insurmountable but can be a daunting task for a shop that has not been involved with web technology. JDeveloper includes a wizard (the JSP Element Wizard) that helps the developer embed JSP tags into the code. This wizard helps ease the learning curve that accompanies learning the JSP tag language.

In addition, since the base language of the application is HTML, you will experience the limitations of that language when constructing a page. However, there are some complex pages on the Web now that use only HTML as their language, so this limitation is solved by employing an imaginative web designer who has a modern HTML development tool.

The HTML limitation is also eased somewhat because HTML can include embedded JavaScript. Although JavaScript does not have as many features as other programming languages such as Java, including JavaScript in an HTML page greatly extends the capabilities of the page. Therefore, developing robust JSP applications requires that the developer (or at least someone on the development team) is skilled in Java, HTML, and JavaScript. For developers accustomed to using a single language for all coding, this will feel like a step backwards.

There is another limitation in functionality because JSP-generated HTML cannot use the rich user interface features included in the AWT and Swing component libraries available for Java applications and applets. In addition, debugging is more difficult because the code is running on the server in the JSP container. JDeveloper offers remote debugging features (mentioned in Chapter 13) that assist in troubleshooting JSP applications.

The Web Bean Solution

A JDeveloper feature called web beans eases the limitation that JSPs cannot use AWT and Swing components. A *web bean* (or web-enabled JavaBean) is a bean that outputs HTML. For example, there is a web bean that creates an HTML version of the NavigationBar class found in the Swing components. Including JSP calls to a web bean runs the bean on the server when the JSP is accessed. The bean contains properties that are set in the code you write that will tailor its behavior. There are also methods in each web bean that you can call to alter the bean's behavior or features. You can write web beans that employ JavaScript for additional functionality.

The following is a sample tag structure that embeds the JSNavigationBar bean into a JSP file:

```
<jsp:useBean   class="oracle.jbo.html.databeans.JSNavigatorBar"
id="deptNavBar"  scope="request" >
<%
    deptNavBar.setShowNavigationButtons(true);
    deptNavBar.setReleaseApplicationResources(false);
    deptNavBar.initialize(pageContext,
       "testBeanPRJ_deptempbuscomp_DeptempbuscompModule.DeptView");
    deptNavBar.render();
%>
</jsp:useBean>
```

Chapter 8 includes further discussion and hands-on practices for web beans.

Where Are JSPs Useful?

JSPs are useful anywhere you would use standard CGI-generated or static HTML pages. Whenever you need a true Internet application that has no firewall limitations or Java requirements for the client, JSPs are indicated.

Using this method can in no way emulate the quality of client/server applications. You will need to embrace a much more rudimentary style of development that takes into consideration the limitations of HTML applications. However, at this point in time, this is still the best alternative for deploying Internet applications, especially applications responsible for e-commerce.

Alternative 4: Terminal Server Strategy

This alternative falls in between the first two alternatives (Java applications and applets) in terms of effectiveness. You can build client/server applications and deploy them over the Internet using a terminal emulator tool (such as Citrix WinFrame or MetaFrame for Windows NT or Unix, respectively). Using this approach, you can create standard client/server applications and deploy them on an application server that allows each user to create his or her own operating system session.

How Does Terminal Server Work?

The terminal server strategy is essentially a mainframe model. The client is a dumb terminal that presents a graphical version of the application that is actually running on the application server. Special software installed on the client emulates the runtime display. The user can interact with the application through this emulator, but there is a process running on the server that represents the actual runtime session.

Figure 7-5 depicts the components of this architecture. The JVM runs on the application server and accesses the business components on that same machine. The business components access the database server in the same way as other architectures. The terminal server on the application server machine sends an image of the application running in the JVM to the client. This is a working image that the user can interact with.

If you remove the client and the terminal server from this picture, the model reverts to the client/server model that the Java application uses. Therefore, you can think of this solution as consisting of client/server with the display on the user's machine.

This strategy is used for standard client/server applications and is available for Java applications and applets as well. It requires no special coding on the

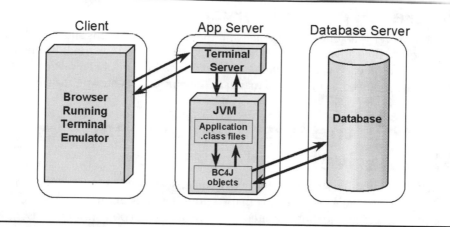

FIGURE 7-5. *Terminal server architecture*

application side, so the developer would be working with JDeveloper in the same way as with a Java application. Therefore, there are no discussions or practices in this book that are specific to the terminal server architecture.

Advantages of Terminal Server

Users access the system through a client machine using a special piece of software. This is equivalent to having multiuser remote access software, which acts like products such as PC Anywhere. As mentioned, this strategy works, not only with Java, but with any client/server applications. For several years, many applications have used this approach to deploy Oracle Forms Developer applications over the web. The terminal software includes built-in security, making it suitable for Internet or intranet use. Using these tools, all that is moving over the Internet is the information about how to change the pixels on the screen, and thus, it even works well with installations that suffer from poor data transfer rates.

This strategy provides all of the benefits of client/server Java applications but does not require installation on the user's machine. The code is centralized as it is using the web solutions, so maintenance and upgrades are easier.

Disadvantages of Terminal Server

The disadvantage of this solution is that every user on the system effectively has a server session running and taking some memory on the server, so there is a limit to the number of users that can be accommodated at any one time. In addition, the client machines must have the terminal emulation software installed and maintained. For intranet or Internet access with a small number of users, this is an adequate solution. However, this strategy would not be appropriate in an e-commerce environment that requires support for a large number of users.

Where Is Terminal Server Useful?

Terminal server is an effective alternative if the number of users is small. It allows developers to take advantage of centralized code architecture without having a JVM installed on each user's machine. However, the benefit of centralized code is lessened by the need to install and maintain the emulation software for each user.

What Is the Best Deployment Alternative?

Of the four alternative strategies presented, the answer to the question "which is best?" is really "all four." The one that you use depends upon your specific environment and application requirements. The factors to be considered, as explained in the preceding discussion, are as follows:

- Complex functionality that needs to be supported

- Scalability

- Performance

- Ease of installation and maintenance

Each alternative requires some trade-offs among these factors.

If you are building applications for internal use only, that require more complex functionality, excellent performance, and scalability to any number of users, the client/server Java application alternative is best, assuming you are willing to put up with client/server development and support issues.

In terms of sophistication and performance factors, the terminal server strategy is the next best solution because it is essentially a variation on client/server. Although scalability is an issue, if the number of users is relatively small, you can deploy sophisticated applications in a poor communications environment and still achieve better performance than with client/server. This is true since all database communications occur between the application server and the database server rather than over the Internet.

Running Java applets works well in an intranet environment or where users are not concerned about page downloading. This option is scalable up to thousands of users. However, the drawback of the initial class files download is worth serious consideration. This drawback is greatly mitigated by a caching scheme (available in Java 1.3) that, after the first download, keeps a copy of the applet on the client hard drive so that the download is only required if the applet code is updated.

TIP

The Release Notes also contain a description of how to install Java 1.3 for your work in JDeveloper. Java 1.3 is available as a download from the Sun Microsystems web site at java.sun.com/products/jdk/1.3.

The alternative of running the applications on an Apache or Oracle9*i* application server with JSPs potentially enhanced by JavaScript code provides good performance, great scalability, no security or firewall issues, but is restricted by the capabilities of HTML and JavaScript. However, currently, this is the only viable alternative for e-commerce solutions.

NOTE

Chapter 5 discusses the differences and similarities between JDeveloper and Oracle Developer. After reviewing this discussion, you may choose to deploy an application using Oracle Developer rather than JDeveloper.

Deciding Where to Put the Code

Depending on the deployment strategy you select, you will have to make decisions about where to place the code. For example, if you settle on the client/server Java application, you have to decide whether to put the BC4J code on the client or on the server in a CORBA Server Object or Enterprise JavaBean (EJB). (You can also place the code on the server using a Remote Method Invocation (RMI) server object, but that is not currently an option in JDeveloper's wizards and would, therefore, require some hand coding.) This particular decision is one you can make for each of the deployment strategies. The factors you will have to weigh when making this decision are the following:

- Will other applications be able to use the same data layer?

- Does any server layer offer data caching of which the business components could take advantage?

- Is it possible that the physical locations of the servers (application or database) will affect the performance of the data layer?

- How much data validation logic do you have in the application code?

The same kind of thought process is required with the database layer because the Oracle database (as of release 8.1.7) includes a JServer that you can use as an application server. Since the application server itself is also an option, this increases the number of possible combinations where specific pieces of code can be placed.

There is no rule of thumb to help you make this decision. The best advice is to be aware of the options and consider them carefully. In addition, keep in touch with Oracle user group sources for success stories on a particular arrangement of servers and code. The good news is that the options are relatively portable, and one of your application tuning steps will likely be moving the code from one tier to another and testing the effect.

> **NOTE**
> *JDeveloper support for EJB and CORBA deployment in the Oracle 8i database varies based on the release of the database and the release of JDeveloper. The JDeveloper Release Notes (available in the Help menu) contain a compatibility matrix with details about various releases of the products.*

JDeveloper Code Deployment Features

Java systems contain many code files. There are class, XML, HTML, and graphics files for most types of deployment, and additional files, such as JSP files, for specific deployment strategies. The number of files for the application and BC4J code alone can be quite large. When you add these to the runtime libraries that contain the Java language and beans you are using in the application, tracking the files becomes a major effort. Fortunately, JDeveloper organizes all of the files required for the application and assists you in packaging them for distribution to whatever deployment layer you select.

The Deployment Profile Wizard is the key tool that you use to assist in this effort. This wizard creates a *profile file* with a .prf extension that stores details about what files will be gathered and where they will be placed. This wizard is reentrant in an edit mode, so you can adjust the settings after initially creating the profile.

Hands-on Practice Preparation

The following hands-on-practices demonstrate the steps required to deploy the code that you create in JDeveloper using the Deployment Profile Wizard. The practices will show the deployment steps for the following alternatives discussed in this chapter:

- Java application
- Applet
- JSP application

The terminal server alternative works in the same way as the Java application with the additional requirement of setting up and running the terminal server and client emulation software. Since these setup and runtime requirements are not specific to JDeveloper, this alternative will not be demonstrated. If you were to use the terminal server alternative, you would create a Java application in the same way as shown in the following practice.

The three deployment alternatives demonstrated require a BC4J library to support their access to the database. Therefore, the first practice will demonstrate how to deploy a BC4J object set.

Sample Starting Files

For the Java application and JSP practices, you will require sample code to deploy. You can download sample code from the authors' web sites mentioned in the author biography page at the start of this book. Alternatively, you can deploy the code you created in Chapter 2 and will create in Chapter 8, for Java applications and JSPs respectively. Chapter 2 provides more detail than is required for the purposes of this chapter, so you might want to spend some time following the instructions in this chapter's practice for creating a sample Java application. Chapter 8 provides details about JSPs if you need more help or information with the JSP deployment practice in this chapter.

For the applet practice, you can, again, download the sample code from the authors' web sites or use the preparation steps in the applet deployment practice later on, to understand the required steps for building the applet.

All presented deployment alternatives will include the steps to build the sample code in case you want extra practice or you want to experience the entire process from application creation to deployment.

The Decision Points

Before you run the Deployment Profile Wizard on a project, you must have already made the major decision about which of the four deployment alternatives you will use. This selection guides you toward one style of coding. When you complete the application and need to create the distribution package, additional decisions are required about how to divide the code (for example, where to place the BC4J objects). These decisions will help you determine the server and directory path in which to install the files that you create in the deployment steps.

Prepare the Workspace

The practices that follow will be clearer if you start with a new workspace. In addition, all of the examples that follow use a common BC4J project. If you have completed the practices in other chapters, you have created this project already. As a review, the following are the primary steps required to prepare the workspace and create a BC4J project. The hands-on practice in Chapter 2 provides further discussion about this process.

1. Start a new workspace by selecting **File | New Workspace**. Select **File | Save Workspace** and create a workspace file called "DeployWS" in a new directory called deploypractice.

2. After you click Save, check to see that the Connections node contains your sample connection for the Scott schema. If it does not exist, create the connection using the steps in Chapter 2.

3. If you have a BC4J project (from the practices in Chapter 1 or 2), select **File | Open** and navigate to the deptempbuscomp directory. Doubleclick the DeptEmpBusCompPRJ.jpr file to load the file into the workspace. Substitute the file and directory name that you used to create a BC4J project if they are different. If this BC4J project does not exist, follow the abbreviated instructions in the next section or the full instructions in Chapter 2 to create the BC4J layer.

4. Click Save All. Your Navigation Pane should look like this:

Use this workspace and project as the starting point for the practices that follow.

Create the BC4J Project

If you did not create a BC4J project in Chapter 1 or 2, or you want more practice in creating a BC4J project, use the following steps. Skip this section if you opened an existing BC4J project in the preceding section.

1. Select **File | New Project**.

2. Dismiss the Welcome page if it appears by clicking Next.

3. Click Browse and, in the Select Project dialog, create a new folder called deptempbuscomp2 and navigate to it. Change the file name to DeptEmpBusCompPRJ.jpr and click Open.

4. Be sure that *A project containing Business Components* is selected and click Next.

5. Click the Browse button next to the package name field and specify deptempbuscomp2. Click OK to dismiss the Package Browser.

6. Click Finish to complete the Project Wizard and to start the Business Components Project Wizard.

7. Click Next if the Welcome page appears. Select a connection, click Next, and log in if the login dialog appears.

8. Accept the default package name and click Next.

9. In the Business Components page, move DEPT and EMP to the *Selected* area. Click Finish to create the BC4J layer. Click Save All.

Hands-on Practice: Deploying the BC4J Project

All useful code needs to connect to the database, and the best way to implement the connectivity in JDeveloper is with BC4J. Therefore, you need to have a BC4J project in all deployment scenarios. One of the steps when deploying an application is to select the libraries that will support the application at runtime. The BC4J code that supports the application must be in one of these libraries. Therefore, a preliminary step for Java application deployment is to deploy the BC4J code and make it available in a library. There are two phases to this process:

I. Create the BC4J archive

II. Add the archive to the libraries list

The following steps for deploying the BC4J project follow the typical method for deploying in local mode. *Local mode* means that the files are copied to the same file system as the application code (Java application, applet, or JSP). For a multi-tier architecture, you can copy the locally deployed files to another machine and set the class path on that machine so that the Java engine can find the files. You can also specify details about a multi-tier *remote mode* or *remotable* deployment for the application module (see the sidebar "Steps for Remotable Deployment"). This encompasses strategies such as CORBA object or EJB deployment to a remote application server.

Steps for Remotable Deployment

A remotable deployment is a multi-tier strategy. The application module of the BC4J layer is copied to another server for centralization and efficiency. You can deploy an existing application module using the following steps:

1. Open the node for the BC4J project in the Navigation Pane.

2. Right click the module name and select Edit from the menu. The Application Module properties dialog will appear, as shown here:

3. Check the *Remotable Application Module* checkbox on the Remote tab.

4. You will now select the platforms on which you will deploy your Business Components. Under the *Available* area, click "Oracle8*i* CORBA Server" and use the > button to move it to the *Selected* area.

5. Under *Target platform*, edit the *Client Project* field to include your package. Use the Browse button or edit the field directly to a value such as this:

   D:\Program Files\Oracle\JDeveloper 3.2\myprojects\
   DeptEmpBusCompPRJO8Client.jpr

6. Click Finish.

TIP
The help system topic on the Index tab "remotable application module, creating" provides details about the remotable option and links to further information.

I. Create the BC4J Archive

Use the following steps to create the BC4J archive.

I. Select the BC4J project (for example, DeptEmpBusCompPRJ) in the Navigation Pane and click Rebuild and Save All.

CAUTION
It is very important that the project files are compiled before deploying. The Deployment Profile Wizard will package whatever class files are in the myclasses directory for the project. If you make changes after compiling, you will not see those changes in the deployed application, even if you had saved the files before deploying. Therefore, it is good practice to rebuild the project before deploying it.

2. Select **Project | Deploy | New Deployment Profile**. Click Next to move to the Delivery page.

NOTE
*Selecting Create Deployment Profile from the right-click menu of a BC4J project will not produce the same results as selecting **Project | Deploy | New Deployment Profile**. Use the main menu instead of the right-click menu for the best results. The right-click menu item on other projects is called New Deployment Profile, and this is the same as the main menu item.*

3. In the *Select a type of deployment* field, select "Web application or command-line application" (or "Web Application to Web Server" in earlier releases). This value is used for code that will reside outside of the Oracle database. Click Next to display the Staging Area page, as shown here. (Your list of files may look different from this one.)

```
Deployment Profile Wizard, Step 2 of 6: Staging Area                    [X]

          Choose a staging area for deployment and select files to deploy
          alongside the project's archive. These files should be in the HTML root
          directory, but they do not need to be in the project.

          Deployment destination

          D:\Program Files\Oracle\JDeveloper 3.2\myclasses\        [ Browse... ]

          Files to deploy

          □─□  🗋 myhtml                                     ▲
             ⊞─□  🗋 deptapplePRJ02_html
             ⊞─□  🗋 deptappletAWTPRJ_html
             ⊞─□  🗋 deptappletBCPRJ_html
             ⊞─□  🗋 deptappletJSP_html
             ⊞─□  🗋 deptappletSwingPRJ_html
             ⊞─□  🗋 DeptEmpBusCompPRJ_html
             ⊞─□  🗋 deptjspPRJ_html
             ⊞─□  🗋 empappletPRJ_html
             ⊞─□  🗋 EmpDeptJSP                             ▼  [ Filters... ]

  [ Cancel ]  [ Help ]                      [ < Back ]  [ Next > ]  [ Finish ]
```

The *staging area* is a directory on some machine (in this case, your local machine) where JDeveloper will copy files required for a particular set of code. The directory will contain all files that the application (or BC4J layer) needs to execute, and you will not need JDeveloper to run the code.

NOTE
For purposes of illustration and discussion, this practice follows the steps for deploying the BC4J as a "web application" that includes all required libraries and the HTML or applet page. In the case of the BC4J project, you do not normally need to use the full web application option because deploying the application project will include the required libraries for BC4J as well as those required for the application. Therefore, your production practice will be to select "Deploy as a simple archive file" to deploy the only BC4J project.

4. Fill in the *Deployment destination* field with "D:\stage\deptempbc4j."
(Use the C drive if you do not have a D drive.) The wizard will create the
directories if they do not already exist. There are no HTML files to deploy,
so you do not need to check anything in the *Files to deploy* field on this
page. Click Next to show the Project page.

5. Click the project checkbox (DeptEmpBusCompPRJ.jpr) at the top level of
the *Select the files for the deployed archive* field. The other levels will
automatically be checked.

6. Click Next to load the Archive page.

7. Select the Zip radio button. You have a choice of creating a JAR (Java Archive)
or Zip file. These are different formats for storing multiple files including a
directory structure inside a single file.

The difference between Zip and JAR is that the JAR file contains a *manifest file*
that stores information about JavaBeans inside the archive. This difference is
not significant for this practice. The name of the file that will contain the class
files for this project will be displayed in the *Archive file* field. Click Next to
show the Applet Tags page.

8. This page is not applicable because the code is not an applet, so click Next
to display the Libraries page.

9. Move all libraries to the right (deployed) side using the arrows, as shown
in the following illustration. (Your list of files may be different from this
illustration.) All files in the deployed area will be copied to the staging
directory, not into the archive file. Click Next to show the Finish page.

10. You can change the name of the profile, but this is not required for this practice. When you need to create different deployment profiles for the same project, the name is important for identifying a particular deployment definition. Click Finish to complete the wizard.

11. A dialog will ask if you want to deploy now. If you click Yes, the files will be copied and the deployment will complete. If you click No, the settings you entered will be saved for when you finally deploy the project. If you click Cancel, the settings will be lost, and you will have to start over when you need to deploy. Click Yes.

12. The project deployment profile will appear in a folder called Deployment under the project node in the Navigation Pane. In addition, the files will copy and the BC4J archive will be created.

13. Click the Directory tab in the Navigator and navigate to the D:\stage\deptempbc4j directory. You will see Zip and JAR files for the libraries that you specified in the deployment profile of your BC4J project. You can open the BC4J .zip file (DeptEmpBusCompPRJ.zip) in the Viewer by doubleclicking it. You will find .class and .xml files that represent the familiar BC4J objects. You can also use a separate utility such as WinZip to open the Zip or JAR file.

What Just Happened?   You ran the Deployment Profile Wizard to create an archive file from the BC4J project. The archive file will serve as a source library for the applications that use this BC4J project. This archive as well as the library files that support it were copied into a separate directory. To deploy the BC4J code, you can just copy the contents of this directory to a location that is in the CLASSPATH of the same machine or is in the CLASSPATH of a different machine. The copying process is described in more detail later.

TIP
*You can edit the Deployment Profile properties by right clicking the profile file name (in the Deployments folder under the project node) and selecting Properties. You can examine settings and cancel the dialog or make changes and redeploy the files by clicking Done. You can also redeploy the files by clicking the project, selecting **Project | Deploy**, and selecting the name of the profile from the menu.*

II. Add the Archive to the Libraries List

Now that the project archive has been created, you have to specify that you want to make it available as a library when you deploy other projects. Whenever you deploy a project or application, you select the library files that contain the classes and other code that supports the project. Since the BC4J files are used by many applications, you want to make the files easily available in the deployment dialogs.

The following are steps for adding the archive to the list of available libraries.

1. Select the BC4J project and select **Tools | Default Project Properties**. Click the Libraries tab and the Libraries button. The Available Java Libraries dialog will appear as follows:

2. Click the New button to add to this list. The fields on the right will then be editable.

3. Fill in the *Name* field with "DeptEmp BC4J."

4. Click the Browse button next to the *Class path* field, and the Edit LibraryClassPath dialog will appear.

5. Click the Add Zip/JAR button and navigate to the BC4J stage directory (for example, D:\stage\deptempbc4j). Select the name of the BC4J .zip file (DeptEmpBusCompPRJ.zip) and click Open. The archive file will be added to the list.

   You can add more than one file for a particular library definition, but that is not required for this example.

6. Click the OK button and OK in the Available Java Libraries dialog. The file is now installed as a library, but you still need to make it available to the project by default.

NOTE
A library in JDeveloper is a bundle of one or more related Java archive (JAR or Zip) files with a meaningful name.

7. Click the Add button. Select "DeptEmp BC4J" in the dialog and click OK. The Default Project Properties dialog will look something like the following illustration:

```
Default Project Properties                                          [X]

 Paths | Libraries | Defaults | Compiler | Run/Debug | CodeCoach | Code ◄ ►

 Java libraries:
┌─────────────────────────────────────────────────────┐
│ JDeveloper Runtime                                    │
│ Oracle 8.1.7 JDBC                                     │
│ Connection Manager                                    │
│ DeptEmp BC4J                                          │
│                                                       │
│                                                       │
│                                                       │
│                                                       │
│                                                       │
│                                              ┌──────┐ │
│                                              │ Add... │ │
│                                              └──────┘ │
│                                              ┌──────┐ │
│                                              │Remove │ │
│                                              └──────┘ │
│                                              ┌──────┐ │
│                                              │Libraries...│
│                                              └──────┘ │
└─────────────────────────────────────────────────────┘

        ┌──────┐   ┌────────┐   ┌──────┐
        │  OK  │   │ Cancel │   │ Help │
        └──────┘   └────────┘   └──────┘
```

8. Click OK. The library will now be listed by default for all new projects. If you need to add the library to existing projects, use the Libraries tab of **Project | Project Properties**.

What Just Happened? You made the BC4J Zip file available as a library and registered it as a default resource for new projects. The list of libraries for a project indicates which libraries will be available to be deployed with the project. The list will be more comprehensive than the requirements of a particular deployment option. You want to be sure that, at a minimum, the libraries in this list support all of the code in the application. When you set up a particular deployment using the Deployment Profile Wizard, you will select from this list the minimum set of library files that will support that deployment option. For example, if you are deploying BC4J in a remotable mode (such as an EJB to the Oracle8*i* server), you would include the libraries for EJB to Oracle8*i* within the wizard dialogs. Those libraries must be available in the library list that you set up in Project Properties, but they would not be required in other deployments.

NOTE

*If you were to create a project now, the "DeptEmp BC4J" library would already appear in the selected libraries list because you added it to the default project properties in the preceding practice. You can select **File | Add Empty Project** and look at the Library properties of that project to verify this.*

Hands-on Practice: Deploying a Java Application

This practice builds on the BC4J deployment practice and demonstrates how to run the Deployment Profile Wizard on a Java application project. This practice steps through the following phases:

I. Prepare a sample Java application

II. Deploy the Java application

You have two alternatives for completing phase I:

 Use the sample Java application from the hands-on practice in Chapter 2 by selecting **File | Open** and opening the Java application project file in the new workspace.

 Use the sample from the authors' web sites.

If you use one of these alternatives, you may skip phase I. In addition, be sure that you have followed the preparation steps described in the sections "Prepare the Workspace" and "Hands-on Practice: Deploying the BC4J Project."

I. Prepare a Sample Java Application

In the interest of saving space and because the subject of creating Java applications has been well discussed in other chapters, the following steps, while complete, are written at a summary level. If you need further assistance with the process of creating a Java application, refer to the hands-on practice in Chapter 2.

1. Select **File | New Project**. Select "A project containing a new" and select "Application." Browse for the file name and enter "DeptAppPRJ" in the deploypractice directory.

2. In the Project Options page, specify "deploypractice" as the package name and finish the Project Wizard. The Application Wizard will appear.

3. Accept the default of "Add a default frame" and be sure that "A new Business Components for Java Data Form" is selected. Click OK to run the Business Components Data Form Wizard.

4. Accept the defaults on pages 1 through 5. On page 6 (Database Objects), select DeptView. On page 7 (Attributes), select all attributes. Finish the wizard using defaults for the Connections page.

5. Click Save All and Rebuild.

6. If the wizard does not create an application file (such as Application1.java), select **File | New** and doubleclick Application. In the Application Wizard, select "An existing frame" and browse to find Frame1 in the deploypractice package. Finish the wizard.

7. Click Save All and Rebuild, and test run the application.

What Just Happened? You created a sample Java application that you will use for the deployment practice.

II. Deploy the Java Application

The steps that you go through to deploy a Java application are similar to the steps for the BC4J project because you use the same Deployment Profile Wizard. As with the BC4J project, the following steps deploy the application in local mode.

1. Right click the Java application project name (for example, DeptAppPRJ.jpr) and select Properties. This will display the Project Properties dialog (also available from the Project menu).

2. Select the Libraries tab. If the DeptEmp BC4J library appears in the list, click OK and skip to step 5. Otherwise, click the Add button. The list of available libraries will appear.

3. Select the BC4J library that you added in the preceding practice (for example, DeptEmp BC4J) and click OK. The library name will be added to the list for this project. Click OK to dismiss the Project Properties dialog.

4. Select the project name and click Rebuild.

5. Right click the Java application project and select New Deployment Profile (also available from the Project menu). Click Next to display the Delivery page.

6. Select "Web application or command-line application" (or "Web Application to Web Server" in earlier releases) from the pulldown and click Next.

7. In the *Deployment destination* field, enter "D:\stage\deptapp" or a similar directory. The wizard will create the directories if they do not already exist. Placing all deployment staging directories under one root directory has an advantage of easier management, but the staging directory structure does not really matter. Click Next to display the Project page.

8. Check the checkbox next to the project file at the top of the list.

9. Click the Advanced button. This area allows you to specify nonstandard options. In this case, check the *Generate scripts...* field. This will cause the wizard to create .bat (Microsoft Windows batch file) and .sh (Unix shell script) command-line scripts that set the CLASSPATH environment variable to include the proper archive files.

10. Click Done and Next to display the Archive page.

11. Select Zip and click Next for the Applet Tags page. Click Next to dismiss the Applet Tags page.

12. On the Libraries page, move all libraries to the right. Be sure that your BC4J project library is represented. If it is not, cancel the dialog and repeat phase II in the BC4J deployment practice and steps 2 and 3 in this section. Click Next and Finish. Click Yes in the confirmation dialog.

13. When the deployment wizard has finished copying files, you can expand the Deployment folder in the application project. There will be .bat and .sh script files that are used to set the CLASSPATH environment variable from the command line in Windows and Unix, respectively.

14. You can test the deployed files from the command line. This is the method by which a Java application is run, although you can also create a Windows shortcut with the command line embedded in it so that your users do not have to struggle with typing commands.

The first step in testing the command line is to open a command-line window. In the Windows Start menu, select Command Prompt or MS DOS Prompt from the **Start** | **Programs** menu. Alternatively, you can select **Start** | **Run** and enter "COMMAND" (for Windows 9x) or "CMD" (for Windows NT and Windows 2000). Click OK to open the command-line window.

15. Navigate to the drive (by entering the drive letter, such as "d:") and directory (by entering the directory name, such as "cd \stage\deptapp"). Press ENTER between each command. The window should change so that the command prompt contains the name of the drive and directory.

16. Enter the command "profile." This will run the profile.bat file that changes the CLASSPATH variable to include all files that you just deployed. To check the CLASSPATH, enter "set classpath." The classpath variable will be displayed as shown here:

```
C:\WINNT\System32\cmd.exe                                          _ □ ×

D:\stage\deptapp>set classpath
CLASSPATH=d:\stage\deptapp\DeptAppPRJ.zip;D:\Program Files\Oracle\JDeveloper 3.2
\java1.2\jre\lib\rt.jar;D:\Program Files\Oracle\JDeveloper 3.2\lib\jdev-rt.zip;D
:\Program Files\Oracle\JDeveloper 3.2\lib\connectionmanager.zip;D:\stage\deptemp
bc4j\DeptEmpBusCompPRJ.zip;D:\Program Files\Oracle\JDeveloper 3.2\lib\javax_ejb.
zip;D:\Program Files\Oracle\JDeveloper 3.2\infobus\lib\infobus.jar;D:\Program Fi
les\Oracle\JDeveloper 3.2\lib\dacf.zip;D:\Program Files\Oracle\JDeveloper 3.2\in
fobus\lib\infobus.jar;D:\Program Files\Oracle\JDeveloper 3.2\lib\LW_pfjbean.jar;
D:\Program Files\Oracle\JDeveloper 3.2\lib\jbodomorcl.zip;D:\Program Files\Oracl
e\JDeveloper 3.2\lib\jbodatum12.zip;D:\Program Files\Oracle\JDeveloper 3.2\lib\j
bomt.zip;D:\Program Files\Oracle\JDeveloper 3.2\lib\jbodomorcl.zip;D:\Program Fi
les\Oracle\JDeveloper 3.2\lib\jboremote.zip;D:\Program Files\Oracle\JDeveloper 3
.2\lib\jndi.jar;D:\Program Files\Oracle\JDeveloper 3.2\lib\xmlparserv2.jar;D:\Pr
ogram Files\Oracle\JDeveloper 3.2\jdbc\lib\oracle8.1.7\classes12.zip

D:\stage\deptapp>
```

The *CLASSPATH environment variable* specifies the names of the classes that are required for an application at runtime. The Java engine reads this variable and locates classes within the archive files by examining the package directory names embedded in the archives. The *import* statements in the Java file contain these directories (that sit under the master directory or package). You can think of the CLASSPATH variable as a PATH variable for Java. The operating system looks for executable files in the directories listed in the PATH variable. Java looks for class and other files in the archive files (treated as directories) that are listed in the CLASSPATH variable.

17. You are now ready to run the application. If you want to prove to yourself that JDeveloper has nothing to do with this test, close JDeveloper. At the command line, enter the following command:

```
java deploypractice.Application1
```

In this string, "java" is the Java runtime (java.exe) that creates the JVM, and "deploypractice.Application1" is the name (including package name) of the starting method that displays the application's first frame. Substitute the appropriate name, such as "deptideapp.Application1" if you are using the Java application from Chapter 2.

CAUTION

The Java runtime engine (java.exe) is case sensitive. Therefore, you need to enter the command-line command with the same case as you used to construct the application.

18. The application should appear after several messages display in the command-line window. The application will run exactly as it did in JDeveloper. The command-line session will be disabled until you close the application.

NOTE

*If you have problems running the Java executable, you may need to reinstall the Software Development Kit (SDK). The SDK was formerly known as the JDK (Java Development Kit). You can download the SDK from the Sun Microsystems web site (java.sun.com). The readme.html file in the JDEV_HOME\java1.2 directory contains information about the SDK. If you receive a message that there is an incorrect version of Java specified in the Java Runtime Environment key of the registry, open REGEDIT using **Start | Run** in the Windows menu. Navigate to the HKEY_LOCAL_MACHINE\software\ Javasoft\Java Runtime Environment node and change the key "Current Version" to the version that the Java engine expects. The SDK installation program should set this key for you.*

The following pages contain sidebars that discuss the details of the script files and how you can create a shortcut for the Java application.

Details About Script Files

The script files that the wizard creates have three calling formats as follows:

- ▪ profile
- ▪ profile *directory*
- ▪ profile copyto *directory*

In the first format, the script builds the CLASSPATH from libraries in JDeveloper directories. It builds the BC4J library from the BC4J staging directory. The libraries in your application staging directory are ignored except for the application library.

In the second format, the script uses the directory name passed in the *directory* parameter instead of the JDeveloper directories. The directory specified must have the same structure as the JDeveloper directories. The script also ignores all other libraries in your application staging directory except the application library.

In the third format, the script copies the library files from JDeveloper directories into the directory specified in the second parameter. The application and BC4J libraries are copied under the specified directory in a directory structure that mirrors the staging directory.

The profile script file does not use the libraries directly inside the staging directory in any of the script formats. The first alternative for deploying the files is to edit the profile script so that it has hard-coded directories that mirror the real directory structure. The script could then be simplified to one SET CLASSPATH= statement.

A second alternative is to use the third syntax with the "copyto" parameter and copy to another directory root. Then use the second syntax and specify the new directory. You have a choice of options, but the simplest is to hand-code a CLASSPATH setting based on a single directory. The drawback is that each application directory will contain a number of the same base Java libraries. Therefore, the more efficient solution is to set up a common library directory structure that all applications can use for the base Java files, as described in the second alternative.

The first format for calling this script is adequate for testing purposes, and will be demonstrated in the practice.

Creating a Shortcut for the Java Application

It is not reasonable to expect users to enter command-line commands. You can create a shortcut for your application that includes the command line so that the user can just doubleclick the shortcut to start the application. The process of creating a shortcut for the Java application is no different from creating a shortcut for any other Windows program.

1. You need to create a batch file that will set the CLASSPATH and run the application within the same session. In the command-line window that is open to the staging directory, enter

   ```
   notepad profile.bat
   ```

   Select **File | Save As** and name the file "rundept.bat."

2. At the end of this file, create a new line and type the following:

   ```
   java deploypractice.Application1
   ```

3. Save the file again and exit Notepad.

4. Minimize all windows and right click the desktop. Select **New | Shortcut** and enter the following:

   ```
   d:\stage\deptapp\rundept
   ```

5. Click Next and enter the name of your application (for example, "Browse Departments"). Click Finish.

6. Doubleclick the new shortcut to test the application. The command-line window will open and show the CLASSPATH setting. Then the application will start.

7. If you are interested in hiding the command-line window, right click the shortcut and select Properties. Click the Shortcut tab and change the *Run* field to "Minimized."

What Just Happened?   You created a deployment file set for a Java application and placed the files in a local staging directory. You can open Windows Explorer and navigate to that directory (for example, D:\stage\deptapp). You will see the following types of files in this directory:

■ **.bat and .sh script files** described before.

- **archive library files** with .jar and .zip extensions that contain the classes required for the application.

- **.zip file for the BC4J project** (for example, DeptEmpBusCompPRJ.zip) that you deployed in the earlier practice. This file and its supporting libraries were copied into this project's staging directory. This means that when you deploy the application, you can just copy the files from one directory and not have to worry about missing a supporting file.

- **.zip file for the Java application project** (for example, DeptAppPRJ.zip). You can open this file and examine its contents by doubleclicking its icon in the JDeveloper Directory tab. You can also use a Zip utility to open this file. You will see class files that support the application and the package (directory) that they were built under (in this case, deploypractice).

The other accomplishments of this phase of the practice were in running the application and examining the deployment files.

Deploying the Library Files

The files you create here can be copied to each machine that will run the application. Each machine would need to have its CLASSPATH variable set with a script file, such as the profile, or in a login script. Alternatively, the BC4J library may be copied to other servers such as an application server Oracle8*i*, VisiBroker CORBA server, or an Enterprise JavaBean (EJB) server. The latter strategies allow the business components to be shared among applications but require some extra steps to create wrappers for the application module object of the BC4J. The JDeveloper help system contains further information about this option.

Hands-on Practice: Deploying an Applet

Deploying an applet shares many of the same steps with the Java application, although running the applet is different. This practice steps through the following phases:

I. Prepare a sample applet

II. Deploy the applet

It is better in this practice if you create the sample application from scratch rather than using the applet practice in Chapter 12. There is a setting in the Applet Wizard that the deployment option requires. This option is not discussed in Chapter 12 because the focus there is on security. Also, to demonstrate deployment, the applet does not need to be complex. Be sure that you have followed the preparation steps described in the sections "Prepare the Workspace" and "Hands-on Practice: Deploying the BC4J Project."

The Swing Class Applet Issue

While the industry trend is toward deploying applications that use the Swing component classes rather than the older and less-featured AWT classes, as mentioned before, there is an issue concerning how Swing classes are deployed in an applet. Browsers cannot natively support Swing classes, although they can support AWT classes. Using either component library in JDeveloper works because JDeveloper runs the applet in its own browser emulation.

However, when you deploy an applet developed with Swing classes, you will find that it will not run (you will get an error such as "applet not inited"). You can run a quick test by developing an applet with Swing classes and deploying it following the steps in this practice. If it works, your browser has been set up to support Swing classes. If it does not, you can try developing a simple applet using the AWT classes. (Be sure to specify that the applet extends the java (AWT) applet, not the javax (Swing) applet.)

The Solution

Sun offers a browser plug-in that supports applets developed with Swing classes. You can download this plug-in as the Java Runtime Environment 1.2 from the java.sun.com web site and install it. The following steps will indicate when you will need to have this plug-in installed.

NOTE
You can use AWT classes for your applet and bypass the plug-in issue. However, if you are accessing the database, AWT classes require much more code to connect. Also, using AWT bypasses a major feature of JDeveloper—Data-Aware Controls—because these controls are built from Swing classes so that the Swing libraries must be available at runtime. If you want to explore how to connect an AWT component to a BC4J layer, examine the SimpleConsumerBean.java demo file in the JDEV_HOME\infobus\demo directory and the BC4JGenericApplet.java demo file in the JDEV_HOME\samples\BC4J\OrderEntry\ LocalApplet directory.

I. Prepare a Sample Applet

The following steps use the wizards to create a sample applet in a new project.

1. Select **File | New Project** and browse to the deploypractice directory. Name the project "DeptAppletPRJ" and click Open.

2. Select "A project containing a new" and specify "Applet" in the pulldown. Click Next.

3. Select the project's default package as deploypractice and click Finish. The Applet Wizard will start.

4. Click Next to move to the Applet page of the Applet Wizard. The defaults will work for this example, so click Next to move to the Parameters page.

5. There are no parameters required by this applet, so click Next to display the HTML Page settings.

6. On the HTML Page screen, check the "Generate HTML file" checkbox. This will create the HTML file that you will use to run the applet.

7. Check the "Generate Java Plug-in code" checkbox to cause the wizard to add tags to the HTML file that will check the state of the plug-in on the client machine. If the plug-in is not installed, the code connects to the Sun download web site. Click Next and Finish to complete the wizard.

   This creates an applet Java file and HTML file.

NOTE
The Business Component Data Form Wizard can create an applet, but it will not add the plug-in lines to the HTML file.

8. Right click the HTML file in the Navigation Pane and select **Open Viewer As | Source Editor**. You will see a large section of code in the middle of this file that checks the browser type (Netscape or Internet Explorer) and checks for the plug-in based on that type.

9. Doubleclick the Applet1.java file and click the Design tab. The UI Designer will be displayed.

10. Drop a SessionInfo component from the InfoProducer's tab into the Structure Pane. Fill in the following properties:

    connectionInfo as "ScottConnection"
    appModuleInfo as the name of the BC4J application module

11. Drop a RowSetInfo component into the Structure Pane. Fill in the following properties:

    session as "sessionInfo1"
    queryInfo as "DeptView" (all columns)

12. Click the "this" frame in the Structure Pane and change the *layout* property to "XYLayout." This will allow you to lay out objects without having a layout manager impose position or size constraints.

13. Drop a TextFieldControl onto the frame from the InfoSwing tab. Set its *dataItemName* property to the "DnamerowSetInfo1" attribute.

14. Drop a NavigationBar control onto the frame from the InfoSwing tab. Set its *dataItemName* property to "rowSetInfo1."

15. Drop a LoginDlg control from the InfoSwing tab onto the Structure Pane. Change its *dataItemName* to "sessionInfo1."

16. Click the Source tab and enter the following line of code at the end of the import section:

    ```
    import oracle.dacf.control.LoginFailureException;
    ```

17. Place this in the `jbInit()` method under the call to loginDlg1.setDataItemName:

    ```
    if (loginDlg1.showDialog() == JOptionPane.CANCEL_OPTION) {
        throw new LoginFailureException();
    }
    ```

18. Click Rebuild and Save All.

19. Select the HTML file in the Navigation Pane and click Run. Try the navigation bar.

What Just Happened?   You created a sample applet by using the wizards and manually adding components. You tested the applet in JDeveloper. The next steps demonstrate how you can deploy this applet outside of JDeveloper.

II. Deploy the Applet

The applet deployment steps are nearly identical to the application deployment steps and are presented in an abbreviated format.

1. Right click the applet project name (for example, DeptAppletPRJ.jpr) and select Properties. This will display the Project Properties dialog (also available from the Project menu).

2. Check that DeptEmp BC4J is listed on the Libraries tab, and add it if it is not listed. Click OK.

3. Select the project name and click Rebuild.

4. Right click the applet project and select New Deployment Profile. Click Next to display the Delivery page.

5. Select "Web application or command-line application" (or "Web Application to Web Server" in earlier releases) from the pulldown and click Next.

6. In the *Deployment destination* field, enter "D:\stage\deptapplet" or a similar directory.

7. In the *Files to deploy* area, check the DeptAppletPRJ_html file. This file must be deployed as well so that the user can start the applet. Click Next for the Project page.

8. Check the checkbox next to the project file at the top of the list. Click Next to see the Archive page.

9. Select Zip and click Next for the Applet Tags. The HTML applet startup file is listed on the left, as shown here:

10. Move the file to the area on the right. If there is more than one file to choose from, select the file name that matches the applet HTML file in the Navigator. This operation defines this HTML file as a deployed applet HTML file. If the file did not have the HTML tags to load the plug-in before

this, including the file in this list would cause the wizard to add these tags. Click Next to dismiss the Applet Tags page.

11. On the Libraries page, move all libraries to the right. Click Finish. Click the Yes button in the confirmation dialog.

12. When the deployment wizard has finished copying files, click Save All.

13. You can open Windows Explorer (or use the JDeveloper Directory tab) and examine the files in the D:\stage\deptapplet directory. This directory will appear to have nearly identical contents as the Java application staging directory. However, there is an additional directory added to this staging area that contains the runtime HTML file.

14. Testing the deployed files is a matter of opening Windows Explorer and doubleclicking the HTML file in the staging subdirectory. (You can close JDeveloper beforehand if you want to verify that the applet is now a standalone package.)

NOTE

The CLASSPATH in the case of an applet is specified by code in the HTML file.

15. If you are not successful when running the HTML file, you probably do not have the Java plug-in installed for your browser. See the following note for a solution.

NOTE

If you have problems running Java code containing Swing classes inside the browser, you will need to install the Java plug-in that is available from the Sun web site (java.sun.com). You can copy the exact location of the plug-in installation page from the HTML startup file into your browser.

What Just Happened?   You created the deployment set for an applet. This practice did not create the script files that were generated in the Java application practice. The reason is that you do not run an applet from the command line, you run it from a browser. The code in the HTML startup file sets the CLASSPATH, which is one of the functions of the script file. If you wanted to copy the files required for this project to another directory, you could generate the script file using the Advanced button in the Project page of the wizard. You would then use the "copyto" parameter to copy the files as described in the sidebar "Details About the Script Files" in the Java application practice.

Deploying the Library Files

The file set is the same as the Java application, except that the applet contains a starting HTML file. All files can be copied to the application server and downloaded by the browser. The application server would have to be configured with project subdirectories and virtual directories mapped to these subdirectories.

Hands-on Practice: Deploying JSPs

As mentioned earlier, you may want to read through Chapter 8 to get a sense of how JSPs work before running through this practice. This practice steps through the following phases:

   I. Prepare a sample JSP application

   II. Deploy the JSP application

You have two alternatives for completing phase I:

- Use a sample JSP application from a hands-on practice in Chapter 8 by selecting **File | Open** and opening the Java application project file in the new workspace.

- Use the sample from the authors' web sites.

If you use one of these alternatives, you may skip phase I. In any case, be sure that you have followed the preparation steps described in the sections "Prepare the Workspace" and "Hands-on Practice: Deploying the BC4J Project."

I. Prepare a Sample JSP Application

In the interest of saving space and because the subject of creating JSP applications is fully discussed in Chapter 8, the following steps are written at a summary level. If you need further assistance with the process of creating JSPs, refer to the hands-on practices in Chapter 8.

   I. Select **File | New Project** and browse to the deploypractice directory. Name the project "DeptJSPPRJ" and click Open.

2. Select "A project containing a new" and specify "Business Components JSP Application" in the pulldown. Click Next.

3. Select the project's default package as deploypractice and click Finish. The Business Components JSP Application Wizard will start. Click Next to dismiss the Welcome page and move to the Web Site page.

4. Change the *Web Application name* field to "DeptWebApp." Click Next for the Business Application page.

5. Click Next after examining the defaults. The Application Template page will be displayed. Select "Oracle." This specifies the look-and-feel template. Click Next.

6. Click EmpView and uncheck the *Generate page* checkbox so that no HTML page will be generated for this view. Uncheck that checkbox for all other views except DeptView. Click Next and Finish. The JSP files will be created and the Navigation Pane will display the list as shown here:

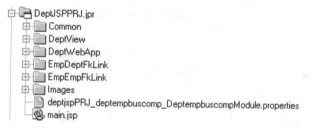

7. Select the project node and click Rebuild and Save All.

8. Select the main.jsp file and click Run. The browser will open and load the opening screen. You can test the application to get a sense of the screens.

What Just Happened?   You created a sample JSP application that you can use for testing the deployment process.

II. Deploy the JSP Application

The JSP deployment steps share a similar process with the Java application deployment steps and are presented in an abbreviated format.

1. Right click the JSP project name (for example, DeptJSPPRJ.jpr) and select Properties. This will display the Project Properties dialog (also available from the Project menu).

2. Check that DeptEmp BC4J is listed on the Libraries tab, and add it if it is not listed. Click OK.

3. Select the project name and click Rebuild.

4. Right click the project and select New Deployment Profile. Click Next to display the Delivery page.

5. Select "Web application or command-line application" (or "Web Application to Web Server" in earlier releases) from the pulldown and click Next.

6. In the *Deployment destination* field, enter "D:\stage\deptjsp" or a similar directory.

7. In the *Files to deploy* area, check the DeptJSPPRJ_html file. Click Next for the Project page.

8. Check the checkbox next to the project file at the top of the list. Click Next to see the Archive page.

9. Select Zip and click Next for the Applet Tags. This is not an applet, so click Next to move to the Libraries page.

10. On the Libraries page, move all libraries to the right. Click Finish. Click the Yes button in the confirmation dialog.

11. When the deployment wizard has finished copying files, click Save All.

12. You can open Windows Explorer (or the JDeveloper Directory tab) and examine the files in the D:\stage\deptjsp directory. This directory will appear to have nearly identical contents as the applet staging directory. However, the HTML subdirectory contains all JSP and other application files.

This completes the deployment preparation process. Testing the deployment for a JSP application has a few more requirements than testing the Java application or applets, and it is an optional activity at this point. The sidebar "Testing the JSP Deployment" provides some notes on how you might proceed with the test if desired.

What Just Happened?　　You created the deployment file set for a JSP application. As with the applet deployment, you do not need to set the CLASSPATH environment variable, as this is set by the starting HTML file. In addition, you can generate the script files (using the Advanced button of the Projects tab in the wizard) if you want to copy the deployment files to another directory.

Testing the JSP Deployment

Testing a deployment set of JSP files outside of JDeveloper requires that you have a web application server running a JServer process that interprets and processes the JSP code. There are a few alternatives for this. The first is to install an Oracle9*i* application server (formerly *i*AS) on the same machine or a different machine. You have to ensure that the installer loads the JServer mod (an Apache module). In addition, you have to configure and note the virtual directories that are set up on the application server so that you can copy your code to a directory that can be accessed by the server.

An easier alternative that does not require the installation of Oracle9*i* application server is to install Oracle8*i* release 8.1.7. This release includes a seamlessly installed Apache application server. The JServer process is automatically loaded, and you do not need to install any other product. The main steps for testing the application are the same as with the separate application server.

The testing process consists of the following general steps:

1. Copying the library and other files to the proper directories on the server. As a quick test, you can use the htdocs directory that already has a virtual directory mapping.

2. Modifying the *index.html* page in the ORACLE_HOME\Apache\Apache\ htdocs directory to include a link to the application's directory and main.jsp file. This is the default file that is loaded when the user accesses your site without specifying another page. For example, if the user enters a URL request for "http://yourserver" the web server fills a default in the rest of the request that usually specifies a virtual directory and file (for example, http://yourserver/htdocs/index.html). The index file usually is the home page for your site that has links to other pages. You can add a link on this page to your JSP application so that the user can access the application by just clicking the link. There are other possibilities for starting the application, as there are for displaying static HTML pages, including making the JSP application the default page using the web server configuration facilities.

3. Clicking the link for the JSP application and testing the application.

Read the Release Notes for Apache or Oracle 8.1.7 Installs   There is an important note in the JDeveloper Release Notes about setting up an Apache web server for use with business components code. This note is titled "Updating Business Components for Java Libraries on Oracle9*i* Application Server (*i*AS)" and also applies to the Oracle 8.1.7 server, although this is not specifically mentioned. The note describes the steps you follow to modify a file called jserv.properties so that it includes additional libraries in the class path (using an entry called *wrapper.classpath*). The CLASSPATH in the operating system environment variable is not used in this scenario.

Be sure that you check the list of libraries in the Release Notes and that all libraries you copy to the server directory are included in the wrapper.classpath statements. In addition, all of the libraries that are specific to your application (BC4J and application code) will require a wrapper.classpath entry. The application module and connections.properties files must also have a wrapper.classpath entry.

You also need to unzip the webapp.zip archive file from the JDEV_HOME\ redist directory into the web server's documentation directory (for example, htdocs) where all the cascading style sheets and images are located.

Another caution is to be sure to overwrite any JAR or Zip files in the application server directories with the staging directory versions, because these were the libraries used to create the application and are more up to date. The versions that exist on the application server may be different, and this may affect your application.

PART III

Implementation Techniques

CHAPTER
8

JavaServer Pages

EVERY man spins a web of light circles
And hangs this web in the sky
Or finds it hanging, already hung for him,
Written as a path for him to travel.
—Carl Sandburg, (1878–1967), Webs (*Good Morning, America*)

ow that you have an idea of how to create the business components layer and deploy the code that you create in JDeveloper, it is time to explore various technical details of how to use JDeveloper to build applications using the three primary deployment alternatives discussed in Chapter 7, namely, Java applications, applets, and JSPs. The chapters in this section will teach you what you need to know to build basic applications of these types. This chapter will discuss how to create JavaServer Pages (JSPs) using JDeveloper. The following three chapters discuss specific components and techniques that you will use in Java applications and applets. The next chapter in this part of the book explores the topic of security that applies to any type of web application. The last chapter explores the subject of debugging any style of application in JDeveloper.

This chapter introduces the topic of how to work with JSPs in JDeveloper. Chapter 7 contains information about the architecture, advantages, and disadvantages of this technology and serves as the necessary background material for these technical discussions. There are many books on the market now that discuss JSPs, and you will want to refer to one or more for further reference material. You can also search on the Oracle technical web site (technet.oracle.com) for white papers in the JDeveloper product area that provide valuable reference material. In addition, search on the www.javasoft.com web site for JavaServer Pages technical information. There is a reference guide on that site for the JSP tag language.

This chapter introduces the techniques needed to develop JSPs in JDeveloper. You should pay particular attention to the practices that step you through the creation of JSPs using different techniques such as the wizards and hand coding. As you work on real applications, you will mix these techniques to accomplish the tasks required for building a full JSP application.

TIP
The JDeveloper help system contains a wealth of information about JSPs. Start at the Contents page topic "Creating JSP Pages" and work your way down from there.

Working with JSP Applications in JDeveloper

Developing JSP applications in JDeveloper is inherently different from developing Java applications and applets. Java applications and applets have a graphical design element to them. You drag and drop objects from the component palette into the Structure Pane or UI Designer. You can view and manipulate the properties of the components using the UI Designer and Inspector.

When you use JDeveloper to work with a JSP application, you do not use a visual editor. Much of the work you do is in the code. The major visual part of the application results from HTML content that will most likely be developed using another tool such as Dreamweaver or FrontPage. These tools can be used in combination with JDeveloper so that you can work on both visual design and JSP construction. In addition, a web designer can work separately on the complex layouts using these tools. You can later merge her or his work with the JSP work that you have done in JDeveloper. This chapter will not explain the use of these visual design tools, but will focus on the JSP development work that is supported in JDeveloper.

More Skills Required

Work in JSP applications requires a broad range of knowledge that is not required for work in Java applications or applets, for which you only need to know the Java language (in addition to database languages). In addition to knowledge of JSP tags, a typical JSP application requires familiarity with the following:

- HTML
- Java
- JavaScript
- Cascading style sheets

All of these are very approachable languages, but may require a bit of study and a good reference book before you become fully fluent and comfortable with development work in them.

Online Information Sources

Free online resources are readily available from the originators of the languages, as follows:

Language	Resource	Online Location
HTML	World Wide Web Consortium	www.w3.org
Java and JSPs	Sun Microsystems	java.sun.com
JavaScript	Netscape	developer.netscape.com

To supplement the information from the originator of the language, use your favorite Internet search engine to find other online reference guides. It is very easy to find additional resources and examples for these languages.

Typical JSP Development Steps

The normal working process in JDeveloper consists of creating a text file with basic JSP elements that identify its nature. A *JSP element* is a piece of code that can be made up of HTML-like tags or other symbols. It can be interpreted by the JSP container running on the server if the server can find the library code that supports the element.

The JSP file that you create can incorporate an HTML template that contains the standard look-and-feel of your site. Alternatively, you can develop the HTML template separately from the JSP file (usually using a tool such as FrontPage or Dreamweaver) and merge the files when both are complete. The HTML template might include a standard background graphic, a company logo in a standard position, a navigation bar containing links to the major areas of your site, a footer graphic, and links to contact information.

The main types of code that you will add to the JSP file are as follows:

- **HTML tags**   These are standard tags used to create browser pages. They are written into the JSP file just as they would be written into a normal HTML file.

- **Standard JSP tags**   JSP elements use the same kind of tag syntax as HTML tags, but contain special characters (such as % signs) to distinguish them from HTML tags.

- **JDeveloper JSP elements**   JDeveloper provides several categories of elements that assist in application development, such as JSP custom data tags, web beans, and data web beans. There is also a supplied set of themes, or cascading style sheets, that make the visual elements of a JSP application consistent.

Refer to the section "Types of JSP Code" for examples of each of these types of code. The sidebar "Working with the JSP Element Wizard" explains the steps for quickly defining syntax-correct elements using this tool.

After embedding the tags in the source file, you can run the file using JDeveloper's built-in web server emulator *Web-to-go*. The pages will be displayed in your browser, and you will be able to check the design, interaction with the database, and user interface functionality. The standard process of code modification and testing continues throughout the development process. You then need to deploy the files to another server so that they may be available to users.

Working with the JSP Element Wizard

The main tool that you use for embedding JSP elements in the file is the JSP Element Wizard. This wizard allows you to easily enter the correct syntax for all supported tags. You can add to the list of elements and properties that the wizard presents using the Web Object Manager. The following are steps for using the JSP Element Wizard.

1. Display the wizard by selecting **Wizards | JSP Element** or selecting JSP Element from the right-click menu in the Source Editor. The wizard will appear as follows:

Be careful of the cursor position when you call the JSP Element Wizard. When you accept the wizard settings, the tags that the wizard creates will be inserted at the cursor position. If the tags are placed in the wrong location, you can always cut and paste them to the correct location (or press CTRL-Z and redo the work with the wizard).

2. After expanding one of the high-level nodes and selecting a tag, you click Next. For tags such as the Output Comment, you will then see the Finish page.

3. Other JSP elements require you to set properties, so a properties dialog will then appear, as in the following example of page directive properties:

4. Some JSP elements, such as data web beans, require another page to define the data elements as follows:

5. When you complete the required pages, click Finish to dismiss the dialog and insert the tags.

Methods for Creating JSP Applications

JDeveloper provides three main categories of JSP elements:

- **BC4J Data Tag Library**   (Called Data Tag Library in the JSP Element Wizard) These tags provide complete access to database operations at a low level using the BC4J layer. Some tags can also display data in a rudimentary way.

- **Web beans (HTML web beans)**   Web beans are JavaBeans that output HTML. The HTML web beans have no links to the database. You need to combine these beans with the Data Tag Library to present data in a JSP file.

- **Data web beans**   These JavaBeans also output HTML and allow you to define data elements as attributes of the web bean. Therefore, you do not need to separate the data and user interface areas—they are both part of the data web bean.

These categories are represented by folders in the JSP Element Wizard and are discussed in more detail later in the chapter. Each category implies a different level of coding that requires a different method. There are many ways to create JSP applications in JDeveloper. The following is a list of some of the most common development methods ranked from hardest and most time consuming to easiest and fastest.

- **Hand code using the Source Editor**   You would also, most likely, be using some kind of HTML editor to supply the look-and-feel. You would then use the BC4J Data Tag Library to retrieve data for the HTML display.

- **Use web beans**   Web beans save you from having to manually code the HTML that displays a particular control object. To retrieve data from the database, you would have to combine the web bean code with the BC4J Data Tag Library tags.

- **Run the DataPage Wizard**   The DataPage Wizard constructs pages one at a time based on the BC4J Data Tag Library tags. This is just a more automatic way of getting the same results as the previous method would provide.

- **Use data web beans**   These beans automatically include database access and display capabilities, so you can more quickly build a data-aware page. The amount of code that you have to write is much less because you do not have to worry about the data source.

- **Run the Business Components JSP Application Wizard**   This wizard creates an entire application quickly from a view object. The problem is that modifying the application is a bit of work because you have to understand how the generator constructs its code.

As usual, the quicker and easier methods are less flexible. Hand coding always yields the most flexible method. However, the quicker and easier methods generate code that is completely modifiable, so you can always get what you want. The best and fastest method for most beginners who still want some control is the data web beans method.

Types of JSP Code

You build JSPs by writing code using JSP elements of different types—HTML tags, standard JSP tags, and JDeveloper JSP elements. The hands-on practices demonstrate these different types, and this section describes and supplies examples. This is not intended to be a complete guide to each of these elements but should get you started and give you a foundation for learning more from the JDeveloper help system and other information sources.

HTML Tags

Most HTML tags are paired to have a starting tag and an ending tag inside which you embed text or other content (such as graphics or JavaScript). The tag (delimited by < > symbols) defines how the browser should process the content. Here is an example:

```
<B>This is bold. </B>This is not bold.
```

The browser will interpret the <B> tag and display everything between it and the matching closing tag </B> in boldface as in the following illustration:

Table 8-1 lists some common tags. An example containing the tags appears in Figure 8-1. Tags are not case sensitive, so that <b> works the same way as <B>.

Opening Tag	Ending Tag	Purpose
`<HTML>`	`</HTML>`	Declares the beginning and end of the page. Anything outside these tags will not be placed in the page.
`<HEAD>`	`</HEAD>`	Page heading that will not print on the page.
`<TITLE>`	`</TITLE>`	This displays the text inside the tags as the window title. It is commonly placed inside the page heading tags.
`<BODY>`	`</BODY>`	Anything inside these tags is treated as display content for the page.
`<H1>`	`</H1>`	Heading level one, which displays text in a larger font. There are also `<H2>` through `<H6>` tags (with corresponding closing tags) for smaller heading levels. You can align the heading (left, right, or center) with the ALIGN attribute.
`<p>`	(none)	An unpaired tag that starts a paragraph. Hard returns and extra spaces in HTML code are ignored, so you need to define the return and space with a tag.
` `	(none)	An unpaired tag that inserts a line break. Line breaks insert a smaller vertical space between lines than do paragraph markers.
` `	(none)	An unpaired tag that inserts a space. The browser will remove consecutive spaces if they are not defined with this tag. The tag does not appear within a set of angle brackets "`<>`."
`<B>`	`</B>`	Displays the text in boldface.
`<I>`	`</I>`	Displays the text in italics.

TABLE 8-1.   *Common HTML Tags*

Opening Tag	Ending Tag	Purpose
`<A>`	`</A>`	An anchor that links to another file, page, or location on the same page. The most common attribute for this tag is HREF, which defines a hyperlink to another page or another location on the same page as shown in the example.
`<!--`	`-->`	Comments that are not processed. Comments, as well as other tags, are displayed when the user selects View Source from the right-click menu on the browser page.
`<UL>`	`</UL>`	An unordered list. These tags surround a list of paragraphs that start with the `<LI>` (list item) tag. Use `<OL>` and `</OL>` for an "ordered list," where list items are numbered.
`<HR>`	(none)	An unpaired tag that inserts a hard rule (horizontal line). The sample code shows two HR attributes: ALIGN and WIDTH.

TABLE 8-1. *Common HTML Tags* (continued)

NOTE
Many tags have documented tag attributes that refine how the tag is interpreted. Attributes appear before the closing ">" after the tag name. For example, the heading tag in the sample code contains an ALIGN attribute (`<H1 ALIGN=CENTER>`) that signals the browser to center the heading text within the browser window. When the window width is changed, the text recenters within the new size.

Sample HTML Code

The following is a sample of HTML code that demonstrates the tags in Table 8-1.

```
<HTML>
    <HEAD>
        <TITLE>Sample HTML Tags</TITLE>
    </HEAD>
    <BODY>
        <H1 ALIGN=CENTER>Samples of Basic HTML Tags</H1>
        The font for plain body text depends on the browser settings.
        <B>This is bold. </B>
        <I>This is italic. </I>This is not.
        <B><I>This is both.</B></I>

        <p>New paragraph before this sentence.<br>Line break before this sentence.

        <p>There are ten spaces between this
             
             
        and this.

        <br>Extra spaces              without tags are ignored.

        <p>The same applies
        to
        line breaks
        in the code.
        <p>

        <!-- A comment: the anchor tag has several attributes. HREF is one -->
        JDeveloper is a product of
        <A HREF="http://www.oracle.com">Oracle Corporation.</A>

        <HR WIDTH=80% ALIGN=CENTER>
        <B>Unordered List</B>
        <UL>
            <LI>An item in a list
            <LI>Another item in a list
            <LI>Yet another item in a list
            <LI>Still another item in a list
        </UL>
    </BODY>
</HTML>
```

Figure 8-1 shows how this code will display in the browser.

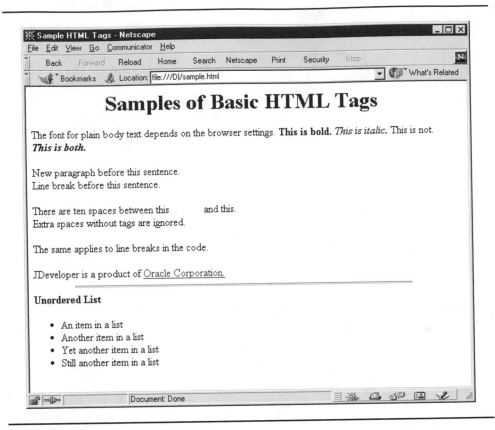

FIGURE 8-1. *Output of sample HTML code*

JavaScript in HTML

You can supplement the functionality of HTML by embedding code written in JavaScript. For example, you can use JavaScript to perform data validation on the client side, which saves network traffic. *JavaScript* is an object-based scripting language designed to extend the capabilities of HTML and allow you to embed structured and object-oriented logic in an otherwise unstructured language. Although it is beyond the scope of this book to describe the basics of JavaScript, the following sample will help you become familiar with what JavaScript looks like. You will then be able to recognize it in the code that JDeveloper creates.

```
<HTML>
<HEAD>
   <SCRIPT LANGUAGE="JavaScript">
   <!--
   function checkRequired(which) {
```

```
        if (which.fname.value == '') {
            alert("The Name field is required.");
            return false;
        }
        else
            which.fname.value = which.fname.value.toUpperCase();
            return true;
        }
    -->
    </SCRIPT>
</HEAD>

<BODY>
    <FORM ONSUBMIT = "return checkRequired(this)">
    First Name:  <INPUT TYPE="text" NAME="fname">
    <P><INPUT TYPE=SUBMIT VALUE="Save">
    </FORM>
</BODY>
</HTML>
```

The HTML tags in the body section display a label, a text item, and a button, as shown here:

The *HTML form* is a construct that allows the user to input values and click a Submit or Reset button. The entered values are passed to the process or procedure defined in the form tag. In this example, the <FORM> tag defines the form as well as what happens when the button that is labeled "Save" (and defined by the < INPUT TYPE=SUBMIT tag) is clicked. When the button is clicked, the JavaScript function checkRequired(), defined in the page header comments, is executed. If a value is input into the field, the checkRequired() function converts the value to uppercase and returns a Boolean true; the submit feature of the form calls the page again and passes it a parameter of the field value (this value will appear in the URL). If no value is input, the checkRequired() function displays an error message and returns a Boolean false; the form is not submitted in this case. This demonstrates one way that JavaScript is defined and called, but you will need to consult a JavaScript reference for further information.

NOTE
It is important to test your application using the browsers that your users will employ to access your application. If you do not know which browsers your users have, you should test your application on Netscape and Internet Explorer. Some JavaScript is not supported in Internet Explorer, so if you use JavaScript, this kind of test is particularly important.

Cascading Style Sheets

Cascading style sheets are another extension to HTML that enable a set of common definitions to serve many uses within an HTML document. Although cascading style sheets can be embedded in the HTML page head, they can also be placed in a separate file that can be used by many pages; JDeveloper uses the separate file strategy because it is the most flexible and maintainable for multipage applications. The file has a .css extension and is located in the JDEV_HOME\myhtml\webapps directory tree. There are two cascading style sheets included with JDeveloper—oracle.css (in the css subdirectory) and cabo_styles.css (in the cabo\images subdirectory). Each has a different set of fonts and colors.

Building a Cascading Style Sheet   A cascading style sheet allows you to define and name a set of attributes that you want to apply to HTML tags. For example, here is an excerpt from the cabo_styles.css file:

```
.LIGHTPANEL {
   background-color:#FFFFFF }
.SOFTPANEL {
   background-image:url(images/page_background_blue.gif);
   background-color:#99CCFF}
.HELPTEXT {
   font-family:Arial, Helvetica, Geneva, sans-serif;
   color:#000000;
   font-size:10pt }
```

In this example, there are three global styles defined: LIGHTPANEL, SOFTPANEL, and HELPTEXT. Each has different attribute settings. A *global style* is preceded by a "." and may be used for any tag.

You can also define styles for HTML tags so that each time the tag is used, the style will be applied. This simplifies the HTML coding a great deal because you do not have to repeat a common set of attributes each time you use a tag. For example, you can use the following in your cascading style sheet to define the appearance of H2 text:

```
H3 {
    font-family: Arial;
    font-style: italic;
    color: green }
```

There are also tag-specific styles that only alter a single tag (for example, H2). The style name would be prefixed with the tag name, for example:

```
H2.DISABLEDFONT {
    font-family:Arial, Helvetica, Geneva, sans-serif;
    color:#CCCCCC
}
```

This means that only the H2 tag will use the DISABLEDFONT attribute.

Using a Cascading Style Sheet   Using a cascading style sheet is a matter of referencing the style sheet location (if it is an external file and not embedded in the HTML comments) and using the styles in the HTML document. An external cascading style sheet file is declared for a JSP page using an HTML tag in the head section, as in the following example:

```
<LINK REL=STYLESHEET TYPE="text/css" HREF="/webapp/cabo/images/cabo_styles.css">
```

When the HTML code requires one of the styles, it uses the CLASS attribute to reference the style. For example, the following tag specifies that the HELPTEXT style will be used to display this heading in the body of the HTML file:

```
<H2 CLASS=HELPTEXT>For more help, contact Technical Support.</H2>
```

The CLASS attribute designates that the HELPTEXT style should be applied to the H2 line. If a style had a specific tag assigned to it (as with the H2.DISABLEDFONT example before), you would not need the attribute, as follows:

```
<H2>This is heading three.</H2>
```

The style that was predefined for H2 would be applied.

While this is not a full discussion about cascading style sheets, it should get you started, just like the brief mentions of the other languages in this chapter.

Adding an HTML Editor to the Menu

Since the recommended methodology for creating a JSP application includes working out the visual layout in a separate HTML tool, it is handy to be able to run that tool from the JDeveloper menu. The following steps allow you to add an editor (in this case MS FrontPage) to the JDeveloper Tools menu.

1. Close JDeveloper. You will be modifying a configuration file, and JDeveloper reads this file only when starting.

2. Open Windows Explorer and navigate to the JDEV_HOME\bin directory.

3. Open Notepad and drop the file Tools.cfg from the directory in Windows Explorer into Notepad.

4. Scroll down to the end of the file and insert the following lines:

```
FrontPage
C:\Program Files\Microsoft FrontPage\bin\fpeditor.exe
.
$NodeName
```

All entries in this file span four lines. The information is position sensitive, so you must place the correct information on the proper line.

5. Substitute the name and path of the executable as appropriate. (For example, if you do not have FrontPage installed, use Notepad for the purposes of testing this technique.) The first line designates the name that will appear in the menu. The second line is the name and path of the program that you will execute. The third line is the working directory name for the file (not used in this example). The last line is a substitution keyword that indicates that the file selected in the Navigation Pane will open automatically in the editor.

6. Save the file and close Notepad.

7. To confirm that this works, open JDeveloper and open a JSP project.

8. Doubleclick a JSP file to open it in the JDeveloper Source Editor. Be sure that the JSP file is selected in the Navigator, and select **Tools** | **FrontPage** from the menu.

9. FrontPage (or whatever program you substituted) will open and load the JSP file. Edit the file, save, and close it.

10. When you return to JDeveloper, a dialog will ask if you want to reload the file into the editor. If you click Yes, you will be able to see the changes that you made in FrontPage.

Standard JSP Tags

JSP tags are nonpaired symbols that may be refined using attributes. Most JSP tags start with "<%" characters and end with "%>" characters. Some use a "<jsp:" prefix and add a method or other word (for example, <jsp:useBean). These nonstandard or custom tags usually end with the characters "/>," although they may use an HTML-style closing tag </keyword>. The contents of the tag between the starting and ending symbols are evaluated by the JSP engine. There are a relatively small number of JSP tags and instructions (or *directives*) as follows:

- **Taglib Directive**   JSP technology allows you to extend the standard JSP tag set by defining your own tags. The taglib directive declares the custom tag library that you will be using and must appear before you use a particular tag. For example, the directive <%@ taglib uri="/webapp/DataTags.tld" prefix="jbo" %> uses the uri attribute to declare a tag library descriptor (.tld file) and defines that the tag will use a prefix of jbo (for example, a custom tag might be <jbo:ApplicationModule   />).

- **JSP Forward**   The forward tag (<jsp:forward>) passes a request to another JSP, servlet, or HTML file. The request may include parameters and values. A simple example would be <jsp:forward page="JSP01.jsp" />.

- **Include Directive**   An include directive (<jsp:include />) allows you to dynamically embed HTML, JSP, or text files when the JSP code runs. The text of the file that you include adds to the text that the JSP file creates. This is a powerful feature that you can use to implement the same look-and-feel if the file you are including is common to all pages. To embed a JSP in another JSP, you would use code such as <jsp:include page="JSP01.jsp" flush="true" />, and both JSPs would be merged.

- **Expression**   This tag (<%=   %>) evaluates its contents and outputs the result. The contents of the tag can be any valid expression in the JSP scripting language (usually Java), such as the return value from a function or a mathematical expression (for example, <%= 5 * 10 %>).

- **Output Comment**   This tag (<!-- -->) is a standard HTML comment that appears in the JSP and the HTML file that it produces. The comment is visible when the user selects View Source from the right-click menu.

- **JSP include (no parse)**   This tag (<jsp:include   />) inserts another file where the tag appears in the JSP file. The included file will be output as is without being interpreted by the JSP container. Therefore, the included file is usually a plain text file or another HTML file.

■ **Page Comment** This tag (`<%-- --%>`), also called a *hidden comment* in the Sun literature, is a comment that is not passed to the HTML file. Its purpose is to give programming comments in the JSP file.

■ **Page Directive** A page directive (`<%@ %>`) sets up statements that apply to the entire JSP page, such as the script language, error page, Java libraries that are required (like the CLASSPATH), and the content type. For example: `<%@ page language = "java" errorPage="errorpage.jsp" import = "java.util.*, oracle.jbo.*, oracle.jbo.html.databeans.*" contentType="text/html;charset=ISO-8859-1" %>`.

■ **JSP useBean** The useBean tag (`<jsp:useBean> </jsp:useBean>`) allows you to embed a web bean inside the JSP file. A web bean is a Java class that outputs HTML. You can pass attributes to this bean to alter its functionality and define its use. For example: `<jsp:useBean id="mainToolbar" scope="page" class="oracle.jdeveloper.jsp.wb.Toolbar"> </jsp:useBean>`.

■ **Scriptlet** A scriptlet is a piece of code written in the JSP scripting language (usually Java) that can accomplish tasks such as declaring variables and methods, writing expressions, and using beans or other objects.

■ **JSP setProperty** The setProperty tag (`<jsp:setProperty />`) works against web beans (described later). It assigns the property of an existing web bean object. The object must be instantiated before you call the setProperty tag. An example is `<jsp:setProperty name="newItem" property="value" value="Harry" />`. This would set the *value* property of the newItem object to "Harry."

■ **JSP getProperty** This tag (`<jsp:getProperty />`) works against web beans. It returns the value of the bean's properties. The bean must be used before this tag so that it has been instantiated. A sample call is `<jsp:getProperty name="newItem" property="value" />`. In this example, the *value* property of the item called "newItem" will be printed on the page.

■ **JSP Plugin** This tag (`<jsp:plugin> </jsp:plugin>`) runs an applet or bean that may require a browser extension (plug-in). The JSP engine returns a tag ("embed" for Internet Explorer or "object" for Netscape). There are a number of attributes that specify the plug-in name, specify the type (bean or applet), set the size of the display window, specify the directory that contains the plug-in, and so on.

A short example is `<jsp:plugin type="applet"
code="ShowVideo.class" codebase="/devices/"
name="MainVideo" align="bottom"> </jsp:plugin>`.
You can embed parameters between the starting and ending tags.

■ **Declaration** This tag declares a variable or method that is used in the JSP code. For example: `<%! int loopCounter = 1; %>`.

The order shown in this list is the same as the order in the JSP Tags folder of the JSP Element Wizard (**Wizards | JSP Element**), as shown in Figure 8-2. Each of these tags is well documented on the Sun Microsystems web site (java.sun.com/products/jsp/tags/tags.html, at the time that this chapter was written), and you should refer to that site for further information about each tag. In fact, the JDeveloper help system points the user to this site from the help system topics instead of repeating the text. Click the Help button after selecting an element in the wizard to display the link page. The hands-on practices at the end of this chapter will demonstrate some of these tags.

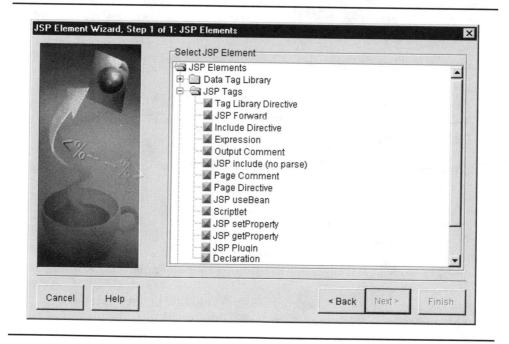

FIGURE 8-2. *JSP Tags folder of the JSP Element Wizard*

JDeveloper JSP Elements

In addition to the standard JSP language elements, JDeveloper provides a number of JSP elements for displaying data items and other components. As mentioned earlier, the JSP Element Wizard divides the elements into the following folders:

- Data Tag Library

- Web Beans (HTML Web Beans)

- Data Web Beans

- Themes

Items in the Folders

As with the other categories of JSP elements, reference material is so readily available that there is no need to provide detailed explanations for each element. The main reference material is available directly in the JDeveloper help system. Therefore, there is no need to search for other online information sources, but you can find white papers about JSPs on the Oracle TechNet web site (otn.oracle.com). For example, as of this writing, there is a white paper on that site that describes how to build JSP applications using the custom Oracle tag libraries.

TIP
The fastest way to navigate to a JSP tag reference topic in the help system is to open the JSP Element Wizard and select the tag in the list. Click the Help button, and the help system will load the topic that is specific to the tag. The wizard folder nodes also have help system topics that describe the category of tags that they contain.

In addition to the reference material and white papers, an Online Orders demo application is provided with JDeveloper. This application builds a JSP application from the ground up and contains examples of how to use various tags. There is nothing like studying working code for learning a programming concept, and this demo provides such code.

For the purposes of this chapter, it is useful to list the tags that each folder contains with a brief description of each tag. This list will give you an idea of the range and scope of functionality and help you recognize the tags when you see them in code that JDeveloper generates. The following list is divided into the main folders in the JSP Element Wizard.

Data Tag Library

This folder contains *BC4J data tags*—JSP custom tags that access data through the BC4J components. The tags allow for all kinds of database operations on the data. Table 8-2 lists the tags in this category using the order in which they appear in the wizard. A similar table in the help system topic "Working with Data Tags for Business Components" also includes the syntax statement. The full syntax for each of the tags includes a jbo prefix (for example, `<jbo.ApplicationModule />`).

Tag	Description
ApplicationModule	Creates an instance of a connection to the BC4J application module. This application module object is accessed when data is required by the other tags.
DataSource	Creates an instance of a data source from a view object that exists in the BC4J components or that is created with the CreateViewObject tag.
CreateViewObject	Dynamically creates a view object from a SELECT statement.
Row	Performs an insert, update, or delete action on a specified row. This tag also locates a row and sets the current record pointer.
RowsetNavigate	Allows you to move to the previous, next, first, or last record in the data source.
RowsetIterate	Loops through all rows in a specific data source.
RefreshDataSource	Re-executes the query that populates the data source. This is necessary after a post or commit operation that affects modified rows.
ShowValue	Displays a value from an item in a data source.
RenderValue	Displays special datatypes such as video, sound, or images that need to be *rendered*, or viewed in a specific tool (*renderer*) that is equipped to handle it.
SetAttribute	Modifies the value of a specified attribute in a data source.

TABLE 8-2. *Tag Library Tags*

Tag	Description
InputText	Displays a text field in an HTML form.
InputRender	Displays a special datatype (video, sound, or images) in a special tool inside a form.
InputSelect	Displays a list in an HTML form. The list can allow single or many selections.
InputSelectLOV	Displays a list-of-values (LOV) in a separate page. The LOV can include more than one column, unlike the InputSelect tag.
InputSelectGroup	Displays a radio button group or checkbox group in an HTML form.
InputDate	Displays a field for a date in an HTML form.
InputPassword	Displays a password for a date in an HTML form.
InputHidden	Inserts a hidden field into an HTML form. This is used if the data must be passed to another application but not displayed on the page.
InputTextArea	Inserts a multiline text field in an HTML form.
Commit	Writes changes to the database that were made in the data source or directly to the database using an ExecuteSQL tag.
Rollback	Reverses changes to the database made in the data source or directly to the database using ExecuteSQL.
PostChanges	Issues a post operation, where data is marked as available for queries but not yet saved to the database.
ExecuteSQL	Issues a SQL statement (except for SELECT) directly on the database.
ReleasePageResources	Sets the state that the application module instance uses to service HTTP requests. The default for JSP pages is "Stateless."

TABLE 8-2. *Tag Library Tags* (continued)

Web Beans (HTML Web Beans)

The term *web bean* refers to special JavaBeans that output HTML tags. There are two categories of web beans: those that do not interact with the database (HTML web beans) and those that do interact with the database (data web beans). The JSP Element Wizard uses the term "web bean" for the folder of tags as a shortened version of "HTML web beans." Therefore, the tags visible in this node of the wizard represent web beans that are not data aware. The syntax for all kinds of web beans is similar. Here is an example of what the JSP Element Wizard inserts for the Toolbar web bean:

```
<jsp:useBean
    class="oracle.jdeveloper.jsp.wb.Toolbar"
    id="mainToolbar"
    scope="request" >
<%
    mainToolbar.initialize(application,session, request,response,out);
    mainToolbar.addButton("/webapp/images/browse.gif",
        "/EmpBrowse_page.jsp", "Browse");
    mainToolbar.addButton("/webapp/images/save.gif",
        "/EmpSave_page.jsp", "Save");
    mainToolbar.render();
%>
</jsp:useBean>
```

The first part of this code is the web bean tag `jsp:useBean`, with attributes that define the class file with its path, the ID that is used in the JSP code to reference the object, and the *scope* (where the ID for the bean will be available). The second part of the syntax is a call to the bean's methods for initializing, setting up, and rendering (drawing) the object. All types of web beans (HTML web beans and data web beans) use this syntax.

Table 8-3 contains a list of JDeveloper web beans ordered as they are in the wizard. You can add your own beans to this list if required.

NOTE
The web beans that have a name prefixed by "JS" use JavaScript for extended functionality. They are similar to the web beans with the same name and no prefix.

Name	Class	Purpose
Toolbar	Toolbar	An HTML toolbar with two default buttons. You can define more buttons and specify the actions that the buttons execute.
Table Control	TableControl	An HTML table structure with columns, rows, and sample content for each cell.
Edit Form	EditForm	An HTML form used for transferring user input to another page or function. Two text fields and a hidden field are created by default.
JS Toolbar	JSToolbar	Similar to Toolbar, but includes JavaScript.
JS Table Control	JSTable	Similar to TableControl, but includes JavaScript.
JS Tree Control	JSTree	A multilevel data display with nodes and folders. The control requires use of the JSTreeData bean to set up the data elements. You need to modify the sample methods to display the data in the proper form.
JS Button Control	JSButton	This displays a button on the page. You have to define the label, name, and action that is taken when the button is clicked.
JS Button Bar Control	JSButtonBar	This sets up a row of buttons that you can modify. The sample code generated by the wizard provides the main parameters to be modified, such as the URL link.

TABLE 8-3. *JDeveloper HTML Web Beans*

Name	Class	Purpose
JS Container	JSContainer	This creates a container with three frames that you can modify to provide a consistent user interface. This control is used by the default theme to show a container with a company logo on the top of the page and a cancel button on the bottom.
JS Tab Container	JSTabContainer	Similar to the JS Container frame arrangement, but includes two tabs that can switch the user from one page to another.

TABLE 8-3.   *JDeveloper HTML Web Beans* (continued)

You can use these controls in conjunction with the Data Tag Library tags to display data from the database. However, it is simpler from the programming standpoint to use data web beans (as described later).

Data Web Beans

The Data Web Beans folder in the JSP Element Wizard represents a type of web bean that is capable of interacting with BC4J components. Data web beans are the HTML counterpart of the Data-Aware Controls (DAC) that Oracle provides for Java applications and applets. The types of available controls are similar to the web bean controls, but have the added feature of easy interaction with the business components layer. They greatly simplify the task of loading data into a web page and formatting it for presentation because they supply not only the HTML formatting but also the database connectivity.

Table 8-4 lists the data web beans that are installed with JDeveloper using the order in which the wizard displays them. The beans with a "JS" prefix include JavaScript-enhanced functionality. You can add your own beans to this list, as you can with the HTML web beans. The hands-on practices will demonstrate how to add a web bean to these lists.

Name	Class	Purpose
Navigator Bar	NavigatorBar	Generates a toolbar with database record navigation buttons similar in function to the InfoSwing NavigationBar component used for Java applications and applets.
RowSet Browser	RowSetBrowser	Creates an HTML multi-row table with data from the data source that is defined in the tags.
Edit Current Record	EditCurrentRecord	Creates an HTML form with controls such as text fields that you can use to edit a row. This supplies the main functionality that you would require from an edit page.
View Current Record	ViewCurrentRecord	Generates HTML text that displays a single record with columns that you specify.
Find Form	FindForm	Displays a page with fields for entering query conditions. There are buttons for executing the query, clearing the query, and adding conditions.
XML Data Generator	XmlData	This tag generates XML data and inserts the tags into the HTML file that displays the data.
RowSet Navigator	RowSetNavigator	This web bean allows you to change the current record in a row set. It is not a visual bean.

TABLE 8-4. *JDeveloper Data Web Beans*

Name	Class	Purpose
Chart	ChartRenderer	Displays a chart object based on the data you associate with the object. The wizard contains custom pages to request the chart type, labels, and data.
JS Navigator Bar	JSNavigatorBar	Similar to the Navigator Bar web bean, but this one is enhanced by JavaScript functionality.
JS RowSet Browser	JSRowSetBrowser	Displays multiple rows from a given row set. It is like the RowSet Browser but includes JavaScript functionality.
JS View Current Record	JSViewCurrentRecord	This bean displays a single record on the HTML page from a row set. It is similar to the ViewCurrentRecord but includes JavaScript functionality.
JS Tree Browser	JSTreeBrowser	This bean displays a hierarchical tree view of a row set using JavaScript. The bean is similar to the HTML web bean JS Tree Control except that it is data aware.

TABLE 8-4. *JDeveloper Data Web Beans* (continued)

This set of controls takes care of a significant percentage of the functions that you might require in a complete application. The Online Orders demo gives you examples of code to change and copy so that you can customize the web bean usage for your requirements. Using the data web beans is an interim level between the method of hand coding low-level HTML and Data Tag Library calls and the high-level method of using the Business Components JSP Application Wizard to create a JSP application. The wizard generates working code quickly but has few options for customization. Hand coding with HTML and the Data Tag Library tags is slower, but provides the ultimate flexibility. Data web beans give you many of the benefits of both techniques.

TIP
The Business Components JSP Application Wizard creates working code that uses many of the data web beans. You can look at a sample that it creates or ideas about how to write your own code using these beans.

Themes

The *JSP theme* defines the visual elements of the generated pages. JSP themes are different from other types of themes used in JDeveloper. They consist of a cascading style sheet file (discussed earlier) that contains predefined styles and tags. The style sheet makes building a common look-and-feel in HTML pages much easier. In addition, they define a set of images that are used for a standard appearance. Table 8-5 shows the themes and their location.

NOTE
The file name for the default theme is oracle.css.

With this background material about the process of creating a JSP and on the languages and tags, you are ready to build some JSPs with JDeveloper.

TIP
Information about creating JSP themes is available in the help system topic "Creating a New JSP Theme" under the "Creating JSP Pages\Creating a New JSP Theme" topic in the Contents tab.

Theme	Cascading Style Sheet File
Default	JDEV_HOME\myhtml\webapp\css\oracle.css
Oracle	JDEV_HOME\myhtml\webapp\cabo\images\cabo_styles.css

TABLE 8-5. *JDeveloper JSP Themes*

What to Do After You Finish the Wizard

The Business Components JSP Application Wizard allows you to quickly build an application with default functionality. For production systems, you will need to go beyond the defaults, and this requires modifying the code that the wizards create. There are several different levels where you can modify the code or which you can use to build the code from scratch.

You can use the data web bean layer with beans such as oracle.jbo.html. databeans.EditCurrentRecord to supply functionality for an edit page. As with all web beans, this bean contains a number of methods that save you time and effort. For example, the setMaximumFieldWidth() method allows you to specify how wide the field will be for a particular attribute. The Javadoc for the web beans that is available in the JSP Element Wizard provides details on all the available methods. You add the calls to these methods inside the JSP jsp:usebean tag. The source code for web beans is located in the JDEV_HOME\src\jbohtmlsrc.zip library file. You can browse and copy this code for use in your own code.

You can create custom data web beans that you use in your JSP code (as in the hands-on practice later). This technique means that you are working on a lower level and there are more manual operations that you need to perform, such as rendering a data value in HTML. This level of working gives you flexibility and power, but there is the additional complexity of handling the data access methods.

The first thing you should do after running the wizard is to examine the code in detail. Then look at other examples provided by Oracle to see how customizations can be performed. An example is worth many explanations. Load and run the sample auction application by opening JDEV_HOME\samples\bc4j\bc4J\ bc4jauctions\bc4jauctions.jws. This sample contains many useful techniques that you can copy. In addition, currently on the JDeveloper product page of Oracle Technology Network (otn.oracle.com/products/jdev/) are the following white papers and demos:

- Building JSP Applications with BC4J Data Tags
- BC4J Data Tags demo script
- Building JSP Internet Applications with Oracle JDeveloper

The time you spend in examining and evaluating how these code examples will pay off when you need to create a production JSP application.

Hands-on Practice Preparation

To prepare a workspace for the practices, use the following steps:

1. Select **File | New Workspace** and **File | Save Workspace**.

2. Create a new folder called "empappjsp" and navigate to that folder. Name the workspace "EmpJSPWS" and click Save. See the sidebar "Alternative Method for Creating a Folder" for a variation on these steps.

Alternative Method for Creating a Folder

Examples in the hands-on practices for this book have used a particular method for creating a folder to hold the project and workspace files. This method consists of saving a new workspace before any project files are added. At that time, you create a folder that represents a package to hold the workspace and project files.

There is an alternative method that you can use when creating the first project in a new workspace. The following technique automates the folder creation step using a feature of the Project Wizard. You may use the following steps wherever the hands-on practices create a folder in the Project Wizard.

1. Select **File | New Workspace**.

2. Select **File | New Project**. In the *What is the project's filename?* field on the Project Type page, add the name of a new folder to the path. For example, the default value in this field is "JDEV_HOME\myprojects\MyProject1.jpr." You can change this by adding a directory and changing the file name, for example, to "JDEV_HOME\myprojects\empappjsp\EmpJSP.jpr." If the "empappjsp" folder does not exist, the Project Wizard will display a confirmation dialog when you click the Next button and create the folder if you click Yes.

3. Select the new directory for the default package in the Project Options page of the Project Wizard. Complete the Project Wizard.

4. When you click Save All for the first time with this new workspace, a save dialog will appear. Navigate to the new directory that the Project Wizard created (step 2), name the workspace file (for example, "EmpJSPWS.jws"), and click Save.

This method requires fewer steps to create the directory so you may find it faster. However, you need to be careful since you may do more work before saving the workspace.

Hands-on Practice: Building a Simple JSP Application

This hands-on practice steps you through creating a simple JSP application that does not connect to the database. The intention is to become comfortable with this style of application and how you work with it in JDeveloper. This practice has the following major phases:

- **I. Create and run a simple JSP file**
- **II. Organize the project with folders**
- **III. Add other JSP directives**
  - **Add code manually**
  - **Add code using the wizard**

Be sure that you have created the blank workspace as described in "Hands-on Practice Preparation."

I. Create and Run a Simple JSP File

The first phase demonstrates how to add an empty JSP file to a new project.

1. Select **File | New Empty Project**.

2. Select **File | Save As** and navigate to the empappjsp directory. Name the project "HellojspPRJ" and click Save. This adds a new project to the workspace.

3. Select **File | New** and navigate to the Web Objects tab. Doubleclick JSP. This will add an empty JSP file inside the new project.

4. Select **File | Save As.** A directory with the name of the project file and a suffix of "_html" will be created in the JDEV_HOME\myhtml directory. In this case, the directory name is HellojspPRJ_html. Name the file "HelloWWW," and click Save.

5. Doubleclick the JSP file in the Navigation Pane to open the source code in the viewer. Although this is a complete JSP file and you can run it as is, it is really only an empty framework to which you add objects and code.

6. Look for the JSP directive (`% out.println("Hello World"); %>`) under the body tag (`<BODY>`). This directive starts with the HTML tag opening symbol (`<`) and the JSP tag symbol (`%`). The instruction within the

JSP tag is a print statement (`out.println()`). Change the printed text to "Hello World Wide Web." Click Save All.

7. Be sure that the JSP file is selected in the Navigation Pane and click Run. The browser will start and display the message as Figure 8-3 shows. Display the page source in the browser (select View Source from the right-click menu). You will see something like the following:

```
<HTML>
<HEAD>
<META HTTP-EQUIV="Content-Type" CONTENT="text/html; charset=WINDOWS-1252">
<META NAME="GENERATOR" CONTENT="Oracle JDeveloper">
<TITLE>
Hello World
</TITLE>
</HEAD>
<BODY>
<H2>The following output is from JSP code:</H2><P>Hello World Wide Web
</P>
</BODY>
</HTML>
```

Compare this source with the JSP file source code. You will see that the JSP directives (<% %> tags) have been processed and stripped out of the output. HTML tags are shown exactly as they are in the JSP source file.

What Just Happened?   You created a project and added a JSP file to it. You also ran the file using the JDeveloper built-in web server emulator (Web-to-go). Building JSP files requires interaction with the Source Editor, and you modified the sample code that is built into the JSP file.

Note for Oracle Developer Users

Web-to-go allows you to test a web server JSP application without having a real web server available. You do not need to create a deployment file set and move it to the web server because the entire server is emulated on your local machine. Oracle Forms Developer offers a similar facility. The Run Form Web button (in Windows NT and Windows 2000) allows you to run your form in a web server-emulation JVM without setting up a web server, installing the Forms Server, deploying the code, and running the test using a browser. These emulators make development testing much easier.

The difference in Oracle Developer Forms is that you can test the form in client/server mode as well as within the JVM. Since web applications using JSP have no client/server mode, this option is not offered in JDeveloper.

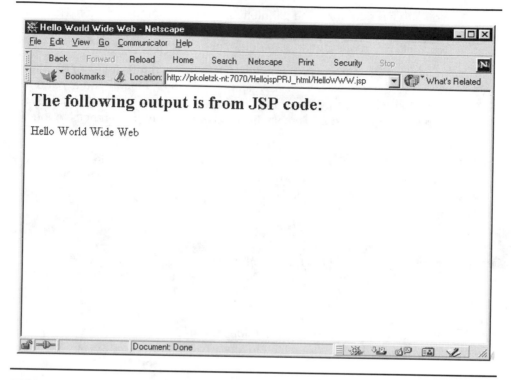

FIGURE 8-3. *Hello JSP running in the browser*

II. Organize the Project with Folders

Since each JSP file represents a page or part of a page, and a web site can require hundreds of files, there can be hundreds of JSP files in an application. To help organize these files, you can create folders within the project. The folders do not represent actual directories or folders on the disk but make it easier for you to find a JSP file.

1. Right click the project file and select Add Folder. Fill in the name as "Examples" and click OK. This will add the folder under the project node as shown here:

2. You now need to move the JSP file into the new Examples folder. This requires add and delete actions. Select the folder and click the "Add to workspace or project" (green +) button in the Navigator toolbar.

3. In the file dialog, navigate to the JDEV_HOME\myhtml\HellojspPRJ_html directory. Select the HelloWWW.jsp file and click Open. If you expand the Examples folder, you will see the file. This is the same file that is directly under the project node. The Navigator now shows two references to the same file.

4. Select the JSP file that is not under the folder and click the "Remove from workspace or project" button (red "x") in the Navigator toolbar. The file reference will be removed. Click Save All.

TIP
If you are adding many files to a folder, you can select them as a group in the file dialog using CTRL *click or* SHIFT *click. When you click Open, all files will be added to the folder.*

What Just Happened?   You added a folder and moved a JSP file into it. This is the method you would use to organize the files in a JSP project.

III. Add Other JSP Directives

As mentioned, the main work when creating a JSP application consists of adding code to the default JSP files. There are two main ways to do this: manually adding code and using the JSP Element Wizard. This phase will demonstrate both methods.

Add Code Manually

Once you become comfortable with the syntax and keywords for JSP tags, you will find it faster to enter simple tags by manually typing them into the JSP source code. These steps demonstrate that method.

1. In the Source Editor window for HelloWWW.jsp, add a blank line before the </BODY> tag that signifies the end of the HTML text body. Type the following into the blank space:

```
<!-- This is an HTML comment -->
<%-- This is a JSP comment --%>
<%// This is a Java comment %>
```

The < indicates the beginning of a tag. The % designates that this code is a JSP directive. For the Java comment, the // after the % indicates that this is an inline Java comment. Symbols after the % are passed on to Java.

2. Run the file and view the page source. You will see a line for the HTML comment but no mention of either the Java comment or the JSP comment. The Java code strips them out before the HTML page is sent to the browser.

3. Use Windows Explorer to find the Java file (HelloWWW.java) in the JDEV_HOME\myhtml\HellojspPRJ_html directory. The JSP engine creates this file when you run the JSP file for the first time. Open Notepad and load the file into it. Search for the word "comment" in this file. You will find both the Java comment and the HTML comment. The JSP comment is stripped out before the Java file is created.

Add Code Using the Wizard

You can also add the JSP and HTML comments using the JSP Element Wizard.

1. Add another blank line before the </BODY> tag and select JSP Element from the right-click menu. The JSP Element Wizard will appear, as in Figure 8-4.

2. Open the JSP Tags node and select the Page Comment element. Click Finish and the JSP comment opening and closing tag (<%-- --%>) will be added to the file. You can add text between the dashes.

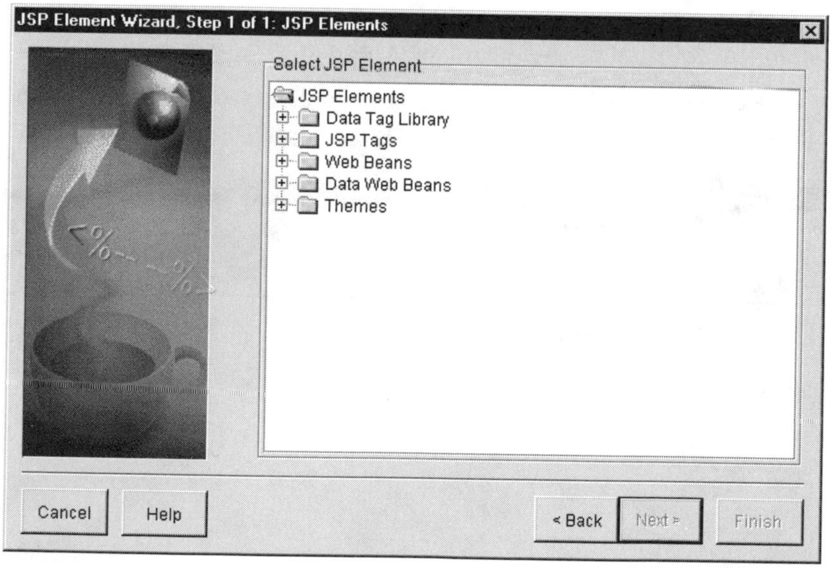

FIGURE 8-4. *JSP Element Wizard*

3. Use the JSP Element Wizard to add an Output Comment. Since the output of a JSP is an HTML page, the HTML comment tags (`<!--  -->`) will be inserted into the file. You can add text between the dashes for the comment.

NOTE
For simple tags such as comments, you will find it faster to type the code manually. However, if you don't know the exact syntax or need a refresher, the wizard is useful. It is also helpful to use for inserting Web Bean code because Web Beans require more complex coding.

4. To see the effect of inserting a web bean into the JSP file, add another blank line in the body area, select **Wizards | JSP Element**, and open the Web Beans node. As mentioned, a *web bean* is a Java class that generates HTML for a specific purpose. For example, the following step inserts a web bean that will generate HTML tags for a toolbar.

5. Select Toolbar and click the Next button. Some elements in this wizard require extra properties, and the Finish button will usually be disabled in those cases. You have to complete the properties before the element can be inserted into your file.

6. In the Property Values page, fill in the *id* value as "mainToolbar." Click Finish. The JSP directives to create a toolbar will be inserted into the file.

7. Click Save All and Run. The application will appear as shown in the following illustration:

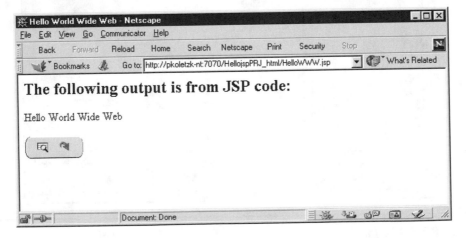

The toolbar elements have been added to the text output. Clicking the buttons displays error pages because the pages for Browse and Save have not been developed.

8. View the source for the HTML page (View Source from the right-click menu in the browser). You will see a number of additional tags that create the toolbar display and links. The *id* property that you filled in using the JSP Element Wizard does not appear in the HTML output. It is used by the Java code to identify a particular element.

9. In Windows Explorer, navigate to the JDEV_HOME\myhtml\HellojspPRJ_html directory.

10. Open Notepad and drop HelloWWW.java into it. Look for the method calls to the web bean mainToolbar (such as `mainToolbar.initialize()` and `mainToolbar.addButton()`). These methods create the HTML output that you saw in the browser.

CAUTION
The JSP Element Wizard is not reentrant for a specific bean. Therefore, you can only modify the bean's code using the Source Editor. The JSP Element Wizard is intended to give you a solid starting point for using the bean.

What Just Happened?   You added comment tags to the JSP file and examined the location of those comments in the runtime and source code files. You also added comment tags and toolbar tags using the JSP Element Wizard.

TIP
For more information and further tutorials on JSPs, look for the JSP topics in the help system Contents tab under the Tutorials and Sample Applications node.

Hands-on Practice: Creating a JSP Data Application Using the Wizard

In this practice, you will use the Business Components JSP Application Wizard to create a JSP project that interacts with the database. You can also run the DataPage Wizard to build a JSP file using BC4J Data Tag Library tags. The practice "Create

Pages with the DataPage Wizard" at the end of this chapter steps through this wizard. There are three phases in this practice:

I. **Set up the Business Components and connection**

II. **Create the JSP files**

■ **Create the JSP application**

■ **Modify the generated code**

III. **Examine the code**

If you did not run the preceding practice, follow the steps in the earlier section "Hands-on Practice Preparation" to create a workspace.

I. Set up the Business Components and Connection

The business component project used in this practice was created in the Chapter 2 hands-on practice. This business component can serve all applications that share the same data source. Although the following steps are technically not required when the database server and Java server are on the same machine, they illustrate the technique you would use when you need to split those servers.

1. With the workspace node selected in the Navigator, select **File | Open** and find the BC4J project that contains the DEPT and EMP tables (for example, DeptEmpBusCompPRJ.jpr in deptempbuscomp directory). Click Open to add it to the workspace.

2. Open the properties for your connection object by right clicking the connection (such as ScottConnection) in the Connections node, selecting Properties, and clicking the Edit button.

3. If the *Host ID* field contains a value of "localhost," change it to match the name of your machine. You can find the name of your machine by right clicking the Network Neighborhood icon on your desktop, selecting Properties, and viewing the Identification tab. Click OK and Done in the Connection dialog.

NOTE

If you move the BC4J components to another machine and the connection is defined to access "localhost," the application will look for the database on the machine that contains the BC4J components, not on the machine that actually contains the database. Defining a specific machine name for the connection will make that connection more portable because it will not matter where the BC4J definitions reside—they will always point to the specific host machine that contains the database.

4. Expand the BC4J project and package nodes. Right click the module node (its name has a suffix of "Module") and select Configurations. The Configuration Manager will be displayed, as in Figure 8-5. A *business components configuration* (also called *configuration*) defines details of the BC4J application module access to the database and the deployment characteristics. This information is stored in a file called bc4j.xcfg that appears under the package node in the Navigation Pane, as shown here. The configuration file is required by the JSP application. This file has an XML format that you can view (but not modify) in the source code viewer.

5. If there is no name in the left column, you may be working with a JDeveloper release before 3.2 or with a module that was created with an earlier release. Release 3.2 added the automatic creation of business component configurations. Follow the steps in the sidebar "Adding a Configuration" if your BC4J project does not have a configuration. Click Done to dismiss the dialog.

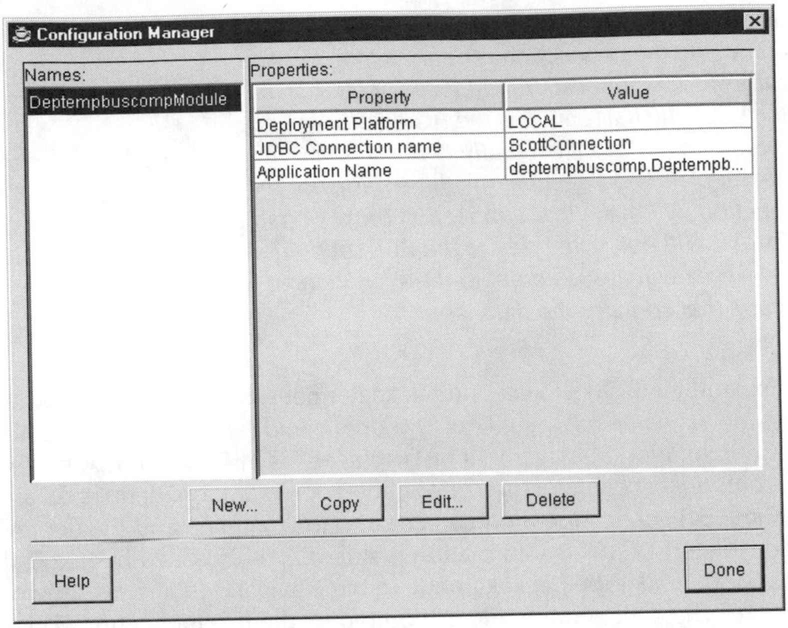

FIGURE 8-5. *Configuration Manager*

Adding a Configuration

The following steps will create a configuration for an existing BC4J project. This will be necessary if you have created the BC4J project with a JDeveloper release before 3.2. You will also need to follow this process if you need to define another set of deployment options for the same project.

1. Click New in the Configuration Manager dialog. This displays the Oracle Business Component Configuration dialog. (The Configuration Manager dialog is displayed by selecting Configurations from the right-click menu on the BC4J application module node.) If the configuration was already created, click the Edit button.

2. Change the name to "DeptempbuscompModuleCFG." The *Middle Tier Server Type* field indicates where the server for this business component will be located. Leave the selection as the default of "Local." The meaning of the choices for this field follow:

- **Local** indicates that the business component objects will reside on the same server as the application.

- **VisiBroker** indicates that you are using the Inprise VisiBroker to deploy the business components. You can select the ORB (Object Request Broker) connection type for local deployment ("Use Collocated"), a specific address ("Use Binding"), or a naming service ("Use Naming"). The help system topic "Choosing Application Module Configuration Options" provides more information.

- **Oracle8i** if the application module will be installed in the database.

- **EJB** if the module will be deployed as an Enterprise JavaBean on a remote server.

- **WebLogic** if you are using the BEA WebLogic Server.

Many of these selections require additional parameters, such as the JNDI path. *JNDI* refers to the Java Naming and Directory Interface, a Sun naming standard for files and directories.

3. Check that the *JDBC Connection* field is set to the connection that you intend to use for the business components (such as ScottConnection). The URL should include the name of the machine as you defined it in the connection properties before.

4. Navigate to the Properties tab. Browse through the properties and their values. Clicking a property will display explanatory hint text at the bottom of the dialog. It is not necessary to change any of these values, but you can get a sense of the details that the configuration stores.

5. Click OK and Done to dismiss the Configuration Manager. The "bc4j.xcfg" file will be added under the package node in the Navigation Pane.

6. Click Save All.

TIP
If you are upgrading to Release 3.2, you may find it easier to re-create your BC4J projects rather than completing upgrade steps such as the creation of the configuration file.

What Just Happened?   You added the BC4J project to the workspace so that the database objects would be accessible to the application. You also modified the connection by defining a specific machine name. In addition, you examined or set up the configuration file that defines how the BC4J application module accesses the database.

II. Create the JSP Files

In this phase, you will use the Business Components JSP Application Wizard to create an application. You will also modify it after the application has been generated.

Create the JSP Application

The following steps use the wizard to create an entire multipage application with a default look and feel.

1. Select **File | New Project** and specify the *a project containing a new* field as "Business Components JSP Application."

2. Click the Browse button and navigate to the empappjsp directory. Name the project "EmpjspPRJ" and click Open.

3. Click Next and fill in the default package name as empappjsp. Leave the other defaults and click Finish to complete the Project Wizard and start the Business Components JSP Application Wizard.

4. Click Next if the Welcome page appears. This will display the Web Site page.

5. Change the *Web Application name* field to "EmpDeptWebApp." The *Project HTML Root* field indicates the top-level directory in which the application directory will be created. The value is not updateable. The *Application directory name* field indicates the location of the project JSP and Java files. The default value for this field is the name of the project with an "_html" suffix. This name falls within the recommended naming convention guidelines.

6. Click Next to display the Business Application page, as shown here:

```
Business Components JSP Application Wizard, Step 2 of 4: Business Application          [×]

                    Select Business Project:
                    ┌────────────────────────────────────────────────┐  ┌─┐
                    │DeptEmpBusCompPRJ.jpr                            │  │▼│
                    └────────────────────────────────────────────────┘  └─┘
                    Select Application Module:
                    ┌────────────────────────────────────────────────┐
                    │deptempbuscomp.DeptempbuscompModule              │
                    │                                                 │
                    │                                                 │
                    │                                                 │
                    │                                                 │
                    └────────────────────────────────────────────────┘
                   ┌─AppModule Deployment────────────────────────────┐
                   │ Select Config : ┌───────────────────────────┐ ┌─┐│
                   │                 │DeptempbuscompModuleCFG     │ │▼││
                   │                 └───────────────────────────┘ └─┘│
                   └─────────────────────────────────────────────────┘

   ┌────────┐  ┌────────┐                  ┌────────┐ ┌────────┐ ┌────────┐
   │ Cancel │  │  Help  │                  │ < Back │ │ Next > │ │ Finish │
   └────────┘  └────────┘                  └────────┘ └────────┘ └────────┘
```

7. Ensure that the business components project and application module
names are selected. In addition, be sure that the configuration that you
created or examined earlier in this practice is selected. Although you have
only one choice in each of these fields, if your project contained more than
one business component project or there were more than one module or
configuration, you would have to select from a list.

8. Click Next to move to the Application Template page. There are two
themes (cascading style sheets and images) included with JDeveloper—
"default" and "Oracle." Each has a different color scheme and set of
images. The *template* that you specify in the Business Components JSP
Application Wizard uses the appropriate theme and preconstructed JSP
files (located in the jsp directory in the same directory structure as the
style sheets) to build the application's pages. You can build a separate
application with each template and run them to compare the differences.
Functionally, the applications will be identical, but they have different
layouts, colors, images, and navigation styles.

9. For this example, select the "Oracle" template and click Next to display the View Selection page.

10. Leave the default check marks on this page. If you did not want to generate a page for any of these views, you would select the view and uncheck the *Generate page* checkbox. There are also options on this page that allow you to specify whether you want to generate specific types of pages (query, browse, edit, and new record) for the view. These options are disabled for the Oracle template. Click Next and Finish to complete the JSP application.

11. Click Save All and Rebuild.

12. To run the application, click the main.jsp file in the Navigation Pane and click the Run button. The browser will start and present a page such as that in Figure 8-6. At this point, you are running the application in the JDeveloper emulation of a web server. You will see the machine name and the default port (7070) in the URL.

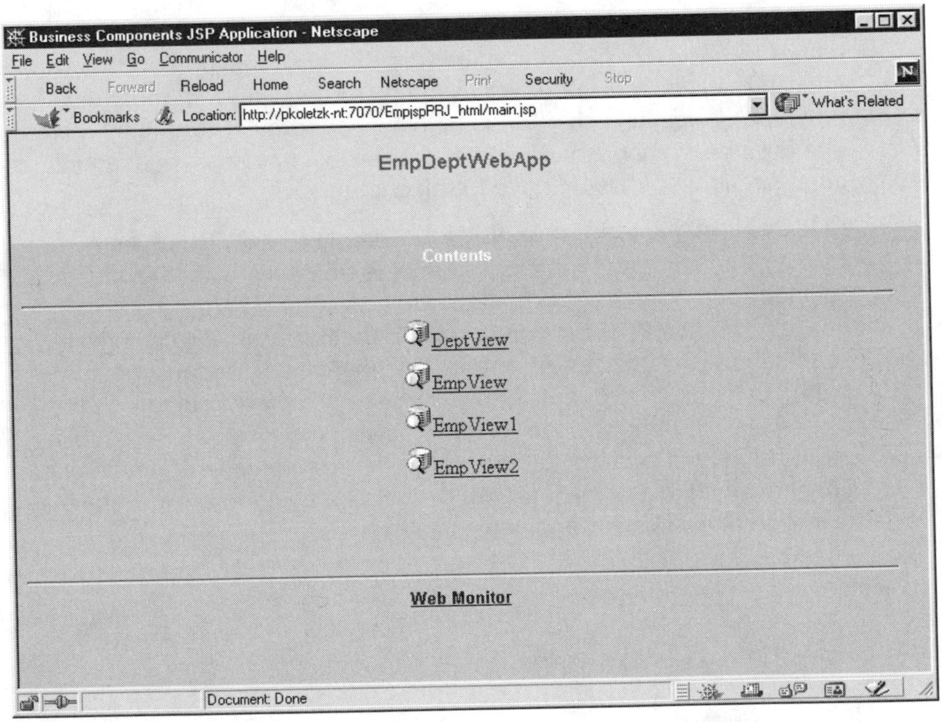

FIGURE 8-6. *Wizard-generated JSP application opening page*

13. Click the Web Monitor link. This will open another browser window with the *Web Monitor* application, which you can use to browse parameter settings for the Java and BC4J runtime as well as details about the application module pool and session. This kind of information is useful for debugging and confirming that the property settings are correctly used. Explore this application to get a feeling for the information that is available. Close the window when you are finished.

14. You can also browse the main application by clicking the view links on the opening page. The application includes navigation bars and text items that act similarly to their counterparts in a Java application or applet. Figure 8-7 shows the employee link tab page of the DeptView page. This page works like a master-detail application.

15. Try viewing, editing, and inserting data through these forms. The application uses JavaScript for some of the functionality, such as changing the icon picture when the mouse passes over a button on the navigation bar. When you use the navigation buttons in a multirecord display, such as the page in the RowSet Browser tab, the screen will redraw and a highlight

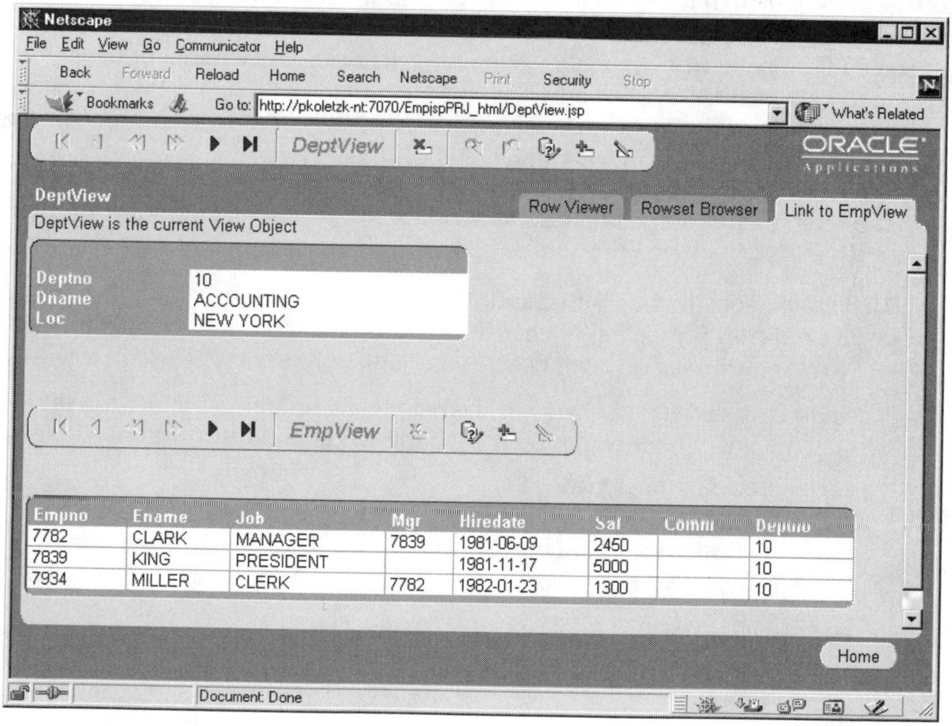

FIGURE 8-7. *Page for department link to the employee*

will appear on the current record. This highlight marks the record that will be deleted or edited by clicking the appropriate buttons in the toolbar.

Click the next record button to display the highlight in the EmpView area. Then click the edit button in that same toolbar. An edit page will open and allow you to change the employee record. There is a calendar window to help you enter the date. Click the icon next to the date field to display this window.

NOTE

The Business Components JSP Application Wizard is not reentrant. It is intended to give you a starting (and possibly ending) point for creating a JSP application using web beans. If you need to edit the application after the wizard generates it, you must modify the code in the Source Editor.

Modify the Generated Code

You can make manual modifications to the generated code if you understand the code. The help system Javadocs contain details about all the web beans, and you can use these details to determine how to change the generated code. You can also get some information from the help system topic that appears when you select the bean in the JSP Element Wizard and click the Help button. Some changes, such as the following, are fairly intuitive. You can change the tab titles in pages such as the one shown in Figure 8-7 using the following techniques.

1. Open the JSP file that represents the page (for example, DeptView.jsp in the DeptView folder) in the Source Editor.

2. Find the code that calls `tbc.addTab()` and modify the second parameter of each call. For example, change "Row Viewer" to "Dept Details," "RowSet Browser" to "Dept List," and "Link to EmpView" to "Employees."

3. Another easy thing to change is the help text that appears in the top of the tab container and the title. Locate the following code:

```
tbc.setTitle("DeptView");

tbc.setHelpText("DeptView is the current view object");
```

4. Change this to the following:

```
tbc.setTitle("Departments in Acme Corp");

tbc.setHelpText("Use the buttons to browse department information.");
```

5. Click Save All, Rebuild, and run the application (main.jsp), and verify that the new help text and tab labels are visible on the DeptView page.

What Just Happened?   You used the wizard to define and modify a JSP application that has insert, update, delete, and select functionality, including a master-detail browser. You also tested the application using the JDeveloper web server emulator.

The wizard generates a number of files that are located under folders used to organize the files in the project node. As mentioned, these folders are not actual directories in the file system. They are really just organizational areas within the project and you can use them for any type of project. The following illustration shows the DeptView folder and other folders that the wizard created.

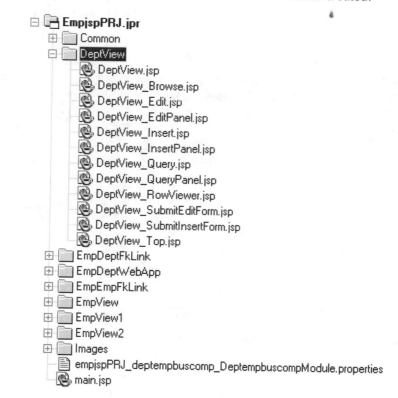

Each folder contains JSP files for the main page (such as DeptView.jsp) as well as JSP files for each of the main functions (such as DeptView_Insert.jsp for adding a record).

You can identify the function by the file name. The additional pages are called from the navigation bar buttons or from buttons on the page. For example, to call the DeptView_Insert.jsp file, the user clicks the Insert a New Record button in the navigation bar of the main page (DeptView.jsp). Try running the application and watching the URL as you move from one function to another. There should be a JSP file in the Navigation Pane for each distinct page that you see in the application.

TIP
The page in this application is built in frames, each of which is assigned a JSP page. You can determine the name of the JSP page for each frame by selecting View Frame Info (in Netscape) or Properties (in Internet Explorer) from the right-click menu on the frame.

III. Examine the Code

Another useful exercise is to view the files that the wizard and runtime engine create.

1. Using Windows Explorer, navigate to the JDEV_HOME\myhtml\ EmpjspPRJ_html directory. You will find all JSP files that are listed under the JDeveloper project node (such as DeptView.jsp). You will also find a Java file for each JSP file that uses the same base file name (such as DeptView.java). This file is created when the application is first run. This file compiles at runtime into a class file, for example, DeptView.class. The project HTML directory may also contain backup copies of the JSP and Java files. These backup files use a file name with a "~" in the file extension.

2. Open Notepad and drop into it a Java file from the HTML project directory. You will be able to recognize the HTML output calls (using the `out.print()` method) as well as calls to Java code that outputs HTML dynamically based on method calls to the web bean object (such as `tbc.setTitle("Departments in Acme Corp");`).

3. Navigate to the JDEV_HOME\myclasses\EmpjspPRJ_html directory and identify the class files (such as DeptView.class) that correspond to the .jsp files. The class file is the compiled version of the Java file. It is run by the web server to generate the HTML output. The Java and class files are stored on the server and regenerated at runtime if the source code was changed.

CAUTION
If you rename a JSP file that has been run, the Java and class files for the old name will not be renamed or deleted. You have to manually delete those files if you want to clean up the project's HTML and class directories.

What Just Happened?   You browsed the project HTML directory to examine the JSP files that are represented in the Navigator. You also found the Java and class files that the JSP files generate at runtime and that create the HTML page.

Hands-on Practice: Building a JSP Data Application Manually

Now that you have created a JSP application using the wizard, it is useful to understand what the process is like without a wizard. As with other JDeveloper wizards, you will often want to modify the code that the wizard creates. If you know the manual process of creating a JSP application, you will be better able to understand the code that the wizard creates.

This hands-on practice is intended to give you another taste of how to work with JSP applications. When you are ready to expand this knowledge, it is useful to examine the code that the wizard creates. Many techniques that you will need, such as linking pages from a navigation bar, will be clear once you analyze how the generated code works.

This practice steps you through the following phases:

I. Create a data browse page with an existing web bean

■ **Create the application**

■ **Modify the web bean directives**

■ **Modify the prompt label properties**

■ **Set up links between pages**

II. Create a data browse page with a new web bean

■ **Build a simple web bean**

■ **Build a data web bean**

■ **Modify the data web bean**

■ **Use the Web Object Manager**

If you did not run the preceding practice, follow the steps in the section "Hands-on Practice Preparation" to create a workspace. You will also need to add the BC4J project to the workspace as explained in phase I of the previous practice.

I. Create a Data Browse Page with an Existing Web Bean

This practice creates a page that displays one record at a time from the department table. It uses a web bean to navigate through the records and another web bean to display one record at a time. You enter both beans using the JSP Element Wizard, which prompts you for the BC4J data specifics.

Create the Application

The following steps show how to create a JSP application by adding web beans for a navigation bar and record browse area.

1. Create an empty project (**File | New Empty Project**) and select **File | Rename**.

2. Navigate to the empappjsp directory (or create the directory if it does not exist). Name the project "DeptjspPRJ" and click Save.

3. Add a folder by right clicking the project, selecting Add Folder, entering the name "JSP Examples," and clicking OK.

4. Create a JSP file by selecting **File | New**, clicking the Web Objects tab, and doubleclicking the JSP icon.

5. Rename the file (**File | Rename**) to "DeptRecBrowse" under the JDEV_HOME\myhtjml\DeptjspPRJ_html directory.

6. Move the JSP file into the JSP Examples folder by adding it to the folder and deleting it from the original location.

7. Click Save All. Your project node should look like the following illustration.

```
DeptjspPRJ.ipr
   JSP Examples
      DeptRecBrowse.jsp
```

TIP

*Since JSP files are located in the myhtml directory path, you need to navigate to that directory each time you want to add files to a folder. To make this easier, create a Windows shortcut in your project directory so that you can doubleclick it to navigate to the HTML directory. To create a Windows directory shortcut from JDeveloper, open the file dialog (right click the folder and select Add to Folder) and navigate to the project directory (such as empappjsp) in Windows Explorer, select **New | Shortcut** from the right-click menu, and type in the name of the directory, "JDEV_HOME\myhtml\project_html," where "project_html" is the project's HTML directory (for example, "D:\Program Files\Oracle\ JDeveloper 3.2\myhtml\deptjspPRJ_html" including quotes).*

8. Open the DeptRecBrowse.jsp file in the source code viewer if it is not already open. Replace the title "Hello World" with "Department Browser." This text will be written into the browser's window title.

9. Remove the H2 line after the body opening tag (<BODY>) and substitute the following:

```
<H1>
    Department Details
</H1>
```

10. Add a line before the body closing tag (</BODY>). This is the space in which you will place the code for the data beans. Select JSP Element from the right-click menu.

11. Open the Data Web Beans node and select Navigator Bar as shown here:

12. Click Next to move to the Property Values page. Fill in the *id* property as "deptNavBar." This property is used as a name of the instantiation of the object in the code. Click Next to display the View Object Selection page.

13. You need to specify the BC4J view object that the navigation bar will interact with. Expand the module node and select DeptView. The *Select Config* field will be automatically filled in with the configuration name. Click Finish. You will see the new section of code in the Source Editor that starts with a "`jsp:useBean`" tag. This code specifies the details, such as the class, ID, and scope, that the web bean requires and includes the calls to the bean's methods for displaying and activating the navigation bar. The lines between `<%` and `%>` will be written into the Java file without modification.

14. You now need to add the browser bean for a single record display. Add another blank line before the body closing tag.

15. Select JSP Element from the right-click menu. Expand the Data Web Beans node, select "JS View Current Record." This bean displays one record at a time in a form-style format. The "JS RowSet Browser" bean displays more than one record at a time in a table format. The beans that have a "JS" prefix use JavaScript and usually have non-JavaScript counterparts that are named without the prefix. Click Next to move to the Property Values page.

16. Fill in the *id* property as "deptRec" and click Next to display the View Object Selection page.

17. Expand the nodes and select DeptView as the view object to be displayed. Click Next to move to the Select View Properties page. This page allows you to select the columns that will be displayed on the page.

18. Select all attributes (using CTRL click or SHIFT click) and click Finish. Code will be added for the JSViewCurrentRecord web bean, including the methods that are required to display the data.

19. Click Save All.

20. Select the JSP file and click Run. An application such as the one in Figure 8-8 will appear. Try the Forward and Back browse buttons to see how the navigation bar bean works.

21. Navigate to department 40 and click the Delete button. The record will be deleted (if there are no EMP records assigned to it) and will not appear when you scroll through records. Click Discard Changes on the toolbar to roll back the delete.

Modify the Web Bean Directives

You can change the way the web bean works by altering the directives in the bean's tag. For example, this data web bean displays the record number by default. You can turn off the record number display with a quick modification to the code.

1. Return to JDeveloper and comment out the line that includes the `setShowRecordNumbers()` method as follows:

```
//      deptRec.setShowRecordNumbers(true);
```

2. Click Save All. Select the JSP file and click Run. Confirm that the record number is not displayed.

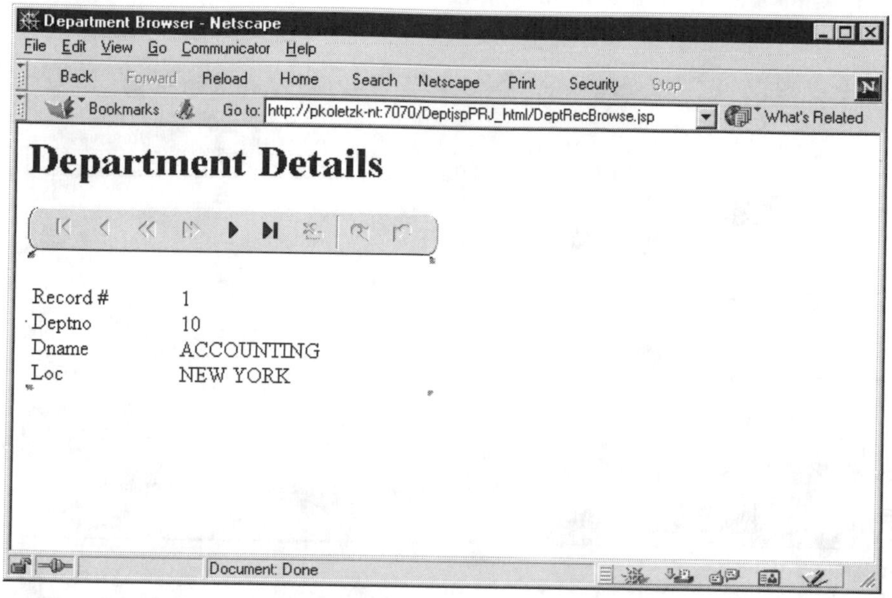

FIGURE 8-8. *Sample JSP data application*

Modify the Prompt Label Properties

By default, the labels for the fields use the attribute names from the view object in the BC4J layer. These labels are not necessarily the most intuitive to the user. However, there is a way to modify the display value associated with the attribute so that the data web bean will use a friendlier label. This technique requires modification of the BC4J layer because the web bean reads all information about the data elements from that layer. The benefit of this technique is that all applications that use the same BC4J project will be able to take advantage of the prompt property because it is part of the common layer.

1. Open the node that represents the BC4J project and navigate to the DeptView view object under the package node.

2. Doubleclick the view object icon to display the View Object dialog.

3. Click the Properties tab and pull down the DEPTNO_LABEL property, as shown in the following illustration:

```
┌─────────────────────────────────────────────────────────────────┐
│ 🌿 View Object: DeptView                                      [X] │
├─────────────────────────────────────────────────────────────────┤
│  Entity Objects │  Attributes │  Attribute Settings │  Query │  Attribute Mappings │
│   Tuning │  Java │   Client Methods │    Client Row Methods      Properties │
│                                                                    │
│                        Name: DEPTNO_LABEL              ▼           │
│                        Value: [                    ]              │
│                        [Add] [Update] [Delete]                    │
│                        Properties:                                │
│                        ┌──────────────────────────────┐          │
│                        │                              │          │
│                        │                              │          │
│                        │                              │          │
│                        └──────────────────────────────┘          │
│                        Hint: Enter a property value and click Add or Update to replace the current │
│                        value.                                     │
│                                                                    │
│  [Cancel]  [Help]  [Apply]         [<Back]  [Next>]  [Finish]     │
└─────────────────────────────────────────────────────────────────┘
```

This property holds the label text that is used when the web bean displays the attribute (column).

4. Fill in the *Value* property with "Department #" and click the Add button. The value will be shown in the Properties box. Click Finish.

CAUTION
Be sure to click the Add button in the view object dialog before dismissing the dialog or selecting another property. If you forget, the change you made will be ignored.

5. Doubleclick the DeptView.xml file under the DeptView node. The Source Editor will display the XML file that describes this view object.

6. Look for the following lines in the properties list:

```
<Properties>
      <Property Name ="DEPTNO_LABEL" Value ="Department #" />
</Properties>
```

This defines the new property value that is associated with the view object. You can add any property through the ViewObject dialog, and the property will appear in the XML file. The code in your JSP web beans can access this code. (This technique is demonstrated in the next phase, "Create a Data Browse Page with a New Web Bean.")

7. Click the BC4J project file and click Rebuild. Click Save All.

8. Select the DeptRecBrowse file and click Run. The new label "Department #" will appear in place of the word "Deptno." You can modify the label properties of the other attributes in the same way. This does not require changing any code in the application, and any other JSP applications that use these same data web beans will pick up the change automatically.

Set Up Links Between Pages

One of the tasks you must complete after creating the JSPs is to link them together. Text links or links from buttons must load a valid page. Fortunately, there are many simple techniques for achieving this goal. The following steps show two techniques that will supply this type of link.

1. Be sure that you have a HelloWWW.jsp file in the HellojspPRJ project. This file was created in the earlier practice "Building a Simple JSP Application." Complete that practice if you have not done so.

2. Open HelloWWW.jsp in the Source Editor.

3. In the tag for the Toolbar web bean, modify the `mainToolBar.addButton()` method call for the browse button as follows:

```
mainToolbar.addButton("/webapp/images/browse.gif",
    "/DeptjspPRJ_html/DeptRecBrowse.jsp", "Department Details");
```

This modifies the default link written for the browse button so that it will load the DeptRecBrowse.jsp page.

4. Rebuild and Save All. Run HelloWWW.jsp.

5. Click the browse button and the DeptRecBrowse screen should load. Click the browser's back button to return. This shows how to link using a button in a toolbar.

6. A second method for linking to another page is to provide a hypertext link. Add the following code just before the body closing tag (`</BODY>`) in HelloWWW.jsp:

```
<A HREF="/DeptjspPRJ_html/DeptRecBrowse.jsp">
  <B>Browse Departments</B>
</A>
```

7. Rebuild and Save All. Run HelloWWW.jsp. Hold the mouse cursor above the link text and examine the URL in the status bar of the browser window. This is the full path to the page that you will load when clicking the link. It is the same as the link for the browse button. Try the text link. It should work the same way as the button link. View the source code to see the HTML tags for the links.

What Just Happened?   You created an empty JSP application and added HTML code and data beans for displaying a single department record. You also modified the generated code to turn off record number display. In addition, you altered the labels of the attributes using BC4J properties and created links between pages.

When you use data web beans, adding data to a JSP is just a matter of being sure that your BC4J layer is set up. The database connection and table details are stored in the BC4J layer, which simplifies the code you have to write for the user interface. The data web bean is hooked to BC4J with the application module name. The connection method for JSP data web beans is analogous to the method used for connecting an InfoSwing bean (data-aware control) in a Java application or applet.

NOTE
The help system topic "About Web Beans" describes the available web beans in more detail. You will find this topic under the Creating JSP Pages/About JSP Applications node of the Contents page. The Javadoc in the help system includes the full description of all web beans. In addition, you can browse the source code (.java) files in the web beans archived in the jbohtmlsrc.zip file in the JDEV_HOME\src directory.

II. Create a Data Browse Page with a New Web Bean

Although the JDeveloper web beans contain a sufficiently wide range of functionality, one of the strengths of this tool and the Java language in general is that you can create your own reusable components—in this case, data web beans—and make them do anything you want. This phase shows how to create a web bean and build a JSP file with it. All work takes place in the HellojspPRJ project.

Build a Simple Web Bean

The following steps build a web bean without any useful code, to acquaint you with the process.

1. Add a folder to the HellojspPRJ project by selecting Add Folder from the right-click menu on the project. Call the folder "Demo Beans."

2. Select **File | New**, navigate to the Web Objects tab, and doubleclick Web Bean. The Web Bean Wizard will open. Click Next to display the Web Bean Name page as shown here:

3. Fill in the following properties on this page:

   Enter package name as "empappjsp"
   Enter Class Name... as "WBDemoViewRow"
   Enter Description as "WB Demo View Row Data"

   The class refers to the Java class name that you will create. Web beans are Java files that are compiled into class bytecode. The description will be displayed in the JSP Element Wizard. The name and description are prefixed by WB to identify that the web beans are defined by the user, not supplied by JDeveloper.

CAUTION
There is no Browse button to find a package name in this page. If you mistype the package name, a folder with the mistyped name will be added to the file system. Therefore, you must be careful when inputting this value. For a production-level web bean, you would normally use a new folder that it is independent from the application code (for example, a systemwide web beans folder). If the web bean is generic to a particular application, you would place it in an enterprise-accessible folder that is not application specific.

4. Uncheck both checkboxes so that no default code will be created. Click Next and Finish. The file will be added to the project.

5. Click Save All.

6. Right click the Demo Beans folder and select Add to Folder. Find the WBDemoViewRow.java file in the empappjsp directory and click Open. (Return to step 5 if you do not see this file.)

7. Delete the version of the file that is not in the folder.

8. Expand the Demo Beans folder and examine the code for the new file. The bean is an Oracle class that extends WebBeanImpl and has a `render()` method that is its starting point (like the Java application `main()` method). This is the simplest file you can create with the Web Bean Wizard.

9. There is no point in using this bean because it contains no useful functionality. However, you can open an existing JSP file (such as HelloWWW.jsp), select JSP Element from the right-click menu, and expand the Web Beans node. You will see the new web bean description under this node because the Web Bean Wizard registered the file with JDeveloper.

NOTE
If you checked the "Add data source support" checkbox in the Web Bean Wizard, the web bean would appear under the Data Web Beans node instead of the Web Beans node.

Build a Data Web Bean

These steps build a web bean that accesses the database and can be used as a data web bean.

1. Select **File | New**, navigate to the Web Objects tab, and doubleclick Web Bean. The Web Bean Wizard will open. Click Next to display the Web Bean Name page.

2. Fill in the following properties on this page:

   Enter package name as "empappjsp"
   Enter Class Name... as "WBViewCurrentRow"
   Enter Description as "WB View Current Row"

3. Leave both checkboxes checked. The wizard will create default code for data connections and presentation of the data in a multirecord display (like the JS RowSet Browser data web bean).

4. Click Next and Finish. The file will be added to the project.

5. Click Save All. Move the file to the Demo Beans folder using the same method as before.

6. Open the file in the Source Editor. You will see a lot more code in the `render()` method than in the first example because you left the checkboxes *Generate Sample Code* and *Add data code support* checked in the Web Bean Wizard's Web Bean Name page. The following code is sample HTML code that is generated from the former checkbox setting:

```
HTMLDiv aDoc;
aDoc = new HTMLDiv();
aDoc.addHeader(1,"Hello from My New Web Bean");
aDoc.render(out);
```

   The `addHeader()` method is only added if the data checkbox is not checked. The rest of the additional code in the `render()` method was generated by the *Add data code support* checkbox. This code loops through a row set and displays data in a table format.

7. To test the web bean, create a JSP file by selecting **File | New**, navigating to the Web Objects tab, and doubleclicking JSP.

8. Select **File | Rename** and call the file "TestCurrentRowWB." Click Save.

9. Open the file in the Source Editor and delete the line that begins with the <H2> tag.

10. Add a line at that point and select JSP Element from the right-click menu.

11. Select WB View Current Row under the Data Web Beans node. This bean will not appear under the Web Beans node because you set it up as a bean with a data source. Click Next.

12. Fill in the *id* property as "deptBrowse" and click Next.

13. In the View Object Selection page, open the module node and select DeptView. The view objects were read from the BC4J project that is open in this workspace. Click Next.

14. Select all attributes and click Finish. The tag syntax for the new file will be inserted into the file.

15. Save All. Move the JSP file to the Examples folder that you created in an earlier practice. It is located in the JDEV_HOME\myhtml\HellojspPRJ_html directory.

16. Select the project node. Click Rebuild and Save All.

17. Select the TestCurrentRowWB.jsp file and click Run. The browser should display the new data web bean as shown in Figure 8-9. The column titles have reverted to the default of the view object attribute names. This is because there is no code in the new web bean to read the label properties.

NOTE
You may see the following "reload buffers" dialog as you work with JSPs and test them. The files that you are generating are changing as you run them because the process of running a JSP will regenerate the Java and class files based on the JSP. This is not an error message and you can just click Yes in the dialog.

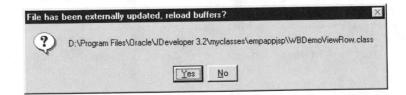

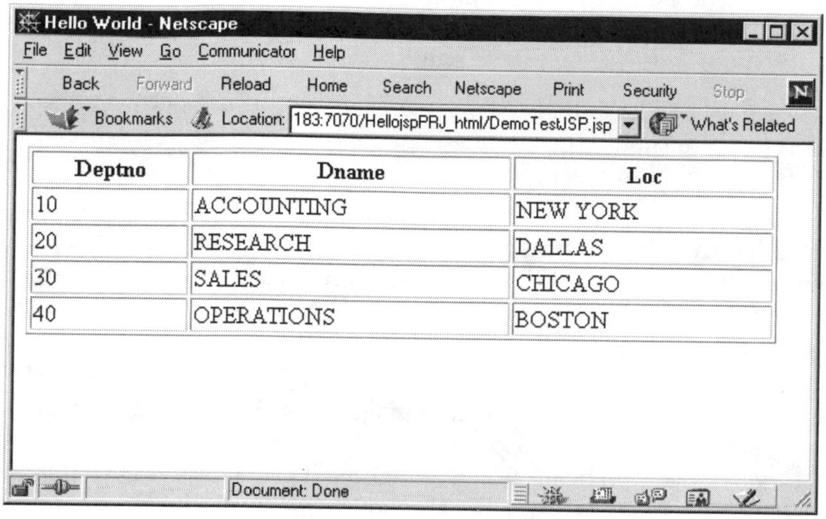

FIGURE 8-9. *JSP with user-defined data web bean*

Modify the Data Web Bean

The following steps will modify the bean so that the label property of the view objects is used instead of the attribute names.

1. Navigate back to the source code for the data web bean (WBViewCurrentRow). Find the section of code that begins with a loop through the attribute list as follows:

```
//This loop iterates through the set of attributes...
for(nIndex = 0 ; nIndex < attrs.length; nIndex++)
{
        if (!shouldDisplayAttribute(attrs[nIndex]))
                                continue;
        aTable.addHeader(attrs[nIndex].getName());)
```

2. Replace the `aTable.addHeader()` line with the following lines:

```
if ((String)rs.getProperty(
        attrs[nIndex].getColumnName() + "_LABEL") == null )
     aTable.addHeader(attrs[nIndex].getName());
else
     aTable.addHeader((String)rs.getProperty(
        attrs[nIndex].getColumnName() + "_LABEL"));
```

This code extracts the label property from the BC4J XML file and uses that as the column heading. If there is no label property set for a particular attribute, it uses the attribute name.

3. Save All and Rebuild. Navigate back to the TestCurrentRowWB.jsp file and run it. You should see modified column labels if you set them in the BC4J layer as discussed earlier.

Use the Web Object Manager

The demonstration data web bean you added first does not need to appear in the JSP Element Wizard list. You can remove the web bean using the Web Object Manager as follows:

1. Select **Wizards | Web Object Manager**. The Web Object Manager shown in Figure 8-10 will be displayed. The *Web Object Manager* is used to add and remove web beans from the registered list of classes available in the JSP Element Wizard. You can also add properties so they appear in the JSP Element Wizard.

2. Expand the Web Beans node.

3. Select Demo View Row Data and click DeRegister. The entry will be removed from the list. You can also add (register) web beans using this dialog. Click the Register button and complete the fields on the screen for name, description, and class file name. This operation would be necessary if you removed a web bean and wanted to add it back or if you developed a web bean in another tool and wanted to make it known to JDeveloper. Web Object Manager will also allow you to add and edit properties that will appear in the JSP. You can explore those dialogs by selecting your bean and clicking the Edit button. Click OK to return to the main dialog.

4. Click OK to dismiss the Web Object Manager.

5. Navigate back to the TestCurrentRowWB file and display the JSP Element Wizard. Look for the change you made to the web beans list.

What Just Happened?   In this phase, you created a simple web bean and a data web bean. You altered the data web bean so that it was able to use the label properties of the view object in the business components layer. You also saw how to register and modify the web beans list using the Web Object Manager.

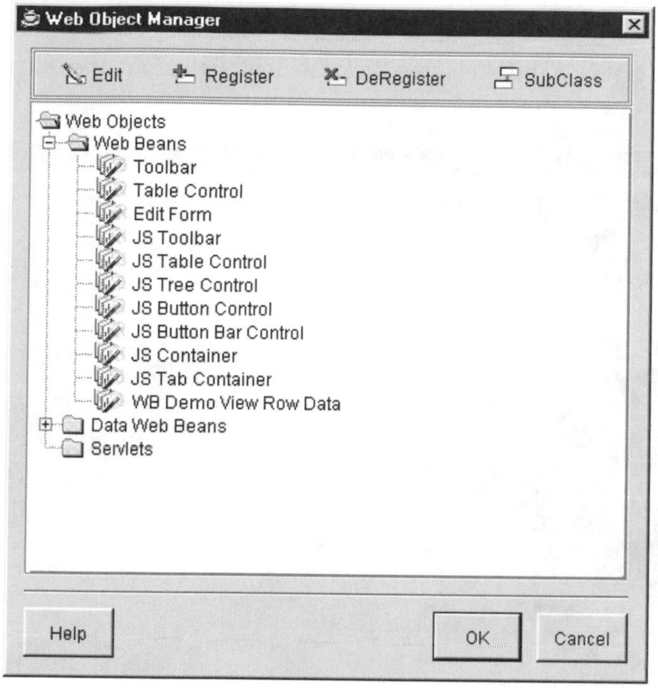

FIGURE 8-10. *Web Object Manager*

Hands-on Practice: Creating Pages with the DataPage Wizard

You have another alternative to use when creating JSP applications. The DataPage Wizard steps you through the task of creating a data-aware JSP. This wizard streamlines the required steps for creating a basic page that you can enhance by changing the code. This wizard gives you a solid starting point for a data-aware page.

If you did not run the earlier practices in this chapter, follow the steps in the section "Hands-on Practice Preparation" to create a workspace. You will also need to add the BC4J project to the workspace as explained in phase I of the practice "Creating a JSP Data Application Using the Wizard."

1. Click the HellojspPRJ project and select **File | New.** Click the Web Objects page and doubleclick DataPage to start the DataPage Wizard.

2. Click Next on the Welcome Page to display the DataPages page, as shown here:

Select Browse Form and click Next to display the View Object Selection page.

3. Expand the nodes and select the DeptView view object. Click Finish. The file (DeptView_Browse.jsp) will appear in the Navigation Pane. Click Save All.

4. Move this file to the Examples folder of the project. The file is in the JDEV_HOME\myhtml\HellojspPRJ_html directory.

5. Click Save All, Rebuild, and Run to test the JSP that you just created. The browser will appear as shown in Figure 8-11.

6. Open the file in the Source Editor and examine its contents. You will see a number of jbo tags that represent the Data Tag Library links to the application module.

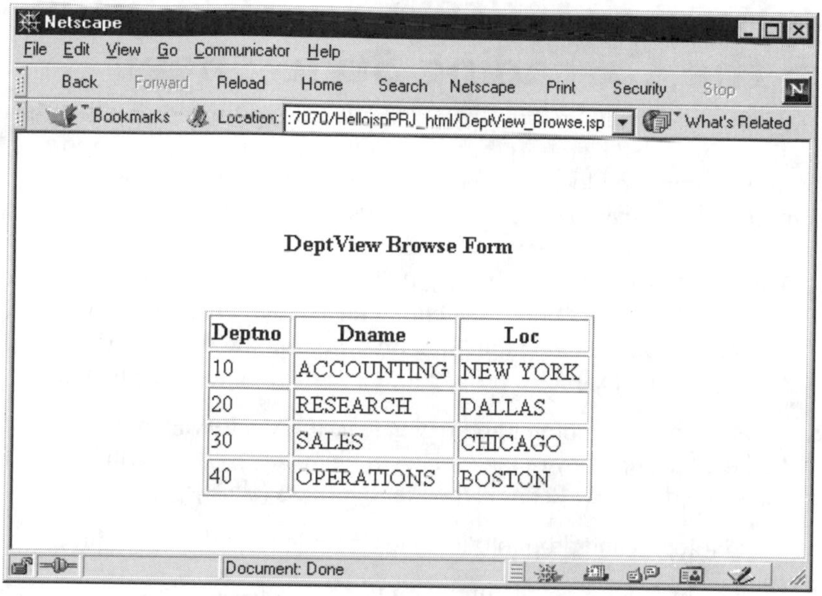

FIGURE 8-11. *A JSP generated by the DataPage Wizard*

What Just Happened?   You used the DataPage Wizard to create a JSP page. This page uses the Data Tag Library to retrieve and display data from the application module of the BC4J layer. This application is not intended to be a full solution, but does provide a good starting point for your own code and a good example of how to use these tags.

The code you create with the DataPage Wizard is at a lower level than that of the previous practices. The source code file contains more HTML tags than the code that uses web beans because the web beans are responsible for generating some of the HTML code. The advantage of this is that you can modify the output by changing the HTML tags directly instead of having to create your own web bean to generate HTML in a certain way. For example, you could easily change the page heading to an H2 style by inserting the tags around the "DeptView Browse Form" string in the source file. You could also remove the rule lines in the table by changing the table tag to BORDER="0" instead of BORDER="1." The drawback, of course, is that there is more code to write and manage.

Hands-on Practice: Experimenting with the Cascading Style Sheet

The cascading style sheet file forms part of the JSP theme as discussed in the earlier section "JDeveloper JSP Elements." The cascading style sheet is an important contributor to a common look and feel for your application. This practice shows how to modify the cascading style sheet and use it in JSP tags.

1. This practice starts with a new JSP file. Create this file by clicking the HellojspPRJ project node, selecting **File | New**, clicking the Web Objects tab, and doubleclicking the JSP icon. Rename the file to "CCStest.jsp." Move it to the Examples project folder and run it to view its output.

2. Open Windows Explorer and navigate to JDEV_HOME\myhtml\webapp\css. Make a backup copy of the oracle.css file. CTRL-C, CTRL-V will make a copy in the same directory. Rename the file to test.css (click F2 to edit the file name).

3. Start Notepad and drop into it the test.css file from the open directory.

4. Browse in the test.css file until you find an entry for "H2." This sets the default font for all heading 2 text to Arial. Now look for an entry for "SOFTPANEL." This style specifies a background color of gray ("EEEEEE") and a background image.

5. In JDeveloper, open the CCStest.jsp file in the Source Editor if it is not already open. Add a blank line after the opening header tag (<HEAD>).

6. Select **Wizards | JSP Element** and select "default" from the Themes node. Click Next and Finish to insert the tag. The tag references the oracle.css file. Change this to reference the test.css file so the tag appears as follows:

```
<LINK REL=STYLESHEET TYPE="text/css"
        HREF="/webapp/css/test.css" >
```

This sets the source of the styles for this page to test.css.

7. Modify the body starting tag from <BODY> to <BODY CLASS= SOFTPANEL>. This defines that the SOFTPANEL style in the style sheet will supply the attributes for the contents of the body section.

8. Click Rebuild and Save All. Run the CCStest file and leave the browser open. You will see the gray background that the style sets. You will also see the special H2 font as defined in the style sheet. View the HTML page source and find the class reference in the body tag.

9. You can change the style sheet and affect the page. In the SOFTPANEL section of test.css, change the background color from "#EEEEEE" to "cyan" (without quotation marks).

10. Save the file and switch to the browser. Click the Reload button in the browser, and the background color should change. Try other colors such as red, blue, yellow, and green.

11. You can also experiment with adding other HTML tags to the JSP file and adding the CLASS attribute to those tags.

What Just Happened?   You added a cascading style sheet to a JSP file and referenced a style. You also changed the style sheet to get a taste for how it can be modified.

CHAPTER

9

User Interface Components

Nothing is less real than realism;
Details are confusing.
It is only by selection, by elimination, by emphasis
that we get at the real meaning of things.

—Georgia O'Keeffe (1887–1986), 1922

he rule of thumb when working with any IDE is to use it to its full potential. For example, it is possible to write code in JDeveloper that creates objects and sets their properties, but this will not take advantage of the IDE features that generate this code for you. Although it is not possible to create an enterprise-class application using only the wizards and components, these features will give you a big head start and greatly minimize the supplemental code that you have to write. If you are careful about how elaborate your GUI becomes, the code you do write will be business specific. The details that Java requires to make the code work, such as imports and constructors, can all be handled by the code generators.

One of the key features that the JDeveloper IDE offers is quick access to commonly used Java components. A Java *component* corresponds to what other languages call a "control," and the words are often used interchangeably. Components are used to create Java applications and applets (not servlets or JSP applications). Typically, a component represents a visual object, but the term can be extended to cover nonvisual data control objects such as row sets. The IDE allows you to drop components into your project, set properties, and define events, all without writing code. The code that is generated from these actions is ready-to-run, error free, and completely available for editing in the Source Editor.

The component palette of the JDeveloper IDE offers high-level control and code generation. Chapter 2 introduced this area with descriptions and examples of how to use some of the components. This chapter will list the components that are installed with the product and give brief descriptions for each. The end of the chapter steps you through examples of how to use two components, the LOV and the Tree control, as examples of the kind of work you can expect the components to accomplish. The hands-on practices also include examples of how to add predefined and user-defined components to the palette. With this knowledge, you will be able to explore the other components and understand where to get information when you need it. As is true in other hands-on practices in this book, there is key information about the objects that the practice manipulates, so it is useful to read and work through the hands-on practices.

Component Palette

The component palette (also called "component toolbar") normally sits under the menu in the JDeveloper window, as shown in Figure 9-1. Each tab page in the palette contains a set of components. The following tabs are installed with the product:

- Swing

- Swing Containers

- AWT

- InfoSwing

- InfoProducers

- Chart

- Other

The following sections describe and show what each tab contains by default so that you can get a feel for some of the controls. The sections are organized by tab and contain a description of the functionality and a representation of how the component will appear in the UI Designer if that is applicable. As you view these lists, remember that you are not bound by the components installed by default on the tabs. Almost any JavaBean can be placed on a tab and used in your application. You can add or remove tabs and add, remove, or move components as described in the hands-on practices.

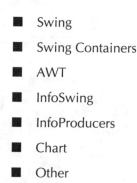

CAUTION
You can place a large number of objects on a single tab and use the tab's scrollbars to access the components. However, the most developer-friendly interface does not require scrolling. Therefore, you should limit yourself to the number of components that may be viewed without scrolling when the window is maximized.

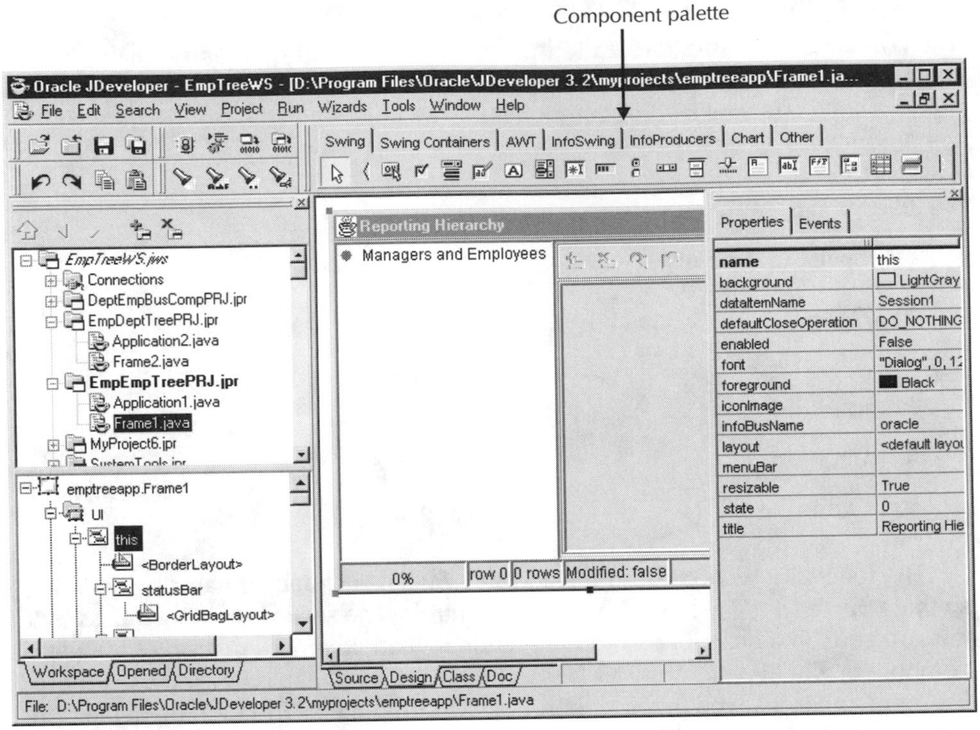

Component palette

FIGURE 9-1. *JDeveloper IDE component palette*

Swing

The Swing components are part of the Java Foundation Classes (JFC). They are available with Java 2 (versions 1.2 and 1.3) as well as in JFC 1.1, which is used in the Java Development Kit (JDK) 1.1. The Swing components' class names start with the letter "J" and are contained in the javax.swing package created by Sun Microsystems. They are an extension of the Abstract Windowing Toolkit (AWT), also created by Sun. Swing and AWT contain many of the same classes, but Swing components offer a more extensive set of properties, and the recent versions are more portable and have been optimized for efficiency. Therefore, the rule of thumb is to use Swing instead of AWT. AWT is included in the tool mostly for backward compatibility. In addition, the java.awt classes are used for event handling. Table 9-1 lists the components on the Swing tab.

Component	Icon	Description and Example
JButton	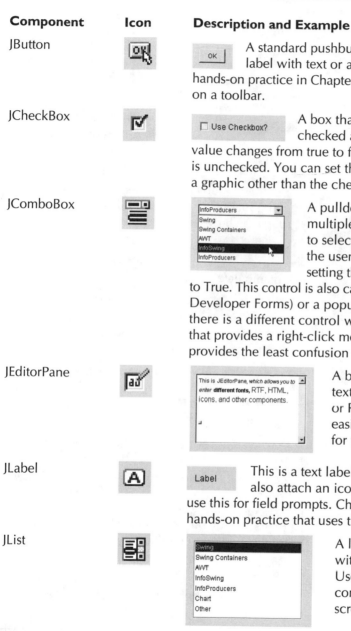	A standard pushbutton that you can label with text or an icon or both. The hands-on practice in Chapter 10 works with buttons on a toolbar.
JCheckBox		A box that toggles between checked and unchecked. The value changes from true to false when a checkbox is unchecked. You can set the *icon* property to use a graphic other than the check mark.
JComboBox		A pulldown list that presents multiple values for the user to select from. You can allow the user to enter a value by setting the *editable* property to True. This control is also called a poplist (as in Developer Forms) or a popup menu (although there is a different control with the same name that provides a right-click menu). The term that provides the least confusion is "combo box."
JEditorPane		A box that can display text formatted in HTML or RTF. It allows you to easily create a help system for your application.
JLabel		This is a text label to which you can also attach an icon. Normally, you use this for field prompts. Chapter 2 contains a hands-on practice that uses this component.
JList		A list of text strings without a scrollbar. Use the JScrollPane container if you need a scrollbar for this control.

TABLE 9-1.   *Swing Tab Components*

Component	Icon	Description and Example
JPasswordField		The same control as JTextField except that this one hides the input by displaying an asterisk character (*) for each character typed.
JProgressBar		A container that graphically displays the completion percentage for a process.
JRadioButton		A single selection button that will be part of a set of buttons in a radio group (ButtonGroup class). Only one button in the group may be selected.
JScrollBar		A vertical or horizontal bar with a button that moves the display or manipulates a value.
JSeparator		This component is used in menus to separate menu items with a horizontal line. It can also be used as a horizontal or vertical straight line or as a spacer in toolbars.
JSlider		A control that is visually and functionally similar to the scrollbar. This control is used more often to change values than is the scrollbar.
JTextArea		Another text editor that shows rows of text strings ending in newline characters. There is no scrollbar on this control, but you can place it in a JScrollPane container if the user will need to scroll.
JTextField		A single-row text editing area. Many of the hands-on practices in this book use the InfoSwing version of this control.

TABLE 9-1. *Swing Tab Components* (continued)

Component	Icon	Description and Example
JTextPane	F♯F	*This is a JTextPane area that displays all test in a single font.* A subclass of JEditorPane that allows you to edit formatted text and embed images and other components within that text. (JEditorPane only allows images within HTML or RTF text.) This means that you can embed other frames or window components as in a Multiple Document Interface (MDI) window.
JTree		Managers and Employees / KING / JONES / BLAKE / ALLEN / WARD / MARTIN / TURNER / JAMES / CLARK Use this to display hierarchical data in a form that emulates the Windows Explorer. A hands-on practice in this chapter includes techniques for working with this component.
JTable		First Name / Last Name / Hobby / # of Years; Harry King Skiing 5; Scott Tiger Swimming 3; Popper Dorsey Frisbee 2; Mohini Koletzke Yard work 20 A spreadsheet-like (grid) display of data. The user can modify column widths at runtime.
JToggleButton		Click Here (Before clicking) / Click Here (After clicking) This control looks like a button but stays depressed when the user clicks it. Clicking again raises the button again. Therefore, this control is useful for Boolean values. You can place sets of JToggleButtons in a ButtonGroup so that only one can be pressed at a time.

TABLE 9-1. *Swing Tab Components* (continued)

Swing Containers

This tab also contains Swing components. In this case, the components are used as *containers*—boxes that other components are placed into. Technically, many Swing controls are containers because they are subclassed from the java.awt.Container class. For example, JButtons and JTextField are both subclassed from Container, although you do not use them as receptacles for other components. The components on this tab, described in Table 9-2, are just a little closer to Container and are more commonly used as holders for other components.

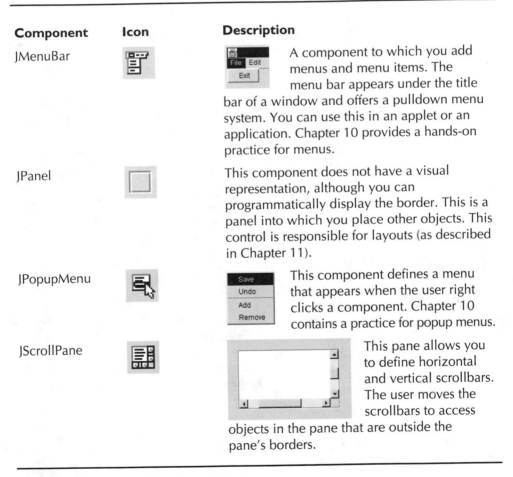

Component	Icon	Description
JMenuBar		A component to which you add menus and menu items. The menu bar appears under the title bar of a window and offers a pulldown menu system. You can use this in an applet or an application. Chapter 10 provides a hands-on practice for menus.
JPanel		This component does not have a visual representation, although you can programmatically display the border. This is a panel into which you place other objects. This control is responsible for layouts (as described in Chapter 11).
JPopupMenu		This component defines a menu that appears when the user right clicks a component. Chapter 10 contains a practice for popup menus.
JScrollPane		This pane allows you to define horizontal and vertical scrollbars. The user moves the scrollbars to access objects in the pane that are outside the pane's borders.

TABLE 9-2. *Swing Containers Tab Components*

Component	Icon	Description
JSplitPane	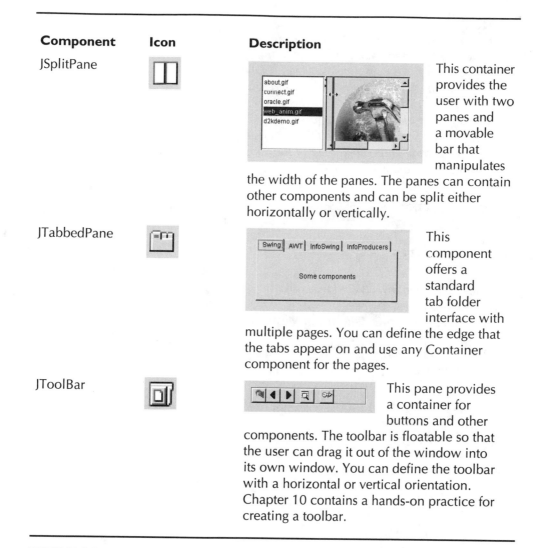	This container provides the user with two panes and a movable bar that manipulates the width of the panes. The panes can contain other components and can be split either horizontally or vertically.
JTabbedPane		This component offers a standard tab folder interface with multiple pages. You can define the edge that the tabs appear on and use any Container component for the pages.
JToolBar		This pane provides a container for buttons and other components. The toolbar is floatable so that the user can drag it out of the window into its own window. You can define the toolbar with a horizontal or vertical orientation. Chapter 10 contains a hands-on practice for creating a toolbar.

TABLE 9-2. *Swing Containers Tab Components* (continued)

NOTE
If you are using Swing classes, you can change the look-and-feel (general appearance) of the runtime. There are three possible styles: Metal, CDE/Motif, and Windows. Metal is the default and is a cross-platform appearance. CDE/Motif and Windows emulate the general user interface of those systems. You can change to CDE/Motif using the following code at the beginning of the main() method (before any constructors):

```
try {
     UIManager.setLookAndFeel(new
        com.sun.java.swing.plaf.motif.MotifLookAndFeel());
}
catch (Exception e) {
}
```

Substitute "windows .WindowsLookAndFeel" for "motif.MotifLookAndFeel" if you want the runtime to emulate Windows. Use "metal.MetalLookAndFeel" if you want to specify the Metal look, but this is the default. You can right click in the UI Designer and select the look of that window during design time.

AWT

The AWT components are contained in the java.awt package. Many of them are similar in appearance and functionality to their Swing equivalents, and you would use AWT only if you need to support work in JDK 1.0 or 1.1. Since the AWT controls have Swing equivalents, the list in Table 9-3 is abbreviated so that it contains references to the corresponding Swing components.

CAUTION
Avoid mixing AWT and Swing components in the same class. They have some elements that are named the same and you might experience unanticipated results if you do not always fully qualify (with the package name) your use of constants and other code elements.

Component	Icon	Description
Button		See JButton in the "Swing" section.
Checkbox		See JCheckBox in the "Swing" section.
CheckboxGroup		This component does not have a visual representation. It is a container for Checkbox components. If you set the *checkboxGroup* property of a checkbox to the group's name, it will be included with that group, and the checkbox icon will change from a box to a radio button circle. The group then acts the same as a radio group, where only one of its members can be selected.
Choice		See JComboBox in the "Swing" section.
Label		See JLabel in the "Swing" section.
List		See JList in the "Swing" section. The AWT control supplies a scrollbar, while the Swing version does not.
MenuBar		See JMenuBar in the "Swing Containers" section. Unlike the Swing versions, the AWT control is not available for applets.
PopupMenu		See JPopupMenu in the "Swing Containers" section. This control is available for applets.
Panel		See JPanel in the "Swing Containers" section.
Scrollbar		See JScrollbar in the "Swing" section.

TABLE 9-3. *AWT Tab Components*

Component	Icon	Description
ScrollPane		See JScrollPane in the "Swing Containers" section.
TextArea		See JTextArea in the "Swing" section.
TextField		See JTextField in the "Swing" section.

TABLE 9-3. *AWT Tab Components* (continued)

InfoSwing

InfoSwing controls are Swing controls created by Oracle that have data intelligence. They are also called Data-Aware Controls (DAC) because they have properties that you can use to link them to the database. All components in this tab have an icon that is similar to the Swing counterpart, but with a green database drum symbol in the lower-right corner that indicates the data awareness. The components are contained in the oracle.dacf.control.swing package and have no special prefix.

Most of these components link to a data control using the *dataItemName* property. This property associates the component to an InfoProducer session info, row set, or row set attribute object that supplies data or connection information. This association carries out the link to the BC4J database layer. The InfoProducer components are listed later.

Since the functionality and visual appearance of most controls are similar to those of the Swing components, the descriptions in Table 9-4 reference the corresponding Swing component if there is one.

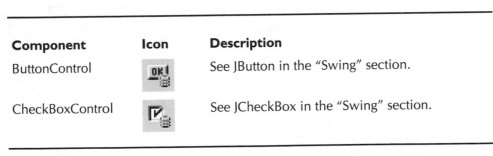

Component	Icon	Description
ButtonControl		See JButton in the "Swing" section.
CheckBoxControl		See JCheckBox in the "Swing" section.

TABLE 9-4. *InfoSwing Tab Components*

Component	Icon	Description
ComboBoxControl		See JComboBox in the "Swing" section.
GridControl		See JTable in the "Swing" section.
LabelControl		See JLabel in the "Swing" section.
NavigationBar		This toolbar provides the user with buttons for the most common database actions: moving forward and backward through the records; jumping to the first or last record; adding, deleting, and committing a record; performing a rollback; and finding records. The hands-on practices in Chapters 2 and 10 contain examples of how to use this component.
TextFieldControl		See JTextField in the "Swing" section.
TextAreaControl		See JTextArea in the "Swing" section. This control contains a scrollbar, unlike its Swing counterparts.
RadioPanelControl		This component has no visual representation. It works the same way as the AWT CheckboxGroup. A set of selection buttons that are contained by this control will force only one selection at a given moment.
RadioButtonControl		See JRadioButton in the "Swing" section.
ListControl		See JList in the "Swing" section.

TABLE 9-4. *InfoSwing Tab Components* (continued)

Component	Icon	Description	
LoginDlg			This component does not display in the UI Designer. It presents

fields for the user to enter user name, password, and connection name. The control logs the user into the database with this information. The hands-on practice in Chapter 2 contains an example of this component.

Component	Icon	Description	
LOV			The LOV displays a list of values from which the user can select one

value. This value can be returned into a field on the form. This chapter contains a hands-on practice to create an LOV.

Component	Icon	Description	
StatusBarControl			The status bar gives details

such as the current row number, the number of rows retrieved in the form, the percentage of the query that has been retrieved, and the display name of the row set that is being queried.

TABLE 9-4.   *InfoSwing Tab Components* (continued)

Component	Icon	Description
FindPanel		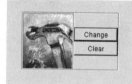

This component presents a dialog in which the user enters search criteria. The conditions that the user enters become part of the filter criteria for the database query. Records are returned to components, such as a grid control on the form.

| ImageControl | | |

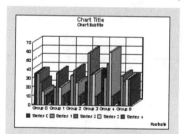 A component that displays JPEG and GIF images from the database. The user can update or delete images using the Change and Clear buttons, respectively.

ChartControl

This component provides data charting based on values in the database.

TreeControl   See JTree in the "Swing" section.

TABLE 9-4.   *InfoSwing Tab Components* (continued)

InfoProducers

The InfoProducer components are Oracle-supplied nonvisual controls that access data from the database through the BC4J layer. They act as an intermediary to pass data to and receive data from the InfoSwing data-aware controls. You can think of them as the conduit from the user interface to the data layer. The user interface InfoSwing components interact with the user and send and receive data from the InfoProducers. The InfoProducers, in turn, send and receive data from the BC4J database layer. The InfoProducers are contained in the oracle.dacf.dataset package created by Oracle and described in the following table.

Component	Icon	Description
SessionInfo		SessionInfo specifies connection information needed to access the application module that you deploy to the middle tier.
RowSetInfo		RowSetInfo is used to access a View Object that your Business Components application defines.
LOVRowSetInfo		LOVRowSetInfo defines a query used by your LOV (list of values) and represents the results of the query.

Chart

There is only one component on the Chart tab, described below, and this appears as a sample of what you can use for charts. The class is distributed in an AWT and a Swing style and available from Three D Graphics (www.threedgraphics.com). Documentation and a full download are available on their web site.

Component	Icon	Description
Perspective		This control offers a charting feature that can produce charts in many different styles, such as pie, 3D, bar, and scatter. The visual representation is similar to the ChartControl in the "InfoSwing" section.

Other

There are no components installed on the Other tab. The intent is that you will add your own components and place any additional components you may need from the existing Swing, InfoSwing, and AWT libraries into this tab. The hands-on practices in this chapter demonstrates how to add components to this tab.

More Information

It would take many hundreds of pages to describe in detail all of these components, their methods, and properties. In addition, as mentioned, these components are the more common of the thousands of components available. Describing all of them is far beyond the scope of this book. The good news is that the components are fully documented in a reference form within the JDeveloper help system. Browse under the Reference node in the Contents page. You will also find some examples and techniques in the same help system. In addition, many reference books on the market provide details about the Swing components and show even more examples of their use. One place to start is on the Web.

As of this writing, the Sun Microsystems web site (java.sun.com) contains an online book called "Java Tutorial." You can reach this from the JDeveloper help system by clicking on "Sun Java Reference" in the Reference node of the Contents tab. Click the node "Sun Microsystems Swing 1.1 Reference." In the middle of that page is a link to the online (Web Access) Java Tutorial. This online book provides the necessary details that you need to become more familiar with the components in the Swing and AWT categories. This tutorial is also available in printed format as the following reference books:

- *The Java Tutorial, Second Edition*, Kathy Campione and Mary Walrath, 1998, Addison-Wesley

- *The Java Tutorial, Continued*, Campione, Walrath, Huml, et al., 1998, Addison-Wesley

- *The JFC Swing Class Tutorial*, Walrath and Campione, 1999, Addison-Wesley

These are just examples of the available books that describe Java components. They describe the Sun components in depth. For more information on the Oracle components, such as the InfoSwing and InfoProducers, look for examples and descriptions on the Oracle Technet web site (technet.oracle.com).

Now that you have seen the range of components, some hands-on practices will help you dig into a few components to see how they work.

Hands-on Practice: Sample BC4J Project

To demonstrate the LOV and tree functionality, you need to start with an application. Each practice creates its own starting application, but you need a BC4J project that is common to all. Use the following steps to create this project. The business components you create in this phase are relatively standard but require one additional step. To save manual effort later, be sure that your sample schema has a foreign key constraint defined for EMP.MGR (referring to EMP.EMPNO). Instructions for creating the proper constraints are provided in the Introduction to this book.

If you need help or explanation for any of these steps, refer to the hands-on practice in Chapter 2. Chapter 6 contains further explanations of the BC4J objects.

1. Close the existing workspace and save the default that is created as "EmpAppWS" in a new folder called "empapp."

2. Create a business components project called "DeptEmpBusCompPRJ" in the empapp folder for the EMP and DEPT tables. Specify the package name as "empapp."

3. Rebuild and save the project.

4. Right click the module name (EmpappModule) in the Navigation Pane and select "Edit EmpappModule."

5. In the Data Model tab, be sure that the module name is selected in the *Data Model* field. Move EmpView from the *Available Views* field to the *Data Model* field. The new entry will be named "EmpView2." The following note explains the need for this step.

NOTE
When you created the module, the BC4J view and link objects were set up to mirror the database tables and constraints by default. When you initially created the BC4J project, JDeveloper read the foreign key constraint between EMP and DEPT and set up a master-detail link. With this type of link, you cannot access the detail table independently. To develop an application based on the detail table alone, the module must be defined with an additional view for the EMP table that is not linked to DEPT. The preceding step added this additional view.

6. Click Finish to close the module edit dialog. Click Save All to save the project.

Hands-on Practice: Using the LOV Control

In this practice, you will add the necessary objects and code to implement a list of values in the application. A list of values provides an easy way for users to insert a value into a code field. The scenario in this example is that the user would be creating an employee record or modifying the department number of an existing employee. The department number is a foreign key code value that points to the primary key of the DEPT table. Users may not know the code values but should be able to select a description from a list. The description will be associated with the code value, and this code will be returned to an item on the form.

Note for Oracle Developer Users

The LOV in JDeveloper emulates the LOV in Forms. The concept is the same, although the implementation is a bit different. The simple functionality of selecting a value from a list that results from a database query is exactly the same. The major concepts of setting up an LOV are the same in JDeveloper and in Forms as follows:

LOV Concept	JDeveloper	Forms
LOV window	An object with properties, no layout possible or required	Same as JDeveloper
Features of the LOV	Find item and button at the top of the window, OK, Help, and Cancel buttons	Same as JDeveloper except no Help button
LOV query	Defined by specifying a row set object that implies a SELECT statement	Usually defined with a SELECT statement in a record group
Return item	Property of the row set that creates the LOV data	LOV property
Associating the LOV and text item	A row set attribute property	A text item property
Allow users to set query criteria prior to data retrieval	Code is required to implement this function	LOV property

This practice runs through the following phases:

I. **Create a project for a sample application**

II. **Create an LOV row set**

III. **Create an LOV object**

IV. **Define an event for displaying the LOV**

V. **Try some variations**

- ■ **Hide the DEPTNO LOV column**

- ■ **Resize the LOV**

- ■ **Set the LOV column label**

- ■ **Add a Department name lookup**

I. Create a Project for a Sample Application

The application you use for this practice can be relatively basic, but it needs some specific elements. The following abbreviated steps will create a minimal application that you can use as a basis. You will use the Business Components Data Form Wizard to create an application based on the business components you defined before.

1. Create a project called "EmpAppPRJ" in the empapp folder. Specify that the project is for a new application. Accept the defaults and in the Application Wizard, accept the empapp package.

2. In the Application Wizard, specify a new Business Components For Java data form.

3. In the Business Components Data Form Wizard, accept all of the defaults and specify a single table form based on the EmpView2 (Empno, Ename, and Deptno).

4. Click Rebuild and Save All. Run the application. The form should look like the following illustration:

This application will serve as the basis for this practice.

II. Create an LOV Row Set

The LOV will display rows from a query. In JDeveloper, the way to create a query is to create a row set object that is defined for a table in the application module. The *LOVRowSet* is slightly different from the normal data row set because it does not include the properties for linking to a master-detail relationship and for allowing updates. An LOV displays query-only data sets.

1. Doubleclick Frame1.java in the Navigation Pane and select the Design tab of the Viewer.

2. Drop an LOVRowSetInfo component from the InfoProducers tab into the Structure Pane. It will appear under the BC4J Data Items node. Set the following properties in the order indicated:
    session to "sessionInfo"
    name to "deptLOVRowSet"
    bindName to "deptLOVRowSet"

3. For the *queryInfo* property, select DeptView (Single Table mode) and specify Deptno and Dname columns in the Selection Order tab. Reorder the columns so that Dname is first. On the Definition tab, specify the ORDER BY as "dname." Click Test Query to check the query and OK to dismiss the dialog.

4. Click Save All.

NOTE
You can view the SQL statement that the BC4J layer will generate (as shown in the following illustration) by clicking the View SQL button in the queryInfo dialog. You can copy and paste the text into a SQL command line (such as SQL*Plus) to debug the statement if you receive a syntax error in this dialog.

```
SQL statement                          [x]
SELECT Dept.DEPTNO,
       Dept.DNAME,
       Dept.LOC
  FROM DEPT Dept
 ORDER BY  dname

                          [ OK ]
```

CAUTION
If the LOVRowSet object disappears from view in the Structure Pane after you set its properties, you will need to force a redisplay. Click the Source tab and doubleclick the deptLOVRowSet object node in the Structure Pane. The Source Editor will display the line of code that creates the LOV row set (LOVRowSetInfo deptLOVRowSet = new LOVRowSetInfo();). Comment out this line by placing "//" at the beginning of the line. Click the Design tab, click the Source tab, and repeat the doubleclick to find the creation line. This time, uncomment the line by removing the "//." When you click the Design tab again, the LOV row set should be visible in the Structure Pane. If you require frequent refreshes, delete and re-create the row sets and do not change the name or bindName properties.

What Just Happened?   You set up the BC4J query object that will retrieve rows from the DEPT table. Specifying an order clause will present the list in a logical order for the user. This query object still needs to be associated with an LOV object.

III. Create an LOV Object

The LOV is an InfoSwing control that has built-in functionality. As with all prebuilt objects, the LOV offers specific properties and behaviors. Although it gives you a quick way to display a selection window, the prebuilt behavior may not be exactly what you intended. However, for most applications, the time you save in using this component should outweigh any functionality that you might miss. For the rare occasions when you need specific functionality that is not native to the control, you can build a new control yourself. The following steps use the standard, unaltered InfoSwing control.

I. Drop an LOV control from the InfoSwing tab into the Structure Pane. It will appear under the Other node. Change the following properties:
   name to "deptLOV"
   title to "Select a Department"
   dataItemName to "deptLOVRowSet"
   This associates the LOV with the row set object that you created before.

2. In the Structure Pane, select the Deptno attribute under deptLOVRowSet, as shown here:

3. Set the *returnItemName* property to the Deptno attribute from Emp view row set, as shown here:

This means that when a row is selected in the LOV, the value in the LOV row set Deptno attribute will be returned into any item that is based on the Emp row set Deptno attribute. Figure 9-2 shows the interaction between the LOV, the items in the frame, and the row sets. The fields on the application take data from the data row set object that is tied to the data model object of the Emp view object; this view object is unfiltered—that is, it is not a detail in a link so that all rows are retrieved. The LOV takes data from the LOV row set object that is tied to the Dept view object. This view object is the master in a master-detail link relationship that contains the other representation of the Emp view object (filtered). The properties that tie the objects together are shown next to the object on which they are set. Chapter 6 contains more information on the concepts behind the BC4J objects.

4. Click Save All.

What Just Happened? This phase added the LOV control to the form and defined the data source as the LOV row set created in the preceding phase. The

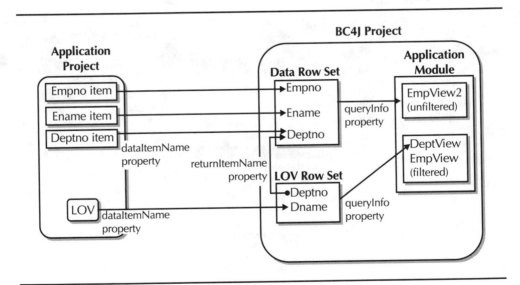

FIGURE 9-2. *Row sets and properties used in an LOV*

return attribute was linked to the LOV so that the selected value in the LOV will populate any item based on that attribute.

IV. Define an Event for Displaying the LOV

The LOV is now completely defined, but there is nothing yet that will cause it to be displayed. The following defines a button with an event that calls the LOV's `show()` method.

1. Click masterPanel in the Structure Pane and change its layout to "XYLayout." This will allow you to place any object anywhere without having to worry about a layout manager enforcing an unwanted size or shape.

2. Drop a ButtonControl from the InfoSwing tab onto the frame in the UI Designer.

3. Select the new button and change the following properties:
    name to "deptLOVButton
    text to "List"
   Move and resize the button so that it looks like this

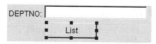

4. Group all fields, labels, and the button (using SHIFT-click) and move the objects to the upper left corner of the frame. Click deptLOVButton in the Structure Pane.

5. Click the Events tab and change the ActionPerformed event name to "deptnoLOVEvent." Press ENTER to move the focus to the Source viewer. The following shell method will appear:

```
void deptnoLOVEvent(ActionEvent e) {

    }
```

6. Replace the blank line with the following:

```
deptLOV.show();
```

7. Click Save All.

8. Compile the project and run it. Test the List button with an existing record and a new record. The LOV will look similar to the following:

Select a Department		
		Find
▼ Department Name	Deptno	
ACCOUNTING	10	▲
OPERATIONS	40	
RESEARCH	20	
SALES	30	
		▼

| OK | Cancel | Help... |

What Just Happened?   You added a button next to the Deptno field and wrote an event to display the LOV when the user clicks that button.

CAUTION
The help system describes how to display the LOV on a navigation event such as the cursor moving into the DEPTNO text item. This method forces the user to select from the list each time the cursor moves into the item. This could be disruptive to the user's interaction with the form, especially if the user is just tabbing through fields without wanting to change the values.

In addition, setting the lovForeignKeyName *to the name of the column (for example, "dept.deptno") as exemplified in the help system will query only the records from the row set that match the number currently in the text item. In the case of the DEPT table query, this will always be one row. The WHERE clause that is constructed from this property is "((99 = dept.deptno))," where "99" is the value in the text item. If the DEPTNO item is null, you will see no rows because the condition will be "null = dept.deptno," which will never be true. This could also be confusing to the user. If you want to use this method, fill in the* lovForeignKeyName *property as "1 = 1 OR dept.deptno." This will create the WHERE clause "((1 = 1 OR dept.deptno = 99))" and display all rows from the row set.*

V. Try Some Variations

You can set properties on the LOV row set to modify the appearance of the LOV. Try the following variations to get a sense of what is possible.

Hide the DEPTNO LOV Column

Frequently, you want to suppress the display of the code value column of your LOV. These steps will show you how to hide the display of the DEPTNO column while still using it as a return value.

    1. With the Design tab selected, click the Deptno attribute under the deptLOVRowSet node in the Structure Pane. Change the *displayed* property to "False." This will hide that column in the LOV, but allow it to be queried and returned into the field.

    2. Compile and run this version. When you click the button, the LOV appears with only the DNAME column displayed. Selecting a name and clicking OK will return the DEPTNO value to the employee record on the frame. The DEPTNO column is still being retrieved, but not displayed.

    3. You can right click in the LOV and select DEPTNO from the popup menu. This will display that column in the LOV. If you set the *displayable* property to "False," the DEPTNO column will not show in the popup menu.

Resize the LOV

The LOV dialog has a default size that is too wide for this particular need. Although the size does not appear in the property list, you can use the following steps to resize the LOV:

    1. Find the following code in the `jbInit()` method:

```
deptLOVRowSet.setAttributeInfo( new LOVAttributeInfo[] {
                        DnamedeptLOVRowSet,
                        DeptnodeptLOVRowSet} );
```

    2. Add the following under that code call:

```
deptLOV.setSize(280, 220);
```

    3. This programmatically resets the starting size in pixels (width of 280 and height of 220) for the LOV dialog.

4. Click Rebuild and Save All. Run the application. Try the List button to see the new size. If you want to modify the location that the LOV appears, use the `setLocation()` method with the X and Y positions as arguments.

Set the LOV Column Label

You can define how the LOV displays the name at the top of the column using a property in the LOV row set attribute as follows:

1. In the Design tab, select the Dname attribute under deptLOVRowSet in the Structure Pane.

2. Change the *columnLabel* property to "Department Name." If this is blank, the *bindName* property is used as the column label.

3. Click Rebuild and Save All. Run the application. Click the List button and see the new column label for the department name.

Add a Department Name Lookup

A friendly interface for users who handle tables that contain code values is to hide the code and display the description. The first variation described before hides the code value (Deptno) in the LOV. What is left to complete this interface is to add the department name field on the form and hide the DEPTNO field. There are two tasks required to implement this solution:

- Set up the BC4J view link
- Modify the Dept entity
- Modify the form

Set Up the BC4J View Link The business components for this application already include view objects for EMP and DEPT. There is a master-detail link defined from DEPT to EMP but not from EMP to DEPT. To add the lookup value, you need to define a link in that direction so that when an employee record is displayed, the corresponding department name from the DEPT table will also be displayed. Although there is no database foreign key constraint defined in this direction, you can set up this master-detail link in the BC4J application module. Since there is a foreign key in EMP already, defining a link from the master as EMP and the detail as DEPT will always retrieve one detail (DEPT) record.

Once the link is defined, you have to create a row set that supplies the data for the detail (DEPT) field. Use the following abbreviated steps and refer to Chapter 6 if you need explanations about where the objects that you are handling fit into the overall picture.

1. Select the business components project in the Navigation Pane.

2. Select **File | New** and click the Business Components tab.

3. Select View Link and click OK. This opens the View Link Wizard. Click Next on the Welcome page.

4. Specify the name as "EmpDeptLookupLink." Click Next to go to the Association Views page.

5. Select EmpView on the left and DeptView on the right. This defines the master-detail relationship between the EMP master and DEPT detail. Click Next for the Source Role Attribute page.

6. Move the Deptno attribute to the right. This defines the attribute in the EmpView that will link to the DeptView attribute. Click Next for the Destination Role Attributes page.

7. Move Deptno to the right. Click Next to display the Association SQL page.

8. Examine the link information on this page. Click Test to test the link, Next to show the Finish page, and Finish to complete the wizard. This creates the link that you will use to display the department name.

9. You now need to add the new link to the data model in the application module. Click the application module as shown here:

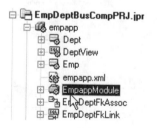

10. Right click and select Edit EmpappModule from the popup menu. The following Data Model page will appear.

11. In the Available Views area on the left, select "DeptView Via EmpDeptLookupLink" under EmpView. In the Data Model area on the right, select "EmpView2." Click the ">" button to move the lookup link to the data model. Be sure to have both nodes selected when you do this. The Data Model field should look like this:

12. Click Finish. Compile the business components project.

13. Click Save All.

Modify the Dept Entity   In the next section, you will create a row set to provide data for the department name lookup field. This row set will be based on the DeptView view object in the BC4J project. The DeptView view is affected by the

Dept entity that defines the DEPT database table. If the user selects a new department name for an employee, the lookup field will be populated with the new name. The problem is that when the user commits the modified employee record, the DEPT table will also be updated because the lookup name field value was also modified and this field is connected to the DEPT table. You can modify the BC4J Dept entity to prevent this update using the following steps:

1. Expand the BC4J project node and the empapp package node under it. Select Edit Dept from the right-click menu of the Dept entity.

2. Click the Attribute Settings tab and select the Dname attribute in the pulldown. The following shows this tab:

3. Normally, the database will be updated when a value is changed on the form. Uncheck the *Persistent* checkbox to indicate that the new values will not update the database. (If you set the *Updateable* radio group to "Never," an error message will result if the user selects from the LOV.)

4. Click Finish to save the entity settings. Select the BC4J project and click Rebuild and Save All.

Modify the Form   You need to create another item for the department name and hide the DEPTNO item. This item requires another row set object to supply the linked DEPT row. When an EMP record is retrieved, the new master-detail link (from DEPT to EMP) will populate the new item.

1. With the Design tab active, drop a RowSetInfo component into a blank area of the Structure Pane. Change the following properties:
   session to "sessionInfo"
   name to "deptDetailRowSet"
   bindName to "deptDetailRowSet"

2. For the *queryInfo* property, select DeptView1 (Detail Table mode). Be sure the Emp view is selected as the master. Select the Dname and Deptno columns in the Selection Order tab. Click OK.

3. Set the *masterLinkInfo* to "EmpView2MasterIter"—the name of the row set that the wizard created.

4. Click the Source tab and use a "//" line comment symbol to comment out the line that starts as follows:

   ```
   masterPanel.add(controlDEPTNO, new ...
   ```

   This will hide the DEPTNO field but retain all other code that links it to the business components.

5. Click the Design tab. Drop a TextFieldControl from the InfoSwing tab onto the masterPanel node of the Structure Pane. Set the following properties of the new item:
   name to "dnameTextField"
   text to blank
   dataItemName to the Dname attribute from deptDetailRowSet

6. Change the *text* property of labelDEPTNO to "DNAME."

7. In the Structure Pane, select the Dname attribute in the deptLOVRowSet and set the *returnItemName* property to the Dname attribute under deptDetailRowSet. This will populate all items built from the detail row set name attribute when a row is selected in the LOV.

8. Position and size the item so that the layout looks like this:

Data Frame

EMPNO:	
ENAME:	
DNAME	

List

0%   Modified: false

9. Click Save All. Compile the project and run the application. Test the LOV and new text item.

10. Make a change to the department for a particular employee and commit the change. Use SQL*Plus (**Tools | Invoke SQL*Plus**) to check that the correct department number has been saved.

What Just Happened?   You tried out some variations on the LOV control to learn some of the possibilities for its behavior.

NOTE
You may want to offer an LOV for a text field in a grid control (multirecord display area). It is not a straightforward task to place a button inside the grid control, but your requirement may be easily met with a single button on the frame or a toolbar button that displays the LOV for the record at the cursor location.

A Note about Hiding Objects

In this practice, you used a code modification to hide the DEPTNO item. The item could not be deleted because it held key data for the database record and was used to hold a return value for the LOV. There are a number of possible methods for hiding objects as follows:

- **Comment out the add() method.** This is a programmatic method used in this practice that removes the line containing the add method that places the item in the panel. For example, `//masterPanel.add(controlDEPTNO,...);`.

- **Set the *displayed* property to "false."** This creates a call to the object's `setDisplayed()` method. Not all objects offer the `setDisplayed()` method.

- **Programmatically set the visible property to "false."** For the objects that do not offer a *displayed* property, you can use the `setVisible()` method, for example, `deptLOVButton.setVisible(false);`.

- **Set the width and height properties to "0."** Some objects have properties for *maximumSize*, *minimumSize*, and *preferredSize*. Setting these to "0,0" (for the width and height) will effectively hide the object. However, if the container for the object has certain layout styles such as BorderLayout and GridLayout, the layout will override your manual size settings.

The technique that you use depends on the situation. The first technique to try is to set a property such as *displayed* in the Property Inspector. This requires no code change and is easier to maintain.

Hands-on Practice: Using the Tree Control

This practice uses the business component layer created in the earlier section "Hands-on Practice: Sample BC4J Project." However, you can complete this hands-on practice without having completed the LOV hands-on practice. This practice creates two applications that demonstrate different uses for this control. If you were adding this control to an existing application, you would already have created the BC4J objects and the application so you would skip those steps. The two applications and the development phases for each follow:

I. **Create a tree display for a self-referencing link**

- ■ **Set up the BC4J view link**

- ■ **Create a single-table application**

- ■ **Define the tree control**

II. **Create a tree display for a master-detail relationship**

- ■ **Create a master-detail application**

- ■ **Define the tree control**

I. Create a Tree Display for a Self-Referencing Link

Hierarchical data is stored in a relational database using a single-table with a self-referencing foreign key constraint, also called a recursive relationship. The recursive foreign key in the EMP table represents a hierarchical reporting structure. The first example creates an interface that allows the user to drill down through different levels of the manager-employee relationship. All employees that report to a particular manager are listed under that manager's node in the tree. The tree serves as a navigational aid that allows you to examine the reporting hierarchy and view the details of that employee in another control. Figure 9-3 shows the tree control of this application.

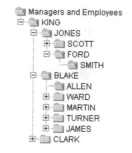

FIGURE 9-3. *Tree control showing manager to employee hierarchy*

Set Up the BC4J View Link

You need to create another view link object in the application module to represent the link from employee to manager, as represented here:

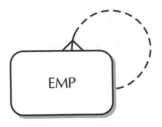

This "pig's ear" relationship is a recursive or self-referencing one. The manager's employee number is stored in the MGR column of the EMP table. This manager number appears in the EMPNO column of another EMP record—the record representing the manager's data. The manager's employee record also refers to a manager that is the manager's manager. In this way, the reporting hierarchy is created.

When you created the BC4J project, JDeveloper extracted the foreign key information from the database and created a view link that represents the recursive relationship. If you did not have a foreign key defined in the database, you will need to create the view link first. Follow the pattern in the example earlier in this chapter called "Set Up the BC4J View Link" in the section "Add a Department Name Lookup."

1. You need to add the view link to the application module so that it can be used as the basis for a row set. Click the module name "EmpappModule" under the business components project. Right click and select "Edit EmpappModule" from the menu.

2. On the left field, select "EmpView Via EmpEmpFkLink." (The link name may vary depending on the name of your foreign key constraint.) On the right side, select "EmpView2." Click the ">" button to move the link under EmpView2 on the right.

CAUTION
Be sure that you click the ">" button to move the link.

3. Click Finish to create the view link code. If the Manager to Empno constraint has not been created, you will not see this option. Exit and create the foreign key constraint for MGR referencing EMPNO. (The Introduction to this book contains the SQL statement that will create this constraint.)

NOTE
If the view link was generated from a database foreign key constraint, it will be named using the constraint name. In this example, the foreign key constraint on the MGR column is called "EMP_EMP_FK." The view link name is generated as "EmpEmpFKLink." Make the appropriate adjustments in this practice if your foreign key was named differently or if you created the view link name manually.

4. Click the business components project node in the Navigation Pane and compile it. Click Save All.

Create a Single Table Application
In this phase, you create an application that will serve as the container for the tree control. For the sake of speeding up the process, you will create the application using the Business Components Data Form Wizard.

1. Click the workspace name and select **File | New Project**.

2. Use the empapp folder and name the project EmpEmpTreePRJ. Specify that this will be a project containing a new application.

3. Specify that the package name is empapp and click Finish to run the Application Wizard.

4. Leave the defaults, including "A new Business Components for Java Data Form." Click OK to run the Business Component Data Form Wizard.

5. Specify a single table.

6. On the Frame page, replace the *Title* field with "Reporting Hierarchy." This will become the window title.

7. Select a grid layout and the default template.

8. Select EmpappModule as the source of the business components.

9. Select the database object "EmpView2." Choose the columns EMPNO, ENAME, and MGR.

10. Specify the connection and click Finish when you reach the final page. This will generate the code for the application and link it to the BC4J application module.

11. Click Rebuild and Save All. Run the application and test it.

Define the Tree Control

You are now ready to add a tree control and link it to the application.

1. Doubleclick the Frame in the Navigation Pane to display the Viewer. Click the Design tab.

2. Click the TreeControl on the InfoSwing component tab. Drop it on the "this" node in the Structure Pane.

3. Change the following properties on the tree control:
    name to "empTree"
    rootNodeLabel to "Managers and Employees"
    nodeDefinitions — click the "..." button to display the nodeDefinitions dialog as shown here:

The *nodeDefinitions* value indicates the data source and the *rootNodeLabel* will be displayed on the top-level node at runtime.

4. Select EmpView2 on the left and move it to the right. This defines the link between the existing row set for the EMP table to the tree control.

5. The *Display column* field is a pulldown where you can select any column in the row set that will be displayed as the tree node label. Set this to "Empno."

6. Check the *self referential* checkbox. This is only checkable if the view link you have selected is defined as self-referencing—that is, the link is to and from the same table. Click the OK button.

7. Click Rebuild and Save All. Run the application. You will see a window such as that in Figure 9-4.

8. Try opening nodes by clicking the + symbol to the left of the employee number. When you click a node in the tree, the corresponding row is selected in the grid control. Conversely, when you click a row in the grid control, the corresponding row is selected in the tree control. This is because both controls use the same row set as their data source.

9. Close the application by selecting **File | Exit**. Clicking the "x" icon at the top of the window may not properly close the window.

10. You can make this application more user-friendly if you specify that the tree node labels use the name of the employee instead of the number. Open the *nodeDefinitions* property of the tree control and click the Empno label in the "Display column" field.

11. Another user-friendly substitution is to place the tree to the left of the grid. Select the tree control in the Structure Pane and change its *constraints* property to "West."

12. Click Rebuild and Save All. Run the application and look for the change in the node labels.

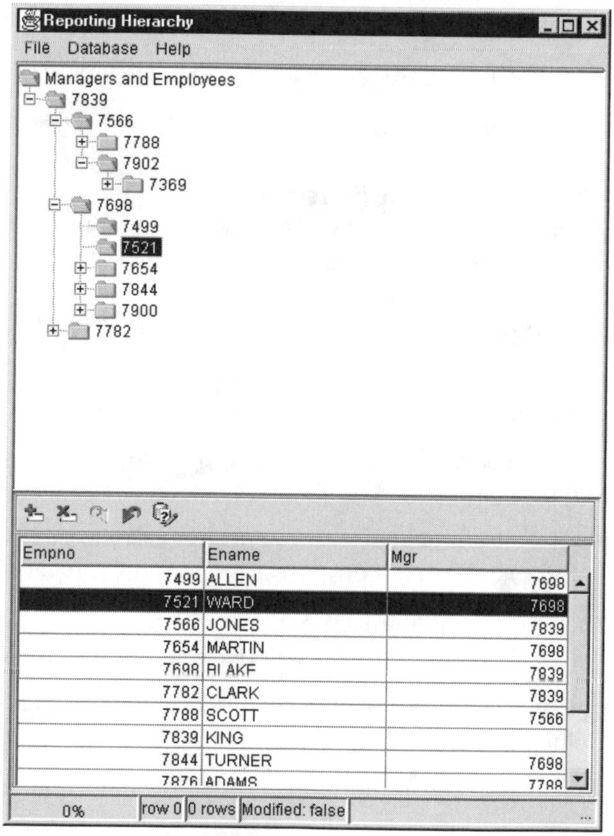

FIGURE 9-4. *Self-referencing tree application*

What Just Happened?   You added another view link object to the application module that represents the self-referencing relationship of manager to employee. You added a tree control that uses this view link and allows navigation among records in the application.

II. Create a Tree Display for a Master-Detail Relationship

You can use the tree display in many other ways. This practice builds a tree that you can use to navigate master-detail information. The master records will be represented in the second-level tree nodes, and the details will be represented under that level. This arrangement provides an even friendlier view of the data and helps the user quickly navigate to a particular record. The data model that this practice implements is the standard master-detail relationship as shown in this diagram:

Create a Master-Detail Application

The starting application for this example is a master-detail form. This practice also uses the Business Components Data Form Wizard to quickly create an application.

1. Click the workspace name and select **File | New Project**.

2. Use the empapp folder and name the project "EmpDeptTreePRJ." Specify that this will be a project containing a new application.

3. Specify that the package name is "empapp," and click Finish to run the Application Wizard.

4. Leave the defaults, including "A new Business Components for Java Data Form." Click OK to run the Business Components Data Form Wizard.

5. Specify a master-detail format. On the Frame page, replace the *Title* field with "Staff by Department." This will become the window title.

6. Specify the master as a vertical layout and the detail as a grid. Use the default template.

7. Select EmpappModule as the source for the business components.

8. Select the master object "DeptView" and select the detail object "EmpView." Accept the join condition.

9. Select the DEPTNO, DNAME, and LOC columns for the Dept view.

10. Select the EMPNO, ENAME, and DEPTNO columns for the Emp view.

11. Specify the connection.

12. Click Finish when you reach the final page. This will generate the code for the application and link it to the BC4J application module.

13. Click Rebuild and Save All. Run the application to ensure that it connects and retrieves data properly.

Define the Tree Control
The next step is to add a tree control to the application.

1. Doubleclick the frame in the Navigation Pane to display the Viewer. Click the Design tab.

2. Click the TreeControl on the InfoSwing component tab. Drop it on the "this" node in the Structure Pane.

3. Change the following properties on the tree control:
   name to "deptempTree"
   constraints to "West"
   rootNodeLabel to "Departments"
   nodeDefinitions — click the "…" button to display the nodeDefinitions dialog.

4. Move DeptView from the candidates field to the right. Move EmpView to the right.

5. In the Display column, select Dname for DeptView and Ename for EmpView from the respective pulldowns. Click OK.

6. Click Rebuild and Save All. Run the application. You will see a window such as the one in Figure 9-5.

7. Try opening nodes in the tree area and notice that the master-detail area stays synchronized with the selection in the tree.

What Just Happened?   You created an application with a master-detail relationship and added a tree control to it. The tree control displays the same information as in the master and detail areas but allows you easy navigation to the records.

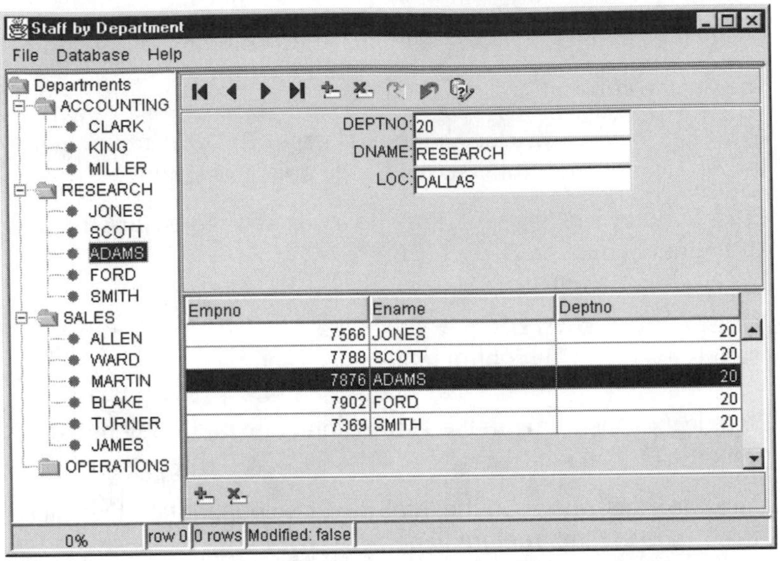

FIGURE 9-5. *Master-detail tree application*

Hands-on Practice: Adding to the Component Toolbar

In this practice, you will add two components to the existing toolbar tabs. The first will be JOptionPane, an existing class in the Java 1.2 library. This practice will also create a JavaBean that you will place on the toolbar. This demonstrates how to create a JavaBean as well as how to customize the component toolbar tabs. After adding each component, you will create a simple application as a test.

This practice will follow these phases:

I. **Add JOptionPane to a tab**

■ **Add the component**

■ **Define the icon**

II. **Test JOptionPane**

   III. **Create a JavaBean**

       ■ **Set up the project**

       ■ **Lay out the bean**

   IV. **Add the JavaBean to a tab**

   V. **Test the JavaBean**

When you first install JDeveloper, the Other tab is empty. You can add components to the Other tab (and any other tab) as well as reorder components within the preinstalled tabs. You can even delete any of the tabs. For example, you could remove the AWT tab entirely. While you are learning the tool, it is probably best to keep the preinstalled tabs intact and add components that you need to new tabs. You will be able to find components more easily when they are referenced in examples and documentation. After you learn the product and components better, you will be able to customize the tabs to match your style.

For ordering the components on the tab, you can either choose a logical organization or an alphabetical organization. By default, the product ships with the components arranged alphabetically. You should probably stay with this configuration. This will make it easier for developers coming from other environments to find the components they are looking for. This practice steps you through adding the components to the Other tab.

I. Add JOptionPane to a Tab

JOptionPane presents a modal dialog window that you can use to display messages to the user, to receive user input through button selections or typed-in text.

Add the Component

These steps will add the JOptionPane component to the toolbar tab. All you need to know in order to add a component to a tab is its filename and location. JOptionPane is located in a JAR file that contains javax.swing classes. The file is called dt.jar, and it is located in the JDEV_HOME\java1.2\lib folder.

   I. To add the component, click the Other tab in the component toolbar. Right click and select Properties from the popup menu. This opens the Palette Properties dialog, as shown in Figure 9-6.

      This dialog allows you to add, delete, and rearrange the components on the toolbars. You can add a page (tab) to the toolbar by clicking the Add

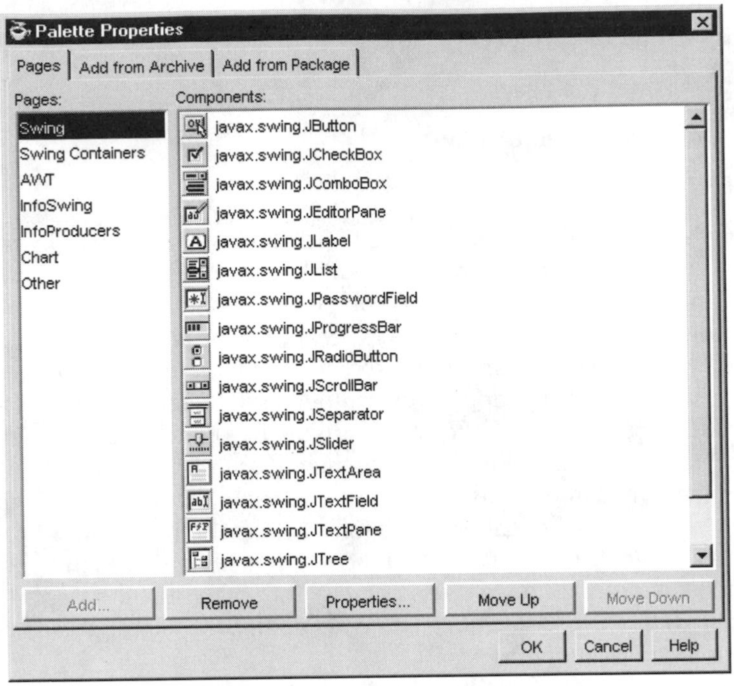

FIGURE 9-6. *Palette Properties dialog*

button. The Remove button allows you to delete a page or a component. The Properties button presents a dialog that you can use to change the icon associated with the component. The Move Up and Move Down buttons allow you to arrange the order of the tabs and the components within the tabs. The Add from Package tab allows you to browse and select class files that are not archived into a JAR or Zip file. The Add from Archive tab allows you to browse and select class files that are in JAR or Zip files.

2. Click the Add from Archive tab. Click the Browse button and navigate to the JDEV_HOME\java1.2\lib folder.

3. Click the dt.jar file in that folder, and click Open.

4. Select the javax.swing.JOptionPane as shown here:

Palette Properties

Pages | Add from Archive | Add from Package

Select a JAR or ZIP file:

D:\Program Files\Oracle\JDeveloper 3.1.1.2\java1.2\lib\dt.jar   Browse

JavaBeans found in archive:

javax.swing.JComboBox
javax.swing.JScrollBar
javax.swing.JSeparator
javax.swing.JOptionPane
javax.swing.JToolBar
javax.swing.JPasswordField
javax.swing.JLabel
javax.swing.JTree
javax.swing.JList
javax.swing.JWindow
javax.swing.JToggleButton
javax.swing.JRadioButtonMenuItem

☑ Only display classes that have BeanInfo

Add component to page: Swing ▼   **Install**

OK | Cancel | Help

5. Ensure that the Other page is selected in the bottom pulldown list. Click the
Install button to add the component.

CAUTION
*Be careful with the Remove button. If you click it
after selecting a component, you will delete the
component. However, if you click it after selecting
a tab page, you will delete that page. If you do this
by mistake, click the Cancel button and start over.
The* DELETE *key is a bit safer because it only
removes the last selected component and will
never remove pages.*

Define the Icon
After creating your components, you need to select a suitable icon that will
make identifying the components easier. The following steps define this icon
for the component.

1. Click the Pages tab and doubleclick the JOptionPane icon. The Item Properties dialog will appear.

2. Click "Select Image" and click Browse to look for an icon file. Select the JTextPane.gif file located in the default icon directory (JDEV_HOME\lib\image16). Click Open and OK.

3. Click OK in the Palette Properties dialog. Check the Other tab for the JOptionPane. The tooltip for this icon will be "JOptionPane (javax.swing)" to indicate the class name and its location.

What Just Happened?   You added the JOptionPane component to the Other toolbar. The main tasks were finding the component and finding the icon file that represents the component in the toolbar. Whenever you use this component, you need to be sure that the import section of the source code includes javax.swing.

II. Test JOptionPane

This phase creates a sample application that uses JOptionPane to create a message dialog. This component has many other uses. The help topic about the JOptionPane class describes the functionality and gives examples.

1. Create a project called TestOptionPanePRJ and specify a project containing an application. Use the empapp folder and package.

2. In the Application Wizard, specify a new empty frame.

3. In the Frame Wizard, accept the default settings.

4. Open the UI Designer by doubleclicking the frame and clicking the Design tab.

5. Select the "JPanel1" node in the Structure Pane. In the Inspector, change its *layout* property to "XYLayout." This will allow you to place objects anywhere in the panel without the panel imposing an automatic layout.

6. Drop a JButton from the Swing tab onto the UI Designer frame. Change the following properties:
   name to "testButton"
   text to "Test"

7. Drop a JOptionPane component from the Other tab onto the UI node in the Structure Frame. Nothing will appear in the "this" window because the pane is not a child of that window.

8. Change the name to "mainOptionPane."

9. Click testButton in the UI Designer and click the Events tab of the Inspector. Doubleclick the actionPerformed field to pass control to the Source pane in the Viewer.

10. Replace the blank line in the new method with the following:

```
mainOptionPane.showMessageDialog(
this,
"This is a dialog box",
"Sample Dialog",
JOptionPane.INFORMATION_MESSAGE);
```

11. Compile the project and click Save All.

12. Run the application and click the Test button to try the dialog. The dialog window title will be "Sample Dialog," and the message will appear in the dialog.

13. Look up the help topic on "Class JOptionPane" and try some other variations, such as using ERROR_MESSAGE instead of INFORMATION_MESSAGE. This will change the dialog's icon. You can also try other methods, such as showConfirmDialog, showInputDialog, or showOptionDialog.

What Just Happened?   You tested the component in a new application. Chapter 13 contains a sidebar "Using the Dialog Class" that describes another method for creating a message window.

NOTE
The code that JDeveloper writes for you in this case is minimal if you do not modify properties in the Inspector, and there seems to be little benefit in creating a component. You have to write some code each time you use this component, because the nature of JOptionPane is that it appears in response to an event. It is still worthwhile to have this component on the tab because any generated code is better than no generated code.

III. Create a JavaBean

A *JavaBean* is one or more classes that form a reusable component. All objects on the component palette are JavaBeans. The benefit of a JavaBean is that it offers reusability—once you design, create, and debug the bean, you can leverage that work by using it many times. The JavaBean hides the complexity of its code and offers an interface that you can control.

Set Up the Project

The easiest way to manage the JavaBean is if it is in a separate project. Therefore the first steps are to set up this project.

1. Create an empty project in the empapp folder and package. Call the project "SystemToolsPRJ."

2. Select the project and choose **File | New**. Click the Beans tab, select Bean, and click OK. The Bean Wizard will display as shown here:

3. Define the *Class* as "SystemToolbar" and *Package* as "empapp."

4. For the *Extends* field, click the Browse button, open the javax package and the swing package under it. Scroll down and select JToolbar. Click OK to dismiss the Package Browser and OK to dismiss the Bean Wizard.

5. Open the UI Designer for SystemToolbar.java. Change the layout of the "this" panel to "XYLayout."

6. Using Windows Explorer, find the gologout.gif file in JDEV_HOME. (Select that directory and press F3 for the Find utility.)

7. Copy the file to JDEV_HOME\myprojects\empapp. This puts the icon in the right place to be packaged with the bean.

8. Drag the file into the Navigation Pane from the empapp folder using Windows Explorer and drop it on the SystemTools project node. This adds the icon file to the project.

NOTE
Since the pane is derived from JToolbar, the Inspector contains properties of that control. The JavaBean that you create in this phase will emulate the toolbar behavior.

Lay Out the Bean

In the following steps, you will define and code the behavior of the bean.

1. Add a JButton from the Swing tab and change the following properties:
   name to "exitButton"
   text to blank (no text)
   icon to "gologout.gif"
   tooltipText to "Exit"
   preferredSize to "25,25"
   The latter property will display the button without a border to emulate the NavigationBar component's behavior.

2. Resize the panel to match the following illustration:

Set the borderPainted property of the button to "False."

3. Click the button. On the Events tab, select the actionPerformed event and type "eventExit." Press ENTER to switch to the Source pane.

4. Type the following in the blank line for the new method:

```
System.exit(0);
```

5. Compile the project and click Save All.

What Just Happened? You created a JavaBean project based upon a toolbar and defined an exit button.

NOTE
This creates a bean in the same folder as your test application. Normally, you would create the bean in another folder to keep it separate from the projects that will use it.

IV. Add the JavaBean to a Tab

The steps to add this component to the Other tab and define its icon are the same as for the JOptionPane and are, therefore, abbreviated.

1. Display the Palette Properties for the Other tab.

2. Click the Add from Package tab. Browse to find JDEV_HOME\myclasses\empapp.

3. Select the SystemToolbar.class file inside that folder and click Open. The dialog will appear as follows:

4. Ensure that the Other page is selected in the bottom pulldown list. Click the Install button to add the component.

5. Click the Pages tab and doubleclick the SystemToolbar row. Choose "Select Image" and browse for an icon file called JToolbar.gif (in the JDEV_HOME\lib\image16 directory). Click Open, OK, and OK.

What Just Happened You added the new JavaBean to the Other toolbar and specified an icon file.

V. Test the JavaBean

Now that you have a new toolbar component, you can use it in your sample application. Use the application from the preceding JOptionPane example (in the TestOptionPanePRJ project) as a basis.

1. Reopen the UI Designer for the tester application by doubleclicking the frame Java file and clicking the Design tab.

2. Click the SystemToolbar icon in the Other tab and draw the object out in the UI Designer above the button as shown here. You may not see the Exit button in the designer, but it will appear when you run the application.

[Figure: A window with a toolbar and a "Test" button]

3. Click Rebuild and Save All.

4. Run the application and try dragging the toolbar out of the window. It will create a floating toolbar. Close the toolbar window to lock it back inside the window.

5. Click the Exit button to exit the application.

Changing the Button Border

The following demonstrates how you can change the bean class and the application will automatically change. A NavigationBar object normally contains buttons without borders. The border appears when the user moves the mouse over the button and disappears when the mouse is no longer over the button, as in the following:

Before mouse entry  After mouse entry

The events involved with this are mouseEntered when the mouse cursor passes over the edge of the button and mouseExited when the mouse cursor is no longer over the button. The following steps will create the code to emulate this functionality.

1. Open the UI Designer for the SystemToolbar java file. Click the button.

2. Define two more events for the exit button. Doubleclick the current name (value) for each and enter the code below for the method that is created in the Source Viewer:

Event	Code
MouseEntered	exitButton.setBorderPainted(true);
MouseExited	exitButton.setBorderPainted(false);

3. Click Rebuild and Save All.

4. Click the tester application (under the TestOptionPanePRJ project), recompile, and run it. Pass the mouse over the exit button and see the effect of the border appearing and disappearing.

What Just Happened   You used the new JavaBean in an application and modified the code for the component in the tab to incorporate the border behavior of the navigation bar buttons. Compiling that code and the base application allowed you to see the change in functionality. It was not necessary to change the component palette definition because the tab just links to the class file and does not contain any code.

CHAPTER
10

Menus and Toolbars

Man is a tool-using animal.... Without tools he is nothing, with tools he is all.
—Thomas Carlyle (1751–1881), *Sartor Resartus*

very user of client/server applications is familiar with the traditional design elements of menus and toolbars. Both provide easy and well-understood user interfaces for many application functions. Menus provide the user with the ability to execute the standard tasks in a particular application. Toolbars provide the ability to execute the most commonly used tasks in the menu. By providing these to your users, you give them the tools they need to perform their work in the most efficient way. Menus and toolbars in Java applications and applets work exactly like their counterparts in the client/server world.

This chapter explains some general considerations for designing menus and toolbars. The best way to describe how to create menus and toolbars in JDeveloper is to step through an example. The hands-on practices at the end of the chapter supply such examples.

Design Considerations

An integral part of any user-interface design is determining how the user will perform the actions required to complete a task. For example, when designing an online transaction processing application, you have to decide how the user will add, search, modify, delete, and save data. The first decision you must make is whether you will use menus and toolbars at all. If you do not use them, you have to decide how to supply the functionality that they normally provide. The deployment method that you select for an application will, to a large extent, help you with this decision.

In a client/server application, menus and toolbars are natural features that users expect to see and easily understand. In a web-deployed application, menus and toolbars are not always a standard feature. If the application will be deployed as a Java applet or Java application, toolbars and menus are natural interface features because the Swing and AWT components used in these deployments closely resemble typical client/server applications. In these cases, using the menu and toolbar components from the Java Swing and AWT libraries is a logical choice.

If the application will be deployed through JavaServer Pages (JSPs) or other HTML interfaces, menus and toolbars are not as automatically supplied. Menus are usually implemented differently than they are in client/server applications. For example, textual or graphical links on an HTML page usually supply the functionality that a client/server pulldown menu supplies. If pulldown menus appear in HTML applications (usually by means of JavaBeans because HTML does not support menus), they are implemented as design elements that look very different from a standard client/server pulldown menu.

Toolbars, on the other hand, may be useful to HTML-style applications if they are designed with components familiar to the user. For example, a client /server-style toolbar made up of a series of iconic buttons would not visually fit into an HTML-based application as well as a series of .gif files that have appropriate links.

Once you have made the decision that you need menus and toolbars, you plan their design and organization and determine which functions you want to provide. There are some general factors to consider and guidelines to follow when creating this design.

What Do You Put on the Menu?

When structuring a menu system, it is important to copy standard menus that users are accustomed to in most Windows applications. This will lessen the learning curve that the user interface may require and will speed up user acceptance of your application. Your menu design should take into consideration the organization of elements that your users expect. For example, if your menu structure contains File, Edit, View, Window, and Help menus, users will quickly understand where to look for a particular function because these menus are commonly used in most Windows applications. While most Windows client/server applications interact with files, your applications will more commonly interact with a database, so you have to stretch the item names a bit in some cases. It is useful to look at a suggestion for how the items will be displayed on these menus, as follows.

File Menu   This menu usually contains Open, New, Save, Close, and Exit items among others. You can provide those same items in your Java applications, even though the concept of file interaction does not apply. An Open item could select a table or application to browse; a Close item could clear current data from the form; and Save could commit the changed data.

Edit Menu   Items may add or remove records or otherwise manipulate data. For example, you can include an item to copy an existing record or fill the current record with default values. Another common item to include on the Edit menu is one for Options that allows users to modify personal preferences such as colors, fonts, and backgrounds. Options may also include how default values are filled in and what is shown when the user opens the application—for example, a find window or an automatic query of all records.

View Menu   Items on this menu may navigate to a particular section or record. The View menu can also contain items for Find, Sort, and Filter to modify how a set of records is displayed. You can also allow the user to display or hide a toolbar using a check menu item.

Other Menus   These menus, which should be placed to the left of the Window menu, will provide functionality that is specific to the application. It is best to keep the number of other menus to a minimum so that the user is not overwhelmed with choices. As a rule of thumb, a maximum of ten pulldowns (main menu headings), each with a maximum of 15 selections, will give users up to 150 choices. This should be plenty of items for a standard application. If they are logically arranged, the user will be able to find a function easily without having to browse the menus frequently.

Selections in other menus might include application-specific functions such as navigating to other applications, stepping the user through a difficult task, using wizards, and copying a record.

Window Menu   The items on this menu can be used to arrange the various open windows and allow navigation between them.

Help Menu   Items perform the expected calls to the help system or Help About dialog.

Other Menu Features

Menus offer other design features. You can take advantage of all of these in JDeveloper, but some may require extra coding.

Nested Menus

Menus can contain nested menus, as shown in an example of the JDeveloper IDE menu in Figure 10-1. In other words, when you select a menu item from a pulldown, another side menu opens for the actual selection. In this example, when you select Toolbar from the View menu, another side menu opens where you can select the toolbar that you want to display.

Design Suggestion   Although you can create menus to virtually any level of depth, a good rule of thumb is to limit yourself to three levels as in Figure 10-1. More than three levels requires some extra dexterity from your user and can lead to frustration if the user cannot easily select a menu item.

Popup Menus

You can define *popup menus* that appear when the user clicks the right mouse button. Popup menus are not attached to the top of the window but normally appear at the mouse cursor location when the right mouse button is clicked on an object. They are also called *context menus* or *right-click menus* because they appear based on the context or location of the mouse cursor. Popup menus are usually customized for the object that was clicked and allow quick access to functions that apply only to that object. For example, right clicking a text item could display a

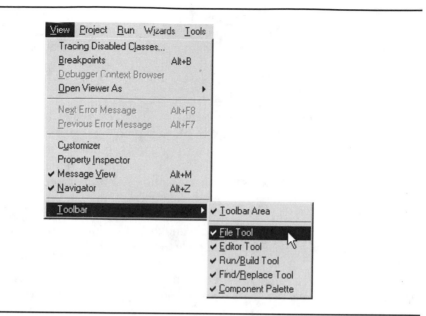

FIGURE 10-1. *Multilevel menu*

menu for Cut, Copy, and Paste to manipulate the text in the item. Right clicking a panel in a data form might display a menu that allows the user to add or remove records and save or undo changes. Users find right-click (more properly called "alternate-button click" to accommodate left mouse users) menus a fast way to get to a particular menu item. They require less movement of the mouse than a normal menu to access the required functions. The following is an example of a popup menu.

Design Suggestion   It takes some training to make users aware of and accustomed to the functionality on popup menus. However, if your application requires repetitive actions to access or input data, popup menus may help. Examine the possible ways that your application will be used when determining what to put on popup menus, and customize them for the most commonly used menu items that a user would require when working with a particular object. Popup menu items are usually items that also appear on the main application menu.

Design the popup menu as simply as possible. For example, nested submenus within a popup menu make the popup menu difficult to use. Popup menus often contain fewer items than a normal pulldown menu, and you may want to set a limit of six or eight items (plus separators).

Check and Radio Group Items

Menu items can appear as normal items or with check marks or radio buttons. A check mark menu item represents a single state of a toggle, such as displaying a toolbar or hiding a toolbar, as Figure 10-1 shows. In this example, if the menu item for File Tool is checked, the file toolbar is displayed. If the user selects the item when it is checked, the check mark vanishes and the toolbar is hidden.

Radio group menu items offer more than one option and display the selected option with a round bullet icon. If you create a group of items, only one of the group will be "checked" at once. The menu item functionality will take care of the visual display, but you need to write code to handle what happens when the user makes a selection.

For example, you might have a main menu item called Sort that is a submenu. When the user selects the item, a nested menu appears with a radio group of items for the columns that will be sorted (such as Name, Hire Date, Salary, and so on). When the user selects one of this group, the radio button will appear by the item and the code you write would re-sort the display based on that column.

Design Suggestion   Check and radio group menu items are not frequently used. It is more common to provide the functionality that they offer using an options dialog.

Mnemonics and Accelerators

Mnemonics are quick access keys that help the user select a menu or menu item without using the mouse. Pulldown menus are typically activated using the ALT key combined with the first letter in the menu text. For example, to activate the File pulldown, the user would press ALT-F. In this example, "F" would be underlined to indicate to the user that this was the key to press with the ALT key. The user accesses a menu item within the pulldown using the underscored letter. For example, the Exit item in the File menu would be activated when the user pressed the x key. The letter used as the mnemonic must appear in the menu item's text property. The following is an example of the underlined letters that indicate mnemonics.

An *accelerator* key is a shortcut to the functionality that is offered in the menu. The user can press this key combination to activate the same code that the menu item activates. Mnemonics and accelerators are similar, but accelerators do not display the menu selection and are a single keypress combination instead of the mnemonic's multiple keypress combination. The accelerator key combination appears next to the menu item, as shown in the following:

File	
<u>S</u>ave	Ctrl+S
E<u>x</u>it	

NOTE
The Swing class JMenuBar uses a property called accelerator *to supply the functionality of an* accelerator. *If you use the AWT class MenuBar, the property name is* shortcut.

Design Suggestion   When you make your decision on which mnemonics and accelerators to include, a good rule of thumb is that you should provide mnemonics for every menu selection so that a user without a mouse can successfully navigate within your application. It is important to respect the standards supported by existing applications. For example, you should provide the commonly known accelerators such as CTRL-S for Save. Examine common Windows programs to get a feeling for the common accelerators. In addition, you should avoid reassigning commonly used accelerators such as CTRL-X, CTRL-C, and CTRL-V that usually represent the functions Cut, Copy, and Paste, respectively.

Disabling and Enabling Items
Many modern applications disable menu options that are not applicable to a certain mode. For example, if you have not made any changes to data on a form, the Save option is not required and therefore should be disabled. When a change is made to the data, the item would be enabled.

Design Suggestion   Although the ultimate in user friendliness, disabling options requires a bit of code, and you have to weigh the benefits of this friendliness against the extra time and effort involved in coding and debugging. In many cases, issuing a dialog to indicate that a function is not available in a certain mode will serve the purpose and not cause undue user frustration.

Menu Item Icons

You can associate a .gif file with a menu or menu item. You can display the menu text with the graphic, as in the following:

Design Suggestion   Although this technique allows you to associate a visual clue with the text, it is not commonly used. The extra space that the graphic absorbs is probably not worth the benefit.

Tooltips

Menu items can have tooltip text associated with them. This text pops up when the user rests the mouse over the item, as the following shows:

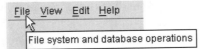

Design Suggestion   Menu tooltips are useful only if menus or menu items are hard to understand. Since you strive for intuitive wording in your applications, you should not need this feature for menu items.

NOTE
You will not see accelerators, mnemonics, or icons in the Menu Designer. If you define them in the properties or code, they will appear only at runtime.

What Do You Put on the Toolbar?

Think of the toolbar as an extension of the menu. All functions on the toolbar should also be available in the menu. Therefore, it is best to design the menu first and repeat menu selections in the toolbar. The main design guideline here is to place menu items in the toolbar that are most commonly used. Examples of commonly used items for a transaction processing system would be Save and Undo. Users need to interact with data frequently, and saving and undoing changes are often-performed tasks. You may have to validate your designation of commonly used functions with a user trial of your application.

Toolbars are usually iconic in nature. In other words, the user selects a toolbar button by identifying an iconic picture located in a panel. This saves space and clutter on the screen over the alternative of identifying the buttons with text labels. Toolbar buttons are also a standard size as opposed to text buttons that are usually sized to their labels. Although there is a bit of a learning curve for users to understand what the pictures represent, it is faster for users to find a picture in the toolbar than a word once that learning curve is overcome.

Other Toolbar Features

Many features of menus are also available in the toolbar. However, the design considerations are different for toolbars and menus, as follows:

- **Icons**   While you would normally not use icons on menu items, you would usually use them on toolbar buttons.

- **Mnemonics and accelerators**   If you follow the guideline that toolbar items are derived from menu items, the menu items will fulfill the need that mnemonics and accelerators serve. Therefore, you do not need mnemonics and accelerators for toolbars.

- **Tooltips**   While you do not use tooltips for menu items, you normally supply tooltips for an iconic toolbar button so that the user can get a hint about the function that the button performs.

- **Enabling and disabling items**   You might want to go through the same process as you do with menus to determine how you will handle enabling and disabling items. Since toolbar buttons duplicate functionality on the menu, you can extend the code you write to disable and enable a menu item to include the toolbar button with the same functionality.

You need to consider a few other features in your decision process when designing toolbars.

Multiple Toolbars

After you decide what to put in the toolbar, you need to make the decision on how many toolbars to supply. Sometimes, there are more items to put in a toolbar than there is horizontal space in the window. Also, there may be logical, task-oriented groupings of buttons that you might want to represent.

The solution for these issues is to supply more than one toolbar. Each user may work with your application in a different way, and you can account for this by allowing the user to select which toolbar is displayed using an options dialog.

Design Suggestion   Use multiple toolbars if you have many functions that need to be represented or if you think some users might want to have control over the groups of buttons that are displayed. If the latter is the case, you have to write code to allow users the ability to define which toolbars are displayed.

Toolbar Arrangements

Although toolbars normally appear on the top of the window just under the menu, you can also build toolbars in a vertical orientation to leave more vertical space for user-interface objects.

You can also define the toolbar as part of a separate window or as a panel that the user can "undock" from the main window so that it floats outside the main window. This gives the user the option to shrink the main window but still have all elements visible without scrolling. The toolbar buttons will be easily available in this arrangement.

Design Suggestion   Horizontal toolbars are a standard and expected interface object. Vertical toolbars are a personal preference that you might want to let the user determine. Floating toolbars are also something that you can supply to the user, but the standard is to have the toolbar initially docked to the main window.

Summary of User Access Methods

When you design your menu and toolbar, you have to consider the functions that the user will need to access. You also need to plan the method that will provide each of these in the application. The following are the main methods available to the application designer:

- Toolbar button
- Menu item (main menu)
- Accelerator key
- Context menu item

For example, the Cut function is usually available in the Edit menu as well as in the popup menu for items that support data editing. In addition, the design could provide for a toolbar button that offers users the choice of clicking the button for the Cut function. As in most applications, the accelerator keys CTRL-X would be mapped to the same function.

There is an additional method that you can offer to particular users—the command line. While this is not the normal method for web applications, there may be some functions that you would allow the user to perform from a command-line prompt (such as opening or converting a file).

Menus and Toolbars in JDeveloper

JDeveloper supports all of the menu and toolbar functionality described earlier. Therefore, you have relatively unlimited scope when designing the features that you want to include. Some features are easier to implement because JDeveloper writes the code for you. For example, to attach an icon to a button, you just fill in the *icon* property of the button object with the .gif file name, and the setIcon() code will be created. Setting the mnemonic and accelerator for a menu item is sometimes possible with properties, but easier by adding a line of code (as explained in the hands-on practice later in this chapter). However, runtime behavior such as disabling and enabling menu items and buttons requires writing custom code.

You can automatically generate default menus and toolbars using the wizards. For example, the Frame Wizard that is called from the Application Wizard contains checkboxes for a menu and toolbar, as Figure 10-2 shows. When you check those,

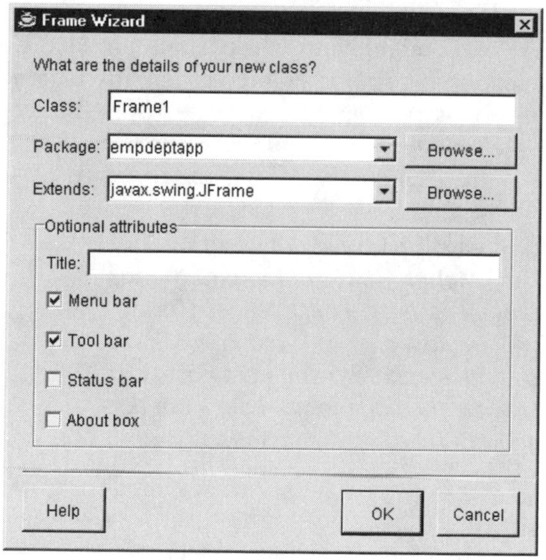

FIGURE 10-2. *Specifying a toolbar and menu in the Frame Wizard*

the Frame Wizard creates a default menu that contains a File menu with an Exit item. The toolbar contains buttons for file open, file close, and help. Both structures contain no code (other than a generic call to exit the application) and are only outlines of what you would use for a real application. Therefore, you need to add code and buttons and modify the contents after the wizard is finished. Other wizards, such as the Business Components for Java Data Form Wizard, also automatically generate a menu and toolbar. In this case, the code for the buttons and menu items is also generated and completely functional.

There are other specific JDeveloper features for menu objects and toolbar objects that are worth exploring. The hands-on practices at the end of this chapter give you some of the practical steps to complete when creating menus and toolbars.

Menu Objects

The object for a menu system that appears on the top of a window is called a *menu bar* (implemented using a component such as JMenuBar). This is the root object that you drag into an application from the JDeveloper component palette. A menu bar is a container that holds two kinds of objects: menus and menu items (implemented by components such as JMenu and JMenuItem, respectively). Menus correspond to the headings that you click for a pulldown or submenu (nested menu or menu within a menu). Menu items are the items in the pulldown menu. In the case of multilevel menu systems, submenus look the same as menu items but are different because they display other menu items. For example, in Figure 10-1, the View menu contains a selection for Toolbar, which is actually a menu because it contains selections such as Toolbar Area and File Tool. Therefore, you can say that menus may contain other menus and menu items.

TIP
*You can quickly create a menu structure using the selection Standard Menus – JFC or Standard Menus – AWT in the Object Gallery (**File | New**). These code snippets will create a class file with File, Menu, and Help menus with standard menu items in each. You still have to write the code for all items, but this saves you the effort of building the layout.*

The Menu Designer

The easiest way to lay out a menu is with the Menu Designer. You access this window by clicking the Design tab in the Viewer. If a menu has been created in the application, right click the menu bar node in the Structure Pane and select "Activate designer" from the menu. You can also doubleclick the icon on any menu object. This will display the Menu Designer, as shown in Figure 10-3. You can switch back to the UI Designer using the same methods: doubleclick an object in the UI node or select "Activate designer" from the right-click menu on a UI object.

The Menu Designer contains a toolbar with functions that you use to create the menu structure. After creating the menu structure, you write code that will be activated when a menu item is selected. The toolbar buttons allow you to create or delete an item or *separator* (horizontal line with no functionality) and create a nested menu. The toolbar also has selections to convert a normal menu item to a checkable menu item and to disable or enable a menu item. The latter just toggles the *enabled* property from "True" to "False." You can also toggle this property at runtime using the setEnabled() method.

Some of the Menu Designer toolbar functions are available using keypresses. For example, you can add a menu item in an empty space below another menu item by pressing ENTER. This will move the cursor to the blank item where you can type the text label. The code and properties areas will update as you make changes to the design area. To edit the text for an existing item, doubleclick the item in the Menu Designer.

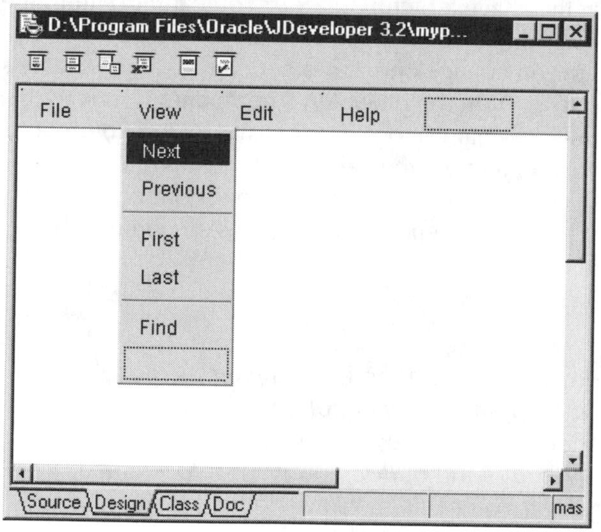

FIGURE 10-3. *Menu Designer*

TIP
You can drag and drop objects within the Menu Designer to rearrange their order. Dropping on top of an item will arrange the dragged item above that item. Clicking a button to add an item or separator will add the item or separator above the selected item.

Toolbar Objects

Toolbars are made up of a set of buttons inside a container called a "toolbar." The toolbar has special properties that allow the user to detach the container from the main window. You can specify that you do not want the user to detach the toolbar using the *floatable* property of the toolbar. Since the toolbar is a container, you can manipulate the group of buttons by manipulating the toolbar. For example, if you want to hide the toolbar buttons, you write code to hide the toolbar. All buttons inside the toolbar will also be hidden.

You lay out the toolbar using the UI Designer. The sequence consists of dropping a toolbar container object in the application and adding buttons inside the toolbar.

Buttons require event code to execute the desired action. You can attach icons to buttons so that they have a picture on top. You can also fill in the *text* or *label* property with a text string that will appear on top of the button. These two properties stay in sync; when you change one, the other changes to the same string. (The *label* property is a carryover from the older AWT components. It is the same as the *text* property.) Normally, toolbar buttons use icons as decoration, but not text labels. Therefore, you need to remove the value of the *text* property (or the setText() call in the source code) so that there will be no text label.

A hands-on practice at the end of this chapter steps through the process of creating a toolbar with buttons.

TIP
You can reorder objects on the UI Designer by dragging and dropping. For example, you can reposition a toolbar button by dragging it and dropping it on top of the button you want it to appear in front of. You can also reorder objects and menu items by cutting them from the Structure Pane (CTRL-X) and pasting them (CTRL-V) on top of another object node in the Structure Pane. The pasted object will be placed on the top or on the bottom of the list of objects beneath the target object.

Note for Oracle Developer Users
Menu items and buttons require code to handle the selection *event*. Events are like triggers except that you have to instantiate them and give them a name. You also need a listener. In Forms, the listener function is automatically taken care of by the runtime engine.

Using a Navigation Bar

A quick way to create a toolbar that has record and database manipulation buttons is to use a navigation bar. The InfoSwing component tab contains a NavigationBar class that you attach to a view object. This navigation bar provides Next, Previous, First, Last, Add, Delete, Save, and Undo functions for the view object that it is attached to. You do not have to write any customized code to make the navigation bar buttons work. Examples of how to create a navigation bar are in the hands-on practice for Chapter 2 as well as in the following section.

Hands-on Practice Sample Application

A menu must be attached to a window so that it can be seen. Therefore, for this practice, you need a window that contains database access controls. You can use the application you created in Chapter 2 as a foundation. If you did not complete that hands-on practice, use the following abbreviated steps to create a minimal application that you can use as a basis for this practice. If you need help on any of these steps, refer to the hands-on practice in Chapter 2. If you completed the hands-on practice for Chapter 2, open that workspace and skip to phase I of this practice. You can also use the application sample file as a starting point. (See the author biographies for the web site address that contains this file.)

1. Create a workspace and save it in a new folder called "menutoolbar."

2. Create a business components project based on the EMP and DEPT tables. Alternatively, if you ran the practice in Chapter 2, you can open the business components project that you created for that practice (DeptEmpBusCompPRJ.jpr).

3. Create a project for an application. Accept the defaults in the Application Wizard.

4. Specify a new empty frame in the Frame Wizard. Accept the other defaults.

5. Add a SessionInfo component and specify a session for the ScottConnection. Specify the *appModuleInfo* property. Add a RowSetInfo component and specify the DeptView (all columns) in the *queryInfo* property.

6. Rename JPanel1 to "formPanel." Specify a BorderLayout. Add a JPanel under formPanel and specify a ColumnLayout. Name this new panel "masterPanel."

7. Add a JPanel under masterPanel and specify a ControlLayout. Call this panel "deptnoPanel."

8. Add a Swing JLabel under deptnoPanel and change its *text* property to "Dept #: " including a space after the colon. Change the *constraints* property so that it is right justified (the value should be "ControlConstraints.ALIGN_RIGHT, 0, 0, -1, -1").

9. Drop an InfoSwing TextFieldControl component under deptnoPanel. Change its *dataItemName* property to "deptno" from the Dept row set. Name it "deptno.TextField."

10. Follow steps 7–9 to add another panel, label, and text item for the DNAME column.

11. Drop in a LoginDlg component. Change the *dataItemName* property to reference the infoSession component. Add the following line to the imports section:

```
import oracle.dacf.control.LoginFailureException;
```

12. Add the following lines after the call to `loginDlg1.setDataItemName()` in `jbInit()`.

```
if (loginDlg1.showDialog() == JOptionPane.CANCEL_OPTION) {
    throw new LoginFailureException();
}
```

13. Drop an InfoSwing NavigationBar component on top of formPanel. Ensure that the *constraints* property is set to "North." Set its *dataItemName* property to the Dept row set. Rename it as "masterNavBar."

14. Test the application. Be sure that the navigation bar works.

Hands-on Practice: Building a Menu

Adding a menu bar to an existing application consists of the following main phases:

I. Lay out the menu elements

II. Set the menu element properties

III. Write the menu item code

As mentioned earlier, there is a preparation step where you design the structure that your menu will use. The menu you will build in this hands-on practice uses the structure shown in the composite Menu Designer session in Figure 10-4.

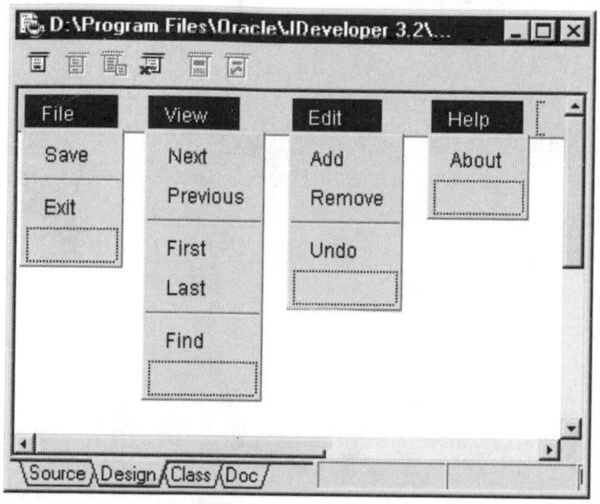

FIGURE 10-4. *Sample menu structure*

I. Lay Out the Menu Elements

The first phase defines the structure of the menu. It constructs the menus and items for the entire menu. At this stage, you do not need to worry about all of the properties or names of the elements. Use the following steps to lay out a menu bar such as that shown here.

1. Doubleclick Frame1.java in the Navigator Pane. The Viewer will open and load the code for this frame.

2. Click the Design tab if it is not already selected.

3. In the Swing Containers component tab, click JMenuBar, and then click anywhere in the Structure Pane to add the menu to the application.

4. Change the *name* property to "frameMenuBar."
At this point, the menu will not be visible. The menu component that you just added is only displayed as an item in the Structure Pane. JDeveloper

contains a *Menu Designer* that you can use to lay out the menu items. This designer displays in the same viewer as the frame. To switch back and forth between editors, doubleclick an element in the appropriate section. For example, if the UI Designer is displayed, doubleclick an element icon in the Menu node of the Structure Pane to display the Menu Designer. Doubleclick an element under the UI node to switch back to the UI Designer. You can also select "Activate designer" from the right-click menu on these elements.

TIP
If you need to show the Menu Designer that is attached to a frame and the Viewer is not displayed, doubleclick the frame in the Navigation Pane. Then click the Design tab and navigate to the Menu node in the Structure Pane. Doubleclick a menu element, and the Menu Designer will open.

5. Doubleclick the icon next to frameMenuBar in the Structure Pane to open the Menu Designer, shown here.

If you see menu items, delete the top-level menu for those items in the Structure Pane.

6. To add the first menu item, doubleclick the dotted rectangle in the upper-left corner of the Design area and enter "File." Press the ENTER key after typing the text. This becomes the *text* property of the menu element. The Menu Designer window will look like this:

When you add a menu, the Menu Designer opens a new menu to the right and a new item below. Each time you add a menu item, the Menu Designer opens a blank item below it. New menu elements are shown with a dotted or selected box. Doubleclicking a new element allows you to type text. The Menu Designer contains a toolbar to assist in setting up a menu as follows:

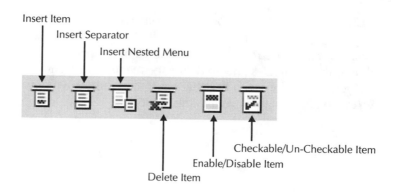

7. Doubleclick the box to the right of the File menu and type "View" for the text. This adds another menu (top-level) element.

8. Add two more menu elements for "Edit" and "Help." Your menu will look like this:

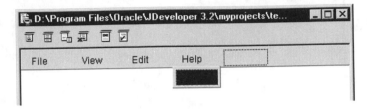

9. Click the File menu and doubleclick the box under it. Type the text as "Save."

10. Click the blank box under Save and click the Insert Separator toolbar button. A *separator* is a thin line that divides one menu item from another. It provides a way to group items logically in the menu.

NOTE
The Insert Item and Insert Separator buttons in the Menu Designer add elements above the currently selected item.

11. Add an item under the separator and type "Exit" for the text.

12. Add items under the View, Edit, and Help menus to match the structure shown in Figure 10-4.

13. Click the Save All icon in the toolbar.

What Just Happened?   You just added a menu component to the application and used the Menu Designer to define the menus and menu items that will be displayed. Since the menu bar attaches to the frame's window title, you do not have to worry about the layout in the frame.

NOTE
If your design required nested menu items, you would have used the Insert Nested Menu button when the selection was on the item. This creates a box to the right of the item that you can treat as another menu item. If your design included check menu items, you would use the Checkable/ Un-Checkable Item button to convert the item.

II. Set the Menu Element Properties

Now that the menu structure is laid out, you need to modify the properties. The primary property that you need to change is the *name* property. The easiest way to make changes to the list of properties is to use in-place editing in the Structure Pane. Use the following steps to accomplish this.

1. Click the file menu (top) icon under frameMenuBar in the Structure Pane. Click the name of that menu to open the edit box. Change the name to "fileMenu" and press ENTER.

2. Change the name of the first menu item to "saveMenuItem."

3. Repeat steps 1 and 2 for all menus and items. You do not need to rename the separators.

4. Add mnemonics for each menu item by writing some code. (Remember, a mnemonic is a letter or character that the user can press to activate the menu item.) For example, you can set the mnemonic for the File menu so it will pull down when the user presses ALT-F. In the Source Editor, place the following code after the call to `fileMenu.setText()`:

```
fileMenu.setMnemonic(KeyEvent.VK_F);
```

This uses a keypress object constant (VK_F) to associate the ALT-F key combination with this menu item. The Inspector property for *mnemonic* will show the Unicode number associated with that letter (70, in this example). You have to be sure that `java.awt.event.*` appears in the imports section of the code for this to compile. This assignment will place an underscore on the matching letter, as the following shows.

The rule is that you need to select a mnemonic letter that is used in the *text* property. Use the values in the following table to assign mnemonics to the menu.

Menu (or Menu Item)	SetMnemonic() Value
Save	KeyEvent.VK_S
Exit	KeyEvent.VK_X
View	KeyEvent.VK_V
Next	KeyEvent.VK_N
Previous	KeyEvent.VK_P
First	KeyEvent.VK_F
Last	KeyEvent.VK_L
Find	KeyEvent.VK_I
Edit	KeyEvent.VK_E
Add	KeyEvent.VK_A
Remove	KeyEvent.VK_R
Undo	KeyEvent.VK_U
Help	KeyEvent.VK_H
About	KeyEvent.VK_A

Some letters are used twice, but not within the same pulldown. Menus are activated with the ALT key combined with the letter. Menu items are activated with only the letter keypress.

TIP

If the cursor focus is in a text field and the user presses the mnemonic, the letter of the keypress may be typed into the field. If this effect occurs, you can use the mouseClicked event to set the focus to the item when the mouse is clicked in the item and the focusLost event to remove focus from the item when the mnemonic is pressed. For example, the code for removing focus on the empno text field is shown here. This code (and the code for the mouseClicked event) would be repeated for each field.

```
void empnoTextField_focusLost(FocusEvent e) {
    empnoTextField.setRequestFocusEnabled(false);
}
```

5. Add an accelerator for Save. Recall that accelerators are shortcut keys that allow the user to access the function of a menu item without activating the menu. For example, if the accelerator was set to CTRL-S for Save, when the user pressed this key combination, the menu's Save function would be executed. The shortcut key appears next to the menu item, as the following shows.

You need to write a line of code for each shortcut key. The shortcut key does not have to be the same as the mnemonic, but it will make more sense to the user if they are the same. The code you will write must appear under the call to setMnemonic() method for each menu item. For example, look in the Source Editor for the saveMenuItem.setMnemonic(); that you just wrote and add the following lines under it:

```
saveMenuItem.setAccelerator(KeyStroke.getKeyStroke(
    KeyEvent.VK_S, ActionEvent.CTRL_MASK));
```

This uses a form of the setAccelerator() method to set the shortcut key to the S key combined with the CTRL key. The constants (uppercase variables) used in this call represent the keypresses.

6. Add an accelerator for nextMenuItem. The call is the same as before except that you need to substitute the correct menu item name (nextMenuItem) and keypress (VK_N) for the N key. Try adding the same kind of shortcut for Previous (use P as a shortcut key).

What Just Happened? You just changed the names of the menus and menu items to comply with the standard that requires a suffix to denote the type of each object. You also added mnemonics and accelerators to assist the user in accessing the menus and menu items.

III. Write the Menu Item Code

You do not need to write code to show menu elements because this function is performed by the control. However, you do have to write the code that each menu item executes when it is selected.

This phase uses a NavigationBar component to supply the functionality for most of the menu items. A navigation bar allows the user to scroll between records and perform basic database activities. The navigation bar is attached to a row set, and its buttons act on that object. Since the buttons perform the necessary actions, all you need to do is write code for the corresponding menu item that emulates a click of the button. It is much simpler to call methods offered by the navigation bar than it is to write corresponding methods from scratch. The following illustration diagrams the code path using a navigation bar method:

You will also write custom code for some of the menu items. This code path is diagrammed in the following:

Attaching code to a menu event is a two-step process. The first step is to identify the type of event the user will activate (such as mouse click, keypress, and focus-gained) and write a code stub for that event. You perform this step using the Inspector. The second step is to fill in the stub with a call to the desired method. You need to write a line of code for this in the Source tab of the Viewer.

Before you begin adding code, click the Source tab for the frame's .java file and navigate to the end. This is where the generated methods will be created. At this point you will only see the default methods for the frame (such as `Frame1()`) and `jbInit()` in your application. As you perform the following steps, you will be switching back and forth to this area to make manual updates to the generated code.

NOTE

If you named your menu items differently from those used in the following steps, be sure to adjust the following steps for those names.

I. Click the Design tab of the Viewer to display the designer. If the Inspector does not pop up, select **View** | **Property Inspector**.

TIP

At any point, if the Inspector does not show the properties of an object selected in the Structure Pane, close it and reopen it or switch back and forth from Design to Source tabs in the Viewer to refresh the Inspector.

2. Click the icon for exitMenuItem in the Structure Pane.

3. Click the Events tab in the Inspector.
   In the Events tab, there are events and event names (used for instantiating the event). You can specify the name that you want the event to have in your code by overriding the default name. The default name is a concatenation of the object name and the event name. For example, the exitMenuItem event for actionPerformed defaults to "exitMenuItem_actionPerformed."

4. Click the *actionPerformed* event, replace the default name with "exitEvent", and press ENTER. This will immediately switch the Viewer to the Source Editor and place the cursor at the stub for the newly created event-handling method. This also creates a listener in the `jbInit()` function body.

   This method has a generic name so that you can use it for other purposes, such as a popup menu item or toolbar button. You could write the code directly in the listener and would not need the extra method; this is not reusable, however, because the listener is specific to an object.

NOTE

If you change the name you assign to an existing event, the method stub that appears in the Source tab will not be renamed, but a new stub will be added with the new name. You will need to delete the old method and rework the listener to call the new method.

5. Look at the code. Starting at the top of the file, search the source code for "exitEvent" as in the following:

```
exitMenuItem.addActionListener(new
        java.awt.event.ActionListener() {
    public void actionPerformed(ActionEvent e) {
        exitEvent(e);
    }
});
```

The code adds a listener that will call the method that the Events tab added, as shown in the next step. Scroll to the bottom of the file.

6. In the Source Pane, the new event-handler method stub should look like the following:

```
void exitEvent(ActionEvent e) {

}
```

Add the following line above this method.

```
// Menu event handlers
```

This will help you find the menu event handlers.

7. Replace the blank line inside the curly braces with the following call:

```
System.exit(0);
```

This is a simple one-line call to exit the application. Other menu items will call methods in the navigation bar.

8. Click Save All in the toolbar. Compile and test the application to check that this menu item works.

9. Click the Design tab at the bottom of your source file to return to the designer.

10. Click the icon for saveMenuItem in the Structure Pane. In the Inspector, replace the *actionPerformed* event name with "saveEvent" (another generic name).

11. Press ENTER. The view will switch to the Source tab. As with the exit item, there will be a code stub for the method name you just entered.

12. Replace the blank line between the curly braces with the following line of code.

```
masterNavBar.doClick(NavigationBar.BUTTON_COMMIT);
```

13. Click the Rebuild icon in the toolbar to check your syntax.

14. Repeat steps 9–12 for each item in the following list. Substitute the event methods and button name constants as appropriate.

Item	Event Method	Button Name Constant
nextMenuItem	nextrecEvent	BUTTON_NEXT
previousMenuItem	prevrecEvent	BUTTON_PREV
firstMenuItem	firstrecEvent	BUTTON_FIRST
lastMenuItem	lastrecEvent	BUTTON_LAST
findMenuItem	findEvent	BUTTON_FIND
addMenuItem	addrecEvent	BUTTON_INSERT
removeMenuItem	removerecEvent	BUTTON_DELETE
undoMenuItem	undoEvent	BUTTON_ROLLBACK

15. Switch to the Design tab to set up the code for the Help menu item. Click the icon next to the aboutMenuItem in the Structure Pane.

16. Change the *actionPerformed* field in the Inspector to "helpAboutEvent" and press ENTER to create the method stub. The control will switch to the source code view.

NOTE

You can also doubleclick the event name to create the method stub.

17. Enter the following inside the blank method stub:

```
JOptionPane.showMessageDialog(
        this,
        aboutMessage,
        aboutTitle,
        JOptionPane.INFORMATION_MESSAGE);
```

This calls a message dialog with the text in the variables.

18. Go to the end of the declaration section by locating the line `JMenuItem aboutMenuItem = new JMenuItem();`. Add the following right after this line. This code declares variables for the dialog box and assigns values to those variables.

```
String    productName      =  "Departments Browser";
String    productVersion   =  "Version 1.0";
String    productCopyright =  "Copyright (c) 2001";
String[]  aboutMessage     =  {productName, productVersion, productCopyright};
String    aboutTitle       =  "About " + productName;
```

19. Click Rebuild and Save All in the toolbar.

20. Run the application and test all menu items.

What Just Happened?   You wrote event-handler code for each menu item in the layout. Some code uses the doClick() methods from the navigation bar, and other code uses specific methods that you wrote. This also gives you an idea of how events and listeners work and are coded.

Hands-on Practice: Building a Popup Menu

The method for creating a popup menu is very similar to the method for creating a regular menu. This practice builds on the preceding practice or on the application created in the practice for Chapter 2. If you do not have the results of that practice, use the abbreviated steps in the menu practice section "Hands-on Practice Sample Application" that appears earlier in this chapter. As before, you can also use the application available in the sample files on the authors' web site. The following steps start after you have opened the workspace containing this application. Figure 10-5 shows an example of a popup menu in action.

The following steps assume that you have completed the preceding practice for menus and are, therefore, familiar with the main operations. If you need further explanation for a particular step in this practice, refer to the preceding practice. There are two main phases in creating a popup menu:

I. **Lay out the elements**

II. **Write the menu code**

■ **Display the popup menu**

■ **Handle an event for each menu item**

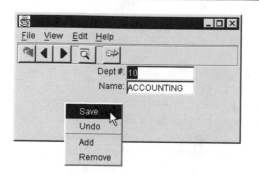

FIGURE 10-5. *Popup menu*

I. Lay Out the Elements

The first phase uses the UI Designer to place the objects on the frame.

1. Click the Design tab of the viewer.

2. Drop a JPopupMenu component from the Swing Containers component tab into the Structure Pane. It will appear in the Menu node.

3. Rename the popup menu to "mainPopupMenu."

4. Right click the popup menu node in the Structure Pane and select "Activate designer." This will change the UI Designer display to show the menu. A *popup menu* is essentially a single pulldown that is detached from the window. It will pop up when the user clicks the right mouse button on an object with which you have associated the popup menu.

5. Add four items and change the *name* properties as in the following table:

Save	savePopupItem
Undo	undoPopupItem
Add	addPopupItem
Remove	removePopupItem

6. Add a separator between Undo and Add. Remember that separators and menu items will be added above the currently selected item. You can drag and drop objects to rearrange them in the Menu Designer.

TIP
When adding items to a menu, pressing ENTER *after entering the name will add an item below and move focus to the new item. All you need to do is start typing the new text at that point. It is not necessary to doubleclick to start editing text on the new item. If you have trouble with this, remember that you can always doubleclick to start editing the text.*

7. Click Save All.

What Just Happened?   You added the toolbar container to the application frame. It appears in the Menu node of the Structure Pane but, unlike normal menus, will not be displayed until you write code to perform that action. In this phase, you also used the Menu Designer to lay out the menu items in a single pulldown. The remaining task is to write some code.

II. Write the Menu Code

You need to write event-handling code for displaying the popup and for performing a function when a menu item is selected. JDeveloper helps you create the code for both purposes.

Display the Popup Menu

While a normal menu is usually displayed at the top of the window, a popup menu usually appears when the user clicks the right mouse button. (You can display a popup menu on a button click or other event, as well.) Therefore, in this example, you need an event handler to display the popup menu on a mouse click. This handler consists of a listener on a panel in the application that calls a custom method. The following steps create this code.

1. Select the formPanel node in the Structure Pane.

2. Enter "formPanelMouseClick" for the mouseClicked event in the Inspector. Press ENTER. The focus will pass to the Source Editor that contains a method stub for the name you just entered. Replace the blank line between the curly brackets with the following:

```
formPanel.add(mainPopupMenu);
if (e.getModifiers() == Event.META_MASK)
    mainPopupMenu.show(formPanel, e.getX(), e.getY());
```

This code adds the popup object to the formPanel, which sets the panel as the popup menu's parent object and displays the menu. You can programmatically attach the popup menu to other objects in the same way. The code also shows the popup menu at the mouse cursor's location (x and y positions) if the right mouse button was clicked (e.getModifiers() == Event.META_MASK;). JDeveloper also adds a listener, formPanel.addMouseListener(), that calls this new method. You do not need to modify that listener.

3. Find and comment out the line (using "//") that adds the popup menu to the "this" frame. The line will look like the following:

```
this.getContentPane().add(mainPopupMenu);
```

This line is generated when you drag in the popup menu component. Although it is required for a normal menu, it is not required for a popup menu because you are executing the add function in the mouse click handler.

4. Click Save All. If you want to compile and run the application to try the popup menu display, you may do so at this point. The menu items will not be functional because you have not written the code.

Handle an Event for Each Menu Item

The code to handle events for each item works the same way as it does with a normal menu. The code you create here for a menu item consists of a new method that calls a method for the navigation bar. If you want to use functionality that is not on the navigation bar, you can write your own code instead of calling the navigation bar methods.

1. Click the Design tab. Click savePopupItem in the Structure Pane. Enter "saveEvent" in the *actionPerformed* name on the Inspector's Events tab.

2. Press ENTER, and the focus will shift to the Source tab. If you created the saveEvent() method in the previous practice, there is nothing more to write. The Events tab creates a listener for the Save item and calls the existing saveEvent() method that you wrote earlier. Skip to step 4 if saveEvent() was created and filled in previously.

3. Replace the blank line in the saveEvent method with the following:

```
masterNavBar.doClick(NavigationBar.BUTTON_COMMIT);
```

4. Repeat steps 5–7 for each item in the following list. Substitute the event and button name constants as appropriate.

Item	Event Method	Button Name Constant
addPopupItem	addrecEvent	BUTTON_INSERT
removePopupItem	removerecEvent	BUTTON_DELETE
undoPopupItem	undoEvent	BUTTON_ROLLBACK

5. Compile the project and test it. You should be able to use the popup menu to perform the stated functions. Click Save All.

What Just Happened? You wrote the code for the main event handler that pops up the menu when the right mouse button is clicked. You also wrote code to execute the appropriate function from the navigation bar by calling the navigation bar's methods. If the function had already been created to call the navigation bar method for that event, you reused that function.

Hands-on Practice: Building a Toolbar

A toolbar is usually an extension of a menu, because it contains the most commonly used menu items. This practice demonstrates how to develop a toolbar that calls methods on a navigation bar, just as the menu created in an earlier practice uses those methods. Why not use a navigation bar instead of a toolbar? The reason is that a navigation bar has a fixed set of functions, and you cannot add to that set. Also, some functions may not be appropriate for some purposes. For example, you may want to add your own, more user-friendly interface for finding a record. You might want to place an exit button in the toolbar. You may not care about offering the user the ability to navigate to the first and last record with the click of a button.

This practice builds on the practice from Chapter 2 or the preceding practices. If you do not have the results of those practices, use the abbreviated steps in the menu practice section "Hands-on Practice Sample Application" that appears earlier in this chapter. The main requirement is that you start with an application that has data controls connected to the database. The data controls must include a navigation bar object. It is not necessary to have a menu before completing this practice, but that will not hurt your efforts.

This practice uses the following phases that are similar to those in the menu practice:

I. Lay out the toolbar elements

- **Hide the navigation bar**

- **Add the toolbar**

- **Find the icons**

- **Add the buttons**

II. Set the button properties

III. Write the button code

At the end of this practice, you will have created a toolbar that looks like the one shown here.

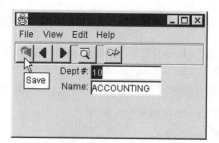

I. Lay Out the Toolbar Elements

As with any GUI container object, you have to be sure that the outer container has the correct layout manager assigned to it. (Chapter 11 describes layout managers in detail.) In this application, you will drop a toolbar onto a panel that is assigned a BorderLayout manager. This will allow you to fix the toolbar to the top of the parent container.

Hide the Navigation Bar

You need to use the navigation bar's methods to provide functionality for the toolbar buttons. However, you do not need to display the navigation bar because the toolbar will duplicate some of its functionality.

In addition to the calls to the masterNavBar methods, you will find code to instantiate (create) the object (`NavigationBar masterNavBar = new NavigationBar()`), set the data item name to the infoSession object (`masterNavBar.setDataItemName()`), and display the navigation bar (`formPanel.add(masterNavBar, BorderLayout.NORTH)`). You want to be able to use the navigation bar, but not see it. Therefore, the object needs to be instantiated and associated with the session, but you do not need the display code.

1. Locate the line of code that displays the navigation bar and comment it out using the "//" comment characters, as in the following example:

```
//   formPanel.add(masterNavBar, BorderLayout.NORTH);
```

2. Check the UI Designer display. The navigation bar should be hidden from view. When you run the application, the navigation bar will not be visible.

Add the Toolbar

You can now add the toolbar container and buttons to the frame.

1. Drop a JToolbar component from the Swing Containers component tab on top of formPanel in the Structure Pane. Be sure that formPanel has a *layout* property of "BorderLayout." The toolbar will have a BoxLayout by default.

2. Change the following properties for the toolbar:

   ■ *name* to "mainToolBar"

   ■ *constraints* to "North" (the default)

   Although you will see the object in the Structure Pane, it will not be prominent in the Design area. The toolbar will grow when you drop a button into it later.

Find the Icons

You have to prepare the icon files that you will be using for the toolbar images. The main preparation is loading them into the project, but this is easier if you have a central location for the icons. Therefore, in this part, you will create a directory for icons and copy files to it.

1. Using Windows Explorer, create a directory called "icons" under JDEV_HOME. This will be parallel to the myprojects directory on your hard drive.

2. Navigate to the JDEV_HOME\myhtml\webapp\jsimages directory using Windows Explorer. If that directory does not exist, perform a file search in JDEV_HOME for .gif files. Copy the files you find into the new icons directory. This is a one-time setup step that will make it easier to find icons for your projects.

CAUTION
You may have problems compiling your code if the icon files in your project have the read-only attribute set. Select Properties from the right-click menu after selecting the files in Windows Explorer. Be sure that the read-only attribute checkbox is not checked.

3. You now have to copy the icon files to your project directory (menutoolbar). Use Windows Explorer to find the following files in the icons directory and copy them into the directory you are using for this project (within the JDEV_HOME\myprojects directory).

browse.gif	nextrec.gif	save.gif
browser.gif	nextrecr.gif	saver.gif
gologout.gif	prevrec.gif	
gologoutr.gif	prevrecr.gif	

NOTE
The icon files will be packaged with your other code files for distribution, and they will be easier to find if they are contained in the same directory. In addition, if the files are in the project directory, the code that the Inspector creates when you set the icon file properties will not include the path, which will make the code more portable.

4. The icon files must now be added to the project in JDeveloper. Click the project node in the Navigation Pane and click the Directory tab. If the Directory tab is not showing, right click the tab area and select "View Directory tab."

5. Navigate to the project directory.

6. Drag the .gif files, one at a time, onto the Workspace tab. You do not need to click the Workspace tab; just drag the file from the Navigation Pane of the Directory tab and drop it on top of the Workspace tab.

If your icon files use different names, you can substitute any file that has a meaningful picture. There are a number of different properties that you can use to assign different icons to a button for different purposes. The *icon, pressedIcon, disabledIcon, disabledSelectedIcon, rolloverIcon,* and *rolloverSelectedIcon* properties define what icon appears on the button in different situations. This practice will assign the icon file with the "r" suffix to the *icon* property and the icon file without a suffix to the *pressedIcon* property.

7. Click Save All in the toolbar. Click the frame Java file in the Navigation Pane.

Add the Buttons
You are now ready to add the buttons.

1. Click the JButton component in the Swing component tab and click the mainToolBar node in the Structure Pane. A button will be added as shown here:

2. Repeat step 1 four times until you have five buttons.

TIP
Although you can doubleclick an image file to open the image viewer window, you will find it easier to work with icon files if you have an image browsing program. Many shareware and commercial programs are available on web sites, such as www.tucows.com. You can use these programs to browse the images and select the files you need for the toolbar.

What Just Happened?   You laid out the main toolbar component and placed buttons in it. You also prepared the project for the assignment of icon images by adding image files to the project. The first part of this phase hid the navigation bar so that you could use its functionality without having to include it in the UI.

II. Set the Button Properties

You will now set the button properties to refine the definitions.

1. Select the buttons as a group by clicking the top button in the Structure Pane and CTRL clicking each button.

2. When all buttons are selected, apply the following properties' values to the group:

- *text* to blank

- *maximumSize* to "25,25"

- *minimumSize* to "25,25"

- *preferredSize* to "25,25"

3. Click the top button in the list in the Structure Pane to ungroup the buttons. Change the following properties:

- *name* to "saveButton"

- *icon* to "saver.gif"

- *pressedIcon* to "save.gif"

- *toolTipText* to "Save"

4. Repeat step 3 to set the following properties for the rest of the buttons, working from top to bottom.

name	icon	pressedIcon	toolTipText
prevrecButton	prevrecr.gif	prevref.gif	Previous
nextrecButton	nextrecr.gif	nextref.gif	Next
findButton	browser.gif	browse.gif	Find
exitButton	gologoutr.gif	gologout.gif	Exit

5. Click the JSeparator icon in the Swing component tab and drop it between the third and fourth buttons in the UI Designer. The fourth and fifth buttons will move to the right. The separator serves the same purpose in the toolbar as it does in the menu—to create logical groupings of functions.

6. Click the separator and set its *maximumSize* property to "10,25."

7. Add another separator between the fourth and fifth buttons and resize it to 10x25. The completed layout should look like this:

8. Click Save All.

What Just Happened?   This phase set the button properties for size and image. You used the object grouping feature to apply common property values to a group of objects. You also added separators to create logical groupings of buttons.

Moving Objects Around

When you finish assigning properties to the buttons and add the separators, it is a good idea to take a few minutes to practice moving buttons around. The techniques you try here on toolbar buttons can be used with any visual object. Start with the UI Designer. You can drag and drop buttons or separators within the toolbar to reorder them. You can also drag them outside the toolbar and they will reparent themselves in the Structure Pane. Try this out, but be sure you restore the layout as in the preceding illustration.

Another method for reordering buttons is to cut and paste them in the Structure Pane. Whenever you paste an object on another object such as a pane, the pasted object will take a position either on the top or on the bottom of other objects in that pane. Try cutting the fourth button by clicking it and pressing CTRL-X. Paste it on top of the toolbar node by clicking that node and pressing CTRL-C. Try this on other buttons, but be sure to return the layout as in the preceding illustration.

III. Write the Button Code

The last step is to add the code to handle the event. You will use the same steps here that you used in the menu practice. The code you write calls the button code on the hidden navigation bar. Since the process for writing the code on menu items is similar, the following steps are abbreviated. If you need more help, refer to phase III in the "Building a Menu" practice that appears earlier in this chapter.

1. Select the saveButton object. Enter "saveEvent" in the *actionPerformed* event on the Events tab.

2. Press ENTER, and the focus will shift to the Source tab. If you created the `saveEvent()` method in the previous practices, there is nothing more to write. The Events tab creates a listener for the Save item and calls the existing `saveEvent()` method that you wrote earlier. Skip to step 4 if `saveEvent()` was created earlier.

3. Replace the blank line in the saveEvent method with the following:

```
masterNavBar.doClick(NavigationBar.BUTTON_COMMIT);
```

4. Repeat steps 1–3 for the items in the following list. Substitute the event and button name constants as appropriate.

Item	Event Method	Button Name Constant
prevrecButton	prevrecEvent	BUTTON_PREV
nextrecButton	nextrecEvent	BUTTON_NEXT
findButton	findEvent	BUTTON_FIND

5. For the Exit button, use the event "exitEvent" and press ENTER. If you do not have that method already coded from the previous practices, enter the following in the method stub:

```
System.exit(0);
```

6. Run the application.

7. Try clicking a button and watch the icon change. When the button is pressed, the icon image is the smaller of the two image files (without the "r" suffix). Normally, the icon image is the larger of the two files (with the "r" suffix).

8. Try displaying the tooltips.

Vertical and Floating Toolbars

Try clicking on a nonbutton part of the toolbar and dragging the toolbar to the right or left side of the window. The toolbar outline will change to a vertical orientation, and when you release the mouse button, the toolbar will stick to the side of the window, as the following shows:

You can resize the outer window if you need to provide more room for the toolbar. You can also drag the toolbar out of the window as in the following:

This creates a separate floating toolbar window that acts in the same way as the JDeveloper toolbars. The NavigationBar component provides this functionality. You can disable this with the *floatable* property of the toolbar. Close the toolbar window using the window's "x" icon to snap the toolbar back to the main window.

What Just Happened?   You added the code that will be executed when the buttons are clicked. This code is similar to the code that you wrote for the menu practice earlier in this chapter because both the menu and the toolbar call methods from the navigation bar.

Note for Oracle Developer Users

In JDeveloper, you need to explicitly create both the menu item and the toolbar button. You also need to write code for both objects although both can call the same method if they perform the same function. In Oracle Forms Developer you can set a menu item property that automatically displays a toolbar button so that you do not need to create a separate object for the toolbar button. The button and menu item share the same code and are treated as one object although they are displayed separately.

CHAPTER
11

Layout Managers

Mad world! mad kings!
mad composition!

—William Shakespeare (1564–1616), *King John (II, i, 561)*

ne of the main strengths of the Java language is the capability of applications built with Java to be deployed to diverse operating systems and platforms. In fact, the principle of platform independence is one on which the language was built. One manifestation of this principle is in the area of user interface design. When applications are deployed on different platforms, the windows and the objects within them are not always the same size. In addition, users may resize the windows in an application to match their preferences.

Developers grapple with this task in many programming languages and often have to develop customized solutions. Java offers a feature—layout managers—that directly addresses the layout problems that occur when displaying applications on different platforms. A *layout manager* is a class that you instantiate and attach to a container (such as a JPanel object). This class determines how objects within the container are positioned and sized at runtime both initially and when the container is resized.

You can take advantage of the layout manager features in your Java application or applet by associating it with a container and by setting a few properties. The layout manager handles the calculations and functions necessary to perform the positioning and sizing manipulations. A number of layout managers are supplied by Java and supported by JDeveloper. Therefore, you need to be aware of what is available and how each of the managers works.

This chapter explains the concepts involved with layout managers and the details about each layout manager that JDeveloper provides. It also provides some hands-on practices to show you how to apply some of the more commonly used layout managers.

Layout Manager Concepts

Tapping into the benefits of layout managers requires some understanding of the concepts. A layout manager (or "layout" for short) is a separate object that exists

Note for Oracle Developer Users

The frame object in Forms contains the same kind of automatic layout features as the FlowLayout manager in Java. However, in Forms, this is a design-time-only feature, unlike layout managers, which also work when the application is running. In Forms, there are some properties that manage how the frame works, but not nearly the number of options that the Java layout managers offer.

This lack of options is not as important because Forms applications are aimed primarily at intranet, client/server, and extranet uses, where the runtime platform can be controlled. For example, the Forms developer can rely on users having a particular screen resolution when running the application. This allows the Forms developer to size the windows and lay out their contents carefully without having to worry about how the application will display on an unknown system.

In Reports, the frame object also corresponds to the Java layout manager concept. Reports provides more control over the frame at runtime, and you can specify whether you want the frame to resize at runtime based on its contents. In this way, the frame emulates the type of functionality that the layout managers provide.

within the context of a container. It determines how objects inside the container will be placed and sized both in design time and at runtime. As a review of Java objects, there are three main levels in what is called the *Containment Hierarchy*:

- ■ **Top-level container**   A top-level container is the visual root for all objects in an application or applet. It appears in a separate window and houses all other components and containers. The top-level containers are Frame (JFrame), Applet, JDialog, and Window. The "this" container in the Structure Pane represents the frame for a Java application.

■ **Panel** This level (also called a *pane*) is an intermediate container, such as a JPanel, that is not visible unless it has been associated with a border object. Toolbars, scroll panels, and tab panels include borders and are visible. Panels contain other components or containers (such as panels). It is common practice to embed panels within panels to more easily manage portions of the frame or dialog.

■ **Atomic components** These are objects such as buttons and text fields that cannot contain other objects. If a component cannot contain other objects, it is an atomic component; otherwise, it is a container.

Laying Out a User Interface

The standard procedure for creating a user interface layout consists of the following steps:

1. **Create a top-level container.** This is a container such as a frame or applet that will act as the outermost container for all other components and containers. While a top-level container can have a layout manager, there are restrictions on its pane (JRootPane), so it is best also to create an intermediate container.

TIP
You can make the top-level container size automatically to its contents using the pack () method. For example, if you place this method in a constructor method (such as Frame3 ()) after the jbInit () method call, the frame will compress to surround its contents when it is initialized.

2. **Create an intermediate container (panel).** This will house all other containers and components. JDeveloper creates this intermediate container when you use the Frame Wizard to create a frame. The following illustration shows how a panel (JPanel1) would appear in the Structure Pane after the Frame Wizard completes:

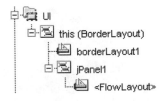

3. **Assign a layout manager and set layout manager properties.** These tasks are described further in the next sections.

4. **Add components.** When you drop components from the component palette into a container in the Structure Pane or UI Designer, JDeveloper creates the code to call the add() method on the panel. This takes an argument of the component name and a constraint that is layout specific. For example, the code JDeveloper creates for adding a button to a panel with a FlowLayout or GridLayout manager would be the following:

```
jPanel2.add(jButton1, null);
```

For a panel that has a BorderLayout manager, the code would be the following:

```
jPanel2.add(jButton1, BorderLayout.SOUTH);
```

5. **Set the component constraints.** The property *constraints* appears on the Inspector window for each component. This property (actually a separate object created by the code shown in the previous step) manages where the component will appear in the container. The *constraints* property takes different values depending on the selected layout manager.

6. **Set component properties.** Other properties on the component, such as *preferredSize*, manage the behavior and display of the component. With some layouts, you can drag and draw out a component (such as a button) into the UI Designer. This will set the size and placement properties for you. If you just drop the component onto the Structure Pane, you will have to set the properties afterwards.

Once you have completed the layout tasks, you can write extra code for handling events. These are the six major steps for creating the user interface layout in JDeveloper.

TIP
Click an object in the UI Designer and press CTRL-SHIFT-F1 *to load the class information about the object's component into a help window. This usually works if you first click the object in the Structure Pane as well.*

Assigning a Layout Manager

When you set the *layout* property for a container component (such as JPanel), the code that is created adds a layout manager to the container. If the layout property is not set, it will have a value of the default layout for that container (enclosed in "< >"). The default indicates that there is a default layout manager in effect, and you can see this in the Structure Pane under the panel, as the example here shows:

The default layout manager is only a placeholder that indicates the style of layout that the object will use by default. This default has no properties that you can manipulate, so it is best to assign an actual layout manager to the container.

Setting Layout Manager Properties

Since it is an object, a layout manager has properties. When you click the layout object in the Structure Pane, the Inspector will show the layout properties, as shown in the following example:

Properties	
name	flowLayout1
alignment	0
hgap	20
vgap	20

Some layout managers use gap properties to declare how much space (in pixels) will appear between components that are inside the container. There is a horizontal gap (*hgap*) and a vertical gap (*vgap*) property. Some layout managers have a property, *alignment*, to define whether the components within the container will be left justified, centered, or right justified. The value for this property is an integer (0, 1, and 2, respectively).

TIP

To verify that the layout manager is working properly, you may want to test your application on different resolutions, different browsers (if it is an applet), and different operating systems (such as Macintosh and Windows).

Layout Managers in JDeveloper

Although some minimal coding is required, most work with the layout managers is accomplished in the JDeveloper UI Designer and the Structure Pane. Table 11-1 contains a list of layout managers supplied by JDeveloper and tells you whether they are referenced from the standard Java Foundation Classes (JFC), have been modified to work with the JDeveloper UI Designer, or are specific to JDeveloper.

Each layout manager is described in the chapter. It is possible to add layout managers from other sources to this set, and it is also possible to create your own layout managers. The JDeveloper help system contains information on how to add to this set, but the group in Table 11-1 should suffice for most purposes.

Layout Manager	Type
BorderLayout	Standard
BoxLayout2	Modified version of the JFC BoxLayout
CardLayout	Standard
FlowLayout	Standard
GridBagLayout	Standard
GridLayout	Standard
OverlayLayout2	Modified version of the JFC OverlayLayout
PaneLayout	Specific to JDeveloper
VerticalFlowLayout	Specific to JDeveloper (a modified version of the JFC FlowLayout)
XYLayout	Specific to JDeveloper

TABLE 11-1. *JDeveloper Layout Managers and Their Sources*

CAUTION
Some containers, such as JPanel, list
ColumnLayout, ControlLayout, and RowLayout
in the layout *property as possible values. These are*
listed only for backward compatibility with older
versions of JDeveloper and require other library
files. If you select one of these for the layout
property, you will receive a compile error unless
you are creating an application with InfoSwing
controls. It is better not to use these layout
managers. Therefore, descriptions of these layout
managers are not included in this chapter although
preceding chapters' practices and the wizards use
ControlLayout for the sake of simplicity.

Overview of the Layout Managers

The following discussion provides some details on the layout managers that
JDeveloper offers. The information in this chapter will get you started,
but, as you progress with your Java work, you will want to refer to other Java
books (such as the "Java Tutorial" mentioned in Chapter 9) for further examples
and explanations.

The layouts are explained in alphabetical order. A table at the end of this
section summarizes the key constraints and properties for each layout. The
hands-on practices that end this chapter further explain three commonly
used layout managers.

Although panels are used in some examples as components within the
container, you can place any component type in a container. Panels are used in
the examples as a generic object that has no implied functionality. The examples
that use panels also create a border so that you can see the panel's sides. The
sidebar "Creating a Border" explains this technique.

NOTE

The examples in this chapter demonstrate a layout manager by setting the layout of the JPanel object that is inside the frame container. The frame container layout manager is left at its default setting (BorderLayout). Since the panel is the only container under the frame, it fills the frame. Therefore, when you resize the window (frame) at runtime, you are essentially resizing the inner JPanel container that manages the layout.

Creating a Border

To create a border for an object, you have to make a border object available in your application. Then the name of that object will appear in the *border* property of components. You can select the border from the pulldown list in the component's *border* property. BorderFactory methods create border objects. Here are some examples of code for different types of borders. This code would appear at the start of your `jbInit()` method.

```
Border etchedBorder = BorderFactory.createEtchedBorder();
Border raisedBorder = BorderFactory.createRaisedBevelBorder();
Border lineBorder = BorderFactory.createLineBorder(Color.black);
Border matteBorder = BorderFactory.createMatteBorder(1, 1, 1,
                        1, Color.red);
```

In addition, you need to add the following to the import section at the start of the class file:

```
import javax.swing.*;
import javax.swing.border.*;
```

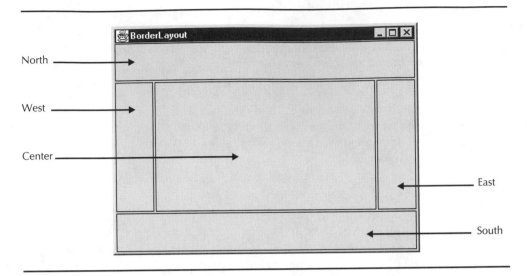

FIGURE 11-1. *BorderLayout areas*

BorderLayout

The BorderLayout manager divides the container into five areas that are named geographically: North, South, East, West, and Center, as shown in Figure 11-1. Each area may contain only one object. If you need to place more than one component in a container, use a panel as the single object and add components to it. BorderLayout takes care of sizing the components within each area.

If the user resizes the window so that it is shorter, the Center, East, and West areas will shorten, as shown here:

Expanding the height will expand the Center, East, and West areas in the same way. If the user narrows the window, the Center, North, and South areas will narrow, as shown here:

Expanding the width will expand the same areas. Components inside the areas will adjust accordingly, as the examples show.

The heights of the North and South areas and the widths of the East and West areas are fixed. If the user moves the sides of the window inside the limits that those dimensions impose, some areas will not be visible.

Layout Properties

The layout manager has two properties as follows:

- ■ **vgap**   The amount of vertical space between areas. This applies to the space between the North, South, and Center areas.

- ■ **hgap**   The amount of horizontal space between areas. This applies to the space between the East, Center, and West areas.

Both properties are measured in *pixels* (picture elements that correspond to dots on the screen). You will be able to see the effect of a change in these values in the UI Designer.

Component Constraints and Properties

The *constraints* property of the component determines in which of the five areas the component will be placed. Although you can set more than one component constraint to the same area, only one component may be visible at the same time. You can get around this limitation by using a panel as the single component and placing objects inside that container.

The heights of the North and South areas are managed by the *preferredSize* property of their contents. Thus, if you place a toolbar object in the North area and a status bar object in the South area, the heights of those areas will be determined by the heights of the objects. If the object height needs to be expanded, reset the second number in the *preferredSize* property of the component. For example, if the property value is "50, 50" and you need a 100-pixel height, change the value to "50, 100." The first number sets the width; BorderLayout ignores this number because it determines the width based on the outer container's size.

Similarly, the widths of the East and West areas are managed by the *preferredSize* property of their contents. The height number in the *preferredSize* value is ignored for East and West areas. The Center area ignores the *preferredSize* property completely.

Uses for BorderLayout

In general, this layout is useful for any situation where one or more edges of the window contain objects and the edges need to be resized automatically when the window resizes. Normally, you would combine this layout with others, as described in the later section "Multiple Layouts."

This layout style is commonly used for placing toolbars or button areas and status bars. Since these objects are normally fixed to the extreme top and bottom of the window, the BorderLayout manager would be set on the first panel under the frame. It is not necessary to use the East and West areas if you are not placing anything in them.

A hands-on practice at the end of this chapter steps through creating an example of this layout.

BoxLayout2

The BoxLayout2 manager (an Oracle extension of the BoxLayout manager) arranges components within it in a vertical or horizontal layout. A container with the BoxLayout2 layout can be defined through the *axis* property as either vertical or horizontal. If it is set to horizontal (components arranged on the X axis), all components placed in the container will be arranged side by side and fill the horizontal space. By default (before setting component properties), each component receives an equal amount of horizontal space and completely fills the vertical space. The manager only allows a single row for each container and

FIGURE 11-2. *BoxLayout2 arrangement*

will not wrap if the container is resized. Figure 11-2 shows this arrangement using three panels inside a container managed by the BoxLayout2 manager.

At runtime, resizing either width or height will resize the components so they still fill the horizontal and vertical space, as shown here:

If you specify that the layout is vertical (components arranged on the Y axis), the components will be arranged top to bottom to fill the vertical space. By default (before setting component properties), each component receives the same amount of vertical space and completely fills the horizontal space, as shown here:

Resizing the outer container preserves this layout, and the components fill the available horizontal and vertical space.

With both arrangements, it is possible to alter the sizes of the components and maintain the stacking effect that this layout offers. This is described in the next "Component Constraints and Properties" section. Examples are given for one axis arrangement or the other, but the effects are similar for both arrangements.

Layout Properties

There is only one property on the layout—*axis*. You set this to "X_AXIS" to specify a horizontal (row) arrangement of components or to "Y_AXIS" to specify a vertical (column) arrangement of components.

Component Constraints and Properties

The component *constraints* property is not used by the BoxLayout2 manager. There are a number of properties that affect the layout:

- **maximumSize** For a vertical (column) arrangement, the first number (width) of this property affects the width of the component. The second number affects the height. If both are set to the default (32676), the component will take up as much space as the layout manager can provide. Set the first number to less than the maximum to make the component narrower.

- **minimumSize**   The layout respects this property, and the component will not resize under the minimum.

- **preferredSize**   This works with the *maximumSize* property to allow you to size the component less than the maximum. For a vertical (column) arrangement, the layout manager uses the largest width value in this property to size all components. If a component has a maximum or minimum size that conflicts, the preferred size will be ignored.

- **alignmentX**   This property is set to "0" to left align the component in its space (for a vertical arrangement). A value of "0.5" indicates a center alignment, and a value of "1" indicates a right-justified alignment. The value is ignored for a horizontal (column) arrangement.

- **alignmentY**   This property is set to "0" to top align the component in its space (for a horizontal arrangement). A value of "0.5" indicates a center alignment, and a value of "1" indicates a bottom-justified alignment. The value is ignored for a vertical (row) arrangement.

The alignment properties can lead to some interesting variations because the alignments are based on the positions of the other components in the container. It takes some experimenting and observation to effectively use different alignments for different components.

Uses for BoxLayout2

Unlike other layout managers, BoxLayout2 can preserve the component alignment and size. Therefore, it is useful in situations where you want to have components stack together in rows or columns and do not want the wrapping effect offered by FlowLayout and VerticalFlowLayout. By default, there is no gap between components, and this is a good layout manager to use if that is required. You can, however, define a gap using a separator if you need to use this layout manager and a gap is important. The sidebar "Using a Separator" explains this technique.

Using a Separator

Some layout managers do not have a gap property, but you can emulate this effect using the JSeparator component on the Swing component tab. For example, with the BoxLayout2 application shown in this section, you can drop the JSeparator onto the outer JPanel object in the Structure Pane. Then reposition it so it falls between the components you want to separate. You can change the *maximumSize* and *preferredSize* properties to suit the need.

The following is an example of two separators that have been added to the sample BoxLayout2 vertical arrangement.

The separators were dropped into the Structure Pane and reordered using the right-click menu's move options in the UI Designer. The *maximumSize* properties were set to "32767, 0." (The "0" height passes control of this dimension to the *preferredSize* property.) The *preferredSize* properties were set to "0, 5" to provide a five-pixel horizontal gap. The separator can be hidden if needed by setting the *background* and *foreground* color properties to match the frame (usually "Light Gray").

CardLayout

The CardLayout manager allows you to place components on top of one another. Only one component is visible at any given time, but you can use the show() method of any component to display it. Each component in a container with this layout fills the entire container. The name of this manager is a representation of a stack of cards, where cards are piled on top of each other and only one is showing.

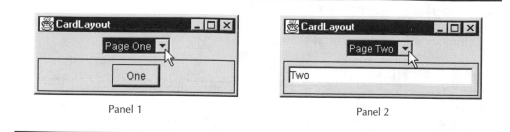

Panel 1   Panel 2

FIGURE 11-3. *CardLayout example*

For example, you might have an interface such as the one in Figure 11-3. This example has two panels—one for the top and one for the bottom of the display. The top panel contains a combo box, and the bottom panel is assigned the CardLayout manager and contains two more panels. One of these panels contains a button, and the other contains a text field. The application displays one panel or another based on code executed when the combo box element is selected.

Layout Properties
CardLayout has the following gap properties:

- **hgap** The distance in pixels between the left and right sides of the container and the component within the container

- **vgap** The distance in pixels between the top and bottom of the container and the component within the container

Note for Oracle Developer Users
The CardLayout in a frame panel is similar to a Forms window with more than one content canvas. The content canvas fills the entire window, but only one can be viewed at a time. You write code to display one canvas at a time.

Component Constraints and Properties

The component *constraints* property is not used by this layout manager. There are no component properties that affect the layout manager.

Uses for CardLayout

This is similar to the functionality of a tab control. The tab control is easier to use because it is a single component instead of several components that are required for this layout. However, if you need to control the display with a component other than the tab interface (such as with a push button, radio button, or combo box), this layout manager will provide the correct functionality.

FlowLayout

The FlowLayout manager arranges components inside it in a row. If the row is filled and there are more components to display, the layout starts another row, as Figure 11-4 shows. Rows span the entire width of the container and are as high as the highest component on a particular row. The contents are centered on the row by default, but they can be right or left justified as well.

The actions that this layout offers are similar to the BoxLayout2 manager with a horizontal (X_AXIS) axis setting. This layout offers the wrapping feature that BoxLayout2 does not offer. FlowLayout does not restrict the container from being sized smaller than the minimum size of the components.

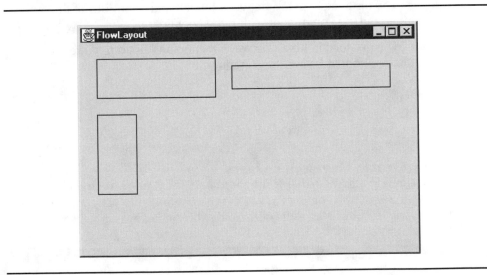

FIGURE 11-4. *FlowLayout example*

When the user resizes the container, the layout wraps the components as required so they will fit in the horizontal space, as shown here:

Layout Properties

FlowLayout offers the following properties:

- **alignment** This is set to "1" by default, which indicates that the components are centered within the horizontal space. A value of "0" indicates that the components will be left justified in the space, and "2" means a right justification.

- **hgap** This sets the amount of space in pixels between sides of components that are on the same line.

- **vgap** This sets the amount of vertical space in pixels between a component and the component underneath it.

Component Constraints and Properties

The component *constraints* property is not used by this layout manager. The component's *preferredSize* property is used to determine the row height and the width that the components use for their display. The row is sized on its height dimension based on the highest component (the one with the largest value in the second number in the *preferredSize* property). The row's width is based on the width of the container.

Uses for FlowLayout

Panels created with classes such as JPanel use this layout as the default. However, the default layout manager cannot be assigned properties or controlled, so a normal step in development is to explicitly assign the FlowLayout manager to containers that you want to manipulate. This creates the layout object.

This layout is particularly useful for a row of buttons that you want to have wrap to another line if the window width is narrowed.

A hands-on practice at the end of this chapter steps through creating an example of this layout and provides more details about property and constraint settings.

GridBagLayout

The GridBagLayout manager creates grid cells to contain components. Like the GridLayout (discussed in the "GridLayout" section), each cell may be assigned only one component. Unlike the GridLayout, containers using the GridBagLayout allow the cells to be different sizes and the components within the cells to span across cells or to be less than the area of the cell. Unlike FlowLayout and FlowVerticalLayout, this layout uses the preferred heights and widths of components to determine the cell height and width. For example, the height of a row of components is determined by the largest preferred size of components in that row. There is a similar effect for column widths.

Figure 11-5 shows a simple layout with four boxes demonstrating the cell and component size concepts. When the user resizes this container, the contents shift and resize according to the values of the component *constraints* property.

The layout manager object does not include any properties to modify its behavior. However, it offers a high level of control through the *constraints* property of the components within the container. With this high level of control comes complexity, and the GridBagLayout is the most complex of the layout managers to set up.

Working with GridBagLayout

As you might expect with a complex layout manager such as GridBagLayout, there are many ways to manipulate it.

Using Drag Handles   When you add a component to the container managed by this layout, a new cell is created. The cell borders are visible in the UI Designer although they will not be visible at runtime. You can turn the grid display on and off using the right-click menu option "Show Grid." When you select the component

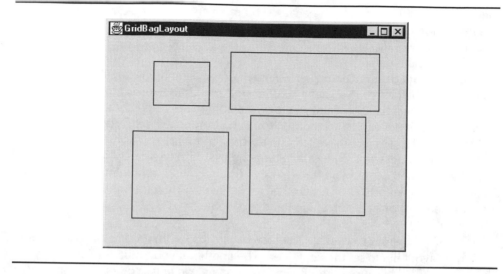

FIGURE 11-5. *GridBagLayout sample*

in the Structure Pane or UI Designer, a set of drag handles will appear both on the cell and on the component inside the cell, as shown here.

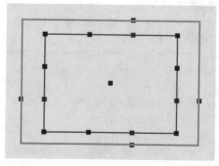

You can resize the cell and the component separately using these drag handles. Initially, both the cell and component are the same size, but you can resize the cell using the blue handles and the component using the black handles. You can also drag the component around within the cell to change its position. This ends up being an exercise in frustration because you often get unexpected and unwanted results, as the new object size affects other components. This is clearly not the best way to work with this layout.

Using the Constraints Dialog　Instead of dragging and positioning components as described before, you can set the constraints values for each component manually through the constraints dialog (available in the Inspector's *constraints* property and in the right-click menu). You can also just write the code that sets the values. In both cases, you have to be fairly certain of the exact values and how they will affect the interaction with other components. This is definitely more scientific than the first method, but you have to be fairly accurate in estimating how large an area (for example, of 100 pixels) will be in the layout. Therefore, this method can generate a lot of manual calculation and take some time.

Converting from XYLayout　The best way to work with this layout is not to work with this layout but to set the container to be another layout initially. The XYLayout is a good choice because it imposes no rules on its contents. You can lay out components freely using the UI Designer and its alignment tools. When everything looks the way you want it, change the container from XYLayout to GridBagLayout. The tool will set the constraints values based on the existing layout. You will need to adjust some of the values, but that is much less work than the other possible methods. In this way, you will be able to take advantage of the power and flexibility of both the UI Designer and the GridBagLayout.

When using this method, carefully consider which objects really require the benefits of GridBagLayout and which objects could be placed in other layouts. The idea is to reduce the complexity of constraints by placing as many objects as possible in simpler layouts and leaving the GridBagLayout manager to handle only the components that require its features.

For example, a typical application uses a toolbar and status line. The BorderLayout is perfectly suited for managing these types of components, so the top-level container should be defined with a BorderLayout. You would assign the *constraints* property of the toolbar to be "North" and the status bar to be "South." You could then place a panel in the layout and define its *constraints* property as "Center." The new panel could be set up initially as an XYLayout container and converted to GridBagLayout after the other objects were positioned.

Layout Properties
There are no layout properties for the GridBagLayout manager.

Component Constraints and Properties
The component constraints, as described earlier, are the heart of this layout manager. The component size properties (minimum, maximum, and preferred) are used to set default initial sizes and are used when the layout manager does not specify a dimension. It is useful to examine each value briefly. The JDeveloper help system and the Java Tutorial (online at java.sun.com) contain further descriptions and examples. Figure 11-6 shows the constraints dialog that you see if you click the button in the Inspector *constraints* property or select Constraints from the right-click menu.

As with other properties in JDeveloper that manage size, the unit of dimension is the pixel. The main areas of this dialog and their values follow. Each description includes the actual name of the property behind the value in the dialog.

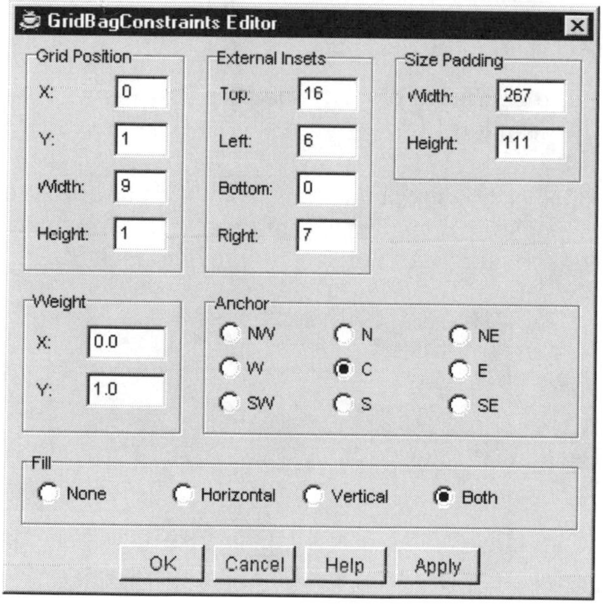

FIGURE 11-6. *GridBagConstraints Editor dialog*

NOTE
If you have problems calling the help system from a Help button such as the one in the constraints dialog, start the help system using **Help | Help Topics** *from the menu and search for the topic. The Index tab lists a topic, "GridBagLayout," that provides descriptions of this layout manager.*

Grid Position   These values manipulate the grid cell around the component:

- **X**   The *gridx* property specifies in which column the upper-left corner of the component appears. A value of "0" indicates the first column, and "1" indicates the next column.

- **Y**   The *gridy* property specifies in which row the upper-left corner of the component appears. A value of "0" indicates the first row, and "1" indicates the next row.

- **Width**   The *gridwidth* property specifies how many columns the component spans. The default is "1."

- **Height**   The *gridheight* property specifies how many rows the component spans. The default is "1."

Here is an example showing part of the layout of a frame. The upper-left corner of the combo box (poplist) component appears in cell "1, 0" and spans two columns and one row. Therefore, the values of X, Y, Width, and Height are "1, 0, 2, 1."

External Insets   This area of the constraints dialog specifies four values that are used in a single property called *inset*. The values specify the number of pixels that act as a margin between the cell border and the component. Each value specifies a component side: Top, Left, Bottom, and Right. The following is part of a frame layout. The text item has a blank space between the cell and three of its sides. The bottom of the component rests on the cell border, but other sides are inset. The Top, Left, Bottom, and Right values for this example are "16, 6, 0, 7."

Size Padding   The padding properties, *ipadx* and *ipady* (for Width and Height, respectively), define an amount of space in pixels that is added to the minimum size of the component. Therefore, a component may end up wider than its minimum height if it has a padding width defined. A padding width of "0" indicates that the component property sizes will be used. You can set the values to be negative, which will make the component smaller than its minimum size.

Weight   When a user resizes a container, there may be extra space into which components can expand. The weight properties (*weightx* and *weighty* for the X and Y values in this dialog, respectively) specify a rule by which the expansion occurs. The value (between "0" and "1" with decimals allowed) represents a percentage of the extra space that the component will take.

For example, there are three buttons in a row. The first and second have an X (width) weighting of "0.2," and the third has an X weighting of "0.6." If the container is widened, the first two buttons will widen by 20 percent of the additional space, and the third button will widen by 60 percent of the additional space.

Components in the same row will be allocated extra width based on their X weight property. If all components in a particular row use a weighting of "1," they will all receive the same amount of extra width. If all components in the row have a weighting of "0," none will be resized. The concepts apply similarly to the Y weighting and the heights of the components.

For example, the following frame contains three equal-sized fields that have X weightings of "0.2," "0.2," and "0.6." As the user widens the container, the fields widen according to their relevant weighting. If the container was widened by 100 pixels, the first two components would widen by 20 pixels each, and the third component would widen by 60 pixels.

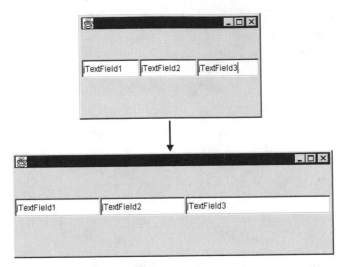

Anchor   This is actually a single property (*anchor*) with one of the following values: NW, N, NE, W, C, E, SW, S, or SE. The value specifies the coordinate area where the component appears inside the cell. For example, the following shows part of a frame in the UI Designer. The field inside the cell is set to an anchor of "W." Changing the value to "E" makes the component move to the right side of the cell. The anchors are preserved at runtime.

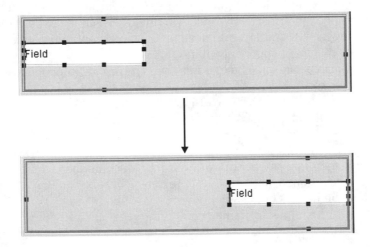

Fill   This is also a single property (*fill*) with one of the following values: None, Horizontal, Vertical, or Both. If the value is "Horizontal," the component fills the width of the cells it is assigned to (less the inset X value). If the value is "Vertical," the component fills the height of the cells it is assigned to (less the inset Y value).

If it is "Both," the component's width and height expand to fill the cells it is assigned to. If the container resizes and the cells resize, the component will resize accordingly. A value of "None" means that the component will be sized using only its size properties. The following is part of a layout that uses horizontal fill on the field and an X inset of "10."

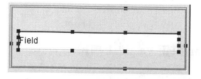

NOTE
The fill properties will take precedence over the component size and padding. Therefore, if you set a fill of "Horizontal," the component will fill the width of its cells, and the padding space will be disregarded.

TIP
When making changes to the properties in the constraints dialog, you can test the results of the change by clicking the Apply button. The dialog will stay open, and you will be able to see the effect in the UI Designer. If you click outside the dialog, the dialog will close.

Component Menu

You can set some values for constraints in a quick way using the right-click menu in the UI Designer. The following are items in this menu. Unless noted, all act on components that are selected before displaying the menu.

- **Show Grid**   This is a check menu item that, as mentioned, displays or hides the cell border lines in the UI Designer. The grid will not show at runtime regardless of this setting. This does not depend on which components are selected.

■ **Remove Padding** This item sets the values of the selected component's *ipadx* and *ipady* properties to the default value of zero. Since the padding adds to the value in the *minimumSize* property, a zero padding means that only the *minimumSize* will define the smallest dimensions of the component.

■ **Constraints** This item displays the constraints dialog for the selected component. If more than one component is selected, the values that the components have in common will be displayed, and the other values will be blank. Any value that you enter in this dialog will be applied to the selected components. This is a powerful tool but one that you must be cautious with because you could easily set values that you did not intend to set. The best practice is to check what is selected before using this menu item.

■ **Fill Horizontal and Fill Vertical** These items set the *fill* property to "Horizontal" or "Vertical," respectively. A horizontal fill means that the component will fill the cell width but not the height. A vertical fill means that the component will fill the cell height but not width. These menu items add to each other. For example, if you select Fill Horizontal for a text item and then select Fill Vertical, the *fill* property will be set to Both.

■ **Remove Fill** Removing the fill for a component means that the size will not be set by the *fill* property but by the component size properties (such as *minimumSize*). To change a vertical fill to horizontal, first select Remove Fill and then select Horizontal Fill.

■ **Weight Horizontal and Weight Vertical** These items set the *weightx* and *weighty* values, respectively, to "1" (the maximum weight). A weight of "1" means that the component will get the full amount of extra space available when a container is resized. The horizontal weight determines the amount of extra space the component will be allocated relative to other components in the same grid row. The vertical weight determines the amount of extra space relative to other components in the same grid column.

■ **Remove Weights** This menu item sets both *weightx* and *weighty* values to "0," which gives them no percentage of the extra space created if the container is resized.

NOTE

The constraints *property for GridBagLayout components is actually an object with properties of its own, such as* anchor *and* fill. *For consistency and because the constraints object shows in the Inspector as a property, you can think of it as a single property when working in the UI Designer.*

Uses for GridBagLayout

Use the GridBagLayout when complex layout is required and you cannot find any other way to place the objects. In many cases, you can accomplish the desired layout using the other layout managers by themselves or in combination. (See "Multiple Layouts" later in the chapter for an example.) However, if you get stuck and cannot find a way to implement a specific design, you will turn to the GridBagLayout manager.

A hands-on practice at the end of this chapter steps through creating an example of this layout.

A Word on Tab Order

Tab order is the sequence of navigation for components on the form. For example, a form might contain three items and a button. When the user tabs from the first item, the cursor will pass to the second item. From that item the cursor will pass to the next item in the tab order.

Different layout managers handle tab order differently. For example, if you place an item in each of the five areas of a BorderLayout panel, the tab order will be based on the areas West, Center, East, South, and North. Other layout managers use similar ordering between objects, usually top to bottom and left to right. For another example, text items in an XYLayout panel will be navigated from left to right and top to bottom. The upper-left corner of the item determines whether it is before (above or to the left of) or after (below or to the right of) another item.

The first item that the cursor moves to when the form starts will be the first item listed under the first container in the Structure Pane. After that, the left to right and top to bottom rules are followed. You can move objects around in the Structure Pane using the right-click menu in the UI Designer, for "Move to First" or "Move to Last." These menu items will move objects around in the Structure Pane list. You can also cut and paste in the Structure Pane.

Another way to alter the tab order is by changing the alignment of objects in the form. You can also alter the tab order by setting the *nextFocusableComponent* property as the name of the object that will receive navigation when the user presses the TAB key. You can effectively remove an item from the tab order in this way. If you do not want the user to click in the item, set the *enabled* property to "False."

GridLayout

The GridLayout manager creates a set of layout areas that consist of rows and columns of equal-sized cells. Each cell can contain one component, and that component fills the entire cell. Figure 11-7 shows a grid with three rows and three columns. This grid contains properties defining a two-pixel horizontal and vertical gap.

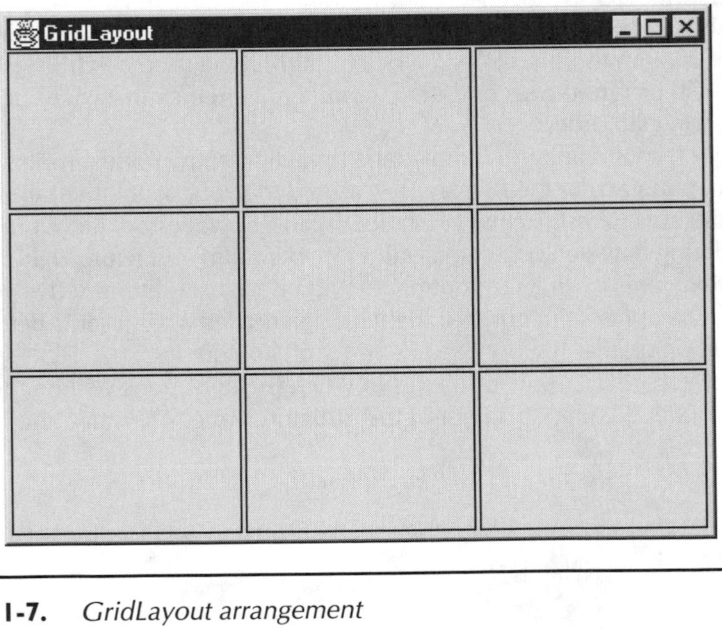

FIGURE 11-7. *GridLayout arrangement*

When the user resizes the container, the cells automatically resize and retain their equal size, as in the following:

When you define this container, you specify the number of rows and columns. As you add components to the container, the layout manager arranges them into equal-sized cells based on the maximum number of rows or columns you specify.

Layout Properties

The GridLayout manager object uses the following properties to define its behavior:

- **columns**   This sets the maximum number of columns that will appear in the grid.

- **hgap**   You specify the number of pixels between columns using this property.

- **rows**   This sets the maximum number of rows that will appear in the grid.

- **vgap**   This property sets the number of pixels that will appear between each row.

If there are more cells than the number of rows times the number of columns, the layout manager will add columns but retain the maximum number of rows. All cells will still be of equal size.

Component Constraints and Properties

No component constraints or other properties are used. The sizes of the cells are taken purely from a calculation of the available space divided by the number of cells (less any defined gaps).

Uses for GridLayout

This layout is perfect for an application that requires same-sized cells that will resize when the container resizes. Examples are a calendar, toolbar, and number pad.

OverlayLayout2

The OverlayLayout2 manager (an Oracle extension of the OverlayLayout manager) allows components to be placed on top of other components. Like CardLayout, all components in the container will be placed on top of other components in the same container. In this respect, it is like CardLayout, but OverlayLayout2 allows the components to be smaller than the container, which means that more than one component may be seen at the same time.

The alignment properties of the component define how the overlap occurs. Figure 11-8 shows an example of a container that is defined with an OverlayLayout2 manager. When the user resizes the container, the components resize in a relative way and retain their overlap.

Layout Properties

OverlayLayout2 has no properties.

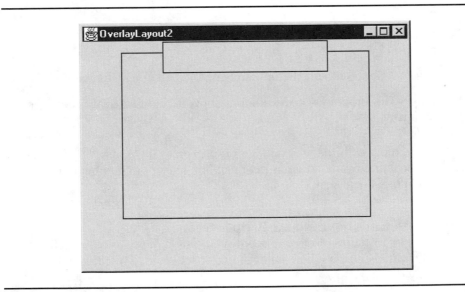

FIGURE 11-8. *OverlayLayout2 sample*

Component Constraints and Properties

The *constraints* property of the component is not used for this layout. The layout manager uses the size properties (*minimumSize, preferredSize,* and *maximumSize*) to determine how large to make the area that holds the component. The layout will respect the minimum size and not allow the outer container to resize so that the component would be smaller than that value. The layout uses the *alignmentX* and *alignmentY* properties to position the component relative to the other components within the container. These properties use the values "0" (for left or top), "0.5" (for center), and "1" (for right or bottom) to set the alignments.

In the example shown in Figure 11-8, the following property values are set on the two components:

Property	Large Panel	Small Panel
alignmentX	0.5	0.5
alignmentY	0.0	0.5
maximumSize	300, 200	200, 50
minimumSize	100, 100	10, 10
preferredSize	10, 10	10, 10

The order in the Structure Pane determines which component will be visible on top. In this example, the small panel appears before the large panel in the Structure Pane list. You can change the order using the right-click menu's move options in the UI Designer. If you set the *opaque* property to "False" for any or all components, the entire border of the underlying component will be displayed.

Uses for OverlayLayout2

Although this layout is rarely used, there are some situations where you would need to place all components on top of all other components in the same container and view them all at once. For example, you may need to attach a scrollbar to a component and have that scrollbar appear on top of the component. This layout would help with that need or if you had separate graphical elements that needed to be overlaid. For example, you might have an image that you want to use as a watermark (behind items and labels on the screen), and this layout would allow you to place the image in back of the other objects.

PaneLayout

The PaneLayout manager allows you to place multiple components in the container and size them proportionally to each other. The logical areas that are created are called *panes*, and the component inside a pane fills the pane completely. The first pane you lay out (by dropping a component into the container) becomes the "root," and all other panes are specified in relationship to that pane. Figure 11-9 shows a container with a PaneLayout manager and four components inside the container. A gap of two pixels has been defined to better show the components within the container.

When the user resizes the container, the layout maintains the placement of one component to another and resizes the components proportionally based on their properties, as shown next:

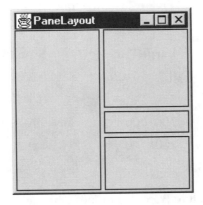

The steps for adding components to an empty container with this layout follow:

1. Add a component. It will fill the entire container. This component becomes the root component.

2. Add another component. It will split the container with the root component.

3. Open the PaneConstraints dialog for this component in the Inspector (from the *constraints* property of the new object). Set the position relative to the previous component and specify the percentage.

4. Repeat steps 2 and 3 for each additional component.

The order in which you add components matters because each time you add a component, it splits the last component. The position and size of the new component are set in relation to the last component.

Layout Properties
The only property offered by PaneLayout is *gap*, which specifies the number of pixels between components.

FIGURE 11-9. *PaneLayout example*

Component Constraints and Properties

You specify the *constraints* property using the following dialog:

The fields in this dialog follow:

- **Name**   This is the name of the component on which you are setting the constraint.

- ■ **Splits** This is the name of the component that you have just split by adding this component. Think of the "splits" component as the parent object that was already added before the component you are working on.

- ■ **Position** You can specify where you want this component to appear in the new pane (Top, Bottom, Left, or Right). This will position all other components in the "splits" pane relative to this position.

- ■ **Proportion** This is a percentage number between 0 and 1. A value of ".5" indicates that 50 percent of the space in the pane will be taken by the new component.

Uses for PaneLayout

An important use for this layout is in a split panel that allows the user to dynamically resize the panes. Otherwise, you can use this layout anytime you need the "diminishing boxes" effect, where each additional component splits the one before it.

VerticalFlowLayout

The VerticalFlowLayout works in the same way as the FlowLayout except that it arranges components in a column. If there is not enough space in the column, the layout wraps the other components to the next column. Figure 11-10 shows an example of this layout.

When the user resizes the container to make it shorter, the components reposition themselves, as shown here:

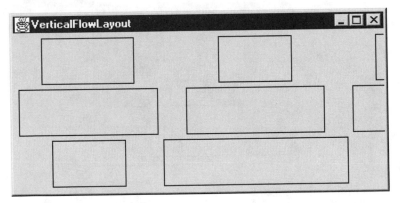

In this example, the user would also widen the window so the components on the right would be visible.

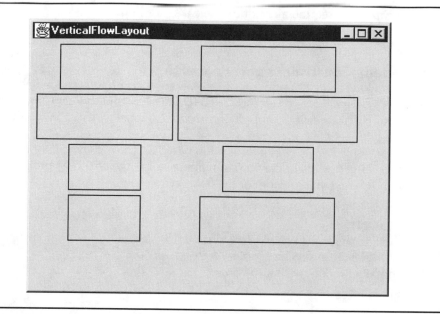

FIGURE 11-10. *VerticalFlowLayout example*

Layout Properties

The VerticalFlowLayout offers the following properties:

- **alignment**   This is set to "0" by default, which indicates that the components are aligned at the top of the container. A value of "1" indicates that the components will be centered vertically. A value of "2" means that the components will be bottom justified.

- **hgap**   This sets the amount of space in pixels between columns of components.

- **horizontalFill**   This is set to "True" by default, indicating that the components will expand to the width of the container. Set this to "False" if you want to set the width using the *preferredSize* property.

- **verticalFill**   This is set to "False" by default, which indicates that extra space at the bottom of the last component will be left intact. Setting this to "True" indicates that if there is empty space after the last component, the last component will expand to fill the space.

■ **vgap**   This sets the amount of vertical space in pixels between a component and the component underneath it.

Component Constraints and Properties

The VerticalFlowLayout does not use the component *constraints* property. The component's *preferredSize* property is used to determine the row height and the width. Be sure that the layout property *horizontalFill* is set to "False" if you want to change the width of the component.

The row is sized on its height dimension based on the highest component (the one with the largest value in the second number in the *preferredSize* property). The row's width is based on the width of the container.

> **CAUTION**
> *You will not be able to change the first number (the width) of the* preferredSize *property if the layout's* horizontalFill *property is set to "True."*

Uses for VerticalFlowLayout

This layout has the same kind of uses as FlowLayout except that it applies to applications where you need a column layout style with wrapping. Vertical button bars are a good use for this layout.

XYLayout

The XYLayout manager allows you to place components anywhere in the container. Components can be any size. When the container is resized, the components will not move or resize. This makes it easy to lay out components because you will not have to work against the rules that a layout manager imposes. You can get any layout possible, but that layout will be static when the application is run. No resizing or repositioning will occur when the user resizes the window. When using this layout manager, you give up the resizing and placement features other layout managers provide. Figure 11-11 shows an application with components inside an XYLayout container.

> **NOTE**
> *You can also select "null" for the* layout *property of a container. This will have the same effect as assigning an XYLayout, but it will not create a layout manager object.*

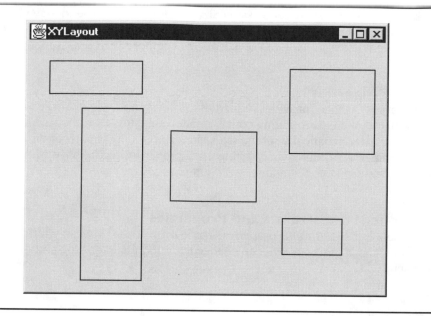

FIGURE 11-11. *XYLayout example*

Alignment Tools

Despite the limitations mentioned, the XYLayout does provide powerful design-time alignment tools. You can use the "Move to First" and "Move to Last" items on the UI Designer's right-click menu to move components in the same way as the other layout managers. There are other tools for aligning grouped components. You can group components by selecting a component and holding the CTRL key while you select another component. Once you have selected a group of components, you can select one of the following from the right-click menu:

- **Align Left, Align Center, or Align Right**   Use these to line up the components with the first selected component's left side, horizontal center, or right side, respectively.

- **Align Top, Align Middle, or Align Bottom**   These menu selections line up the components with the first selected component's top, vertical center, or bottom, respectively.

- **Even Space Horizontal or Even Space Vertical**   These allow you to lay out the selected components with the same horizontal or vertical gap between each. These items are enabled only if you select more than two components.

■ **Same Size Horizontal or Same Size Vertical**   Use these to assign the width or height of the first selected component to all other selected components. These items are enabled only if you select more than one component.

Layout Properties

The XYLayout manager provides properties for *height* and *width*. You can set these for a container if the surrounding container allows it. However, the surrounding container may automatically set the sizes. For example, if the surrounding container were managed by BorderLayout, setting these properties would have no effect because the surrounding container would impose a size.

Component Constraints and Properties

The component's *constraints* property is made up of four numbers: width, height, X position, and Y position. You can change these manually or drag and drop in the UI Designer.

Uses for XYLayout

This layout is useful only for prototyping or if you don't care about resizing. A dialog or window that you do not allow the user to resize is a possible candidate. However, you also have to take into consideration the resizing that occurs due to another platform, operating system, or screen resolution.

NOTE
Regardless of which layout manager you select, you can prevent the user from resizing the window by setting the resizable *property on the "this" frame to "False."*

Layout Manager Comparison

Some layout managers have properties that you can set. Some interact with settings of the *constraints* property of components inside the container. Some have extra right-click menu items for managing the display other than "Move to First" and "Move to Last" that reorder components within the Structure Pane list. Table 11-2 summarizes these concepts for each layout manager.

Layout Manager	Layout Manager Properties	Uses Component Constraints	Additional Right-Click Options on Component	Notes
Border	gaps (vert, horiz)	Yes (values of North, South, East, West, Center)	(none)	Used to place components in five areas. It is particularly useful for a status bar and toolbars.
Box	axis (X or Y)	No	(none)	Used to cleanly align components in a row or column without wrapping.
Card	gaps (vert, horiz)	No	(none)	Used to change the contents of an area. Components take the entire space, and you write code to display one component at a time.
Flow	alignment (0, 1, 2), gaps (vert, horiz)	No	(none)	Used to align components in a row with the ability to wrap to the next row if required. It is useful for button bars.
GridBag	(none)	Yes (complex dialog)	Show Grid, Remove Padding, Constraints, Fill Horizontal, Fill Vertical, Remove Fill, Weight Horizontal, Weight Vertical, Remove Weights	Used when complex layouts are required. Useful in situations where you cannot use another layout manager.
Grid	gaps (vert, horiz), number of rows, number of columns	No	(none)	Used whenever cells of the same size are required. An example is a calendar object.

TABLE 11-2.   *Features of JDeveloper Layout Managers*

Layout Manager	Layout Manager Properties	Uses Component Constraints	Additional Right-Click Options on Component	Notes
Overlay	(none)	No	(none)	Used to place components on top of one another and allow all of the multiple components to be visible. Rarely used.
Pane	gap	Yes (Constraints dialog)	Constraints (no Move menu items)	Used to define panes for layout that need to keep their proportional size and placement when the container is resized.
Vertical Flow	alignment (0, 0.5, 1), gaps (vert, horiz)	No	(none)	Used to align components in a column with the ability to wrap to the next row if required. Like FlowLayout, it is useful for button bars.
XY	height, width	Yes (X, Y, width, height)	Align (Left, Center, Right, Top, Middle, Bottom)	Used for prototypes and applications where automatic resizing and placement is not required. Rarely used because it does not manage anything.

TABLE 11-2. *Features of JDeveloper Layout Managers* (continued)

Multiple Layouts

When you are designing an application, one of the key considerations is in how you will best use the layout managers. Keep in mind that one layout manager may not suffice for a particular application. It is common practice to nest containers that have different layouts and take advantage of the strengths of each layout manager. To get an idea of the possibilities, it is useful to look at an example. The master-detail application created by the Business Components Data Form Wizard contains instances of four different layout managers. The running form is shown here:

The results of the wizard are shown in Figure 11-12 as they appear in the Structure Pane. Figure 11-13 is a diagrammatic representation of the frames and major objects with a designation of the assigned constraints and layouts where applicable. Most of the objects in this diagram are containers (created from the JPanel object). The interplay of objects is best described by describing the contents of this application as follows:

- The "this" frame is assigned a BorderLayout object by default. Actually, there is another panel associated with the frame that is not diagrammed in the hierarchy. This pane (called "contentPane" in this example) is a normal JPanel object that acts as the outer container. It, too, is assigned a BorderLayout manager. While it may seem redundant to add a panel that fills the window entirely and acts as an additional layer, this is a standard technique. The problem is that the layout manager for a top-level container such as a frame or window is limited in behavior. The solution is to add this extra panel and assign a layout manager to it.

- Inside the "this" contentPane is a status bar assigned to the South area. The BorderLayout ensures that the status bar always appears at the bottom of the frame, that the status bar height will be maintained, and that the status bar width will resize as the window width is resized. The formPanel object is assigned to the Center area, and there are no other objects directly within the contentPane container. Therefore, the formPanel fills the rest of the frame, and its height and width are resized as required when the outer window is resized. The East, West, and North regions of the layout manager are not used.

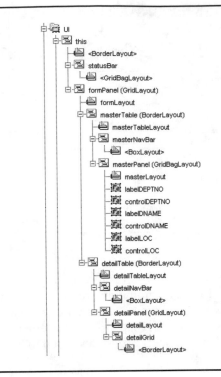

FIGURE 11-12. *Structure Pane view of a master-detail form*

- The formPanel is assigned a GridLayout manager. It contains two equal-sized panels (specified as two rows) for the master and detail views (called "masterTable" and "detailTable," respectively). The *columns* property of the layout manager is set to "1" so that the two panels will be stacked vertically. The layout manager ensures that the panels are always the same size regardless of the size of the window.

- The masterTable panel uses a BorderLayout manager and contains a navigation bar (masterNavBar) assigned to the North area of the layout and a panel (masterPanel) assigned to the Center area of the layout. If the window is resized, the cells in the grid will resize, causing the BorderLayout areas to resize according to the BorderLayout rules. Thenavigation bar will retain its height and allow its width to resize. The masterPanel area will resize along its height and width because it is assigned to the Center area.

- The masterPanel is assigned a GridBagLayout manager that contains the labels and text fields for the DEPT table. The GridBagLayout causes its

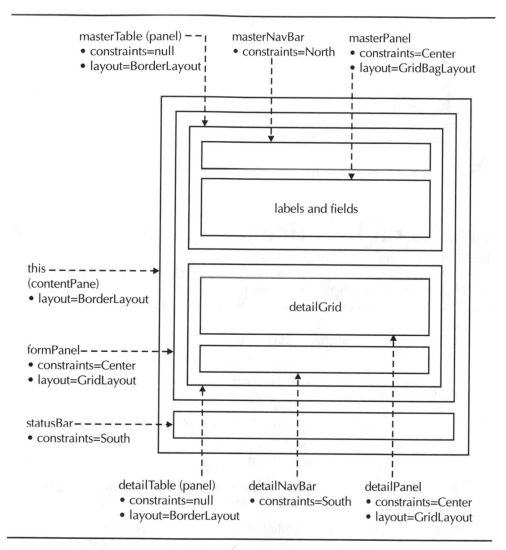

FIGURE 11-13. *Master-detail form panels and major objects*

contents to retain their relative positions and centering within the panel if the window is resized.

■ The detailTable panel uses a BorderLayout manager and contains a navigation bar (detailNavBar) assigned to the South area of the layout and a panel (detailPanel) assigned to the Center area of the layout. As the detailTable's cell area is resized, it imposes the BorderLayout rules on the contents so that the navigation bar retains its height and the panel resizes on both height and width dimensions. The detailPanel's component, detailGrid, represents the grid display of EMP table fields.

This application demonstrates a number of major principles. The first is that you can nest containers created by the JPanel class. The second is that you can assign different layout managers to different containers depending on the behavior that you want their contents to adopt. The last principle is that the layout managers offer an easy way to achieve complex functionality that would otherwise require many lines of code to implement.

Hands-on Practice Sample Application

Each practice in this chapter requires a very basic application that contains an empty frame as a starting point. Use the following steps to create this application. The steps are abbreviated because there is an assumption that you have completed the practice from Chapter 2, which contains more complete descriptions for these steps.

1. Create a new workspace called "LayoutAppWS" in a new directory called "layoutapp."

2. Create a new project called "LayoutPRJ" and specify a new application in the Project Wizard.

3. In the Application Wizard, specify a new empty frame. Use the default names.

4. Accept all defaults in the Frame Wizard.

5. After the application and frame have been created, doubleclick the frame file in the Navigation Pane to open the Viewer.

6. Click the Design tab. The following will appear in the Structure Pane:

The practices that follow will create additional applications for each layout style.

TIP

*Remember the trick for restoring the Inspector view. If the Inspector disappears, click the Design tab of the Viewer and select **View | Property Inspector** from the menu. If the Inspector window is blank at that point or any other point when you click an object in the Structure Pane, click the Source tab and then the Design tab. The Inspector should refresh and show properties at that point.*

Hands-on Practice: Layouts

This practice creates applications that contain specific layouts to give you experience with some of the layout managers. The sections are not sequential. Therefore, if you want to try a specific layout manager, you can skip to that section. Each section creates a separate application and frame to run it. There is no database connection required, as the objective is to practice a user interface feature.

This practice shows how to do the following:

I. **Use the BorderLayout manager**

- **Add the components**

- **Add a border**

- **Resize the side panels**

- **Try some variations**

II. **Use the FlowLayout manager**

- **Add the components**

- **Change the component sizes**

- **Try some variations**

III. **Use the GridBagLayout manager**

- **Add the components**

- **Align and size the objects and convert the layout**

- **Set the constraints property**

NOTE
Although the authors believe in rigidly adhering to naming conventions, the practices in this chapter do not spend time in resetting the default names that the tool creates. If these demonstration applications were to be used for a real application, the names of all objects would be changed to conform to the naming conventions explained in Chapter 3.

I. Use the BorderLayout Manager

This practice steps through creating a layout using the BorderLayout manager. You can, of course, place any component inside the areas of this layout manager, but this practice will lay out panels to illustrate the technique. Since panels are normally not visible, you will also create a border for the panels so you can see them. This demonstrates the technique of applying a border to objects that have this capability.

Add the Components

The following steps start with the application created in the "Hands-on Practice Sample Application" section.

1. Click the default JPanel object (called "jPanel1" by default). Set the *layout* property to "BorderLayout." The display will change to the following:

> ⊟ ▣ jPanel1 (BorderLayout)
>   ⌊ ▣ borderLayout2

This creates an actual layout manager object for this container that you can manipulate.

2. Click the JPanel component in the Swing Containers component tab.

3. Drag the mouse over the frame. Watch the lower-right corner of the status bar in the UI Designer window as you hold the mouse over various locations. The hint will indicate the orientation, as shown here:

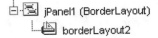

jPanel1 (BorderLayout): West

The orientation will change, indicating what the constraint property will be if you drop the component at that point (North, South, East, West, or Center). Drop the component on the North area.

4. Drag the panel and reposition it to the South area. Watch the status bar and the drag outline as you move the mouse to ensure that you will drop the panel in the proper area. The idea with this step is to give you practice in repositioning while being aware of the indicators that help you place the component. Try dragging to other areas if desired.

5. Drop a new JPanel in each of the other areas. You will not be able to see the panels yet. Check to make sure that you have a panel in each of the areas by examining the *constraints* property for each panel.

Add a Border

Adding a border to the panels will make them visible. A border is an object that you have to create with a few lines of code.

1. Click the Source tab to view the code. In the imports section, add the following:

```
import javax.swing.border.*;
```

2. Add the following after the line `private void jbInit() throws Exception{`

```
Border etchedBorder = BorderFactory.createEtchedBorder();
Border raisedBorder = BorderFactory.createRaisedBevelBorder();
```

This creates two different styles of borders.

3. Click the Design tab and select the East, West, South, and Center panels as a group. (Hold the CTRL key as you click the nodes in the Structure Pane.)

4. Select "etchedBorder" from the pulldown list in the *border* property. The pulldown presents the borders that you created in the source code. The borders of the selected panels should now be visible in the designer.

5. Select the panel assigned to the North area and set its *border* property to "raisedBorder."

6. You will be able to see the panels now because of the borders.

Resize the Side Panels

Panels are laid out in a BorderLayout with default sizes. You can change these most easily in the Inspector.

1. Click the panel on the west and SHIFT-click the panel on the east to group the two panels. Set the *preferredSize* property to "50,14."

2. Do the same for the North and South panels. Click the North panel and SHIFT-click the South panel to group them. Set the *preferredSize* property to "14,50." The UI Designer should appear as follows:

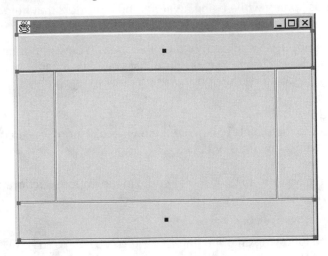

3. Compile and run the application. Test resizing the frame.

Figure 11-14 shows the default size and the results of resizing the window in various ways. A few things to observe with this test follow:

■ The North and South panels resize only their widths.

■ The East and West panels resize only their heights.

■ The Center panel resizes both its height and width.

Try Some Variations
You can set properties of the layout manager to add gaps between components.

1. Click the Design tab. Click the layout object under jPanel1. Set the following properties:

     hgap to "5"

     vgap to "5"

The layout will show the gaps between components, as follows:

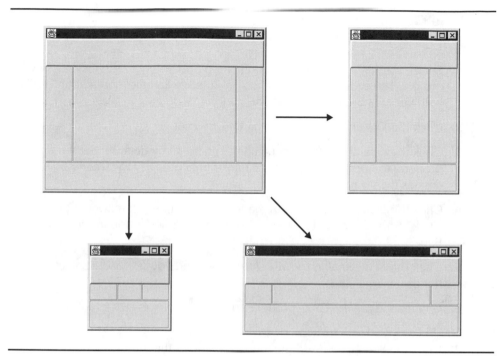

FIGURE 11-14. *Running and resizing a BorderLayout container*

2. Compile and run, and try resizing the window to check the effect on the gaps.

What Just Happened? You specified a BorderLayout manager for a panel and added other panels inside it. You also made the panels visible by adding border objects and resized the areas by resizing the components assigned to them.

NOTE
In a BorderLayout, an area can display only one object at a time. You can, however, make that object a container such as a panel, which contains other objects. The container would require a layout manager of its own that is appropriate to its contents.

11. Use the FlowLayout Manager

This practice steps through the use of the FlowLayout manager using a simple frame and panels inside the frame.

Add the Components
The first set of steps adds the components to the frame.

1. Before starting, create another application and empty frame inside a new project. The earlier section "Hands-on Practice Sample Application" will help you prepare this application.

2. Click the Design tab to display the UI Designer.

3. Click the default JPanel object (called "jPanel1" by default). Set the *layout* property to "FlowLayout" and the constraints property to "Center." This creates the layout manager for this panel.

4. Click the JPanel component in the Swing Containers component tab. Click the frame in the UI Designer or on the jPanel1 node in the Structure Pane.

5. Click the new panel in the Structure Pane, and you will see it selected in the designer.

6. Change the *preferredSize* property to "150,50." Press ENTER, and you will see the new panel resize in the designer.

7. Click the Source tab. Add the following line to the import section:

   ```
   import javax.swing.border.*;
   ```

8. Enter the following code at the start of the `jbInit()` method:

   ```
   Border etchedBorder = BorderFactory.createEtchedBorder();
   ```

9. Return to the Design tab and click jPanel2 in the Structure Pane. Click the pulldown in the *border* property. The new "etchedBorder" object should appear in that list because you have added it to the source code. (If it does not appear, check the import statement.) Select "etchedBorder."

10. Select jPanel2 in the Structure Pane and copy it (CTRL-C). Select jPanel1 and paste (CTRL-V) to add this panel. The designer should show the new panel. The border is copied with the panel.

The panels appear side by side because the layout manager's rules place new objects in the same row.

11. Compile and run the application. Resize the window so the right side of the frame is on top of the rightmost panel. The layout manager will wrap the panel to the next row. This is an effect that this layout manager provides.

12. Try resizing the window so that the bottom side of the frame is on top of the bottom panel. The layout manager does not resize the components to account for this action. Therefore, the bottom component will not be fully visible.

13. Close the application and add another panel using the copy and paste method. The new panel will wrap to the next line, as shown here:

So far, all components have appeared in the center of the layout because the outer panel's *constraints* property specifies a center alignment.

14. Compile and run the application. You see the same effects as before when you resize the window. If you increase the width of the window sufficiently, the second row's panel moves up to the first row.

Change the Component Sizes

The next set of steps uses the Inspector to change the component sizes.

1. Click the second panel in the UI Designer and change its *preferredSize* to "50,100." The first component moves down so that all components are vertically centered. This is another effect of the layout manager.

2. Click the third panel and change its *preferredSize* property to "250,20." The designer should appear as follows:

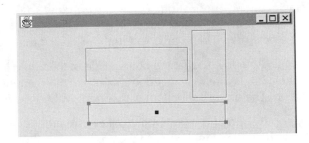

3. Compile and run the application. Move the right side in to the left until the tall panel moves to the second row. The top row component will move up because the first row is now shorter. Rows in this layout manager are sized to the height of the tallest component.

4. Move the right side out so that all components appear on the first row. The row height will resize to accommodate the highest component.

5. Move the right side, trying to keep all components on the first row. The components will always be centered within the available space. This is another function of this layout manager. Close the application.

Try Some Variations
You can try a few things to test more of the capabilities of this layout.

1. Click the flowLayout1 node under jPanel1 in the Structure Pane. The layout manager properties appear in the Inspector. The *alignment* property is set to "1" by default. This indicates that the components will be centered within the width of the row.

2. Change *alignment* to "2." This right justifies the components within the container. Run the application if you want to see how changing the window size changes the layout.

3. Change the *alignment* to "0." This left justifies the components.

4. Change the *hgap* property to "10." The effect is to increase the horizontal space between the left side of one and the right side of the next component.

Increase the *vgap* property to "10." You can see that this property increases the vertical space between the bottom of one component and the top of a component under it.

5. Compile and run. The gaps and alignments are preserved regardless of how you resize or move the window. Close the application.

6. Click the second panel in the UI Designer. Select "Move to First" from the right-click menu on that object. The panel will move to the left. This shows that the order of the components in the Structure Pane will determine the layout within the container.

What Just Happened?   You specified a FlowLayout manager and added panels to it. You also resized the components and set the alignment and gaps to experience the effects of the layout manager's placement logic.

III. Use the GridBagLayout Manager

This practice demonstrates how to work with the GridBagLayout manager by building a simple application with components and a design similar to the Save As file dialog shown in Figure 11-15.

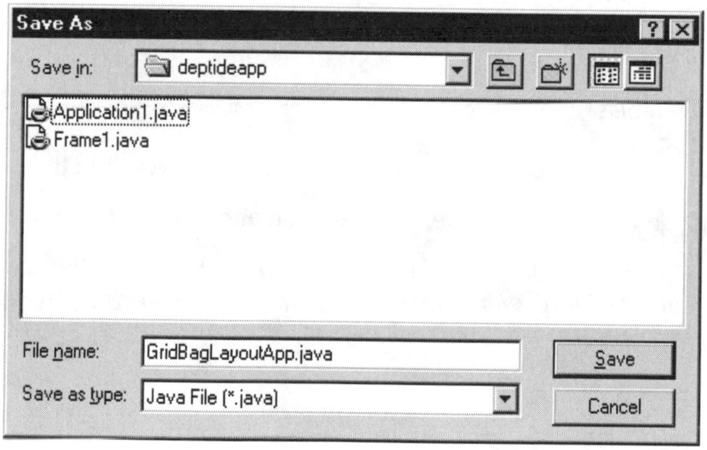

FIGURE 11-15.   *Save As file dialog*

Add the Components

The first part uses the XYLayout manager to place objects on the frame in the approximate positions. The exact positions and sizes are set in the next phase.

1. Before starting, create another application and empty frame inside a new project. The earlier section "Hands-on Practice Sample Application" will help you prepare this application.

2. Switch to the UI Designer and change the *layout* property for JPanel1 to "XYLayout." Be sure that the panel's *constraints* property is set to "Center." This gives you a full-frame container (JPanel1) that will allow you to place and size objects in any way that you want.

3. Create the following objects using the layout in Figure 11-16 as a guide to placement. All components are from the Swing components tab.

UI Object	Component
Combo box	JComboBox
Four buttons	JButton
Multiline text area	JTextPane
Text field	JTextField
Combo box	JComboBox
Two buttons	JButton
Three labels	JLabel

4. Change the *text* property of the labels to match the text in the sample.

5. Change the *text* property of the text pane and text fields to blank (no text).

6. Change the *text* property of the buttons in the bottom of the screen to match the sample. Don't worry about the icons in the buttons on the top of the screen. This is not a functional demo.

7. Click Save All.

Align and Size the Objects and Convert the Layout

When converting a layout to the GridBagLayout, it is important that objects line up as much as possible. The reason is that the conversion process calculates grid cells for the components, and if a component is slightly out of alignment with another

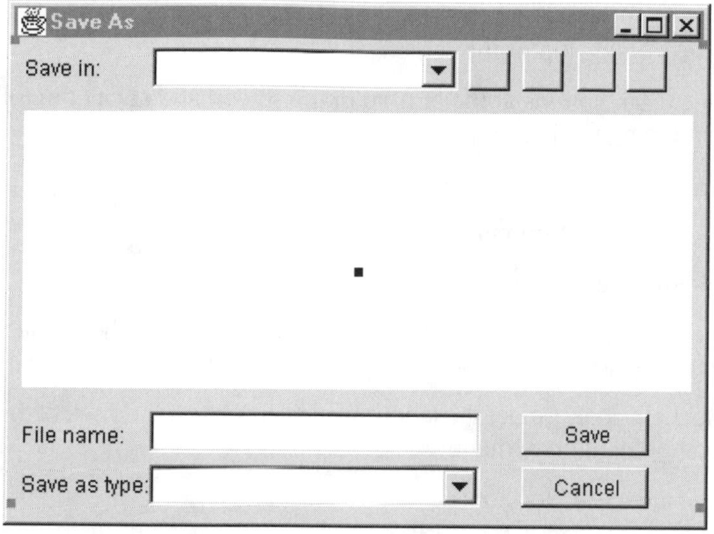

FIGURE 11-16. *Save As dialog layout with JDeveloper components*

component, two rows or columns will be created even if one would suffice. If the objects are aligned, the conversion process will use fewer cells, which makes the layout easier to manipulate.

1. Carefully size the leftmost button on the top of the screen by setting the last two numbers in its *constraints* property to "23," for example, "238, 7, 23, 23."

2. Select the button and CTRL-click on the other buttons on the top of the frame to select them as a group. Select the following from the right-click menu in this order:

   ■ Same Size Horizontal

   ■ Same Size Vertical

   ■ Align Top

   ■ Even Space Horizontal

   This makes the button sizes more consistent and aligns them.

3. Select all objects in the first row (four buttons, a combo box, and a label) and select "Align Middle" from the right-click menu. This lines up all objects on the top of the screen.

4. Select both buttons at the bottom of the screen and select the following from the right-click menu:

   ■ Same Size Horizontal

   ■ Same Size Vertical

   ■ Align Left

5. Select the text field and combo box on the bottom of the frame and select the same three menu options as the buttons.

6. Select all labels (select the label "Save as type" first) and select the following from the right-click menu:

   ■ Same Size Horizontal

   ■ Align Left

7. Click Save All.

8. Compile and run this application. When you resize the window, no resizing or repositioning occurs because the container is managed by XYLayout. Before proceeding, be sure that you used the alignment tools in the previous section to line up and size the components. The better aligned the components are, the fewer cells you will create when you convert to GridBagLayout.

9. Set the *title* property on the "this" object to "Save As."

10. Click the JPanel1 object and set its *layout* property to "GridBagLayout." If the components resized or repositioned, you may want to revert to XYLayout and use the alignment menu items again on those components.

11. Be sure that the *constraints* property of JPanel1 is "Center," which will ensure that both horizontal and vertical sizes will be affected when the window is resized.

12. Click Save All.

13. Compile and run this application and notice the difference in behavior when you resize the window.

Set the Constraints Property

Now that the layout is a GridBagLayout, you can set the *constraints* properties of the components to fine-tune the behavior. This is an application that you can use to experiment with the constraints settings.

1. Select a component in the UI Designer and you will see the grid borders of the cells that were created when you converted to GridBagLayout, as in the following illustration. The following instructions refer to this setup, and you may need to adjust the steps if your grid is slightly different. In this section the effect of the properties is more important than the exact layout.

2. The button in the upper-right corner is not spaced evenly with the other buttons. Select the button in the UI Designer and select Constraints from the right-click menu.

3. Change the *External Insets – Left* value to a smaller number. Remember that negative numbers are allowed. Click the Apply button and check the layout without closing the constraints dialog.

4. Adjust the number and check the effect if the spacing is not even. The insets modify the space between the edge of the cell and the component.

5. When you run this application, the combo boxes resize in a horizontal and a vertical direction when you resize the window. Resizing horizontally when the width of the container changes is fine, but resizing vertically is not. Group the combo boxes together using CTRL-click, and select the following from the right-click menu in this order:

■ Remove Fill

■ Fill Horizontal

6. Display the constraints dialog and verify that the Fill is set to "Horizontal."

7. Compile and run the file. Check the effects of resizing the window on the combo boxes. They should resize horizontally but not vertically.

8. Group the four buttons at the top of the frame and display the constraints dialog. The horizontal and vertical weights should be set to "0." Close the dialog and run the application. When you resize the window, the buttons do not resize because they have no weighting.

9. Change the horizontal weighting of the group of buttons by selecting Weight Horizontal from the right-click menu. Compile, run, and watch the effects of resizing.

10. The buttons may not resize if their *preferredSize* property is set. If this is the case, group the buttons and change the *preferredSize* to "100,25." Compile and run to check the effect of resizing.

 This shows that the *constraints'* weighting properties interact with the component's size. In this case, the size takes precedence over the weighting.

11. Click the text field at the bottom of the frame and display the constraints dialog.

12. Change all insets to "0" and click Apply. If the *anchor* property is set to "C," you will see the component reposition to the center of the cell. Set the *anchor* property to "N" and click Apply. You will see the component attach to the top (north) border of the cell, as in the following:

Top of cell and top of component

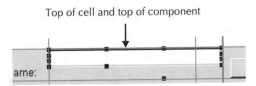

13. Set the anchor to "S" and apply the change. You will see the component reposition to the bottom (south).

14. Verify that the *fill* property is set to "Horizontal," and select an anchor of "W." The component will not move horizontally because it is set to fill the

horizontal space within the cell. Therefore, it is already attached to the left border of the cell, which is what the anchor of "W" would accomplish. This shows the interaction between the *fill* property and the *anchor* property.

15. In the constraints dialog for the same text field, set the Height padding to "0" and click Apply. The height will change if the padding was more than zero.

16. Change the Width padding to "0" and click Apply. The width will not change because the *fill* property is set to Horizontal, which means that the component fills the width of the cell regardless of sizes or other properties.

17. Change the Fill to "None" and click Apply. The component width will change because it is no longer set to fill the width of the cell, as follows:

18. Modify the padding Width to "20" and click Apply. You will see the padding increase the component width because the *fill* property is no longer set.

What Just Happened?   You added components to an XYLayout container and set their properties. You then converted the layout to the GridBagLayout manager. The GridBagLayout is influenced mostly by the *constraints* values. For proper understanding of the power of this layout, you might want to take some time to further explore other constraint properties such as Grid (X, Y, Width, and Height). Watch how the settings interact with one another and how they affect the runtime behavior.

TIP
This layout uses complex logic to determine the interaction and precedence of components. However, while initially learning to use this layout, use common sense to determine how the interactions will occur. For example, common sense would dictate that if the fill *property is set to horizontal, the component's size properties will be ignored because the component must "fill" the cell's horizontal space. With this approach, you will quickly come to an understanding of the complex logic that this component uses and be able to better predict the effect of a change in properties.*

CHAPTER
12

Security

...How little security have we when we
trust our happiness in the hands of others.

—William Hazlitt (1778–1830), *On Living to One's Self*

omputer security has become part of our daily lives. Almost everyone is familiar with the term "computer virus," and almost every business transaction requires sensitive information to be exchanged electronically. Unfortunately, security is often only thought of after a security breach. However, it is important to consider security issues at the outset, when you are developing the requirements for your system. The security issues for any system are not limited to potential fraud or mischief. There is always some overlap between application design issues and security concerns. For example, consider what you would like to happen when you accidentally delete information at the wrong time. Critical assets should not be lost or mistakenly altered due to a lapse in concentration or a tap on the wrong key.

When considering security, it is important to ask several questions about what you want to accomplish:

■ What needs to be kept safe, and what cost or effort are you willing to expend to safeguard those assets?

■ What measures should be taken during system design to ensure security?

■ What harmful events (exposures) could happen to your software and hardware?

■ Are you secure from both internal and external interference or malicious manipulation of your data and/or systems?

■ Who will be the final authority for providing and maintaining consistent security for your system?

This chapter discusses the issue of security and what steps you can take using JDeveloper to ensure the integrity of your system. Many of the concepts are not JDeveloper specific, but are still necessary for your consideration and will, therefore, work into the design and development of your application. The hands-on practice demonstrates how to work with security within JDeveloper as well as the steps you will need to take outside of the JDeveloper product to implement an effective security system.

Security Issues

Application security in various contexts is not a new topic. There are always numerous types of exposures that must be taken into consideration. However, too often the "solution" selected for handling these exposures is to do nothing. Large, well-managed companies and IT shops handle security by identifying all possible exposures and systematically designing a set of controls to adequately protect against security breaches.

The first rule in considering your security requirements is to identify potential losses, then to base your efforts on the potential impact of those losses to your business and the probability of that loss. Any security scheme can be breached, but it is in your best interests to add sufficient security to your system to offset the possible loss of critical data at a price that justifies the effort.

An example to illustrate this point is a situation in which a costly cash register system was being proposed for use in a 15-branch library network. The purpose of the system was to track the account activity for a variety of discrete sources of fees collected over the counter (overdue-book fines, lost item replacement costs, used book sales, photocopy charges, Internet printer copy charges, etc.). It quickly became obvious that, as good as the elaborate new cash register system was, the traditional approach was still the most economical way to proceed. The few dollars in discrepancies that could be resolved by the cash register system would require several lifetimes to offset the cost.

If the cost of a loss can be very large, then even a very expensive control that protects against that breach can be appropriate. In one case, a bank was processing paper requests for wire transfers. Each request was duplicated and manually entered twice until one instance when two data entry personnel inadvertently and coincidentally made the same error resulting in an unrecoverable loss of $1million to the bank. After a careful analysis of the error indicated that no fraud was involved, the bank modified its data entry procedure so that each wire transfer was independently input by three different data entry people. The bank perceived that both the monetary and political costs of these kinds of data entry errors justified the additional expense.

Exposures and Controls

It is very difficult to stop all unauthorized system access. With the widespread access to the World Wide Web, you need to consider the possibility that someone may have malicious intent to commit fraud or otherwise interfere with business transactions. The larger and more visible your enterprise, the bigger a target it is for all types of security breaches.

Sometimes, computer controls can help prevent human errors and fraud. Automated and manual controls can also sometimes help detect programming errors. For example, requiring a physical sign-off of purchase orders means that the orders were actually handled by a person. Using an approved vendor list and approved purchase order items can help decrease data entry errors. Periodical audits, such as physically counting inventory, can help detect a computer error in a purchasing system. All controls and all exposures (potential opportunities for harmful events) must be considered together.

Controls that are not commonly implemented are worse than no controls at all. At a large multi-national retailer, formal sign-off procedures were required for documents such as purchase orders. Users of the system were unaware of the importance of these controls and largely ignored them. Only when the internal auditors arrived for an audit would someone hurriedly go through all documents, adding the required authorizations without any real review of the documents taking place.

It is important to remember that database controls, application-level controls, and accounting controls are not three separate topics. A coherent security strategy mandates integration of all three types of controls. Traditionally, this integration has not been considered. Database people, in general, do not understand accounting controls, and internal auditors have little understanding of database technology. Even now, the most common way that external auditors evaluate an internal control system is by first sending in a team of computer specialists to evaluate the computer controls and then sending in traditional auditors to independently evaluate the accounting controls. Such a strategy is conceptually flawed. The goal is to prevent exposures. Any type of control can assist in decreasing the risk of an exposure. It is only by reviewing all potential moderators of that risk that you can rationally assess whether the protection is adequate.

You can prepare a matrix with one axis listing all of the exposures that have been identified. Across the other axis, list all of the plausible controls. At the intersection of each control and exposure, rate how effectively that control decreases the risk of that exposure. This is referred to as a control/exposure matrix. An example of such a matrix is shown in Table 12-1. If a control has no impact on the exposure, leave the cell blank. If the control decreases the risk of exposure, rate its effectiveness as low, medium, or high.

Filling out this type of matrix requires many judgment calls. You can identify your exposures in broad terms such as "fraud" or "hardware theft," or you can be specific to whatever level of detail you deem appropriate such as "programmer writes fraudulent code to divert goods legitimately ordered by a vendor to a fictitious address." If you list exposures at that level of detail, you might also want to list your controls at a similar level of detail such as "do visual inspection of module SHIPGOODS to make sure that there is no fraudulent code." In some cases, very general controls can support a wide range of exposures. For example: "Have a code supervisor visually inspect each piece of code to guarantee that there is no fraudulent code prior to implementation." Of course, such controls can be prohibitively expensive.

The assessment of how effective a particular control is with respect to a particular exposure is a matter of professional judgment and should be subjected to review by a systems auditor. The matrix shown in Table 12-1 was intended to be illustrative. A fragment of a real control/exposure matrix is shown in Table 12-2.

Once the matrix is complete, you can evaluate the quality of your internal control system by its ability to protect the system from each exposure. You may also find redundant controls that can be eliminated. After the design of the internal control system is complete, a report can be prepared concerning the level of security that is in place for the system. Decisions can then be made about whether the existing level of protection is adequate.

Controls Exposures	Backup System	Double Entry System	Manager Approval	Passwords	Overall Risk
Hardware Failures	High				Low
Human Error		High			Medium
Fraud		Medium	Medium	Medium	Medium

TABLE 12-1. *Control/Exposure Matrix*

The same strategies for handling exposures also apply to JDeveloper projects. However, if you deploy in a web environment, there are new exposures to handle that are not normally considered in a client/server environment.

There are four main exposure categories specific to the web environment: interception of data, system hacking, interception/alteration of a business event, and overloading attacks.

Controls Exposures	Each transaction entered by three different people	Transactions are randomly assigned to data entry	Passwords	Overall Risk
Manual error on data entry	High			Low
Two-person fraud collusion on data entry	High	High	Low	Low
Three-person fraud collusion on data entry	Low	High	Low	Low
Duplicate entry of data	High	High		Low

TABLE 12-2. *Control/Exposure Matrix Fragment*

Interception of Data

The most obvious security exposure is theft of information. When you buy something over the Internet and provide your credit card number, you do not want anyone to see the information being transmitted.

This exposure requires some type of secure encryption so that, as the information moves from place to place, the bytes cannot be decoded if they are intercepted.

System Hacking

Because the users you want to access your system can do so through the Internet, what is to prevent someone from using the same portal to enter your system with malicious intent?

To prevent system hacking, you must ensure that access to your site is limited to the way that you want your site to be accessed. You need to provide access to the appropriate people for the appropriate tasks. This makes for a complex security problem since you need some applications accessible to everyone but with limited capability. For example, a visitor to a commercial website should be able to place an order for a product by entering the relevant information. Other capabilities that might be required include allowing customers to access their own account information. At the other end of the spectrum, your web administrator may need to access the entire system remotely and be able to make substantial modifications to your web site from a remote location. Obviously, this capability should not be accessible to the public.

You also need to make sure that the Oracle server is not visible outside of the firewall. If the server needs to be visible outside of the firewall (for remote DBA access), you will need to change all of Oracle's default passwords. Don't forget about the Scott schema since it has resource privileges.

Most web sites have reasonable audit trails. If an employee wants to inappropriately access company information, the risk of being caught can be reduced by gaining access from a remote site (such as an Internet café). You need to plan for security controls not only to prevent outsiders from damaging your system but also insiders who may have intimate knowledge of your system.

Interception/Alteration of a Business Event

In some systems, the interception or alteration of a business event may not be a major concern. If you are a retailer, you probably have little risk that anyone would go to the trouble of intercepting and altering orders. However, special guards against interception of any credit card information transmitted should be in place. If the transaction is of significant size or involves the transfer of large sums of money, the motivation to alter such a transaction is high. You must pay special attention to security measures to prevent this type of fraud.

This is a very difficult type of fraud to carry out since the perpetrator must intercept the transmission, modify it, and pass it along. The solution to this exposure is essentially the same as for the interception of data. If the data is encrypted in such a way that it cannot be intercepted, then it also cannot be altered. The key to a good security plan is not to have only a single control for any one type of exposure. If one control fails, there should be additional control measures for all exposures.

Overloading Attacks

This exposure involves crashing a web site by malicious generation of large numbers of fraudulent transactions. Although this may appear to be a difficult exposure to prevent, it is not as hard as you might think. The only web sites that can be damaged by this type of attack are those that do not anticipate and plan for it.

Most overloading attacks come from the same Internet Provider (IP) address. Therefore, you can detect and count transactions from any one IP address. If the transactions from any one IP address exceed a certain number, access from that address can be cut off.

Multiple Controls Impacting All Exposures

There are two important ideas to keep in mind regarding exposures. First, any control can be circumvented by a determined person. Second, the more secret you keep your controls, the more effective they are likely to be. As few people as possible within any organization should know what type of security measures are being used and how they are implemented. In addition to security breaches from the outside, you also need to protect against fraud and malicious attacks from disgruntled employees or other insiders.

Controlling Access

Controlling access has many implications when you are considering the design for your security system. You must understand the logical and physical architecture of your system before you can determine the appropriate security solution. For instance, you will have a stricter set of requirements if you are going to allow users to access your system via the Internet than if you are implementing an isolated LAN for trusted employees. Natural security boundaries such as routers and firewalls can help facilitate a secure environment for your system, as shown in Figure 12-1. All systems should have at least one firewall (the first one in Figure 12-1) if they are using the Internet. In addition, systems using web and application servers should have at least two firewalls: the first one between the Internet and the servers, and a second between the servers and the database. In critical applications, a third firewall should be installed between the database and the internal network. This third firewall is helpful in preventing hackers from reaching your database through your internal network.

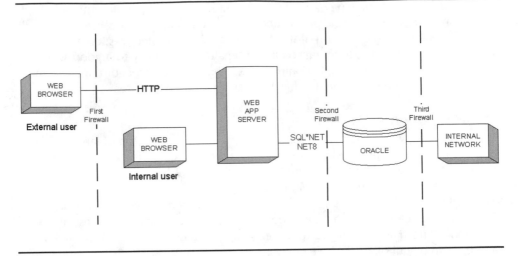

FIGURE 12-1. *Firewall placement*

Types of Users

In solving security problems, there are two classes of users to consider:

- **Internal users** These include customer service representatives on the road, managers, and other employees requiring remote access to information.

- **General access users**   These are members of the general public using the Internet.

The tools available for internal users are much richer than those for general access users. Users may have tokens or secret steps, as in the old days of dial-up modems that connected with no visible cues. Users needed to know what to enter in order to access the system. Other methods of keeping the system secure can include displaying only certain pieces of information to specific types of individuals.

Implementing Controls

Controlling access to critical assets is based on the sound implementation of four key concepts: identification, authorization, verification, and encryption.

Identification

The process for determining who is attempting to communicate with your system is known as identification. This is typically accomplished through user IDs and passwords. In newer systems you will find biometrics (such as fingerprints or eye scans), digital media (smart-cards), and digital signatures being introduced.

Authorization
Authorization is the process that determines which applications, files, and data users will be allowed to access. Some of your web applications may be open to everyone in a read-only mode to promote your products or services, while the ability to edit, update, and delete files will certainly be limited to individuals or groups within a predetermined set of trusted users.

Verification
Any time you transfer information, it is important to know if the data sent was actually received exactly as it was sent. In the past, this process was generally performed using parity checks on the local hardware. When your critical data is exposed to open environments such as the Internet, other techniques such as digital signatures and hash-codes can be employed to ensure that the data has not been tampered with.

Encryption
In today's Internet commerce environment, applications must be secure in many ways. As data travels across the Internet, it travels in packets across multiple servers, allowing others access to your data packets. When you are transferring sensitive data (such as bank account number, Personal Identification Number, or Social Security Number), it is imperative to use some sort of encryption to reduce the risk of others being able to view the contents of your transfers. Encryption techniques backed up by digitally signed certificates can give your remote clients the ability to interact with your systems with complete confidence. Public and private keys can be certified through trusted agencies, giving your remote clients the ability to interact securely with your systems.

Other Security Factors

Application security centers on your hardware and on the communications that occur between your application and other resources. When evaluating the overall integrity of your application, you must explore how memory is utilized in your CPU, what happens when buffers overflow, and what privileges have been granted to applications that may be running on, or interacting with, your machine. Also, you should consider what happens to the data after your application receives it. There is a popular protocol developed by Netscape called the Secure Sockets Layer (SSL) that provides a software layer in between your browser application and the TCP/IP layers. It does little good to implement a Secure Sockets Layer transfer from your client machines, and then use an open email link across the Internet to communicate the results. A security system is like a chain—it is only as strong as its weakest link. You must consider the strength of each link in the entire chain of your data flow in order to ensure full security.

Your choice of operating system and peripheral applications can have a significant impact on overall security. For example, older-style file transfer programs (FTP) can leave big holes in your security if they are based on the older FTP protocol. Newer extensions of HTTP such as HTTPS that can be protected with SSL can often replace these older programs. It is also important to review your user accounts and the privileges that you have granted them. Since any account can ultimately be compromised, it is important to limit the system-level privileges that you grant, thus reducing the chance that you will compromise the entire system. Hardware decisions such as the prudent use of routers and firewalls can also help to isolate data paths in your network, thus giving you better protection for your critical assets.

After reviewing the security for your system, don't forget the physical environment that surrounds your system. Everything—leaky roofs, water lines, chemical exposure, dust, temperature controls, humidity, earthquake, flooding, lighting, electrical surges, locked doors—should be considered in your security plan. At an Internet company that one of the authors worked at recently, the security experts deliberated long and hard about how protected their servers would be if someone tried to drive an armored truck through the plate glass walls of their building. It makes little difference what you include in your system assessment if anyone can walk up and gain access to your servers or if you locate your critical machines in an environment where they can be easily compromised.

Security in Java

Security issues have been a top priority in design considerations from the inception of the Java language. Traditional constructs such as pointers were eliminated to prevent Java routines from accessing other parts of memory. Flexible security mechanisms such as permission levels, digital certificates, cryptographic keys, and signed files were added. These mechanisms are used to control code and machine access, identify users, hide data, and provide additional privileges to trusted sources.

One of the traditional deployment options for Java uses a client browser to display a Java applet. Applets are very secure by design and, unless they are given special permissions, cannot interact with other system resources (such as reading or writing files). Java uses a combination of policy, security, and certification files to track and control your security preferences. You may find several sets of these files on your system, as each Java-related product might have its own set. The default security files used by Sun Microsystems follow:

- **java.policy** Basic policy file that stores your default permissions to access specified properties, allow thread stopping, and grant socket listening privileges.

- **java.security**   Master security properties file that stores information about your registered Cryptography Package Providers, system-wide policy files, IdentityScope use, keystore type, and package access definitions.

- **cacerts**   System-wide repository for trusted certificates. This file currently ships with a limited number of trusted certificates from certification authority providers, such as VeriSign.

You can find these Java security-related files in directories such as:

- **JDeveloper**   JDEV_HOME\java1.2\jre\lib\security

- **Oracle8i**   ORACLE_HOME\javavm\lib\security

- **Oracle runtime**   D:\Program Files\Oracle\jre\1.1.7\lib\security

Other security files may also exist on your system depending upon which client tools and applications you need to support. Microsoft has its own set of security utilities designed for Internet Explorer. Whereas Sun and Netscape use JAR and Zip files to store their Java code, Microsoft uses a slightly different format called a cabinet (CAB). Microsoft also stores its public and private keys in a different way, requiring the use of additional tools to provide security across the contending technologies.

Keep in mind that, by default, Java class files are vulnerable to decompilation. In other words, it is very easy to produce source code from Java classes or jars. Most IDEs now have code obfuscators that remove all the things developers do to make source code readable (e.g. descriptive variable naming, indentation, etc.). Unfortunately, as yet, JDeveloper does not include a code obfuscator. If you want your Java code to be proprietary and remain proprietary, you will need to take specific actions to protect it.

Java Applet Permissions

Java programs can be deployed in many ways, including Java applications, applets, servlets, and JavaServer Pages (JSPs). Learning the security tools that are used with applets and Java applications will give you a basic introduction to the principles involved in controlling the security for your Java programs whether they are deployed as Java applications or applets. Security in JSP applications follows the same model as basic HTML, for example, using a software layer such as SSL.

Traditional Java applications are designed to run in a standalone mode on a client machine and have few security restrictions or requirements. Applets, on the other hand, are designed to run on a client browser after being downloaded from the Internet. Since the Internet is an open environment, applets have significantly higher security requirements. The default security level for applets prevents them from having any potentially damaging interaction with your operating system by limiting their ability to see or modify other assets on your system. For instance, they cannot read or write to the file system, or have access to system memory outside of a well-defined area.

You can change this default security behavior by using the Java security APIs or other third-party toolsets. For example, you can modify the permissions for a specific applet, giving it the ability to interact with the operating system and perform file-handling commands that are generally limited to applications. On the other hand, by packaging an application in a JAR file and specifying the appropriate permissions, you can modify the security requirements for an application until it is constrained just like an applet. Each browser has minor variations in how it handles these modified security requirements.

The first part of the hands-on practice that follows will focus on the tools provided by Sun Microsystems to manage security preferences. In the last practice of the chapter, similar tasks will be repeated using the Microsoft Software Development Kit (SDK) to demonstrate how the security tools for Internet Explorer differ. As the Internet continues to evolve, standards will likely emerge to unify the current compatibility issues. Undoubtedly, you will eventually be able to use a single set of security tools to deploy your Java programs. In the meantime, in order to deploy them, you will need to use several container types and certificate formats to accommodate different browsers—Netscape Navigator and Microsoft Internet Explorer.

NOTE
It is important for novice Java programmers and designers to understand how database connectivity affects applets. Applets can only communicate (via TCP/IP) with the web server from which they are invoked. Therefore, you either need to put the database on the web server (this is not recommended) or delegate all database access to a servlet, JSP, Remote Method Invocation (RMI) Service, or CORBA service that is used by the applet (this is recommended).

Hands-on Practice: Test Basic Security with an Applet

To demonstrate how to modify the basic security, this practice will allow you create an applet that will write "Hello World" to a text file. Under normal circumstances, applets do not need to write to the client file system. However, this method is used in this practice for the purpose of demonstrating Java security. By using the tools from Sun Microsystems, you can modify the basic applet's security permissions by creating a security profile that includes a Java file permission. This permission will allow your applet to perform read/write file operations.

Sun's *Policy Tool* will help you alter the basic permissions granted to your Java code. Using the concepts in this example, you will be able to understand what is necessary to change the default security behavior for Java programs in general.

This practice includes the following phases:

    I. **Prepare your path**

    II. **Create a Java applet to write a text file**

   III. **Deploy the applet**

   IV. **Test the applet in a browser**

       ■ **Download the plug-in**

       ■ **Run the applet**

    V. **Create a security policy file**

   VI. **Test the applet in Appletviewer**

I. Prepare Your Path

Before you can use the tools in the following practice session, you must add their home path to the environment settings on your operating system. This allows the operating system to find the executable files from any subdirectory.

For example, in Windows 2000 or NT, you can append the appropriate Java 1.2 tool location to the path by following these steps:

1. Find the correct path by locating the file named "policytool.exe."

2. Select **Start | Settings | Control Panel**. Doubleclick System and select Advanced (in Windows 2000) and Environment Variables. Append the path under System Variables to reflect the correct tool path, for example:

   ```
   PATH = ... ;d:\Program Files\Oracle\JDeveloper 3.2\java1.2\bin; ...
   ```

II. Create a Java Applet to Write a Text File

The first step is to write a simple applet to illustrate how the default security prevents an applet from writing to a file. Later you will add the policy file that alters the default security, which allows the applet to write "Hello World" to a file successfully.

1. If you have an open workspace, select **File | Close Workspace**.

2. Select **File | New Project** to display the Project Wizard.

3. If necessary, click Next to dismiss the Welcome page.

4. On the Project Type page, change the project file name in the *What is the project's filename?* field *("MyProject1.jpr")* to "myprojects\myfileout\MyFileOutPRJ.jpr."

5. In the *What type of project would you like to create* pulldown, select "A project containing a new" and keep the Applet default selection.

6. Click Next, and a message asks if you want to create the myfileout directory. Click Yes to proceed.

7. On the Project Options page, enter "myfileout" in the *What is the name of the project's default package?* field. Accept the other default directories and click Next to go to the Project Information page.

8. You may leave the default information fields unchanged, and click Next and Finish. This creates the project file and starts the Applet Wizard.

9. If necessary, click Next to dismiss the Welcome page.

10. On the Applet page, rename the *Class* to "MyFileOut."

11. In the *Extends* field, use the pulldown menu to select java.applet.Applet. This specifies an AWT class for the applet. Then click Next.

12. On the Parameters page, click Next to go to the HTML page. Then check the checkbox next to *Generate HTML File.*

13. Reset the *Width* to "750" and the *Height* to "250," as shown in Figure 12-2. This sets the size in pixels of the applet window in the browser. Click Next and Finish to build your applet and the HTML file that calls it.

14. In the Navigator window, select the workspace node (for example, Untitled1.jws), and then select **File | Save As**.

15. Select the myfileout folder and enter "myfileout\FileOutWS" and click Save. Click Save All.

16. In the Navigator window, doubleclick the applet source file MyFileOut.java to open the editor.

17. Add the line "import java.io.*;" to the bottom of the import list.

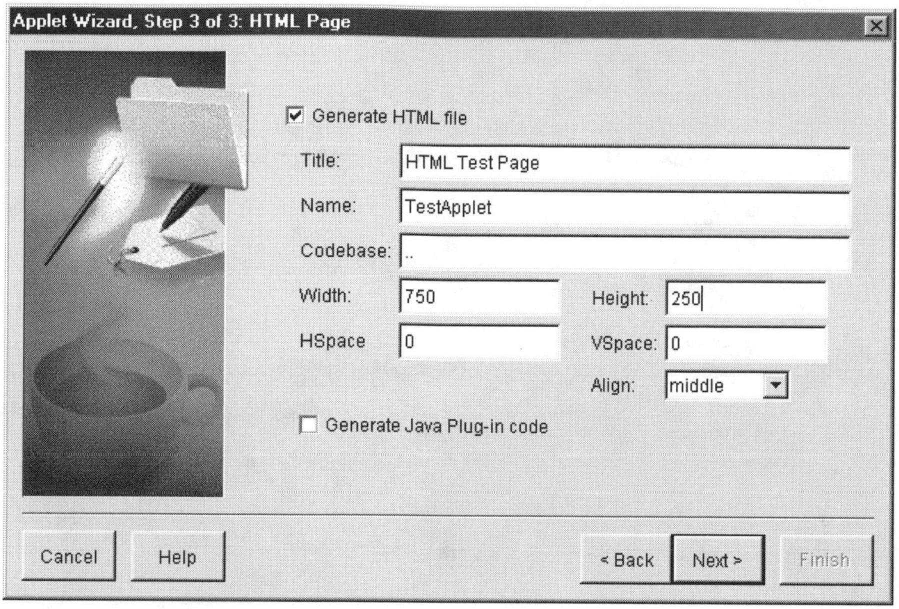

FIGURE 12-2. *Applet Wizard*

NOTE

The * wildcard in the import statement is used for example purposes only. It causes the entire library path under the io directory to be included at runtime. In general, it is not good coding practice to use wildcards in import statements, particularly for applets. Most deployment tools, including JDeveloper's, will include all classes referenced in the import statements in the deployed JAR (typically, applets are deployed via .jar files). The size of the .jar file greatly impacts the user's perceived performance due to the time required to download the JAR. Explicitly listing objects with import statements (for example, java.io.IOException) is a better strategy because fewer files need to be included in the JAR.

18. Insert the following method, just before the closing } at the end of the file:

```
public void paint (Graphics g) {
  try{
    String dirName = "C:\\test";
    BufferedWriter out = new BufferedWriter (new OutputStreamWriter (
    new FileOutputStream(dirName + File.separator + "fileout.txt") , "UTF8" ));
    out.write("Hello World - This is a successful test");
    out.newLine();
    out.close();
    g.drawString("You just completed writing to: fileout.txt ", 10, 10);
    }
  catch (SecurityException se) {
    g.drawString("FileOUT: SecurityException: " + se, 25, 25);
    }
  catch (UnsupportedEncodingException uee) {
    g.drawString("FileOUT: UnsupportedEncodingException", 25, 25);
    }
  catch (IOException ioe) {
    g.drawString("FileOUT: I/O Exception", 25, 25);
    }
}
```

This code is available on the web sites mentioned in the author biographies at the front of the book.

NOTE
*You can also use PrintWriter instead of
BufferedWriter. If you use PrintWriter,
the code within the "try" block changes
to the following:*

```
PrintWriter out = new PrintWriter (new FileWriter ("C:\\test\\fileout.txt") );
out.println("Hello World - This is a successful test");
out.close();
g.drawString("You just completed writing to: fileout.txt ", 10, 10);
```

*If you use this code, you would no longer need the
"catch" for the UnsupportedEncodingException.*

19. Compile your project by selecting **Project | Rebuild Project
"MyFileOutPRJ.jpr"**.

20. Save your work by choosing **File | Save All**.

21. Create a directory "C:\test" for your text file using Windows Explorer. After you have created the test directory, you may test your applet using the open security policies in JDeveloper.

    JDeveloper has its own test browser for running applets. The test browser has relaxed security constraints, so you can verify how your applet will work when it is deployed with an appropriate policy file.

22. Open the HTML file in the source code editor. The APPLET tag should set the HEIGHT attribute to 250 (`"HEIGHT = 250"`). Change it if it does not appear correctly.

23. Test your applet by right-clicking MyFileOutPRJ_MyFileOUT1.html in the Navigation Pane and select Run. Accept the copyright notice the first time you run this.

If your applet ran successfully, you should see the text "You just completed writing to: fileout.txt" displayed in the Applet Viewer window, as shown in Figure 12-3.

Also verify that C:\test\fileout.txt was correctly written onto your hard drive. After you have verified that the applet works in the test environment, delete fileout.txt from the C:\test directory.

What Just Happened?   You created an applet that writes a string into a file. JDeveloper applet runtime allows you to bypass the normal security features of a system to facilitate testing. When you actually deploy the applet, you will need to take care of these security requirements so that it may be run successfully.

FIGURE 12-3.   *Output of file-writing applet*

III. Deploy the Applet

This phase will lead you through deploying the applet to your hard drive and running it from your browser. Since the appropriate policy permissions do not exist for your applet to perform a write operation, you can expect it to generate an error when running outside of JDeveloper's test environment.

1. Before you can run your applet outside of JDeveloper, you must prepare it for deployment. Select the node MyFileOutPRJ.jpr in the Navigation Pane. Then select **Project | Deploy | New Deployment Profile** to invoke the Deployment Profile Wizard.

2. If necessary, click Next to dismiss the Welcome page.

3. Using the pulldown menu in the *Select a type of deployment* field, select "Web application or command-line application" and click Next to display the Staging Area page.

4. Change the *Deployment destination* to "C:\test."

5. Under *Files to Deploy*, check the checkbox next to MyFileOutPRJ_html, as shown in Figure 12-4, and then click Next to go to the Project page.

6. Check the checkbox next to MyFileOutPRJ.jpr to select all files for deployment.

7. Click Next to go to the Archive page.

8. Under *Delivery Options*, select Zip and click Next to go to the Applet Tags page. The JAR file would also work for this exercise.

9. Move the file in the Project HTML files window to the *Applet HTML files* area by first selecting it and then clicking on the ">" button. Click Next to go to the Libraries page.

10. Click the ">>" button to move all libraries to the *Deployed libraries* area. Click Next, accept the default profile name and click Finish. Click Yes when asked "Deploy now using these settings?" to deploy your applet to the C:\test directory.

11. Save all your work by selecting **File | Save All**.

12. Now that you have completed the deployment profile for your applet, end your JDeveloper session by selecting **File | Exit**. You will run the applet outside of JDeveloper in the next phase.

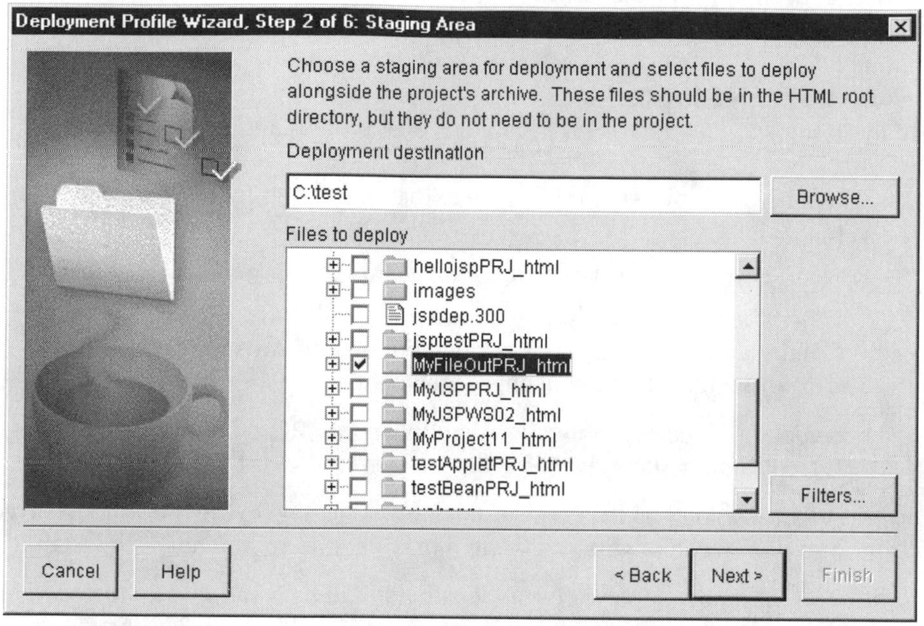

FIGURE 12-4. *Staging Area page of the Deployment Profile Wizard*

What Just Happened? You created the deployment profile that identifies how the project will be installed on a server. This profile is stored in a file with a .prd extension that is associated with the project. You can create more than one profile for each project to store different deployment settings. Chapter 7 contains more information on deployment alternatives with further information and practices for the Deployment Profile Wizard.

IV. Test the Applet in a Browser

The next few steps will test your applet using your browser's default Java security. It is recommended that you have an Internet connection running before you attempt to run your applet for the first time. You may obtain the latest plug-in code and Java Runtime Environment (JRE) for your browser by going to the Sun Microsystems site and downloading the files for your operating system. You will be prompted to download a 5–10MB library depending upon which version you need. This entire process may take from five minutes to an hour depending upon the speed of your

Internet connection. Once the download is installed, you will not have to re-download the code except when future updates become available.

Download the Plug-in

Use these steps to download and install the latest plug-in and JRE.

1. Open your browser and navigate to the following site (current as of this writing):

   `http://java.sun.com/products/plugin/1.3/plugin-install.html`

2. When the page displays on your screen, scroll down until you see the Continue button. Click the Continue button and save the code to your hard disk, accepting the license agreement.

3. Select the directory where you would like the JRE to be installed; the default is C:\Program Files\JavaSoft\JRE\x.x where "x.x" is the release number.

4. After downloading the code, install it by navigating to the file you just saved and doubleclicking it. Your system may need to reboot after the install.

5. You must now append the tool location to the path variable for the operating system in your client machine. For example, in Windows 2000 you can append the appropriate tool location to the path by selecting **Start** | **Settings** | **Control Panel**. Doubleclick System and select Advanced (in Windows 2000) and Environment Variables.

6. Append the path under System Variables to reflect the correct tool path, for example:

   `PATH = ...C:\Program Files\JavaSoft\x.x\bin;...`

Run the Applet

Once the plug-in is installed, you can run the applet.

1. To test run your applet, go to the directory C:\test\MyFileOutPRJ_html\, and doubleclick MyFileOutPRJ_MyFileOUT.html. The browser will start and load your applet.

2. You should see a message in your browser that looks like "myfileout.MyFileOUT will appear below in a Java enabled browser."

3. The applet will try to run under the default security restrictions that your browser uses for applets. Since this applet will attempt to access your file system, which is beyond the normal boundaries given to applets, it will generate a security exception such as

"SecurityException:java.security.AccessControlException:access denied"
or "SecurityException:netscape.security.AppletSecurityException:security.
checkwrite:"

What Just Happened?   You installed the Sun Java plug-in and ran the applet
to test security outside of JDeveloper. To successfully run this applet, you will need
to modify its default security. Unfortunately, each browser uses slightly different
tools to accomplish this. The next phase will alter the default security by adding the
java.io.FilePermission tag to a policy file. The policy file will be generated using a
Sun Microsystems utility named Policy Tool.

V. Create a Security Policy File

To create a security policy file for the applet in this hands-on practice, use the
following steps:

1. Open a command-prompt window (**Start | Run** and enter "cmd " in
Windows 2000 or NT or **Start | Run** and enter "command" in Windows 95
or 98). Some people may still refer to the command window as a "DOS
window" because of its similarity to the old DOS system window.

2. Navigate to the C:\test directory by typing "cd test" and pressing ENTER.

3. Type "policytool" at the prompt and press ENTER to start the Policy Tool,
shown in Figure 12-5.

4. Click OK to dismiss the warning message, which tells you that you have not
opened a default policy file. Click the Add Policy Entry button to start the
Policy Entry dialog.

5. In the *CodeBase* field, enter the deployment directory in the form
of a URL, `"file://C:/test/-"` using the forward slashes for all
systems (Windows or Unix). The dash ("-") at the end of the URL extends
permissions to all of the sub- directories below C:\test. If you use an
asterisk (*) in place of the dash, the permissions are only for class files
stored directly in C:\test. Click Add Permission to open the Permissions
dialog box.

6. In the Permission pulldown, select "FilePermission." You should see an
entry appear in the field to the right: "java.io.FilePermission."

7. In the blank field below "java.io.FilePermission," enter the Target File name
"fileout.txt." This limits the write permission to just one file name. You could
also use the pulldown and select "<<ALL FILES>>" to give permission for
all file names.

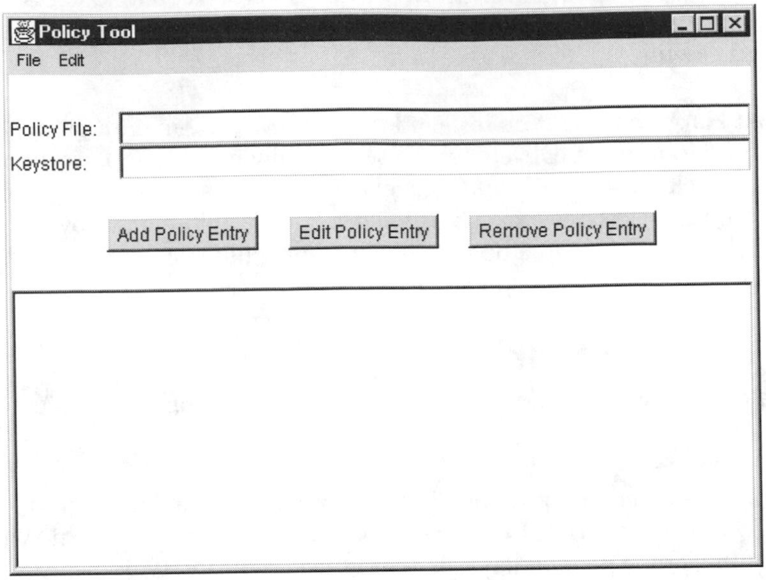

FIGURE 12-5. *Policy Tool's opening screen*

8. On the left-hand side, select "write" from the bottom pulldown on the *Actions* field. When you click Write in the pulldown, you will see the word "write" appear in the third field down on the right-hand side. Leave the *Signed By* field blank and click OK and Done to return to the Policy Tool.

9. To save this new policy file, select **File | Save As** to open the Save As dialog. Since you started the Policy Tool from the deployment directory C:\test, you are ready to save the new policy file in this location.

10. Type "file.policy" in the *File name* field and click Save to save the file. Click OK to acknowledge the successful write operation, and notice that the *Policy File* box now shows the correct location as shown in Figure 12-6.

11. To close the Policy Tool, select **File | Exit**.

What Just Happened?   You used the Policy Tool program to create a policy file. This file is required to run an applet.

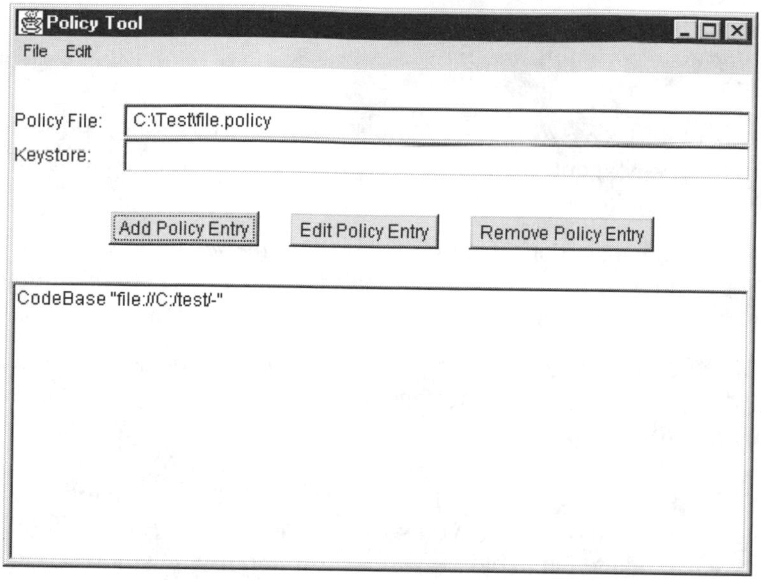

FIGURE 12-6.   *The completed policy*

VI. Test the Applet in Appletviewer

You are now ready to test your applet and policy file with another utility from the Java Development Kit (JDK) called "Appletviewer." *Appletviewer* is a Java program that runs an applet in a window outside the browser. Since a large amount of typing is required to execute the applet, you will build a batch file to store the required keystrokes. You must pass the name of the policy file and HTML file to the Appletviewer. You can create this batch file using any text editor, such as Notepad, that can accommodate long single-line entries. The entire command must be typed on one line, even though it is broken up in this book due to line width limitations.

Use the following steps to create a batch file and test your applet.

1. Start Notepad in Windows (**Start | Programs | Accessories | Notepad**) and enter the following command on one line, leaving one white space between segments. You must use the forward slashes for all operating systems. The trailing & means to run asynchronously (do not wait for command to terminate).

```
appletviewer -J-Djava.security.policy=file:/c:/test/file.policy
   file:/c:/test/MyFileOutPRJ_html/MyFileOutPRJ_MyFileOUT.html &
```

CAUTION
Be sure to enter the line exactly as it appears here
including case sensitivity and forward slashes.

2. Select **File | Save As** and navigate to the directory C:\test; then click in the *File name* box, enter "run.bat," and click Save to store your batch file. Then exit Notepad.

3. Now you need a command prompt to run the batch file. If your command line window is not open, run through the earlier steps to open it and navigate to the C:\test directory.

4. Test your applet by typing "run.bat" at the command prompt and pressing ENTER. You should see a message in the Appletviewer: "You just completed writing to: fileout.txt."

What Just Happened?   You created a batch file for the command line and ran your applet using Appletviewer. If you wish to run your applet in another browser such as Netscape or Internet Explorer, you will need to use other toolsets to duplicate the security steps that you have just completed. You may need several sets of tools if you wish to run your applet on several browsers. An appropriate set of steps will be introduced later in this chapter for Internet Explorer.

Hands-on Practice: Implement Certificate Security

When you leave the protected environment of an in-house network, you must consider the appropriate level of security necessary to protect your business transactions as they travel across the Internet. It may be important for you to know if the information you sent or received was altered in any way during its travel. The current solution to this problem is to have the sending party add a digital signature that can be verified by the receiver. Digital signatures for your Java applications can be created using several different tools. The security benefits of any given technology are usually short-lived. Improvements in computing power and in the science of cryptography continue to expand almost daily, soon rendering today's secure solution vulnerable to attack. Therefore, you will need to revisit your security requirements periodically to ensure that you are adequately protecting your business assets. One of the current toolsets for creating and managing digital signatures comes with the JDK that ships with JDeveloper. The toolkit includes many useful utilities, including the Appletviewer used in the previous practice. To implement a digital signature for your applications, you will need to use utilities from the JDK to help you maintain the following items:

- Public and private keys

- Certificates

- Keystores

After you have become familiar with these basic tools, you will be ready to deploy your applications using a few additional tools that are compatible with the browsers installed on the client machines from which you intend to run the applet.

The diagram in Figure 12-7 depicts the kind of verification process that this practice will build. This process is only responsible for validation of the identity of the sender, not for any other security measure such as encryption. The receiver and sender in the practice are physically on the same machine but the appropriate files

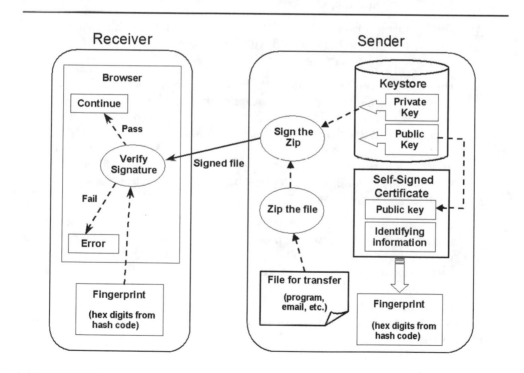

FIGURE 12-7. *Sample certificate verification process*

are created to emulate a multi-machine system. The process shown in the figure represents the following concepts:

- The sender's *keystore* holds private and public keys in this example. In a real production situation, the private key would be stored in a more secure location such as a separate keystore.

- A *certificate* is created to hold the public key and other identifying information such as the name, serial number, and address of the sender.

- For a self-signed application such as this example, the fingerprint consisting of hexadecimal digits representing the private key is generated by a *hash code program*. The fingerprint (in a self-signed application) is copied by some secure means (FedEx or hand-delivery) to the receiver. Alternatively, a certification authority such as VeriSign can hold the fingerprint. In this scenario receivers request verification from VeriSign and do not need to store the fingerprint file.

- The file that is transferred to the receiver is converted to a Zip, JAR, or CAB format. The Zip file is combined with the private key from the sender's keystore and sent to the receiver.

- The receiver transfers the file to the browser, which sends it through an identity verification process. The hexadecimal numbers are extracted by means of a hash code program and those numbers are matched with the fingerprint that the browser has access to. If a certification authority is in charge, the receiver requests a fingerprint from that site and matches the return value with the result of the hash code program. In addition, all other information from the certificate must be matched such as company name, address, and serial number.

- Other programs on the receiver's side may be in charge of verifying the identity. If this is the case, the program will read the fingerprint file from the browser location and go though the same kind of validation. The fingerprint can be stored in different places such as a file, executable DLLs, or the registry.

These concepts will become clearer as you proceed through the practices. You may wish to refer to this diagram as you work to clarify the role a component plays in this process.

This practice uses the following phases to explore this subject:

I. Prepare the sender to use a digital signature

- **Create a keystore**

- **Create a self-signed certificate**

- Obtain a fingerprint for the certificate

- Sign a JAR or Zip file with a private key

II. **Prepare the receiver to use a digital signature**

   - Prepare the fingerprint and keystore

   - Create a client policy file

   - Test the applet on the client machine

I. Prepare the Sender to Use a Digital Signature

The first step in building a digital signature is to create a pair of security keys, one public and one private. These keys are tokens that are required to decode the encrypted message and act as a unique validation pair. The receiving party uses the public key to verify that the information received is in fact from a source that had the matching private key. The keys can be used just as they are generated from a utility such as the keytool in the JDK, but for additional security, they should be generated and validated as part of a certificate process.

A *certificate* contains the public key, plus information that identifies the sender, and, in most cases, an additional verification of authenticity by a third party known as a certification authority (CA), such as VeriSign or Thawte. The certification process was established to eliminate the need for passing public keys face-to-face. The ultimate question is always, "Is the public key I hold an authentic one?" The certification authority signs your digital signature with their own well-known digital signature, ensuring that the receivers can trust your key, even though it has passed through an insecure environment such as the Internet. When you use keytool to generate public and private keys, they are stored in an encrypted repository called a *keystore*.

Before beginning the practice exercise, whether you are sending code, data, or documents, you will need to store them in a JAR, Zip, or CAB container before you can sign them. The digital signature is added to the container, ensuring that the contents cannot be altered without detection. The keytool command uses the following parameters to create a pair of keys and store them in a keystore:

- **-genkey**   The parameter that generates the key pair

- **-alias**   The name that is used to access the key pair

- **-keypass**   The password used to access the key pair

- **-keystore**   The name of the storage repository

- **-storepass**   The password to use the repository

- **-validity**   The duration in days that your certificate will be valid

After you enter the command, you will be prompted for information to identify yourself as part of the certification process.

Create a Keystore
Use the following steps to create a keystore that holds a public key and a private key.

1. If you do not have a command line prompt open, use the earlier steps to open one and navigate to the C:\test directory.

2. Type "keytool -help" at the prompt and press ENTER to start the Key Tool and see a list of the valid parameter usages.

3. To create your first set of keys, enter the following command at the C:\test prompt. The entire command must be entered on a single line.

```
keytool -genkey -alias signfilekey -validity 365 -keypass xyzzy123
    -keystore MyKeyRepository -storepass Plough#1974
```

4. Next you will be asked to identify yourself for the certificate information. Follow the script:

```
What is your first and last name?
  [Unknown]:  Mark Jones
What is the name of your organization unit?
  [Unknown]:  Sales
What is the name of your organization?
  [Unknown]:  Dulcian
What is the name of the City or Locality?
  [Unknown]:  Iselin
What is the name of your State or Province?
  [Unknown]:  NJ
What is the two-letter country code for this unit?
  [Unknown]:  US
Is <CN=Mark Jones, OU=Sales, O=Dulcian, L=Iselin, ST=NJ, C=US> correct?
  [no]:  y
```

This process may take a minute or so, on slower machines. When it completes, you will have created your first encrypted key repository.

Create a Self-Signed Certificate
The next step in a production environment is to prepare your public key for distribution by sending it to a certification authority. In this practice session, you will follow the steps to create a self-signed certificate. The person or application receiving the data will use this certificate to verify that the transfer process completed without any tampering.

1. To create a certificate, enter the following command at the C:\test prompt. The entire command must be entered on a single line.

```
keytool -export -keystore MyKeyRepository -alias signfilekey
    -file MarkJonesSun.cer
```

2. Next you will be prompted for the security passwords you entered when you created the key. Follow this script:

```
Enter keystore password: Plough#1974
Certificate stored in file <MarkJonesSun.cer>
```

After you have created and sent your self-signed certificate to the party that will be receiving your data, you should have a way to verify receipt of the proper key. If both parties run a *secure hash algorithm* (SHA) against their respective keys and find that the results match, you can be confident that the keys have not been altered. The SHA will return a 20-byte hex code that associates the keys with one in 2^{260} possible fingerprints, which, for all practical purposes, guarantees that the keys match.

Obtain a Fingerprint for the Certificate

To obtain a certificate fingerprint, use the following steps.

1. Enter the following command at the C:\test prompt. The entire command must be entered on a single line.

```
keytool -printcert -file MarkJonesSun.cer
```

The system will respond with something like this:

```
Owner: CN=Mark Jones, OU=Sales, O=Dulcian, L=Iselin, ST=NJ, C=US
Issuer: CN=Mark Jones, OU=Sales, O=Dulcian, L=Iselin, ST=NJ, C=US
Serial number: 38e1c806
Valid from Mon Feb 12 09:28:34 EST 2001 until Sun Apr 13 09:28:34 EST 2001
Certificate fingerprints:
        MD5:  74:A4:91:5A:91:2F:B6:F5:2C:B7:E5:19:EB:48:F5:11
        SHA1: B4:27:0c:B4:AD:E1:AB:6A:33:DF:59:19:F4:40:CC:B3:41:72:D6:DF
```

Make a note of the values after MD5 and SHA1. These are the hexadecimal numbers that the receiver needs to match.

2. By duplicating the previous steps on the receiving end, you can use two-way signed communication with confidence that your communications cannot be tampered with without detection.

Sign a JAR or Zip File with a Private Key

Use the following steps to add a digital signature to your JAR or Zip file:

1. Navigate to the C:\test directory and rename MyFileOutPRJ.zip to "unsigned.zip" using this command line command:

```
ren MyFileOutPRJ.zip unsigned.zip
```

2. Next, enter the following command at the C:\test prompt. The entire command must be entered on a single line.

```
jarsigner -keystore MyKeyRepository -signedjar MyFileOutPRJ.zip
    unsigned.zip signfilekey
```

3. You will be prompted for the security passwords you entered when you created the key. Follow this script:

```
Enter Passphrase for keystore: Plough#1974
Enter key password for signfilekey: xyzzy123
```

What Just Happened?   You have now completed the following tasks:

- Prepared private and public keys

- Stored the keys in an encrypted repository, known as a keystore

- Created a self-signed certificate for your public key, using the keytool

- Generated a fingerprint that you used to validate the certificate delivery

- Placed the material you wished to send in a jar or zip file and signed it with your digital signature using the jarsigner utility

You are now ready to send your material across the Internet. The receiving party will use the public certificate to validate receipt of the material, thus ensuring a secure and tamper-proof method of transferring data across an open system. In the next phase, you will go through the steps that the receiving party must take to set up his or her own key repository.

II. Prepare the Receiver to Use a Digital Signature

The public key, which is used as a digital signature, is typically provided in the form of a certificate that has been issued by a third-party certification authority (CA). By validating the signature using the known fingerprints of the CA, the receiving party is able to trust the certificate without needing to contact the sender. However, care should be taken regarding how much trust you put in the CA validation. VeriSign is a well-known certification authority that issues several classes of authentication. In a "Class-1" ID, all that is required is an unverified relay of information that someone sends over the Internet. A requestor can input any name and any organization and obtain a Class-1 ID, thus making a Class-1 ID not particularly reliable. At the other extreme, a "Class-3" ID requires that the requestor's representative appear before a notary public, and the associated corporate financial rating may be verified as well. Keep in mind that no matter who acts as the third-party CA, you must understand what their authentication is telling you about the certificate. How much trust you place in the certificate will be based on your business situation.

In this phase you will act as the person receiving the material and set up a key repository to store the self-signed certificate that you created in the previous section. When you receive a certificate, you need to verify its authenticity. In a production environment, you could do this through a third-party CA or directly from the sender using a self-generated fingerprint. For this practice, a self-generated fingerprint method will be used.

Prepare the Fingerprint and Keystore

The first thing you will need is the keytool utility from Sun Microsystems. The keytool utility is shipped as part of the JDK and JRE in JDeveloper, but you can obtain this tool directly from the Sun web site in the form of a plug-in for your browser.

NOTE
When using the JDeveloper Applet Wizard, you can check the checkboxes called Generate HTML File *and* Generate Java Plug-in code, *and tags will be placed in the generated HTML file that, at runtime, automatically connect to Sun Microsystems' web site and receive the appropriate plug-in. This only occurs if the browser had not been set up with the plug-in. You must have a valid Internet connection open when you run the HTML file.*

The following steps create and configure the fingerprint and keystroke files.

1. To act as the receiving party, copy C:\test and its subdirectory to a folder with the same name on another machine, or just continue to use the same machine and pretend you are now the client machine.

2. If you did not download and install the browser plug-in in the "Download the Plug-in" section of the earlier practice, go back and complete those steps now.

As the receiving party, you are now ready to fingerprint the certificate file that you simulated receiving across the Internet. After you obtain the fingerprint, you would contact the sender and compare fingerprints to see if the certificate is valid, or use the known fingerprint of a certification authority (CA) if a trusted CA validated the certificate.

3. To obtain a certificate fingerprint, use the following script on the C:\test prompt command line. The entire command must be entered on a single line.

```
keytool -printcert -file MarkJonesSun.cer
```

The system will respond as follows:

```
Owner: CN=Mark Jones, OU=Sales, O=Dulcian, L=Iselin, ST=NJ, C=US
Issuer: CN=Mark Jones, OU=Sales, O=Dulcian, L=Iselin, ST=NJ, C=US
Serial number: 38e1c806
Valid from Mon Feb 12 09:28:34 EST 2001 until Sun Apr 13 09:28:34 EST 2001
Certificate fingerprints:
        MD5:   74:A4:91:5A:91:2F:B6:F5:2C:B7:E5:19:EB:48:F5:11
        SHA1:  B4:27:0c:B4:AD:E1:AB:6A:33:DF:59:19:F4:40:CC:B3:41:72:D6:DF
```

This fingerprint must exactly match the one generated by the sender, or the certificate is invalid. Compare the numbers for MD5 and SHA1 with the numbers that you noted in the steps for setting up the sender before. Once you are convinced that the certificate can be trusted, you are ready to add it to your own encrypted key repository.

Depending upon the browsers and third-party tools you intend to support, you may need more than one certificate. A second toolset that supports Internet Explorer, called the Microsoft SDK, will be introduced later in this chapter. Additional minor changes will be required to the HTML file that calls your applet if you wish to have it run in both Netscape Navigator and Internet Explorer. In a production environment, you would probably implement these modifications so your applet could run on either basic browser.

4. To store your certificate, enter the following command at the C:\test prompt. The entire command must be entered on a single line.

```
keytool -import -alias signfilekey -file MarkJonesSun.cer
  -keystore ClientKeyRepository
```

5. You will be prompted for new security passwords. Enter the following information:

```
Enter Passphrase for keystore: *!*ClientPlover
```

The prompt may read "Enter keystore password." Your answer is the same, whatever the prompt. The system will respond with something like this:

```
Owner: CN=Mark Jones, OU=Sales, O=Dulcian, L=Iselin, ST=NJ, C=US
Issuer: CN=Mark Jones, OU=Sales, O=Dulcian , L=Iselin, ST=NJ, C=US
Serial number: 38e1c806
Valid from Mon Feb 12 09:28:34 EST 2001 until Sun Apr 13 09:28:34 EST 2001
Certificate fingerprints:
        MD5:  74:A4:91:5A:91:2F:B6:F5:2C:B7:E5:19:EB:48:F5:11
        SHA1: B4:27:0c:B4:AD:E1:AB:6A:33:DF:59:19:F4:40:CC:B3:41:72:D6:DF
```

You will then be prompted to decide whether you trust this certificate:

```
Trust this certificate? [no]: y
Certificate was added to keystore
```

Create a Client Policy File

The next step for the client is to create a policy file that grants the signed material permission to operate on the client machine. To create a client policy file, use the following steps:

1. If you closed the command line window, open it and navigate to the C:\test directory. If you did not close the window, switch back to it.

2. Type "policytool" at the prompt and press ENTER to start the policy tool.

3. Click OK to dismiss the warning message, which tells you that you haven't opened a default policy file.

4. To set the keystore, select **Edit | Change Keystore**. The keystore window shown in Figure 12-8 will appear.

5. Then enter your client repository as a URL address by entering "C:/test/ClientKeyRepository," and click OK.

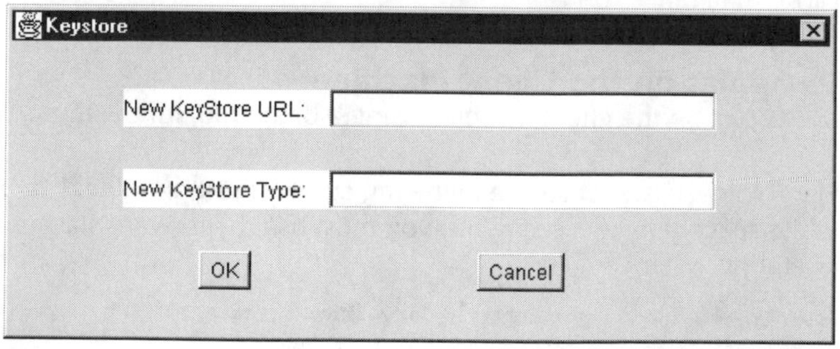

FIGURE 12-8. *Policy Tool Keystore window*

NOTE
*You must use forward slashes "/" in the path for
your repository for all operating systems, including
Windows.*

6. Click Add Policy Entry to start the entry dialog.

7. In the *SignedBy* field, enter "signfilekey"—the alias from your certificate.
   Leave the *CodeBase* field blank, indicating that any code signed by the
   signfilekey will be granted permission regardless of the JAR in which it
   is located.

8. Click Add Permission to open the Permissions dialog box.

9. Using the Permission pulldown, select FilePermission. You should see
   an entry appear in the box to the right for "java.io.FilePermission."

10. In the blank box below "java.io.FilePermission," enter the target file name
    "fileout.txt." This limits the write permission to just one file name.

11. Select "write" from the bottom pulldown (on the *Actions* field). When you
    click Write in the pulldown, you will see the word "write" appear in the
    third box down on the right-hand side. Leave the *Signed By* field blank,
    and click OK and Done to return to the Policy Tool.

12. To save this new policy file, select **File | Save As** to open the Save As
    dialog. Since you started the Policy Tool from the deployment directory
    C:\test, you are ready to save the new policy file in this location.

13. Type "clientfile.policy" in the *File name* field and click Save to save the file.
    Click OK to acknowledge the successful write operation, and notice that
    the *Policy File* field now shows the correct location.

14. Close the Policy Tool.

Test the Applet on the Client Machine
To test your applet on the client machine using a batch file, follow these steps:

1. Start Notepad and enter the following code on just one line, leaving one
   white space between segments: you must use the forward slashes for all
   operating systems.

```
appletviewer -J-Djava.security.policy=file:/c:/test/clientfile.policy
    file:/c:/test/MyFileOutPRJ_html/MyFileOutPRJ_MyFileOUT.html
```

2. Select **File | Save As** and navigate to the directory C:\test. Then click in the *File name* field, enter "runclient.bat," and click Save to store your batch file. Exit Notepad.

3. If a command line window is not open, open one and navigate to the C:\test directory.

4. Test your applet by typing "runclient" at the command prompt and pressing ENTER. You should see a message in your browser that looks like "You just completed writing to: fileout.txt."

What Just Happened?   You set up the receiver with the files required for successful processing of signed material.

Hands-on Practice: Creating Security Files to Support Internet Explorer

The Internet Explorer browser from Microsoft uses a slightly different system to manage security. Along with specific permissions like the toolset from Sun, the Microsoft browser also uses a zone and level architecture, which allows Java different default security levels based on where the code is run. This is convenient when dealing with applets that are intended to run on an isolated intranet. An applet running on an intranet can automatically receive lower security requirements, similar to an application, without any extra work on your part. But with this complexity comes additional overhead requiring a different toolset to handle the security model used by Microsoft.

This practice uses the following phases to explore this subject:

I. Install the Microsoft SDK

II. Set up the Internet Explorer security files

- **Create a certificate**

- **Create a cabinet file**

- **Create a permissions file**

- **Sign the code and test the applet**

CAUTION
Internet Explorer security is different from security in Netscape. Be sure to test security in both browsers.

I. Install the Microsoft SDK

To prepare your applet to run in a form that is compatible with Internet Explorer, you must download and install the "Microsoft SDK for Java 4.0" (or a higher version) product from the following site (current as of this writing):

`http://www.microsoft.com/java/download.htm`

CAUTION
This is a 18 MB file that requires 140 MB of disk space to install.

After you have installed the tools, you must append the Microsoft SDK Java 4.0 bin directory to the path variable of your operating system. For example, in Windows 2000 you can append the appropriate tool location to the path with these steps:

1. Find the correct path by locating the file named cabarc.exe. This will indicate the directory into which the installer placed the SDK program files.

2. Select from the Windows start menu **Start** | **Settings** | **Control Panel**, doubleclick System, select Advanced and EnvironmentVariables. Append the path under System Variables to reflect the correct tool path, for example:

   `PATH = ...;C:\Program Files\Microsoft SDK for Java 4.0\bin" directory;...`

What Just Happened?   You installed the Microsoft software development kit to support application security in Internet Explorer.

II. Set up the Internet Explorer Security Files

This phase uses the SDK tools to create public and private keys, a certificate, and a cabinet file to modify the security requirements for your applet to run on Internet Explorer. If you need keys signed by a certification authority (CA), you will need to request a separate set to run your applet on Internet Explorer. This practice session uses a self-generated set of keys to demonstrate the deployment process for your applet.

The following utilities from the SDK will be utilized in the practice to prepare your applet to run on Internet Explorer:

- Makecert
- Cert2spc

- Cabarc

- Signcode

- Piniedit

Using the makecert utility, you will create a new certificate to use with Internet Explorer. This step will also create a key file (.pvk), which you will use when signing code for Internet Explorer.

Create a Certificate

Use the following steps to create the certificate files:

1. If your command prompt window is not open, open it and navigate to the C:\test directory.

2. Type "makecert -!" at the prompt and press ENTER to see a list of the extended options.

3. To create a new certificate and key file for Internet Explorer, enter the following code on a single line and press ENTER.

```
makecert -n "CN=MarkJonesIEcert" -m 99 -r -sv MarkJonesIE.pvk MarkJonesIE.cer
```

4. The system will request a new password. Enter and confirm a new private key password: "clientpw2345" and "clientpw2345," and then click OK.

5. When prompted for the password again, enter "clientpw2345" and click OK. If all went well, the system will respond with a success message.

6. To convert your certificate file to a Microsoft-compatible file (.spc), enter the following command at the C:\test prompt and press ENTER.

```
cert2spc MarkJonesIE.cer MarkJonesIE.spc
```

The system will respond with a success message.

Create a Cabinet File

The next step in the process is to create a cabinet file holding your Java code. The cabinet file is similar to JAR and Zip files, and will contain a copy of your code that is compatible with Internet Explorer. You will copy the compiled class file from JDeveloper to the test folder you have been working with. Then, using the cabarc utility, you will create the cabinet file. Next you will prepare a permissions file, using the piniedit utility, to give your applet the ability to write a file. Finally, you will use the signcode utility to digitally sign your code with the modified security requirements stored in the permissions file.

To create the cabinet file, use the following steps:

1. Copy MyFileOut.class from its source:
JDEV_HOME\myclasses\myfileout\ MyFileOut.class
to your deployment area C:\test\myfileout\MyFileOut.class.

2. To store your Java code in a cabinet file, enter the following code on a single line:

```
cabarc -p n MyFileOutPRJforIE.cab myfileout/MyFileOut.class
```

The system will respond with the following output:

```
Creating new cabinet 'MyFileOutPRJforIE.cab' with compression 'MSZIP':
  --adding myfileout/MyFileOut.class
Completed successfully
```

Create a Permissions File
Use the following steps to create a permissions file.

1. Navigate to your test directory and enter the following code on a single line:

```
Piniedit
```

This will start the Permission INI File Editor.

2. Under the File tab, change the *Access type* to Write using the pulldown.

3. In the box below *Include files*, enter "C:\test\fileout.txt" and click the Add button to the right of the box.

4. Then save the file by clicking **File** | **Save As**, and navigate to the C:\test directory. In the *File name* box enter "permissions.ini" and click Save.

5. Exit the editor.

Sign the Code and Test the Applet
The steps listed here can be used to sign your code.

1. To sign your code with your digital signature, and to specify the modified security requirements, enter the following code on a single line. You may view the signcode options by entering "signcode" at the prompt.

```
signcode -j javasign.dll -jp permissions.ini -spc MarkJonesIE.spc
   -v MarkJonesIE.pvk  MyFileOutPRJforIE.cab
```

2. Enter the password when requested as "clientpw2345." The system will respond with the following:

```
Warning: This file is signed, but not timestamped.
Succeeded
```

Since Internet Explorer recognizes cabinet (not .jar or .zip) files, you will need to convert the Zip file containing the unique JDeveloper classes (C:\test\jdev-rt.zip) into a cabinet file.

3. Create a folder under the test directory called "unzip. "

4. Utilizing any standard zip utility, unzip the jdev-rt.zip file into the C:\test\unzip directory, including the original paths.

5. Next, using a command prompt, change to the C:\test\unzip directory and enter the following command:

```
cabarc -p -r n jdev-rt.cab *.*
```

6. Copy the new cabinet .cab file to C:\test\jdev-rt.cab by entering

```
copy C:\test\unzip\jdev-rt.cab C:\test\jdev-rt.cab
```

You must now edit the HTML file that calls your applet and add a parameter that identifies the new cabinet files you have created for Internet Explorer. It is important to note that Internet Explorer will recognize the cabinet files identified by this parameter tag, and Netscape Navigator will automatically ignore them.

7. Using Notepad or another text editor, insert the following line just above the ending applet tag "</APPLET>" in the file C:\test\MyFileOutPRJ_html\MyFileOutPRJ_MyFileOut.html:

```
<PARAM NAME = "cabinets" VALUE = "jdev-rt.cab,MyFileOutPRJforIE.cab">
```

8. To add the certificate to Internet Explorer and test the applet, right click the Internet Explorer icon on your desktop.

9. Select **Properties | Content | Certificates**, select Import, and click **Next** to open the Certificate Wizard.

10. Click Browse and change the *Files of type* to "X.509 Certificate." Navigate to the C:\test directory and click MarkJonesIE.cer, Open, and Next.

11. Leave the selection of certificate store in the Automatic mode and click Next, Finish, Yes, and OK to add the certificate to the root store. Then select Close and OK to exit the Certificate Wizard.

12. To run your applet with Internet Explorer, open Internet Explorer and enter the following address:

```
C:\test\MyFileOutPRJ_html\MyFileOutPRJ_MyFileOUT.html.
```

If everything was completed successfully, the applet should respond with "You just completed writing to: fileout.txt."

What Just Happened? You set up the proper security files to allow Internet Explorer to validate security in an applet. This requires different steps and files than shown in the practice that used the Sun plug-in files. An important concept that is worth repeating is that security is handled differently by each browser and you need to set up your application with an awareness of what your expected audience will use. Otherwise there may be surprises when you deploy the application.

Implementing a Secure Sockets Layer (SSL)

Successful implementation of a Secure Sockets Layer must be accomplished independent of any code or feature of JDeveloper. Accomplishing this task involves all of the principles mentioned earlier in the chapter, including identification, authorization, verification, and encryption. It is important to use reliable certification authority certificates, public and private keys, and a suitable encryption algorithm in your web server.

SSL technology is based upon a handshake between the client browser and the web server, where keys are passed back and forth to provide encryption and decryption of the data being transmitted to keep the packets secure. If you install Oracle's *i*AS product, the web http server will automatically be configured with SSL and a trial set of keys for testing security.

Do not use these test keys for production purposes. You must go to a certification authority such as VeriSign (www.verisign.com) or Thawte for production-ready keys.

The most common web servers are Oracle's *i*AS (based on Apache technology), Apache, Microsoft's Internet Information Server (IIS), and IBM's WebSphere. The instructions for using each of these can be downloaded over the Internet. The most effective option for production systems is Oracle's *i*AS implementation of Apache. Accessing the SSL is simply a matter of typing in the web server address using an "https" prefix to generate the security alerts.

CHAPTER
13

Debugging the Code

Debugging is anticipated with distaste,
performed with reluctance,
and bragged about forever.

—Anonymous

he concept of software testing is broader than simply debugging your software application programs. You need to think critically about testing long before you get to the point of developing and implementing your application. This type of awareness and planning will go a long way to ensure that your applications can be brought quickly to production quality.

Finding design and coding defects early in the development life cycle can result in huge benefits. Perhaps you will only need to spend hours correcting code errors that are discovered early in the process, rather than the days to weeks otherwise required to retrofit code errors discovered after a product is deployed or shipped to a customer.

In other words, testing, quality assurance, and other configuration management methods should pervade your system development process from start to finish. These measures will help you to ensure that the highest quality software product is delivered using JDeveloper 3.2.

It is not the intent of this chapter to discuss the topic of software quality in general. Rather, this chapter discusses some of the techniques that can be easily used within JDeveloper to help with the unit testing of your Java code as it is being written. The chapter explains how the major features of JDeveloper's native debugger handle the debugging process and the essential debugging activities—program control and value checking. The chapter concludes with a hands-on practice that illustrates these concepts.

Most of the techniques in this chapter apply equally to debugging a Java application, applet, or JSP application that is running in the client machine's JVM. When you deploy and run JSP code, you may need to perform additional debugging on the server. The section later in this chapter called "Remote Debugging" explains where to find more information on the subject of debugging code on the server.

Overview

Debugging is the process of locating and fixing errors in your software programs. Most developers would readily agree that debugging source code, regardless of the language, is tedious and time consuming. The objective of debugging is to find and fix the problem as quickly and easily as possible. There are a number of ways to debug a program, many of which do not involve a dedicated debugging tool. However, Java includes a full-featured debugger that allows you to perform activities that are required to find problems in the code. JDeveloper provides a graphical interface for this debugger and adds many features to ease the debugging process.

Before explaining how debugging works in a JDeveloper environment, it is necessary to step back and examine the types of program errors and the activities required in the debugging process to understand where the errors occur.

Types of Program Errors

There are four general types of program errors with which to be concerned:

- **Syntax errors**   These are the result of incorrectly formed statements. They are easily detected by the JDeveloper compiler, which displays errors in the Message View window. You can just doubleclick an error in this window and the Source Editor will highlight the problem code line.

- **Data condition errors**   These are a result of inputting or passing a value to the program that causes the program to abort, such as a divide-by-zero error. The error is reported by the Java runtime system (JVM in the case of a Java application or applet). Data condition errors are much more difficult and challenging than syntax errors because your testing may miss the data value that causes the error. Developer experience and better program design can eliminate these types of errors. The trace feature of the debugger assists in fixing this type of bug.

- **Logic errors**   This type of error also shows up only at runtime. A logic error is a result of poor design or of coding mistakes and often manifests itself if the program does something that it is not intended to do. This type of error is the most difficult to catch because it may not occur consistently or early in the development process. In fact, these errors can occur for the first time long after a program is released to production use. The best guard against logic errors is a very thorough test plan and testing cycle. Once you experience this type of error, the debugger will help you locate the problem.

- **Resource errors**   This type of error occurs due to lack of a required resource such as network availability, server availability, memory, disk space, or other "physical" (nonprogrammatic) resource.

Correcting Syntax Errors

Of course, little advice for fixing a syntax error is necessary. Developers normally read the error text carefully and closely examine the code based on that text. If an error indicates that a method that you call does not exist, check the spelling and use of upper- and lowercase because Java is a case-sensitive language. If the spelling is correct, you should check to see that you are passing the correct argument types. The Javadoc for a method will indicate which arguments are expected and allowed. If the spelling and arguments are correct, you may be missing an import statement. You also need to be sure that the package is accessible by including it as a library in the Project Properties dialog (**Project | Project Properties**).

Other common errors that are easy to check for are mismatched braces or parentheses, missing quotation marks, and missing semicolons at the end of an executable line. The Message View window will be of some help in identifying these errors. Other than honest mistakes with a misunderstanding or misuse of the Java language, the errors mentioned will probably cover 80 percent of the syntax errors that you experience.

Since syntax errors must be corrected before you run the program, and since the debugger only works at runtime, this chapter will not discuss them further.

Correcting Data Condition and Logic Errors

The JDeveloper debugger assists in resolving runtime data condition and logic errors. This chapter focuses mainly on the generic debugging process that you can apply to these types of errors.

One of the most pernicious errors for novice Java developers to watch out for results from the automatic casting of numeric data types. Be especially careful of odd rounding errors involving integer data types.

The best defense against logic errors is well-constructed, object-oriented code. Java programming is very different from programming in other languages, such as PL/SQL. The best resource for learning good Java programming "style" is Martin Fowler's book on writing object-oriented programs in Java called *Refactoring: Improving the Design of Existing Code* (Martin Fowler, Kent Beck, John Brant, William Opdyke, and Don Roberts, Addison-Wesley, ISBN 0-201-48567-2).

Correcting Resource Errors

Resource errors may be intermittent, and these are difficult problems to fix. If you can consistently reproduce the problem, the JDeveloper debugger will help you to determine at which point a program is failing. If you determine that there are no logic or data condition errors, you can then turn to external resources. Follow the process of elimination by substituting hardware or network resources and testing the problem. This should lead you to a solution. Sometimes such errors result from a recursive routine that is not terminating.

Debugging Activities

The debugging process normally combines two interrelated debugging activities: running and stepping through the code and examining the values of variables, parameters, data, and array items. The process follows the steps and activities diagrammed in Figure 13-1. You normally test an application first in normal runtime mode to see if there are potential errors. If you find errors, you run the debugger and set up breakpoints to stop execution of the code. At those points you can stop the program execution and examine data values. When you are finished with those tasks, you exit the debugger.

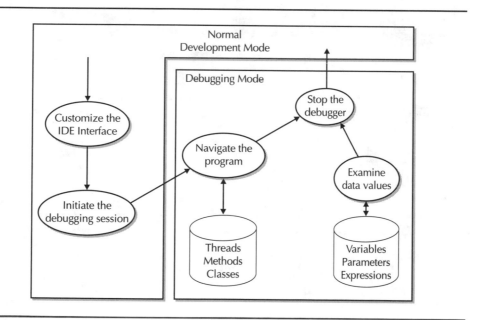

FIGURE 13-1.   *A typical debugging session*

Help with the Debugger

The JDeveloper help system topics that apply to debugging fall under the "Debugging Java Programs" node in the Contents page. For example, the topic "Debugging a Project in JDeveloper," shown in the following illustration, explains the debugger in great depth. Drill down through this node in the Contents page for other applicable topics.

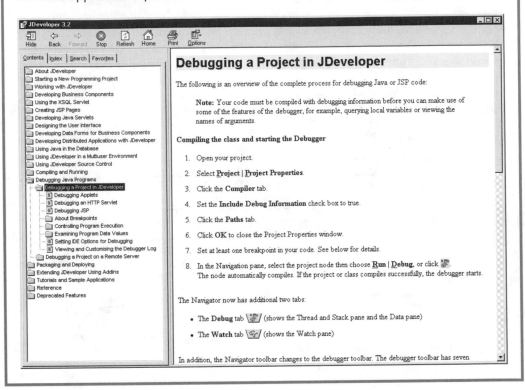

Do You Really Have to Run the Debugger?

The JDeveloper debugger is a powerful tool for repairing defects in code that you create. As with many powerful features, there is a bit of complexity. You may not need to employ the debugger for a problem that seems to be relatively simple. There are some simple debugging techniques that you can use to determine problem areas. These may lead you to a solution without having to run the debugger. The following techniques are described in a section called "Troubleshooting the Application" at the end of Chapter 2. These techniques provide alternatives to running the debugger for specific kinds of problems. They are your first line of defense in the battle against bugs.

- General debugging tips
- Testing and editing the connection
- Testing and editing the row set
- Testing with the Oracle Business Components Browser

There are some other techniques that you can use outside of the debugger.

Displaying Messages

A simple but effective technique that works in selected situations is to temporarily add code to display a message while the program is running. The message can contain information about the method that is being run, and it can include variable values. This is usually useful only if you have a clear picture of the potential problem area and just need to quickly verify a value or that the execution path reached a certain line of code. For other debugging situations, the debugger might be easier and more informative. The drawback with using messages is that you have to modify the code and strip out the messages when you are finished debugging.

There are two methods you can use when you want to display a message. Both can accomplish the main debugging objectives of program control and value checking.

NOTE
Some developers define Boolean variables in the code and set the flag to "true" to turn on the messages. Each section of code that has a message tests the flag to see if the message should be displayed. When the developer is finished with the messages, she or he sets the Boolean variable to "false" so that messages will be suppressed. When the program is completed, the developer either strips out all message code or leaves it in for future debugging efforts.

Console Window
You can embed a call to this method in key positions in your code. For example, if you wanted to determine the value of a variable called `totalSalary`, you would add the following line in a Java application or applet:

```
System.out.println("total salary = " + totalSalary);
```

This would display the text "total salary = 999" (if the variable value were 999) in the console window (or the Message View, depending on the settings in Project Properties). In a JSP file, you would use the following line:

```
<% System.out.println("This is a debugging message"); %>
```

If you needed to pass variable values, you could use the names as declared in previous statements in the JSP file.

Message Dialog

For Java applications and applets, you can display a message box (dialog) that contains text (optionally concatenated with variable values). This allows you to stop and look at the dialog before the program continues. A message box is useful if you need to check the output on the screen in the middle of an operation. The console window technique described earlier does not provide this capability.

The code that you write calls a method of the Swing class JOptionPane. JOptionPane offers a number of features, including specifying more than one button and providing a text input area that the user can fill in. It is an easy way to show a dialog box. For debugging message purposes, you only need its simplest format, shown in this example:

```
JOptionPane.showMessageDialog(this,
    "The debugging message.",
    "Debug Message",
    JOptionPane.INFORMATION_MESSAGE);
}
```

The following shows the output of this code. This technique results in showing the same kind of message (normally including variable values) as you would show using the console window technique.

This technique is not applicable to JSP applications.

Using the Dialog Class

Although JOptionPane will suffice for most debugging message requirements, you may require more functionality and additional components. The Dialog class demonstrated in the following steps displays a window with a customized dialog.

1. Create a project (TestDialogPRJ) that contains an application with an empty frame.

2. Open the frame source code and click the Design tab. Change the *layout* property of JPanel1 to "XYLayout" so that the container does not impose sizing or positioning logic.

3. Add a button to the frame in the UI Designer. Select the button and change the *text* property to "Test Dialog."

4. Click Rebuild and Save All. Test run the application.

5. Add a dialog class by clicking the project file, selecting **File | New**, and doubleclicking Dialog on the Objects tab. Note the name of the dialog in the Dialog Wizard and accept the default values. This will create a file in the project called Dialog1.java which contains constructors for a dialog window.

6. Open the source code for the new dialog file and click the Design tab.

7. Click JPanel1 and change its *layout* property to "XYLayout." Although you can place any component in this dialog panel, for this demonstration, just add a text field. Doubleclick the frame file and click the Design tab.

8. Click the Test Dialog button in the UI Designer and click the Events tab in the Inspector. Doubleclick the value of the actionPerformed event to insert the event handling code and switch the control to the Source Editor. In the blank line between curly brackets, insert the following code:

```
Dialog1 myDialog = new Dialog1();
myDialog.show();
```

9. Click Rebuild and Save All. Run the application. Click the Test Dialog button and the dialog with the text field will display. Use the window closing buttons to close both windows.

A variation on this technique is moving the instantiation (new) line to the class level (under `public class Frame6` in this example). This allows the dialog to be called from any method in that class. You can also instantiate the dialog with arguments (parent window, dialog title, and modal flag) as follows:

```
Dialog1 myDialog = new Dialog1(this, "My test dialog", true);
```

The help system topic "Adding a Dialog Box" (called "Dialog Box, adding" in the Index tab) contains more information on the Dialog class.

HTML Messages

For JSP applications and applet HTML startup files, you can use HTML messages to show the program section that is being executed. Simple message text embedded in the HTML body section can show that a particular code line was reached. You can also use hidden field values to show the parameter values that were passed to the page. (Consult your favorite HTML reference for details on hidden fields.)

TIP
Browsers usually offer a way to display messages from the server. In Netscape, you can select **Communicator | Tools | Java Console** *to show a window that will display messages about the session (for example, when running an applet). Internet Explorer has a checkbox called* Disable script debugging *on the Advanced tab of the Internet Options dialog (**Tools | Internet Options**). If you uncheck this checkbox, the browser will use whatever script debugger you have installed in Internet Explorer.*

BC4J Web Monitor (Admin Utility)

When you create JSP applications, the user interface you create is written in HTML. While the program is running, you can get a list of session-level variables and parameters for the application and the BC4J code using the Web Monitor. This is a page (as shown in Figure 13-2) that is accessed using an address of server:port/ webapp/admin/bc4jadmin.htm (where server:port is the host name and port number of your JSP listener).

This page offers details about the runtime status and parameters for the BC4J and Java layers that can help you detect an error in the BC4J code.

TIP
You can also set a command-line parameter to assist with diagnostic output for BC4J. The help topic "Controlling Diagnostic Messages" (found in the Index tab's "diagnostic messages, business components" entry) explains how to set up this parameter.

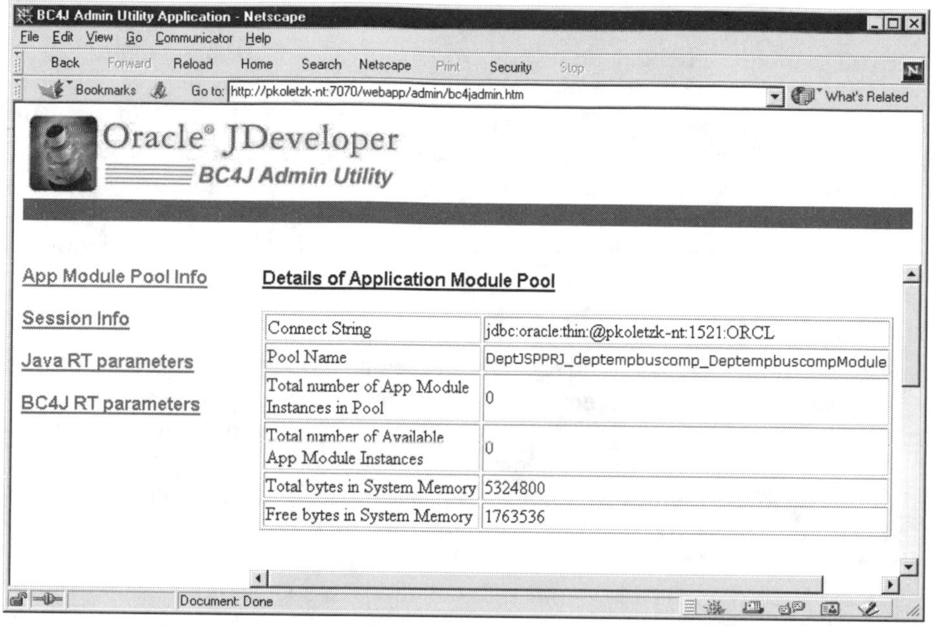

FIGURE 13-2. *BC4J Web Monitor (Admin Utility)*

Note for Oracle Developer Users

Oracle Developer provides a debugging tool that offers the same main features as the JDeveloper debugger for controlling program execution and examining data values. You will find, however, that the JDeveloper debugger contains many additional features that are offered in other 3GL environments but not in 4GL environments such as Oracle Developer. The traditional method for debugging Oracle Developer forms is to temporarily add message statements to the code so that you can check the execution path and variable values as the form is running. This technique parallels the use of `System.out.println()` to display messages in the console (Message View) window. You can also call SHOW_ALERT to display a message in a dialog window, which is similar to calling `JOptionPane.showMessageDialog()` in Java.

CodeCoach

After you complete a debugging session, you may want to test the efficiency of your code to make certain that the application program is of the highest quality and performs at an optimum level. This is a useful exercise to go through before debugging as well so that the code is tuned as early in the development process as possible. JDeveloper provides a tool to serve this purpose called CodeCoach. When you activate CodeCoach, your program will run as usual. After you exit the program, you will find a list of suggestions for improving your code in the Message View window.

Setting Up CodeCoach

You can customize the way CodeCoach runs using the CodeCoach tab in the Project Properties dialog (**Project | Project Properties**), as shown in Figure 13-3. You can request help for different areas by checking the appropriate checkboxes. The level of help that you request indicates whether CodeCoach will advise only on the most important findings (1), on all findings (10), or something in between. You can override or refine the settings by inserting *pragmas* (comments that are specially formatted) in your code.

Each advice type has a keyword with which it is associated, for example, "CFIN" for "Possible final class" advice or "LFIN" for "Possible final local variable." These keywords (all of which are documented in the help system) are displayed in the Message View after you run the program.

Running CodeCoach

To start CodeCoach, select the project file in the Navigation Pane and select **Run | CodeCoach *<appname>*** (where "appname" is the program name). If you receive a warning stating that a class must be compiled with debug information, either exclude the class or check the *Include debug information* checkbox in the Compiler tab of the Project Properties dialog. As you run the program, be sure you test all features of your application so that the CodeCoach can receive a full picture of all aspects of the application.

CAUTION
CodeCoach will consider only loaded classes. If your code calls a method in a class, but during the program operation does not access that class, the class will not be loaded. CodeCoach will construct its findings based on that situation and may, therefore, alert you to a problem that does not exist. The main warning is to think carefully about what the advice implies.

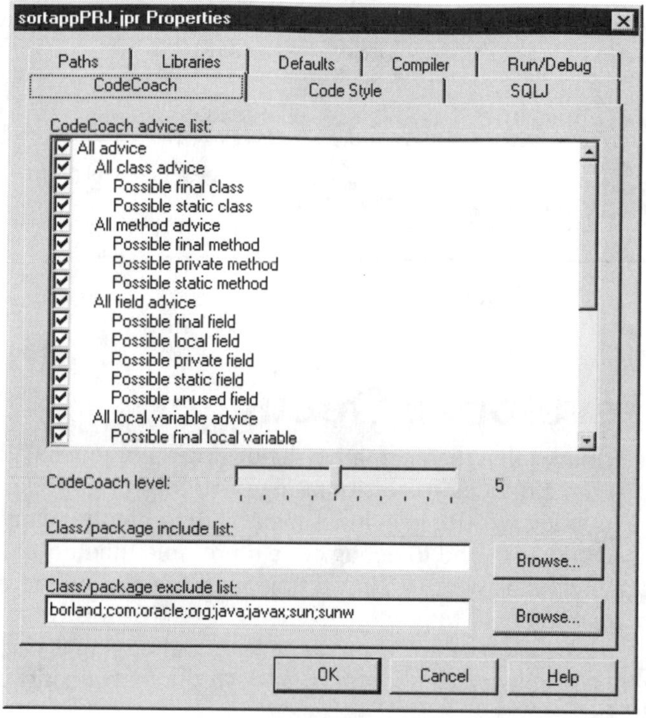

FIGURE 13-3. *CodeCoach properties*

Output from a CodeCoach Session

Upon completion of a CodeCoach session, a CodeCoach tab in the Message View window will display the results, as shown in Figure 13-4. The popup menu in this window contains options to save the results to a file, obtain help about the message, remove the message page, and hide messages of the same type as the selected message. It also allows you to apply some of the suggested fixes to the source code, such as adding a keyword. Clicking a message will display the referenced line of code in the Source Editor.

TIP

The help system Contents page node "Working with JDeveloper\Writing More Efficient Java Using CodeCoach" contains topics with more information.

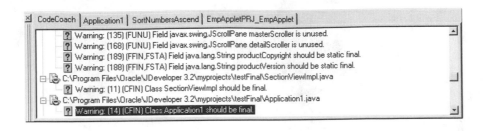

| CodeCoach | Application1 | SortNumbersAscend | EmpAppletPRJ_EmpApplet |

       ? Warning: (135) (FUNU) Field javax.swing.JScrollPane masterScroller is unused.
       ? Warning: (168) (FUNU) Field javax.swing.JScrollPane detailScroller is unused.
       ? Warning: (189) (FFIN,FSTA) Field java.lang.String productCopyright should be static final.
       ? Warning: (188) (FFIN,FSTA) Field java.lang.String productVersion should be static final.
  C:\Program Files\Oracle\JDeveloper 3.2\myprojects\testFinal\SectionViewImpl.java
       ? Warning: (11) (CFIN) Class SectionViewImpl should be final.
  C:\Program Files\Oracle\JDeveloper 3.2\myprojects\testFinal\Application1.java
       ? Warning: (14) (CFIN) Class Application1 should be final.

FIGURE 13-4. *CodeCoach output*

The JDeveloper Debugger

If you have determined that the alternative debugging techniques will not suffice, you will want to run a debugging session using the debugging mode. JDeveloper uses the Java 2, debugging API. It includes the ability to handle many JDK versions (such as 1.1, 1.2, and 1.3), and to debug code on remote machines. Debugging is an essential activity that is worth an initial time investment. The more time you spend up front learning how to use the debugger, the more easily you will be able to respond to a problem program. The time to learn debugging is not when you encounter the first problem in a high-pressure development situation.

Starting a Debugging Session

You start a debugging session from the IDE by clicking the Debug button, pressing SHIFT-F9, or selecting **Run | Debug "<*program name>*"** from the menu (where "program name" is the file name, such as SortNumbersAscend). You also need to check the *Include debug information* checkbox on the Compiler tab of the Project Properties dialog (**Project | Project Properties**). Another requirement is that you set at least one breakpoint that will halt the program execution, or use Trace Into to stop at the first line of executable code. The file compiles with special debugging information and runs in a modified JDeveloper window such as that shown in Figure 13-5.

NOTE
Another way to stop execution in the code is to start the debugger and click Pause to stop. The trick is to stop in the right place, but if the code execution is paused or stopped (such as when the program awaits user input), this is a reasonable technique to use.

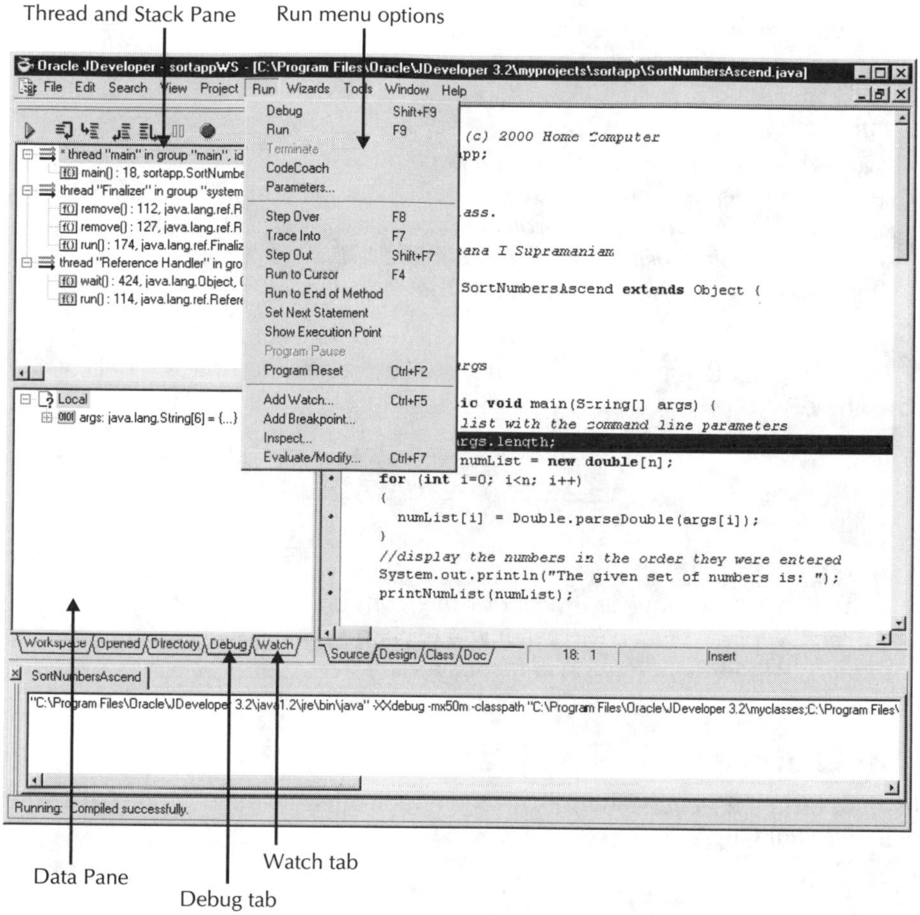

Thread and Stack Pane   Run menu options

FIGURE 13-5. *JDeveloper running in debug mode*

Figure 13-5 shows a number of special debugging features that appear in debugging mode. Debugging menu options are enabled in the Run menu. In addition, two tabs are added to the Navigator as follows:

■   **Debug**   This tab contains the Thread and Stack Pane that shows the methods called and *threads* (lines of program execution). The tab also shows the Data Pane that displays data values. There is a special toolbar for this window (described later) that contains debugging actions.

■ **Watch**   You use this tab to display the current values of the expressions you are watching. The tab offers a split pane that you use to view more than one set of watches at a time.

TIP
You can change the contents of each pane by selecting Properties from the popup menu in any pane. In addition, you can set colors of the various debugging displays using the Fonts tab in the IDE Options dialog that is available in the Tools menu.

The Navigator tabs may appear with icon labels instead of text labels, as shown here:

NOTE
If you expand the Navigator window, the icons on the tabs will be replaced by text. If you expand it further, both text and icons will be displayed.

The Debug Tab Toolbar

The buttons in the Debug tab toolbar shown here offer the main actions that you need when running a debug session.

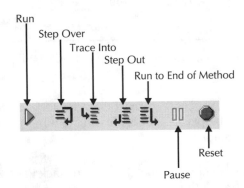

The actions and the keypresses that you can alternatively use to activate them follow.

- **Run**   Execute the program to the next breakpoint or to the end of the program if no subsequent breakpoints are defined (F9).

- **Step Over**   Execute the next method called and stop at the next executable line following the method call (F8).

- **Trace Into**   Execute the program and trace step by step into the next method called (F7).

- **Step Out**   Step out of the current method and return to the next instruction of the calling method (SHIFT-F7).

- **Run to End of Method**   Execute the program to the end of the current method or to the next breakpoint in the current method.

- **Pause**   Temporarily stop the program at a specific location or when a certain condition is met.

- **Reset**   Abort the program that is in debugging mode. The debug settings will be saved (CTRL-F2).

When you are in debugging mode, the toolbar and menu contain around 15 debugging commands that you can select for controlling program execution. In addition, the popup (context) menu contains items such as Run to Cursor, Add Watch, and Evaluate/Modify.

The Run Menu Debug Items

The Run menu options that are enabled in debugging mode repeat the toolbar options and add the following functions:

- **Terminate**   Stops a program that is running outside of debugging mode.

- **Run to Cursor**   Runs the program from its current execution point to the line of program code containing the cursor (F4).

- **Set Next Statement**   Allows you to skip from the stopping point to the code at the location of the cursor even if the cursor is before the stopping point.

- **Show Execution Point**   Displays the section of code that is currently running.

- **Add Watch**   Displays the Add Watch dialog, where you can set up a new watch to evaluate an expression or value (CTRL-F5).

- **Add Breakpoint**   Opens the Breakpoint Options dialog, where you define a new stopping point for your program in the debugger.

- **Inspect**   Displays the Inspect window, where you can enter and track expressions in Java, such as variable values.

- **Evaluate/Modify**   Displays the Evaluate/Modify dialog that you use to change or view the value of variables and other expressions (CTRL-F7).

It is usually much easier to click a toolbar button or press a key than select a menu item, so you will probably not use the Run menu often.

Controlling Program Execution

The first main debugging objective is to track and control the *execution point*—the section of code that is about to be executed. In a typical session, the debugger stops the program execution, highlights the execution point, and waits for you to resume the program. You use one of the debug actions (button, keypress, or menu selection) to resume the program execution.

Debugging Actions

While the program is stopped, you can evaluate the *stack* (the sequence of method calls that preceded the execution point) and order that the program executed to determine whether the program execution path is the problem. The Thread and Stack Pane of the Debug tab displays this information, as shown next. In the pause, you can also evaluate data values (as mentioned in the later section "Examining Program Data Values").

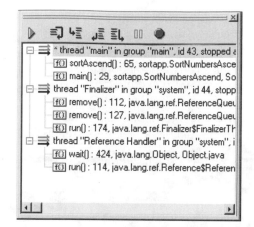

As you step through the code in this way, you are *tracing* its path. You can choose to skip tracing each line of code in a particular method that is called by *stepping over* the call. The method will still execute, but you will not stop in the method code. This is useful if you are certain that a method works and you do not want to take the time to look at it in detail. If you start tracing in a method and determine that the rest of the code works, you can choose to *step out* of that method. Each of these actions is represented by a menu item, toolbar button, and/or keypress.

These are the main actions in a debugging session. There are other actions you can take in the debugger, such as viewing the method's source code by selecting Goto Method from the popup menu in the Thread and Stack Pane.

This and other techniques such as stepping back, disabling tracing for classes that have not been loaded, and tracing into a class that has no source code file, are explained further in the help system.

Breakpoints

A *breakpoint* is a defined pause point for the debugging session. It is the primary method that you use to control the program execution. When the program reaches a breakpoint, it stops and waits for an action. There are two types of breakpoints—a *source breakpoint* that is set to pause at a particular line of code and an *exception breakpoint* that is set to pause when an exception is thrown.

Conditions   For both types of breakpoints, you can define a condition so that the program will stop only if a variable value is within a certain range or a flag variable is set. You can also set a *pass count* that specifies that the execution will stop only after passing the breakpoint a certain number of times. This is an additional condition that is placed on the breakpoint that is added (using AND logic) to the other conditions that are defined.

You can set and define conditions for breakpoints in the Breakpoint Definition tab of the Breakpoint Options dialog (**Run | Add Breakpoint**) shown here:

Defining Breakpoints   Breakpoints are marked with a red circle icon in the Source Editor's left-hand margin so that you can easily identify the lines of code at which the execution will stop. You can get a list of breakpoints using **View | Breakpoints** to display the Breakpoints window, as shown here:

You can enable and disable or delete breakpoints using the popup menu in this window. You can also delete or set a breakpoint by clicking in the line in the Source Editor and pressing F5 or by doubleclicking the left-hand margin on that line. The Action tab of the Breakpoint Options dialog, shown here, allows you to specify what occurs when the execution reaches the breakpoint:

TIP
You can enable and disable breakpoints as a group. A breakpoint group is a set of breakpoints that share the same group name. You can set or select the group name in the Breakpoint Definition tab of the Breakpoint Options dialog for any breakpoint in the group. This group can then be enabled or disabled in the Action tab of that same dialog.

Examining Program Data Values

The other main debugging objective is to examine the values of *expressions* that represent variables, constants, and data structure values and the operators that act on them. You may not use method calls in a debugging expression. You also may not use local variables or static variables that are not available (because of scope) to the code line you are executing. There are a number of JDeveloper features that you can use to examine expressions.

Data Pane   This part of the Debug window contains a list of data elements (variables, constants, and so on) that are defined for the class. This window is shown here:

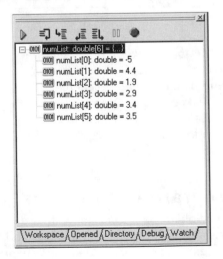

Watch Pane   This is the only pane in the Watch tab, as shown here:

It shows the data values that are part of the expressions being tracked. A *watch* is an expression that contains program variables or other data elements and their operators. You set up a watch and monitor its value as the program executes. The watch displays the value for the context (current) execution.

You can add a watch using the Add Watch dialog as the program runs (using **Run | Add Watch**) as shown here:

Add Watch

Enter watch: numList

OK   Cancel   Help

You can modify the watch expression using the Edit Watch Expression dialog shown next. To display this dialog, right click the expression in the Watch Pane and select Edit Watch.

Edit Watch Expression

Modify expression to watch

storemax * 100

OK   Cancel

NOTE
You can delete a watch expression by highlighting it in the Watch Pane and selecting Remove Watch from the popup menu.

Evaluate/Modify Dialog   Use the dialog shown here (using **Run | Evaluate/ Modify**) to display the state of a defined expression (watch) within the context of the current program execution point. Click the Evaluate button to show the value. This dialog also allows you to change the values of data during the debugging session. This allows you to test a bug fix that would modify a value. The value type must match the type of the variable to which it is assigned. The change you make does not change your code.

Evaluate/Modify

Expression:

numList[0] < 5.0

Result:

true

New Value:

Evaluate   Modify   Log   Watch   Inspect   Done   Help

Debugger Context Browser   The Debugger Context Browser is a separate window that shows watch information when you have selected the Debug tab. Normally, you would need to select the Watch tab to display this information, but you may also want to show the Debug tab information. The following shows this window. You can alter the contents of this window, as with any pane in the debugger, by selecting Properties from the popup menu. You can also open more than one browser at the same time and monitor different information in each one, such as watches, threads, or stacks.

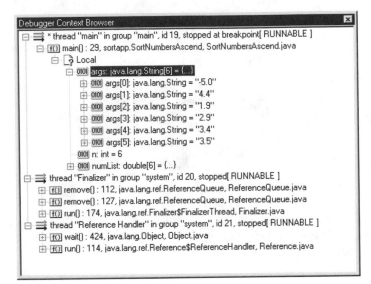

TIP

The best arrangement of windows in a debugging session is to keep the Debug tab active and use the Context Browser to display watch information.

Inspector   A *data inspector* also allows you to examine and modify the data values just as with a watch. The difference with an inspector is that it shows the state of the expression based on when the inspector was created, not based on the current context as do watches. Display the Inspector window by selecting **Run | Inspect** or selecting the variable in the Data Pane, right clicking, and selecting Inspect. The functionality is similar to the normal watch.

You can also modify the expressions by right clicking the variable in the Data Pane and selecting Modify Value. The Change Data Value dialog will be displayed as follows:

The easiest way to inspect a variable is to right click the expression you want to inspect in the Data Pane and select Inspect. The expression is always evaluated within the current scope.

Remote Debugging

Debugging an application that is running on a remote server (such as a JSP application, servlet, or Java Stored Procedure) is a challenge because error and execution messages must be generated by the server instead of just in the IDE. Although the basic approaches to debugging code are possible, such as adding calls to `System.out.println()` and logging this output to a file, these debugging methods do not always suffice. The new debugging support provided by the Java Platform Debugger Architecture (JPDA) has led to a solution enabling software vendors, including Oracle, to build debuggers that can serve distributed applications.

JDeveloper's support for remote debugging of server-side Java includes many of the features built into the local IDE debugger, such as controlled execution, breakpoints, watch expressions, and examination of variable values and properties during execution. Therefore, with JDeveloper, the same intuitive GUI can be used for both local and remote debugging. Remote debugging of Enterprise JavaBeans, CORBA server objects, and Java Stored Procedures running in Oracle8*i* Release 2 from JDeveloper leads to significant productivity gains for application developers. In addition, JDeveloper has a feature (*debug on demand*) that allows you to remotely debug any Java object running in an Oracle8*i* database called by external programs.

In addition to using the JPDA protocol for remote debugging of servlets, you can also use the Oracle Java Virtual Machine protocol, which is faster and has more features.

More Information

If you decide that you need to use remote debugging, there are some configuration steps required on the server as well as on the client. The topic of remote debugging is beyond the scope of this book but is well documented in the JDeveloper help system. Start in the Contents tab node "Debugging Java Programs\Debugging a Project on a Remote Server." In addition, technet.oracle.com's JDeveloper area offers a white paper titled "Remote Debugging Server Side Java" (look for the link titled "Remote Debugging White Paper" currently under the JDeveloper 3.1 Technical Information heading).

Hands-on Practice: Debugging a Java Application

The best way to understand how the debugger works is to apply it to a task and examine the activities required to find a problem. In this practice, you will walk through all of the major steps for carrying out the two essential debugging activities of controlling program execution and examining program data values. The practice follows these phases:

I. **Create a buggy application**

II. **Prepare for the debugging session**

III. **Control program execution**

- **Run the debugger and step through the code**

- **Disable and enable tracing of classes**

IV. **Examine data values**

As with other practices in the book, this practice assumes that you have mastered the basics of creating a workspace, project, and Java application as detailed in the hands-on practice in Chapter 2.

I. Create a Buggy Application

Normally, you do not intentionally create buggy code. The sample application for this practice requires code with bugs to illustrate the debugging process and techniques. The application used in this practice processes a list of numbers entered as command-line parameters and sorts the numbers in ascending order. The results print in the Message View window. A logic error in the program results in an incorrect sort, and the aim of the practice is to discover this error. Once the bug is found, a fix can be applied.

1. Select **File | New Workspace** and select **File | Save Workspace**. In the Save As dialog, create a new folder/package called "sortapp" (using the Create New Folder button) and navigate to it. Name the workspace "SortAppWS" inside that folder.

2. Select **File | New Project** to start the Project Wizard.

3. Click Browse and navigate to the sortapp directory. Name the project "SortAppPRJ."

4. Select "An empty project" and click Next.

5. Click Browse for the project package and select "sortapp." Click OK and Finish.

6. Select **File | New** and doubleclick the Class icon. This will open the Class Wizard.

7. Enter *Class* as "SortNumbersAscend." Leave the defaults for *Package* and *Extends*. In the *Optional attributes* area be sure that the *Public* and *Generate main function* checkboxes are checked as shown in Figure 13-6.

8. Click OK to create the file, and click Save All.

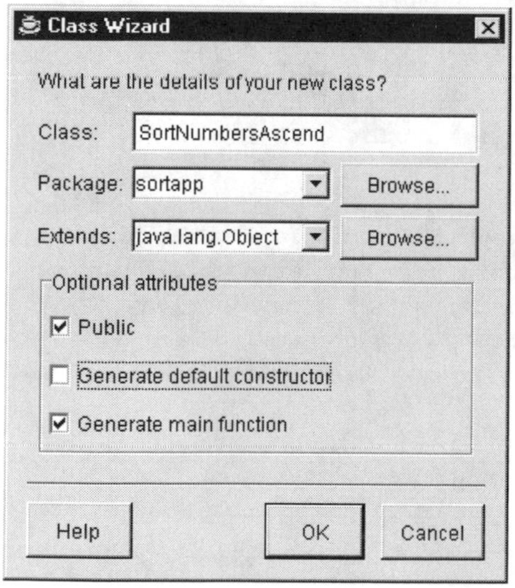

FIGURE 13-6. *The Class Wizard*

9. Open the Source Editor for this class file and add and edit it to match the following code (this code is available on the authors' web sites):

```java
package sortapp;

public class SortNumbersAscend extends Object {

  /**
   * main
   * @param args
   */
  public static void main(String[] args) {
    // Fill a list with the command line parameters
    int n = args.length;
    double[] numList = new double[n];
    for (int i = 0; i < n; i++) {
      numList[i] = Double.parseDouble(args[i]);
    }

    // display the numbers in the order they were entered
    System.out.println("The given set of numbers is: ");
    printNumList(numList);

    // sort the numbers in ascending order by calling a method
    sortAscend(numList);

    // Print the sorted list
    System.out.println("The numbers arranged in ascending order");
    printNumList(numList);
  }

  // The method for displaying the numbers in the message window
  static void printNumList(double[] numList) {
    for (int i = 0; i < numList.length -1; i++)
      System.out.print(numList[i] + ", ");
    System.out.println(numList[numList.length - 1]);
  }

  // The method for sorting the numbers
  static void sortAscend(double[] numList) {
    double storeMax;
    int    storeIndex;

    for (int i = numList.length - 1; i >= 1; i--) {
```

```java
        // store the current number from numList[0..i] in storeMax
        storeMax = numList[i];
        storeIndex = i;

        // Step through the array comparing the stored number
        // with the previous number
        for (int j = i - 1; j >= 0; j--) {
          if (storeMax < numList[j]) {
            storeMax = numList[j];
            storeIndex = i;
          }
        }
        // Swap the numbers if the current number is greater
        if (storeIndex != i) {
          numList[storeIndex] = numList[i];
          numList[i] = storeMax;
        }
      }
    }
  }
}
```

10. Click Rebuild and Save All.

What Just Happened?   You created a new workspace and project. You then added a Java class file with some buggy code that you can use for testing the debugger. The intended logic for this program follows.

1. Loop through the command-line parameter list of numbers and build an array variable with one number in each array element.

2. Display the unsorted list in the Message View window.

3. Sort the numbers using the `sortAscend()` method.

4. Display the sorted list.

The logic for the `sortAscend()` method follows.

1. Loop through the array that was passed from the `main()` method.

2. Store the value of the current element in `storeMax` and current index in `storeIndex`.

3. Loop through all numbers in the list before the current element. If `storeMax` is less than the number, swap the current element number with the number that is less than `storeMax`.

II. Prepare for the Debugging Session

The first stage in running the debugger is to prepare the project properties. You then compile your program to generate the required symbolic debugging information required by the debugger.

1. Click the SortAppPRJ node in the Navigator. Select **Project | Project Properties**.

2. On the Paths tab, be sure that the Target JDK version is 1.2 or later.

3. Click the Compiler tab (as shown next in the top part of the dialog) and check the checkboxes *Include debug information* (to compile special debugging information into the .class file) and *Show warnings* (to show compilation error messages in the Message View window).

```
SortAppPRJ.jpr Properties                                    [x]

   CodeCoach         |      Code Style    |       SQLJ
   Paths  |  Libraries  |  Defaults    |  Compiler  |  Run/Debug

  ┌─Default compiler options─────────────────────────────────┐
  │  ☑ Include debug information   ☑ Update imports           │
  │  ☑ Show warnings               ☐ Including .zip/.jar imports│
  │  ☐ Show deprecations           ☑ Show compile progress     │
  │  ☐ Obfuscate                                              │
  │                                                           │
  │  Exclude class: [_____▼]       │
```

4. Click the Run/Debug tab and be sure the *Compile project before running or debugging* checkbox is checked. This causes JDeveloper to automatically compile the code when you click Run or Debug. The alternative is to explicitly click Make before clicking Run or Debug.

TIP
*If the Project Properties dialog is not displayed, you can display it and jump to the Run/Debug tab by selecting **Run | Parameters**.*

5. Since the application you want to run requires command-line parameters (the numbers to be sorted), you have to specify them before running the application. Fill in the *Parameters* field with the following string of numbers, each separated by a blank space:

```
-5.0 4.4 2.9 3.4 3.5 4.4 1.9
```

The next illustration shows the top part of the Project Properties dialog with this string entered in the *Parameters* field.

6. Click OK to close the Project Properties dialog. Click Save All.

What Just Happened?   You set the project properties and command-line parameters to prepare for the debugging session. The debugger requires special instructions in the class file that are inserted when you set the project properties.

> **CAUTION**
> *It is important that you remove the check on the "Include debug information" checkbox before generating the final production code so that the final code does not incur the slight overhead of the extra debugging information.*

III. Control Program Execution

Before starting the debugger, be certain that you have properly set the project properties as in the last phase. This phase will start the debugging session and illustrate how you track the program execution.

Run the Debugger and Step Through the Code

You can run the debugger by selecting Debug (using a menu item, button, or keypress). The code will compile and run in debug mode. If there are any breakpoints defined, the program execution will stop at the first breakpoint. If there are no breakpoints, the program will proceed to completion. You can alternatively select Trace Into, which also compiles and runs the code in debug mode. The difference is that Trace Into will stop at the first executable statement whether or not breakpoints were defined. Since this phase of the practice has no breakpoints, the Trace Into technique is used.

1. Select SortNumbersAscend.java in the Navigation Pane and select **Run | Trace Into**.

   If the program compiles without errors, the debug session will start. The Navigator will add the Debug and Watch tabs, and the Source Editor will show the execution point. Each executable line of code will have a blue bullet next to it in the left-hand margin.

   The Debug tab contains the Stack and Thread Pane (to show methods) on top and the Data Pane (to show data elements and values) on the bottom.

CAUTION
As mentioned, data will be shown in the Data Pane only if the project property "Include debug information" checkbox is checked.

2. Exit debug mode by selecting **Run | Program Reset** or by clicking the Reset button.

3. Select **View | Message View** and undock the Message View window by dragging the double bar at the left side of the window. Place this window on the screen in a location that does not obstruct the Navigation Pane.

4. Press F7 to start the debugger (the same action as **Run | Trace Into**). The green arrow indicating the execution point should point to the following line, which is the first executable line of code in the `main()` method:

   ```
   int n = args.length;
   ```

5. Place the cursor on the line of source code, making the first call to the method `printNumList(numlist)`.

6. Select **Run | Run to Cursor**. The Message View shows the output from the execution of the line of code prior to the call to the `printNumList()` method. This line causes the string "The given set of numbers is:" to be printed in the Message View window.

7. Select **Run | Step Over** (or click the Step Over button). The Message View shows the numbers that were input as parameters as the output from the `printNumList()` method. This is because the Step Over command allows all of the code invoked by the call to execute to completion before pausing again.

8. Place the cursor on the line of code that makes the second call to the `printNumlist(numList)` method.

9. Press F4 (the same function as selecting **Run | Run to Cursor**). You will see the output of the text string argument to the `println()` method—the text string "The numbers arranged in ascending order."

10. Select **Run | Trace Into**. The execution point jumps to the first line of the `printNumList()` method.

11. Watch the Message View window as you click the **Trace Into** button on the debugging toolbar twice. Continue clicking the button four more times to watch the loop iterate.

12. Select **Run | Run to End of Method**. The program executes the remaining iterations of the loop, and the execution point moves to the closing curly bracket of the `printNumList()` method.

13. Select **Run | Program Reset** (or click the Reset button) to terminate the debugging session. If you look in the Message View, you will see that the output order of the numbers is the same as the input order. The sort function is not working, and this is the bug you need to fix.

Disable and Enable Tracing of Classes

In this application you have only one file, which you created and need to debug. However, when you have many source code files in your project and want to debug only one of these files, you will need to change the Trace Into settings. The following steps demonstrate this technique, although the only other files used by this program are the library classes.

1. Start the debugging session again by pressing F7.

2. Select **View | Loaded Classes**. The Loaded Classes window appears, as in Figure 13-7, showing a hierarchical display of all classes that have been loaded (called) so far during this debugging session.

3. You can be relatively certain that the Sun classes are problem free. Therefore, the icon by the node for "sun" shows an icon with a red circle and a slash indicating that it will not be traced. Turn tracing on for the "sun" classes by selecting "Enable tracing" from the popup menu on the "sun" node.

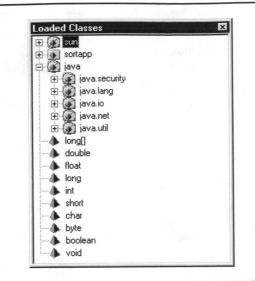

FIGURE 13-7. *Loaded Classes window*

4. Click Reset to end the debugging session. Select **View | Tracing Disabled Classes** to display a window called List of Packages and Classes With Tracing Disabled. This window lists all class parent nodes that have been disabled in debug mode. You can edit the text in this window (shown here) to add or remove classes.

5. Click F7 to start debugging the file and select **View I Loaded Classes**. Disable tracing on the "sun" class node by selecting "Disable tracing" from the right-click menu on the "sun" node. Click the Reset button.

CAUTION
Clicking outside the Loaded Classes window closes it.

What Just Happened?   You started the debugging session and practiced stepping into and stepping over code. You also got a feeling for the messages that you can see in the Message View window and tried a technique for enabling and disabling the tracing of specific classes and their child classes. Disabling tracing on a particular class or tree of classes will save you having to step out of or step over a set of code that you know to be problem free.

IV. Examine Data Values

Now that you know how to control the program execution, you can practice defining watches, setting breakpoints, and examining data element values. This will help you locate the problem area in the code.

1. Select **Run I Trace Into** to start debugging. The execution point is in the first executable line of the `main()` method (`int n = args.length;`).

2. Click the Watch tab in the Navigator. Since you have not defined any watches, the pane will be blank.

3. Move the cursor to any letter of the variable `numList` declared in the second line of the `main()` method (`double[] numList = new double[n];`). Do not select (highlight) the word "numList."

4. Select Add Watch at Cursor from the popup menu to display the Add Watch dialog, as shown here:

5. Click OK, and you will see the `numList` variable added to the Watch Pane as shown next. The **???** symbol indicates that the variable has no value assignment.

6. Click Trace Into twice. You will see a + symbol appear by the variable name in the Navigator Pane. If you expand this, you will see that the array has been declared and the values of all rows in the array set to "0."

7. Click Trace Into twice more, and you will see that the value of the first row of the array has been filled in as the loop proceeds through the list of numbers.

8. Since there are no errors until the sort method, you can skip all lines of code until the call to the `sortAscend()` method. You could just click the Step Over button until you reached that code, but there is a better way using a breakpoint. If you set a breakpoint on the line on which you want to stop, you can easily skip all lines of code before that. There are several ways to set a breakpoint:
   Click the blue bullet in the left border next to the line of code or
   Select Toggle Breakpoint from the popup menu or
   Press F5
Create a breakpoint for the line that calls `sortAscend()` using one of these methods. You do not need to be in debug mode to set breakpoints.

9. Click the Run button in the Navigator (or select **Run | Debug**) to execute all lines until the breakpoint. The Watch Pane will show that values are assigned to all rows of the `numList` array.

10. Click the Trace Into button (or select **Run | Trace Into**) to follow the code in the `sortAscend()` method.

11. Place the cursor at the `if` statement immediately after the comment "Swap the numbers." Select Run to Cursor from the popup menu. The execution point will transfer from the breakpoint to the `if` statement.

12. Click the Debug tab. In the Data Pane (as shown in the following illustration) look at the values for the variables `i`, `storeMax`, and `storeIndex`. The sort routine correctly picked the largest number as 4.4 for the first iteration of the outer loop, but the array position of this number is not 6 and is the same as the value in i. This means that the exchange of values did not occur, as it should for a proper sort.

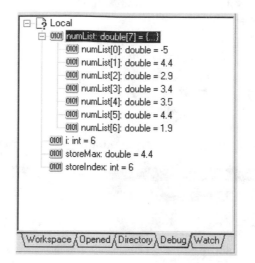

The watch for numList that was set earlier tracked the values of this variable, and these are displayed in the Watch Pane and the Debug tab Data Pane. All variables that appear in the current line of code are also displayed in the Data Pane, but, since they have no watch defined, they do not shown in the Watch Pane.

TIP
You can examine the value of a variable by holding the mouse cursor over the variable name. The value will be displayed in a tooltip next to the name, as shown here:

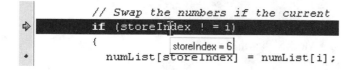

```
            // Swap the numbers if the current
            if (storeIndex ! = i)
            {
                                storeIndex = 6
                numList[storeIndex] = numList[i];
```

13. If you examine the code before this line, you can determine that the problem is that the correct value is not being saved in the storeIndex variable. In the Source Editor, change the assignment to storeIndex in

the j loop to j instead of i (`storeIndex = j;`). (The file is still in debug run mode while you are editing it.)

14. Select **Run | Step Over**. A dialog prompts you to recompile. Click Yes. The debugging session will restart.

15. Run completely through the program and verify that the sort is successful by examining the Message View output.

The Evaluate/Modify Dialog

You can use the Evaluate/Modify dialog, shown here, to provide an alternative for evaluating and modifying the value of expressions. The following demonstrates how to work with this dialog using the example program in this practice.

1. Remove all breakpoints by selecting **View | Breakpoints** and selecting Remove All from the right-click menu in the Breakpoints window. Start a debugging session using Trace Into.

2. Click on the line in the `sortAscend()` method `if (storeMax < numList[j])`. Select Run to Cursor from the popup menu to run all code before that line.

3. Select Evaluate/Modify from the popup menu to display the Evaluate/Modify dialog.

4. Enter "storeMax*20" in the *Expression* field and click the Evaluate button to display the result. This is a simple arithmetic expression. You can also examine the values of variables (such as storeMax) on their own.

5. You can examine logical expressions using this tool. In the *Expression* field enter "numList[0] < storeMax." Click Evaluate, and you will see the result "true," as shown here:

The *New Value* field is disabled in this case, because you are evaluating an expression and it does not make sense to modify the value of an expression. However, you can modify a variable.

6. Enter "storeMax" in the *Expression* field. Click the Evaluate button to see the value.

7. Enter "2" in the *New Value* field and click Modify. The value "2" will replace the previous value of 1.9 and will display in the *Result* field.

8. Click Done to close the window. Click Reset to end the session.

What Just Happened?   You successfully debugged a logic error by setting up a watch and a breakpoint and examining data values during the program execution. This simple example showed the basic techniques that you can use to find and fix problems in your code. There are some more advanced features, as mentioned earlier, that you will want to explore once you have mastered these basics. The JDeveloper help system is the source for information about these techniques.

APPENDIX
A

JDeveloper Wizards

We're off to see the Wizard...
  —Dorothy and the Scarecrow, *The Wizard of Oz* (1939), MGM

racle JDeveloper includes many wizards to make development faster and easier. A wizard is a quick and easy interface routine that helps you perform tasks and create files of various types. The standard wizard interface is a modal dialog with many pages. Each page contains descriptive text about how to complete a part of the task. There are input areas on this page that allow you to enter information by typing or selecting from predefined values. Some wizards in JDeveloper consist of a single page so there are no navigation buttons.

The intention of the wizard is to guide you in accomplishing a complex task and to ensure that you have filled in the required properties. Wizards usually contain a set of standard buttons:

- Next and Previous to navigate between the pages

- OK to accept the definition and dismiss the dialog

- Cancel to abort the definition routine

- Help to load a help topic about the wizard's page

- Finish to indicate that your interaction with the wizard is complete.

It is difficult to generalize about wizards, since there are many more differences than similarities between them. Not all wizards can be invoked in the same way—for example, the Deployment Profile Wizard can be invoked in several ways, but not the way many other new elements are created (with **File | New**). Different wizards may or may not be available under the JDeveloper Wizards menu, depending upon what is selected in the Navigation Pane.

The wizards are listed in alphabetical order in Table A-1. Wizards are usually named starting with the element that they create. Therefore, if you know what object you are creating, you should be able to easily find the wizard in this table. This list of wizards includes only those wizards where something is actually created rather than simply modified.

Most wizards set properties and create objects that you can modify after running the wizard. In many cases, there is an edit dialog that you can load by selecting Edit from the popup menu on a created object. This edit dialog has many of the same elements as the wizard, but will either add to existing code, or create new files. For example, you can select Edit <modulename> from the right-click menu on a BC4J application module to display the edit dialog for that application module.

Accessing the Wizards

Wizards often have several ways in which they can be accessed. The most common ways to access wizards are through the menus, the Navigator, and the Source Editor.
To access the wizards using menus:

- Select ***<some main menu>*** | **<Wizard Name>**, where "some main menu" is a menu pulldown in the JDeveloper IDE.

- Select **File** | **New**, click *<some tab>* in the Object Gallery and select the element type to create. "Some tab" is the group within the Object Gallery.

- Select **Wizard** | **<Wizard Name>**.

There are some additional ways to access wizards in JDeveloper. For example, within the Source Editor, various wizards can be invoked using standard editing techniques. For example, the JSP Element Wizard and XSQL Element Wizard are accessed using the right-click menu in the source code for the appropriate file.

For more specialized (restricted context) wizards, often the viewers, designers, or dialogs can invoke various other wizards. This is done by pressing a button on a toolbar. Keep in mind that the wizard invocation points are accessible from the places where they would most logically belong (main menu/context menu/within dialogs, within editor, etc.).

NOTE
The JDeveloper help files sometimes refer to the same wizard by different names. These alternate names are listed in the Wizard column of Table A-1.

Wizard	Description	Access Method
Applet Wizard	This wizard helps you create a class with the code necessary for an applet containing a default frame and optional components.	Select **File	New**, and then on the Objects tab, doubleclick Applet. (See Application Wizard for alternative methods.)
Application Wizard	Creates a Java application. If you select "Add a default frame," the Business Components for Java Data Form" in the Application Wizard, the Business Components Data Form Wizard will open. If you select "Add a default frame – A new Business empty frame," the Frame Wizard will open. If you select "Add a default frame – An existing frame," you will need to fill in the existing frame name by clicking Browse or entering the name manually. If you select "Do not add a default frame," the wizard will create the application without a frame.	■ Select **File	New**, and then on the Objects tab, doubleclick Application or ■ Specify a new application in the Project Wizard or ■ Call the Business Components Data Form Wizard.
Application Module Wizard	This wizard creates the BC4J application module used to connect to view objects.	■ Select **File	New**, and then on the Business Components tab, doubleclick Application Module or ■ Right click on any package file in the Navigation Pane and select Create Application Module from the right-click menu.
Association Wizard	Use this wizard for Business Components projects, to create new associations between entities.	■ Select **File	New**, and then on the Business Components tab, doubleclick Association or ■ Right click any package and select Create Association.
Bean Wizard	This wizard generates the code for a new JavaBean. You will also need to select the class to extend for your bean.	Select **File	New**, and then on the Beans tab, doubleclick Bean.
BeanInfo Wizard	This is a single panel that allows you to specify the details for a new JavaBean class.	Select **File	New**, and then on the Beans tab, doubleclick BeanInfo.

TABLE A-1. *JDeveloper Wizards and Their Access Methods*

Wizard	Description	Access Method
BeanInsight Wizard	This wizard checks to see that a component is a valid JavaBean and shows any detailed information about the selected bean.	Select **Wizards** | **BeanInsight**.
Business Components Data Form Wizard	This wizard assists you in creating a Java application or applet using the BC4J-defined view objects. It generates the Java source code required to implement the Java form.	You can start this wizard in one of four ways: ■ **File** | **New** and select Business Components Data Form from the Objects tab. Calling the wizard in this way adds the data form to an existing project. You get a choice of creating a frame, panel, or applet, which, if you select Frame, will translate to a single frame.java file inside the selected project. The wizard connects the frame to BC4J objects and creates complete code for the frame. However, it does not create an application.java file that is required to run it as a standalone. The idea is that this object will be added to a system where you are calling forms individually with some kind of navigation scheme between forms. ■ **File** | **New Project** and specify "A project containing a new" and select Business Components Data Form. Complete the Project Wizard, and the Business Components Data Form Wizard will start. This option works in exactly the same way as the first option. ■ **File** | **New Project** And specify a project containing a new application. When the Project Wizard completes, the Application Wizard will appear. Specify "Add a default frame" with "A new Business Components for Java Data Form" selected. When the Business Components Data Form Wizard starts, the options for panel and applet will be disabled. You will only be able to create a frame. Completing the wizard will create the frame.java and application.java files. ■ **File** | **New** and doubleclick Application in the Objects tab. This starts the Application Wizard. If you specify "A new Business Components for Java Data Form," as in the preceding method, the wizard will go through the same steps and create the same results. The general rule is that if you specify a data form, the result will be a frame only (or applet or panel) without the application to call it. If you start the Application Wizard, it will create the application.java, and if you specify a frame using a business components data form, it will add the frame.java.

TABLE A-1.   *JDeveloper Wizards and Their Access Methods (continued)*

Wizard	Description	Access Method
Business Components JSP Application Wizard	This wizard generates a JavaServer Page application that contains full database access.	Select **File	New**, and then on the Web Objects tab, doubleclick Business Components JSP Application.
Business Components Project Wizard	This wizard consolidates all of the business components files including entity objects, associations, view links, view objects, and an application module.	■ This is automatically invoked when you have selected "A project containing Business Components" on the Project Type panel of the Project Wizard or ■ Select **Wizards	Business Components** when working on a business components project or ■ Select **File	New** and doubleclick the Business Components icon on the Business Components tab.
Business Components System Properties Wizard	This wizard allows you to select the desired options for the entity schema panels (of the Business Components Wizard) as well as the definition, object, and row information for the entity objects, view objects, and application modules.	Select **Wizards	Business Components Properties**.
Class Builder Wizard	See Class Wizard.	
Class Wizard	This is a single panel where you can specify the details of a new Java class.	Select **File	New**, and then on the Objects tab, doubleclick Class.
CORBA Server Object Wizard	This wizard allows you to enter the CORBA object's Java interface name (including its package) and source file used by the Caffeine compiler.	Select **File	New**, and then on the Objects tab, doubleclick CORBA Server Object.
CORBA Wizard	See CORBA Server Object Wizard.	
Customizer Wizard	You can enter details for your new customizer class in this single window. The customizer offers an interface for setting many properties of an object.	Select **File	New**, and then on the Beans tab, doubleclick Customizer.

TABLE A-1. *JDeveloper Wizards and Their Access Methods* (continued)

Wizard	Description	Access Method
Data Form Wizard	See Business Components Data Form Wizard.	
DataPage Wizard	This wizard uses BC4J custom tags to create data-aware JSP pages.	Select **File** | **New**, and then on the Web Objects tab, doubleclick DataPage.
Deployment Profile Wizard	The purpose of this wizard is to collect information to generate and deploy an archive file. The pages of this wizard require you to identify project files to archive, provide a file name, and select library files to prevent from being archived.	■ Select a project. Select **Project** | **Deploy** | **New Deployment Profile** or ■ Right click a project file and select New Deployment Profile. BC4J projects have a right-click menu option for Create Deployment Profiles. This option produces as simpler profile file that is not the same as the previously mentioned options. Use the main menu method for BC4J projects instead of the right-click menu.
Dialog Wizard	This creates a non-JavaBean class file that displays a dialog window. Also called Dialog Builder.	Select **File** | **New**, and then on the Objects tab, doubleclick Dialog.
Domain Wizard	Creates a BC4J domain that defines allowable values and validations for a data element. In the Name page, you can specify a name. Select a datatype and storage properties in the Settings page.	■ Right click a package in the Navigation Pane, to display its popup menu, and then select Create Domain. ■ Select **File** | **New** and doubleclick the Domain icon in the Business Components tab.
Enterprise JavaBean Wizard	Use this wizard to create enterprise bean classes. This wizard will also generate the interface required for an EJB object, generate the remote interface, and select remote interface methods.	Select **File** | **New**, and then on either the Objects or Beans tab, doubleclick Enterprise JavaBean. *Note:* JDeveloper 3.2 fully supports EJB 1.1.
EJB Wizard	See Enterprise JavaBean Wizard.	

TABLE A-1. *JDeveloper Wizards and Their Access Methods* (continued)

Wizard	Description	Access Method
Entity Constraint Wizard	This creates BC4J objects that represent database constraints. Using this wizard, you enter the key constraint and database constraint names, select attributes for the constraint, and enter additional details about the constraint.	Right click any entity in the Navigator and select Create Entity Constraint.
Entity Object Wizard	This wizard creates a BC4J entity object. With this wizard, you can specify the entity name and package, attributes and attribute properties, entity object definition, database object, and Java files and methods to generate.	▪ Select **File** ❘ **New**, and then on the Business Components tab, doubleclick Entity Object or ▪ Right click any package and select Create Entity Object.
Frame Builder Wizard	See Frame Wizard.	
Frame Wizard	This single panel allows you to enter details for a new frame class, including any optional attributes such as title, menu bar, toolbar, status bar, or About box.	▪ Select **File** ❘ **New**, and then on the Objects tab, doubleclick Frame or ▪ Called from the Application Wizard.
Generate CORBA Server Classes Wizard	Creates a CORBA Server object class files.	Accessed through **Wizards** ❘ **Generate CORBA Server Classes** only when a CORBA object is selected in the Navigation Pane. *Note:* You will not see any windows or dialogs when this wizard is run. The message bar will show "Compiler: Successful with no errors" upon completion.
Generate Javadoc Wizard	This wizard automatically creates documentation (Javadoc) for a Java class file.	Select **Wizards** ❘ **Generate Javadoc.**

TABLE A-1. *JDeveloper Wizards and Their Access Methods (continued)*

Wizard	Description	Access Method
HTTP Servlet Wizard	This wizard creates an HTTP servlet and allows you to specify the name, package, file, methods, and parameters for the servlet.	Select **File	New**, and then on the Web Objects tab, doubleclick HTTP Servlet.
IDL to Java Wizard	This wizard converts Interface Definition Language files to Java CORBA files.	Select **Wizards	IDL to Java** when a .idl file is highlighted.
Implement Interface Wizard	This wizard creates a signature framework at the end of the source file for the Java class. Each method of the interface must then be implemented by code that you write.	Select **Wizards	Implement Interface** when a .java file is highlighted.
Import Project Wizard	This wizard adds existing files to a project. You can specify the file source directories and archives, as well as any libraries, classes, or packages that you want to add to your project.	Right click on any .jpr file and select Import Classes/Packages.
Javadoc Wizard	See Generate Javadoc Wizard.	
JPublisher Wizard	JPublisher creates java interface source code for accessing database object types, collection types, reference types, and PL/SQL packages.	Doubleclick the Connection icon in the Navigator to display the Database Browser. Expand the Database Schemas node. Expand one of the schemas and right click an object type or package. Select Generate Java from the menu to open the JPublisher Wizard. You can also right click a folder, such as the Object Types folder or the PL/SQL Packages folder, to generate Java classes for all of the objects or packages it contains.
JSP Application Wizard	See Business Components JSP Application Wizard.	
JSP Element Wizard	This wizard allows you to add JSP elements that contain reasonable default property values. Use this wizard to add JSP tags, themes, web beans, and calls to servlets on a JSP page.	■ Open the JSP source file and place cursor where you would like JSP tags inserted. Right click and select JSP Element from the menu. ■ Select **Wizards	JSP Element.**

TABLE A-1.   *JDeveloper Wizards and Their Access Methods* (continued)

Wizard	Description	Access Method
New Java Class Wizard	See Class Wizard.	
Override Methods Wizard	This wizard creates the code framework needed to override a superclass method.	Select **Wizards** | **Override Methods Wizard** when a .java file is highlighted.
Package Wizard	Use this wizard to create a Business Components package and other BC4J files.	■ Select **File** | **New**, and then on the Business Components tab, doubleclick Package or ■ Right click on any .jpr or .jpx file and select Create Package.
Panel Wizard	The Panel Wizard can be used to add a new panel class (a top-level container) to the open project.	Select **File** | **New**, and then on the Objects tab, doubleclick Panel.
PJC Wizard	To create a Pluggable Java Component that you can use to extend the functionality of an Oracle Forms Developer application that will be deployed on the Web.	Select **File** | **New**, and then on the Beans tab, doubleclick Oracle Forms PJC.
Project Wizard	Two files are created by the Project Wizard: one project file to store the project properties and an optional HTML file that includes default project information.	Select **File** | **New Project**.
Property Editor Wizard	This wizard creates a property editor that allows you to customize the value list presented by properties in your class files.	Select **File** | **New**, and then on the Beans tab, doubleclick Property Editor.

TABLE A-1. *JDeveloper Wizards and Their Access Methods* (continued)

Wizard	Description	Access Method
Resource Wizard	This wizard facilitates localizing your Java program by grouping resource strings into a separate class.	Select **Wizards** | **Resource Wizard** when a Java file is selected in the Object Navigator.
SQLJ Wizard	This creates a SQLJ file that allows you to embed SQL in your Java class files.	Select **File** | **New**, and then on the Objects tab, doubleclick SQLJ File.
View Link Wizard	You can create BC4J view links with this wizard to synchronize your master-detail usages.	▪ Select **File** | **New**, and then on the Business Components tab, doubleclick View Link or ▪ Right click any BC4J package and select Create View Link.
View Object Wizard	Use this wizard to create BC4J view objects for the purpose of connecting to the entity.	▪ Select **File** | **New**, and then on the Business Components tab, doubleclick View Object or ▪ Right click any BC4J package and select Create View Object.
Web Bean Wizard	Creates web beans and data web beans for JSP applications.	Select **File** | **New**, and then on the Web Objects tab, doubleclick web bean.
Web Object Manager	This wizard registers servlets and web beans.	Select **Wizards** | **Web Object Manager**.
XSQL Element Wizard	This wizard will add XSQL elements with reasonable default values to an XSQL source code file.	▪ Open an XSQL source file and place the cursor where you would like to have the XSQL tags inserted. Select XSQL Element from the right-click menu or ▪ Select **Wizards** | **XSQL Wizard**.

TABLE A-1. *JDeveloper Wizards and Their Access Methods* (continued)

APPENDIX B

Customizing and Extending the IDE

Pay no attention to the man behind the curtain.

—Wizard, *The Wizard of Oz* (1939), MGM

evelopment work is, by nature, repetitive work. Without an IDE, you create code for an application by manually typing the same commands and structures many times. Traditionally, developers working outside of an IDE used programmable text editors such as Brief or SlickEdit to create customized macros and shortcuts that eased the load of repetitive tasks. As time passed, these tools added more and more features and ended up fulfilling many of the same functions as a full-fledged IDE. However, even in an IDE, you find repetitive tasks as you run through the same sequence of menu options and toolbar buttons many times.

Automating this kind of repetition can make you more productive and the code you create more accurate. You have probably experienced this effect with a favorite software tool. After working with the tool for a while, you find easy and fast ways to complete a particular function. Your productivity benefits because you are not slowed down (and bored) by the repetition, but free to apply your skill and thought to more challenging endeavors.

The development tools that are the most useful allow the developer to customize the tool to a particular style and set of tasks. They also offer a way to add features that are not native to the tool but that assist in completing a particular job. JDeveloper is in this category. In addition to its fully featured IDE it offers the ability to customize and extend its feature set. Therefore, you are not stuck with a particular method for performing a task. If the native method does not suit your particular style, you can create a new tool that lets you be more efficient. This is an extremely strong feature of JDeveloper, and as a developer, you need to know what possibilities exist in the tool that allow you to customize your working environment.

This appendix explains the main features that you can use to tailor your JDeveloper working environment to your style and to the types of tasks that you perform. The discussion focuses only on the specific features. Some of the extensions require many steps, and a full explanation of those techniques would exceed the allotted space in this book. Fortunately, the techniques used to create these extensions are well documented, with examples published in various locations. This appendix will give you a sense of the complexity level of each method of customization and point you to the information sources where you can find more detailed information.

What Should You Customize?

Extending and customizing the development environment is a useful and necessary undertaking. The reason that this subject is in the back of this book is that some of the techniques discussed in this appendix are fairly advanced features and require many steps to complete. In most cases, the steps do not take much time, but they may require careful testing and debugging. For these complex techniques, you should decide whether the time required for the customization will save a greater amount of time in future development work. The answer to that question may not just be a personal one. You may be able to share customizations with your team and, in doing so, set a standard for the methods that the team uses to create applications. The payback will, of course, be greater in this case. You may also share the customizations with the JDeveloper user community at large. The main guideline, as in most business applications, is to examine the return-on-investment for the time spent.

Another guideline that you can use in deciding what to customize is to closely examine how you work with JDeveloper. You need to use JDeveloper for a project or two to become familiar with your personal style and the type of code that you typically create. This is not necessarily an easy thing to do. You have to remove yourself from the thought processes that you go through when creating an application and watch the steps that you follow to complete a task. In essence, you have to be your own efficiency expert. It might pay to have someone else with an expert level of knowledge about JDeveloper and the types of applications you create fulfill this role. That person could watch you work or interview you and come up with an improved process that could be more automated by using the extensions. This takes some "thinking out of the box."

Note for Oracle Developer Users

You use templates in Oracle Developer to help implement the application standards that you have created. The objects in the template act as archetypes or patterns on which you base other objects. This implements a form of *subclassing*, which is similar to the Java concept of subclassing. JDeveloper uses templates in some areas to effect a standard look-and-feel for a user interface. In other areas, you can create wizards or extensions that create objects and set properties based on your standards. This usage for JDeveloper customizations corresponds closely to the Oracle Developer use of templates.

In addition, some of the extensions you create in JDeveloper correspond to Oracle Developer user exits or calls to the Foreign Function Interface (FFI). FFI allows you to include functionality in an external, non-Forms library (such as a call to the Windows registry reading and writing functions located in an external Windows DLL). These extend the Forms tool and the PL/SQL language. In addition, when you web deploy forms, you can use *Pluggable Java Components* (PJCs) as Forms widgets. PJCs are JavaBeans that provide functionality that is not included in Developer Forms. (JDeveloper contains a PJC template in the Object Gallery to help you get started.)

The Possibilities

The rest of this appendix lists the possibilities for customizations and extensions to JDeveloper's IDE. It does not repeat the tips and techniques mentioned in Chapter 2 for moving and rearranging windows and toolbars in the tool.

Information Resources

The main resources for information about JDeveloper extensions are the JDeveloper help system and Oracle Technology Network web site.

JDeveloper Help System

The main Contents page node for "Extending JDeveloper Using Addins" contains topics that explain the concepts of the Addin API that allows you to extend the JDeveloper IDE. In addition, the node "Working with JDeveloper\Customizing the IDE" holds additional topics for modifying the interface. Specific topics are mentioned later.

CAUTION
As mentioned earlier, the Contents node path to the help system topics and the titles of the topics may change with new releases of JDeveloper. If you do not find a topic that matches the path or exact name, use the help system's Search tab to find the topic.

Oracle Technology Network (OTN) Web Site

This web site (otn.oracle.com, called previously "TechNet") is the main source of Oracle-published information for all Oracle products. At this writing, the JDeveloper home page (otn.oracle.com/products/jdev) contains a number of white papers that demonstrate and explain techniques and concepts for the product in its various releases. There are also links on that page to download a trial copy of JDeveloper, view the system documentation (the same as in the help system), and obtain sample code. OTN also offers a discussion forum that focuses on JDeveloper.

CAUTION
Due to the dynamic nature of the Web, the web site addresses provided in this appendix (and in the rest of the book) may change over time. If you find this to be the case, use your favorite search site to look for keywords on the applicable concepts. Similarly, the help system topic names and paths to reach the topics may change with new releases of JDeveloper. Use the help system's Search tab if you cannot find a topic mentioned in this text.

Techniques for Customizing and Extending the IDE

The following list describes the main features of the JDeveloper IDE that you can customize and extend. It also mentions where to find more detailed information on the feature. Two key samples are currently available in the sample code section of the JDeveloper page on OTN as follows:

- **Exploring JavaBean Development with Oracle JDeveloper**   This is a sample that offers prebuilt code to demonstrate various customization techniques. The sample also leads you through the steps to follow if you want to re-create the sample. (This is also called "Advanced JavaBeans and JDeveloper" and "Developing JavaBeans" on the web site.)

- **Oracle JDeveloper 3.1 Custom Addins**   This area (currently listed in the Addins section of the web site) supplies a number of code samples that demonstrate various extensions.

The following discussion also assigns a complexity level to the technique based on these criteria:

- **Easy**   This indicates that you use a native JDeveloper wizard or other IDE dialog to activate the change. It should take you less than 5 minutes of effort.

- **Medium**   This is a simple procedure that you need to perform outside of the JDeveloper IDE and should take less than 15 minutes of effort.

- **Difficult**   This requires extra Java class files that you need to write (although you may be able to use the wizards to obtain starting code). You also may need to reconfigure some system files. This will take you more than 15 minutes of effort.

The following techniques are described in this appendix:

- Modify and add JavaBeans to the component palette

- Add items to the Tools menu

- Add a snippet to the Object Gallery

- Add a web bean and web bean properties to the JSP Element Wizard

- Add a layout manager

- Create a JavaBean property editor

- Create a JavaBean customizer

- Create a wizard using the Addin API

Modify and Add JavaBeans to the Component Palette

Complexity   Easy

Description   Using a dialog in the JDeveloper IDE, you can add buttons that represent JavaBeans to the component toolbar. This allows you to incorporate your own (or someone else's) JavaBeans into the component palette that you use to build Java applications and applets. The elements that you add will normally be visual elements, but you can also add elements that will not show in the UI Designer window, such as a login dialog. The idea is that you can click the button and drop the component into the UI Designer or Structure Pane to add its instantiation code to the source code.

You can also add tab pages to the component toolbar. This allows you to organize the components in a way that better suits the way in which you work. For example, you may find that the text field, label, panel, and rowset objects are the components that you use 90 percent of the time as you are creating an application. In this case, you may want to create another tab (called "Main") that contains these objects. You can then click that tab and use its controls for the greater amount of your work. This saves you from having to switch tabs frequently to access commonly used objects. You also might want to add a tab to hold frequently used components that you add to the toolbar.

TIP
Another useful customization is to arrange your windows to make working with JDeveloper most efficient. This takes some analysis of how you work best with the tool, but there is a suggestion to get you started in Chapter 2's section "Arranging the JDeveloper Windows." Also think about the arrangement of the toolbars when you are designing your work area.

More Information   Chapter 9 contains a hands-on practice ("Adding to the Component Toolbar") that steps through the process. The JDeveloper help system contains an appropriate topic for "Customizing the Component Palette" (in the Contents tab node "Working with JDeveloper\Customizing the IDE\Customizing the Component Palette").

Add Items to the Tools Menu

Complexity   Medium

Description   Adding an item to the main JDeveloper Tools menu allows you to easily access an external tool. In addition, you can specify that the tool will load the file that is selected in the Navigator. This is particularly useful if you want to open an HTML editor for a JSP file (that contains HTML tags). There is no wizard interface; you need to edit a JDeveloper configuration file to add to the Tools menu. You can also add items to other menus and to right-click (context) menus using the Addin API (described in the section "Create a Wizard Using the Addin API" in this appendix).

> **CAUTION**
> *Make a backup of any system configuration file (usually in the JDEV_HOME\bin directory) that you need to modify manually. If you make a change that breaks something else, you can revert to the previously working copy of the file.*

More Information   Chapter 8 contains a section "Adding an HTML Editor to the Menu" that describes the steps for installing a Tools menu selection for the FrontPage HTML editor. The JDeveloper help system contains a topic "Adding Tools to the Tools Menu" (in the Contents tab node "Working with JDeveloper\Customizing the IDE") that provides more information. In addition, the file that you need to modify in this technique, JDEV_HOME\bin\Tools.cfg, contains extensive comments in the file header that explain the structure of the file.

Add a Snippet to the Object Gallery

Complexity   Easy

Description   Snippets are another type of template that are available in the Object Gallery (**File | New**). Some objects in the Object Gallery launch wizards that help you create files that are customized to property values set in the wizards. Other elements in the Object Gallery just create a file that contains default code that you need to modify using the Source Editor. Snippets are in the latter category; therefore, selecting a snippet from the Object Gallery will create a file containing a copy of the text that is in the snippet file. This technique is most useful if the file you are adding is a snippet that will be incorporated as a file in the project. You add a snippet using a wizard from the JDeveloper IDE.

CAUTION
Adding a snippet modifies the JDEV_HOME\bin
Gallery.ini file. If you need to add a wizard, this file
needs to be manually modified. Be sure to make a
backup if you need to modify the file manually.

More Information   The sidebar "Adding a Snippet for the Login Dialog"
describes the steps for adding an object to the Object Gallery. The JDeveloper help
system contains a topic "Adding Snippets to the Object Gallery" (in the Contents tab
node "Working with JDeveloper\Customizing the IDE") that provides the steps to
accomplish this task.

Add a Web Bean and Web Bean Properties to the JSP Element Wizard

Complexity   Easy

Description   When you work with JSPs and other code that uses web beans or
servlets, you use a wizard to present the list of available beans. This wizard corresponds
to the component palette, where you select object types to place in your application.
The wizard presents a list of beans that are registered in the tool. If you develop a
new bean using the Web Bean Wizard, the tool will automatically register the bean,
and it will be available in the JSP Element Wizard.
    If you develop a web bean outside of JDeveloper, you can use the Web Object
Manager to register the bean. The Web Object Manager also allows you to add and
modify the properties that the JSP Element Wizard presents in its dialog.

More Information   Chapter 8 contains a hands-on practice section "Use the
Web Object Manager" that describes the steps for adding a web bean or servlet to
the list of beans presented in the JSP Element Wizard. The help system topic that
supports this task is "Registering a Servlet Using the Web Object Manager" (in the
Contents tab node "Developing Java Servlets").

Add a Layout Manager

Complexity   Difficult

Description   You can develop your own layout manager that extends the
capability of an existing layout manager or provides new functionality. (Chapter 11
discusses the native layout managers.) This requires writing the code for the layout
manager and registering it in JDeveloper using the procedure in the help system.

Add a Snippet for the LoginDlg

The following steps add a snippet to the Object Gallery for the code you would manually insert into a Java application or applet file to present a login dialog. The steps assume that you have dropped the login dialog component into the Structure Pane and that its name is the default "loginDlg1."

1. Open Notepad and type in the following code:

```
// place this in the imports section
import oracle.dacf.control.LoginFailureException;
// place this in the jbInit() method under the call to loginDlg1.setDataItemName
if (loginDlg1.showDialog() == JOptionPane.CANCEL_OPTION) {
    throw new LoginFailureException();
}
```

2. Save it as a file called LoginDlg.snippet in the JDEV_HOME\snippets directory where "JDEV_HOME" is the directory into which you installed JDeveloper.

3. Select **File | New** and click the Snippets tab.

4. Right click the background white space and select Add Snippet from the menu.

5. Fill in the fields as follows:
   Description as "Login Dialog"
   Snippet Filename as "JDEV_HOME\snippets\en\LoginDlg.snippet"
   Image Filename as "JDEV_HOME\snippets\en\icon4.gif"
   Use the Browse buttons to assist in entering the file names.

6. Click OK.

7. To use the snippet, select **File | New** and click the Snippets tab.

8. Doubleclick the LoginDlg snippet. A new file will be added to the selected project.

9. Open the new file in the editor and copy and paste its text into the current project.

10. Delete the snippet file.

There are a few extra steps in adding the file, copying the contents, and then closing the file. You need to decide if the work involved with using this technique is worthwhile in the long run.

You can also register a layout manager that you have obtained from another source. The layout manager will then be available from the *layout* property of the Inspector for a user interface component.

More Information   The help system topic "Adding Custom Layout Managers" (in the Contents tab "Designing the User Interface\Working with Layout Managers" node) has information on this process.

Create a JavaBean Property Editor

Complexity   Medium to difficult

Description   A *property editor* is a Java class that supports editing of a single property value for a JavaBean. Using the Inspector, you enter values for properties in different ways. You just type in values for properties such as *text* and *name*. For properties such as *layout* and *dataItemName*, you interact with a pulldown list or a new dialog. A property editor manages the latter type of property value and, as with other properties, writes the code that sets the property. When you create your own bean, you need to think about how developers will edit the properties. You can create a property editor for a specific property using the Bean tab object Property Editor in the Object Gallery (**File | New**). You then register the property editor with the BeanInfo class that you have generated for your bean.

Property editors can be simple text selection lists (that will create a pulldown list in the Inspector) or more complex dialogs that contain a separate visual interface such as a color selector.

More Information   Details about property editors may be found in the white paper and sample code called "Exploring JavaBean Deployment with Oracle JDeveloper" on the OTN web site. The help system also contains instructions for creating and registering the property editor. Start with the topic "Ways to Create a Property Editor" (in the Contents tab node "Working with JDeveloper\Developing a JavaBean").

Create a JavaBean Customizer

Complexity   Difficult

Description   A *customizer* is another supplementary feature for a JavaBean. It works in the same way as a property editor but allows the developer to edit the entire object (many properties at a time) rather than a single property as with the property editor. For example, you may want to create a customizer to set the height, font, and colors of a text item. The customizer would allow you to input all of these characteristics and would then write the code to implement the settings. After the customizer is registered with the BeanInfo class for your JavaBean, the developer activates the customizer using **View | Customizer**.

More Information Details about customizers may also be found in the previously mentioned white paper and sample code "Exploring JavaBean Deployment with Oracle JDeveloper" on the Oracle Technology Network web site. The help system also contains instructions for creating and registering the customizer. Start with the topic "Creating a Customizer" (in the Contents tab node "Working with JDeveloper\Developing a JavaBean").

Create a Wizard Using the Addin API

Complexity Difficult

The complexity level for using the Addin API is greater than the other techniques, and you should examine whether the other techniques will fulfill the need before launching into an Addin project. The payback may be enormous if it helps you implement your standards, save repetitive steps in development, or generate code that would otherwise require much effort. Think of how easy it is to create a data-aware master-detail Java application using the Business Components Data Form Wizard, and imagine how much time you and your team would save if you had that kind of wizard for creating the functionality that you frequently require.

Description The Addin API is a set of Java Application Programming Interfaces (APIs) that allows you to extend the JDeveloper IDE to fulfill nearly any requirement. You can use it to create your own customized wizards that generate code or files. (Other uses are mentioned in the sidebar "Create Other Addin API Extensions.")

The best feature of the Addin API is that it allows you to write the wizards or extensions using Java. In fact, you can start with a template class file located in the Object Gallery. You can use this template by selecting **File | New** and clicking the Snippets tab. The file is called "Example Wizard/Addin." You then add functionality to the file and install it. The installation process registers the new addin class with JDeveloper. You then need to specify the way in which the function will be invoked. For example, the new wizard can be called from a main menu (for example, the Wizards menu) or a popup menu. It can also be available in the Object Gallery along with other JDeveloper wizards.

More Information Documentation on developing addins is located in help system topics under the "Extending JDeveloper Using Addins" node on the Contents tab. The white paper and sample on OTN called "Oracle JDeveloper 3.1 Custom Addins" contains examples that supplement the help system information.

> **Create Other Addin API Extensions**
> The Addin API can be used for adding features other than wizards. You can use it to create menu items on the main menu and right-click (popup) menus. You can also extend JDeveloper with external editors or viewers for file types that are not natively supported (such as multimedia). The information sources and sample code are the same as those listed in the technique "Create a Wizard Using the Addin API."

CAUTION
It is important to document any extension that you create so that it may be understood, enhanced, and fixed by others. This is particularly important if you are going to share the extension with another developer or group of developers. You also have to be aware that customizations you write will not be supported by Oracle Support unless you experience a problem with a feature such as the JDeveloper Addin API.

Other Customization Tips

There are some other customizations mentioned in Chapter 2 that are easily accomplished using the native IDE features.

■ **The Treat as Text menu item** This item appears on the Tools menu. This item allows you to add or modify file extensions that JDeveloper can display and edit in the Source Editor. For example, you can add "*.log" as a file extension in the dialog you see when you select this menu item. If you open a file with that extension in JDeveloper, the source code editor will load the file and allow you to edit and save it.

■ **Source Editor macros** You can record and play back keyboard macros by pressing CTRL+SHIFT+R, entering the keystrokes that you wish to repeat, and pressing CTRL+SHIFT+R again to stop the recording. Pressing CTRL+SHIFT+P plays the keystrokes back. This is intended for keystrokes only (not menu selections), and there is no way to save the macros between JDeveloper sessions.

■ **Select Tools | IDE Options** This item displays a dialog that you can use to set a large number of Source Editor behavior and visual aspects such as colors and fonts. The procedures are documented in the help system node "Working with JDeveloper\Customizing the IDE\Customizing the Source Editor."

APPENDIX
C

Java Security and
Oracle8i File Handling

I'll get you my pretty...and your little encryption key too...
> —Apologies to the Wicked Witch of the West,
> *The Wizard of Oz* (1939), MGM

 common task for application developers is server-side file handling. This simple task can become fairly complicated when you start integrating Java security requirements with the traditional Oracle database environment. For the Java that is stored in and executed from the database (using Java Stored Procedures), specific file read/write permission must be granted to any schema in which you wish to use Java. In addition, if you wish to work with files on remote machines, you will need to alter the user for the listener and database instance in which you plan to execute your Java procedures. A more common way to provide file access is to embed the logic in a CORBA or RMI service, not in a Java Stored Procedure.

Java Security Manager

The Oracle8*i* database uses the Java Security Manager (part of the Java security model) to control which operations it will allow Java code to perform. For operations dealing with files, the Java Security Manager checks to see if the JAVAUSERPRIV role has been granted for reading and writing files. If the file creation operation is requested, the Java Security manager checks to see if the JAVASYSPRIV role has been granted. The SYS user grants these roles using statements such as the following:

```
GRANT javasyspriv TO scott;
```

Prepare the Database

To prepare the Oracle8*i* database to use Java stored procedures for file handling between machines, you must change the logon account for the listener and database service to a user that has privileges to perform file handling across systems. You can do this in Windows 2000 using the following steps:

1. From the Windows Start menu, select **Start | Settings | Control Panel**, doubleclick Administrative Tools, and select Services.

2. Locate the listener service OracleOraHome81TNSListener and right click it.

3. In the popup menu, select **Properties | Log On** and click This Account. Set it to a user who is a member of ORA_DBA and Administrators.

4. Repeat the account change for your database service, for example, OracleServiceORCL.

The steps in Windows NT 4.0 are similar:

1. From the Windows Start menu, select **Start | Settings | Control Panel** and doubleclick Services.

2. Click the listener service OracleOraHome81TNSListener, and then click Startup.

3. Under *Log On As*, click This Account and set it to a user who is a member of the ORA_DBA and Administrators groups. You may need your administrator to add a new user for this purpose.

4. Repeat the account change for your database service, for example, OracleServiceORCL.

CAUTION
Be careful about granting privileges and changing logon accounts since allowing access to the operating and file systems can pose a significant security and data integrity risk.

Note to Index

This index contains some specialized listings that you may find useful, including the following entries:

- "Hands-on practices," includes a list of all of the practices scattered throughout the book.

- "More information," contains a list of page references where additional sources for information about your work with Java and JDeveloper, including books and web sites, can be found.

Index

D

G

H

N

INTERNATIONAL CONTACT INFORMATION

AUSTRALIA
McGraw-Hill Book Company Australia Pty. Ltd.
TEL +61-2-9417-9899
FAX +61-2-9417-5687
http://www.mcgraw-hill.com.au
books-it_sydney@mcgraw-hill.com

CANADA
McGraw-Hill Ryerson Ltd.
TEL +905-430-5000
FAX +905-430-5020
http://www.mcgrawhill.ca

GREECE, MIDDLE EAST,
NORTHERN AFRICA
McGraw-Hill Hellas
TEL +30-1-656-0990-3-4
FAX +30-1-654-5525

MEXICO (Also serving Latin America)
McGraw-Hill Interamericana Editores S.A. de C.V.
TEL +525-117-1583
FAX +525-117-1589
http://www.mcgraw-hill.com.mx
fernando_castellanos@mcgraw-hill.com

SINGAPORE (Serving Asia)
McGraw-Hill Book Company
TEL +65-863-1580
FAX +65-862-3354
http://www.mcgraw-hill.com.sg
mghasia@mcgraw-hill.com

SOUTH AFRICA
McGraw-Hill South Africa
TEL +27-11-622-7512
FAX +27-11-622-9045
robyn_swanepoel@mcgraw-hill.com

UNITED KINGDOM & EUROPE
(Excluding Southern Europe)
McGraw-Hill Education Europe
TEL +44-1-628-502500
FAX +44-1-628-770224
http://www.mcgraw-hill.co.uk
computing_neurope@mcgraw-hill.com

ALL OTHER INQUIRIES Contact:
Osborne/McGraw-Hill
TEL +1-510-549-6600
FAX +1-510-883-7600
http://www.osborne.com
omg_international@mcgraw-hill.com